EXPERIMENTAL METHODS
IN PSYCHOLOGY

EXPERIMENTAL METHODS IN PSYCHOLOGY

Gustav Levine
Stanley Parkinson
Arizona State University

LAWRENCE ERLBAUM ASSOCIATES, PUBLISHERS
1994   Hillsdale, New Jersey   Hove and London

Lawrence Erlbaum Associates, Inc., Publishers
365 Broadway
Hillsdale, New Jersey 07642

Library of Congress Cataloging-in-Publication Data
Levine, Gustav.
    Experimental methods in psychology / Gustav Levine & Stanley
Parkinson.
        p.   cm.
    Includes bibliographical references and index.
    ISBN 0-8058-1438-8 (alk. paper)
    1. Psychology, Experimental—Methodology.   2. Psychology—
Research.   I. Parkinson, Stanley.   II. Title.
BF181.L48   1994
150'.724—dc20   93-35652
                                                                      CIP

Books published by Lawrence Erlbaum Associates are printed on
acid-free paper, and their bindings are chosen for strength and
durability.

Printed in the United States of America
10 9 8 7 6 5 4 3 2

Contents

Preface

This text's unique contributions are found in two features. First, there is a detailed discussion of the process of theorizing that is coupled with a close examination of psychological constructs. This focus is evident in reading through some of the chapter headings: "The Problems Encountered in Theorizing about Internal Events"; "Changes in the Construct of Iconic Memory Over 30 Years of Research"; "A Close Look at the Methods and Logic Used in Evaluating a Theory of Short-Term Memory Search"; "Testing Theories when Internal Events Can Be Monitored or Manipulated." Thus, the reader of this text is offered an opportunity to see how psychologists think about, develop, and modify their theories, and the part played by research in changing explanations for behavior.

The second unusual focus in this text is an overt analysis of the logic of drawing conclusions from research. It is common for psychologists to be self-conscious in their reasoning. But it is uncommon to see an analysis of the logic that they use to draw conclusions. For example, chapter 7 closely examines the commonly encountered logical error of affirming the consequent, an error frequently made when predicted results are interpreted as confirmation of a theory. Conditions promoting the error, and conditions that avoid it, are described in both chapters 7 and 13. Other logical problems that are commonly encountered are also examined.

There are probably more chapters here than can be comfortably completed in one semester. The purpose was to offer options to the instructor. The "excess" chapters are in the latter half of the textbook, where there are choices among particular areas in psychology. The instructor using this text can teach a broad-based course including material on research methods in experimental, social, and clinical psychology, or a course that is exclusively focused on experimental psychology.

Whatever the final decision about which chapters to use, it is recommended that the first seven chapters be included. Chapter 13 is also highly recommended. Whereas chapter 7 describes the logic most commonly encountered in experimental psychology, chapter 13 describes a different form of logic that is more common to the area of social psychology. Neither form of logic is exclusively used in either subdiscipline, so it is helpful to understand both approaches regardless of a reader's major area of interest. A close examination of the two different approaches, and the problems they each pose, serves to increase understanding of the entire research enterprise.

Chapter 5 is a relatively complete summary of the material typically presented in an introductory statistics class, with an emphasis on what the students need to know for a course on experimental methods. The chapter includes an appendix that offers the formulas for commonly used statistical tests, and illustrates their use. This material was deliberately kept separate from the chapter itself, in order not to distract from the chapter's discussion of the logical relationship between statistics and the research enterprise.

Whereas all of the later chapters (beginning with chaper 7) integrate psychological content and experimental methods, the initial chapters focus more exclusively on methods and associated terminology. In chapters 1 through 4, only simple examples with single independent variables are described, so as not to distract from the information on research technique. After the summary of the more elementary statistical concepts in chapter 5, chapter 6 presents a discussion of designs with multiple independent variables. It defines and illustrates blocking variables and moderator variables, and offers an extensive discussion of tests of interactions. Chapter 6 also describes the ways in which additional independent variables can sometimes affect the estimate of variability, and the consequences this can have for statistical significance. Such topics are only occasionally covered in introductory statistics classes. They were included in this methods text because of the insights they contribute to the discussion of multifactor designs.

The two authors have enjoyed teaching experimental methods. The special pleasure this course provides is the opportunity to broaden the ways in which students think, to offer new templates that will help in their later approaches to problems in very different areas of concern. It is for this reason that the text emphasizes ways of thinking. Although this suggests that the specific content covered is secondary, we took special care in its selection. We wanted the students to have contact with questions that were initially intuitively interesting, that had been made more interesting by their research histories, and that involved clever solutions to the problems encountered in the quest for understanding. We have increased our own level of understanding through the writing of this text, so we have high hopes for its readers.

Gustav Levine
Stanley Parkinson

CHAPTER 1

Introduction: The Function of Research Methods

People were gathering information, and successfully using much of this information, long before science came along. The survival of the species is evidence that humans are capable of obtaining useful information without invoking the scientific method. Yet we are all familiar with incorrect information that was believed for long periods of time by intelligent people. For example, there was the belief in bloodletting to reduce fever (which weakened the patients and sometimes killed them), and there was the use of boiling oil to cauterize battlefield wounds when soldiers or sailors lost limbs (which created a toxic reaction from the burnt tissue, increasing the death rate). Remedial procedures sometimes appear reasonable, and are reported by observers to be effective, yet are in fact useless, or even harmful. It must be concluded that there are circumstances where experience and observation can be misleading, and that prior beliefs, or other factors, can affect what is observed or remembered (Nisbett & Ross, 1980). Some of the observational circumstances that are most vulnerable to such errors have been identified. Ways of rearranging the collection of observations to avoid these errors have been developed. These better arrangements for making (and interpreting) observations constitute the largest part of what is meant by research methods. In fact, an informal definition of science might be that science is a series of techniques to help people avoid fooling themselves.

1

The special arrangements for collecting observations that are integral to research procedures are detailed throughout this text, but an example is useful at this point. There is an interesting accidental experiment that occurred naturally and resulted in the abandonment of the use of boiling oil for cauterization. Boiling oil cauterization was used during the 15th and 16th centuries, having been recommended by Giovani Divego (1460–1520) in his classic text on surgical procedures. During military battles army and navy surgeons always had boiling oil handy, which they would apply after amputating a mangled arm or leg. Civilian surgeons followed the same procedures when accidents produced similar injuries.

The 16th century French army physician Ambroise Paré ran out of oil during a battle. The result was two groups of wounded men, one group receiving the burning oil cauterization, and another group, otherwise similarly wounded and similarly treated, who did not have the burning oil applied after the amputation procedure. Contrary to expectations, the surgeon found far more survivors, and better healing, among the noncauterized group, and reported this finding to his colleagues. Paré was something of a nay-sayer, and so was probably happy to be able to show that an established treatment was incorrect. If this dissident physician were simply to claim that in his experience cauterization was an undesirable treatment, his colleagues would have ignored him. As discussed in the following section, it was the form of the evidence that caused the profession to treat the new information seriously.

CONTROL GROUPS

The contrast of two similar groups, the only difference being that one group receives a specific treatment and the other does not, is an excellent situation for testing a treatment's effectiveness. It permits two conditions to be compared, where only one contains the component being tested. This is an example of one kind of observational circumstance that a researcher would deliberately create in order to test a treatment. In this research design, the group without the treatment is called the **control group** or **control condition**, and the group with the treatment is called the **experimental group** or **experimental condition**. It took the presence of a simultaneous control condition, along with an experimental condition (the subjects in the experimental condition receiving the treatment), for the surgeon to be able to recognize that the boiling oil treatment was a poor one. The opportunity, simultaneously, to compare the results in a control group with the results in an experimental group made it easier for other physicians with faith in the treatment to attend to the new contrary information.

Control Variables

In planned experiments care is taken to maintain identical conditions and influences in the experimental and control conditions, to see to it that the situations are the same. Only the treatment that is being tested is permitted to vary from one condition to the other.

The influences and details that could vary if permitted to do so, but that are deliberately kept identical in the two groups, are called **control variables**. If an experimenter wished to test boiling oil cauterization, he or she would include the same kinds of amputations, same ages of patients, same conditions of hygiene, same aftercare, etc. in both the control and experimental conditions. The control variables would then include types of amputations, ages of patients, hygienic conditions, and aftercare.

CONDITIONS THAT FOSTER MISPERCEPTION OF EVIDENCE

A reasonable question is, why do people need such sharp contrasts, that is, the simultaneous presence of both a no-treatment control group and an experimental group, to recognize when a treatment does or does not work? For example, surgeons saw many oil-cauterized patients prior to the accidental experiment of Ambroise Paré, and occasionally saw patients who lost limbs under conditions where no oil was available at the time of their accidents. Why couldn't those surgeons use their memories and accumulated experience to recognize that the use of boiling oil increased deaths? There are a number of conditions that can foster misperception of evidence.

A major cause of distortion of evidence is an observer's prior belief that a treatment works (or does not work). People attend more to information that is consistent with their beliefs and are prone to more often miss evidence that contradicts their beliefs (Greenwald, Pratkanis, Leippe, & Baumgardner, 1986). When evidence accumulates slowly over time, prior belief can permit a person to recall events selectively, forgetting some of the evidence. One way of reducing the effects of prior belief is to have all of the evidence (outcomes) simultaneously present for examination. With planned research, all of the outcomes are recorded and then simultaneously viewed at the end of the experiment.

An additional basic ingredient in self-conscious use of research design is the careful maintenance of similarity between the control and experimental conditions, so that the only difference between the two groups is the presence or absence of the treatment being tested. This requires scrutiny of the two conditions, and searching for control variables that should be held constant. This can be compared with informal (nonexperimental) gathering of information and experience by a physician in practice in Paré's time. It is possible that a particular surgeon only used boiling oil when he removed a limb in his office, but usually did not when patients arrived with a severed limb from a street accident (because the bleeding had stopped). In this case, there would be a number of differences between those treated and not treated with boiling oil. Street accidents could introduce more filth into the wounds, or there could be greater loss of blood, and so on. Thus, extraneous factors (that should have been kept identical in the two conditions for a proper comparison) could be responsible for making a useless or harmful treatment appear effective. The maintenance of identity between the experimental and control conditions (with the exception of the treatment being tested) is probably the single most important principle in good research design. Unfortunately, it can sometimes be a difficult task, with unwanted differences being subtly introduced. Undesired factors that additionally differentiate the experimental and control conditions are called **confounding factors**. A confounding factor is differentially present in the two conditions, just as the treatment is present in one condition but absent in another. Thus, with a confounding factor present, there are two differences between the experimental and control conditions, which then make it impossible to know whether the treatment or the confounding factor is responsible for any effects. The avoidance of confounding factors is discussed in chapters 2 and 3.

There is another interesting phenomenon that operates to prevent people from reaching proper conclusions from evidence. Sometimes when an accepted treatment is applied, if it fails, the patient is blamed. For example, those who die despite receiving a standard treatment are sometimes declared to have been constitutionally weak. On the other hand, if the patient gets well, the treatment is credited for the success. Prior beliefs are similarly maintained when the treatment is not applied. Those who die are thought to have died because they could not receive the treatment. Those who live are thought to have lived because of unusually strong constitutions, or perhaps because of the intercession of prayer.

Similar explanations have operated quite dramatically to maintain confidence in some inadequate forms of psychotherapy. Many different kinds of psychotherapeutic treatment have been developed over the years, and although a number of them can be helpful, some of them lack convincing evidence of effectiveness, yet all of them have their devoted advocates. The claim has generally been made by those using most treatments that patients who do not respond are not motivated, or are not ready for therapy, or do not want to get well. This offers a ready explanation for any individual lack of success. Because a certain percentage of people spontaneously recover with or without therapy (more favorable circumstances at work, a new love or friendship, discovery of a new source of pleasure, a new philosophy or faith, etc.), even an ineffective but busy therapist will see some people whose state of mind appears to improve. By dismissing those who did not improve as in some sense not ready for therapy, and accepting those who improve as having benefited from the therapy, any therapy, and any therapist, can appear efficacious.

The point is that given an assumption that something works, the occasions when it does not work are often explained away. It is rare to find a phenomenon that human beings cannot explain to their own satisfaction, when they are motivated to do so. Research methods are arrangements for making and interpreting observations that make it difficult to explain away evidence selectively—that make it difficult to ignore information that contradicts old assumptions.

A DEFINITION OF SCIENCE

The preceding discussion should make it clear that **science** is not just the organized information that has accumulated from the application of research methods, but includes the research methods themselves. The research methods are arrangements for making and interpreting observations in a manner that minimizes the probability of reaching incorrect conclusions. Thus, science could be defined as both an accumulation of knowledge and an accumulation of research methods that function to limit self-deception by serious observers. It offers some protection against the influence of prior beliefs and the various forms of bias that often are spawned by enthusiasm about an original idea.

OBJECTIVE METHODS, NOT OBJECTIVE SCIENTISTS

The point has been made that good research design is necessary because personal bias can distort observations and conclusions. Yet it is occasionally implied that scientists are objective individuals, and that it is their scientific detachment and tradition of careful observation that yields the more reliable information on which the society depends. Nothing could be further from the truth. Scientists, including psychologists, like other human beings, can (and usually do) fall in love with their own hunches, ideas, and theories. This is in fact desirable. Interesting new ideas are often difficult to validate. It frequently takes a great deal of passionate conviction and excitement about an idea to pursue the difficult path of confirmation. Therefore, the passion that scientists have for their own ideas is in fact useful, and probably necessary. Scientists can be expected to be protagonists for their own explanations, and to seek to find data in support of their own theories. On the other hand, this is what makes it so necessary for the scientist to use a set of techniques that can identify useless concepts and incorrect conclusions, and that can force the scientist to recognize unexpected facts. The scientific method and its research procedures perform this function, permitting the scientist to maintain his or her enthusiasm and the bias that this sometimes entails. Although the goal of avoiding the effects of the researcher's bias is not always realized by the use of standard research procedures, these procedures are far more effective than just a reliance on careful observation and the best of intentions. An additional factor strengthening the scientific method is the requirement of recording not only what was observed, but what was done. This too involves special procedures and concerns, because descriptions of what procedures were followed could themselves be affected by bias. Thus, in each scientific specialty, characteristic ways have developed for how an experiment is to be described, permitting other scientists to check and see if the scientist doing the research has overlooked possible confounding factors or has otherwise compromised the experiment. This standardization of procedural description allows other scientists to repeat the experiment and see if the results do in fact come out as reported by the prior observer. Thus, the entire enterprise is geared to permit the rest of the scientific community to peer over the shoulder of the person doing the research, and to minimize the influence of the expectations or hopes of the researcher.

The goals of avoiding bias and confounding factors are not always met, so future researchers sometimes have to ferret out the experimental errors of earlier researchers. But the requirement of full description of what was done permits the members of the scientific community within a discipline to keep track of the details of each other's research, and to criticize each other, and to redo or improve each other's experiments. The result is that the scientific community, in its research role, does offer the best source of unbiased information that the society has. Yet there is no requirement, or assumption, that scientists are personally any more objective than any other group of people. *Objective evidence* refers to evidence gathered in a specific fashion, and does not refer to evidence gathered by mythical, unbiased people.

SUMMARY

There are circumstances where even careful observations can lead to incorrect conclusions. Some of these situations have been identified, and procedures to reduce the probability of reaching erroneous conclusions have been developed. These procedures constitute the methods used by researchers. Use of these procedures is synonymous with good research design.

An important component of good research design is the use of (at least) two similar groups, the only difference between the two groups being the specific condition or treatment being tested for effectiveness. The group with the treatment is called the experimental group, and the group without the treatment is called the control group. The factors in the situation that are deliberately kept identical in the two conditions are called control variables. When it is time to draw conclusions from a research project, to avoid distortions in memory, all of the evidence is simultaneously examined.

Although maximal effort is devoted to avoiding any systematic differences between the experimental and control conditions, this attempt is not always successful. Factors that differentiate the experimental and control conditions in addition to the treatment difference being tested are called confounding factors. Confounding factors are specifically those factors that are differentially present in the experimental and control conditions, in addition to the treatment being tested. The presence of confounding factors thus prevents clear conclusions as to the cause of any differences observed between the experimental and control conditions. Usually, the presence of confounding factors is not recognized by the experimenter, or else they would be removed. If they are recognized but cannot be avoided, the experimenter limits her or his conclusions.

Science is defined here as both an accumulation of knowledge and an accumulation of research methods that function to limit self-deception by serious observers. It is assumed that scientists are no more objective than people in other professions. In fact, with regard to their own work, they are likely to be highly enthusiastic and to have strong emotional stakes in their own ideas. This could lead to bias in observations and recollection of results, and to distortions of conclusions. This is why good experimental procedures are so necessary. It is the use of such procedures that provides an external basis for objectivity. That is, good research design limits the extent to which even a prejudiced person can draw incorrect conclusions. Thus, it is not necessary for scientists to be objective; rather, they employ methods that are likely to avoid the kinds of errors that have been recognized as common in all data collection procedures. Scientists use methods that are most likely to yield objective results, and so it is their methods that we study in order to become scientists.

NEW WORDS AND PHRASES IN CHAPTER 1

confounding factors
control condition
control group
control variables
experimental condition
experimental group
science

CHAPTER 2

Variables: Thinking of the World in Terms of Relationships Between Variables

It should be clear from the preceding chapter that research methods can be understood as means of minimizing the probability that observers will distort the facts. But what is the nature of the facts that psychologists seek? And what need researchers observe to obtain these facts? The point is made in this chapter that what have to be observed are things called *variables*, and that the facts sought are relationships between variables. Psychological questions are more readily answered when they are restated as questions about the relationships between variables.

PSYCHOLOGICAL VARIABLES DEFINED

Events and phenomena that are potentially variable, and in which observers have some interest, are called **variables**. Deciding what is of interest, and what needs to be observed, is still part of the creative process of psychological research and psychological theorizing. The range of variables that are of interest to psychologists continuously expands and changes, but generally concerns overt and covert responses and characteristics that fall into the following five categories: abilities (such as intelligence or memory), responses (such as reaction times or helping behavior), attitudes (such as being religious or liking some individual), cognitive states (such as attention or certainty), and subjective experiences (such as moods or anxiety). These all refer to characteristics of people. In addition, variables can be defined by differences in circumstances, circumstances that affect people. In summary, psychologists are interested in observing and learning about personal and situational variables.

When abilities, responses, attitudes, cognitive states, and experiences vary, psychologists search for explanations; that is, they attempt to learn what causes the variability in interesting variables. When variables can vary but on specific occasions do not, psychologists search for what maintains the constancy. Things that never vary usually lack interest. If there is interest in intelligence, it is because intelligence varies. This is also true for mood states such as depression, or for cognitive states such as attention, or for aspects of learning such as memory, which is better or worse from time to time or better for one thing and worse for another. It is the variability that poses the meaningful questions, and so variable phenomena, and phenomena that can vary but do not, are of potential interest. If these variables are in any way related to people's abilities, responses, attitudes, cognitive states, or experiences, they attract the attention of psychologists.

RESTATING QUESTIONS AS RELATIONSHIPS BETWEEN VARIABLES

In describing the conditions under which a particular variable (some response, or perhaps some attitude) varies, it is generally necessary to refer to the influence of some other variable. For example, when someone expresses anger on one occasion but not on another, the question of what is causing these variations in behavior is usually best expressed by asking what other variable has to be present or absent for the occurrence (or absence) of anger (low blood sugar, an interpersonal slight, frustration of some desire, etc.). Conversely, when the influence of a particular variable is questioned (e.g., what is the effect of low blood sugar?), the question achieves specificity only after naming a second variable on which it potentially impacts (e.g., what is the effect of low blood sugar on patience?).

As another example, suppose that a question is raised about the extent to which noise interferes in a particular task. Although the question sounds reasonable as stated, it is not a clear question because it only identifies a single variable, level of noise. The desired improvement in clarity is seen after the identification of a second variable. In this example the second variable is implied by the word *interferes.* The second variable is identified by asking what is meant by interferes. Perhaps what is meant is that an increase is expected in the number of errors with noise. In this case the second variable would be *number of errors,* and an experiment would be done on the relationship between level of noise and the number of errors. Interference could have been defined differently, for example, in terms of time to complete the task. If that had been the definition of interference, then time to complete the task would be the second variable, and the experiment would have been a study of the relationship between noise and time to complete a task. For example, there would be two situations for some task, one with and one without noise. Time to complete the task in the two situations would be compared.

In summary, the question of whether noise interferes in a task would have been profitably restated as a question of the relationship between two variables. The variable noise would be varied within the experiment, and a second variable, say, number of errors, or time, would have been observed to see if it varied consistently with noise levels. A second variable is generally implied in any meaningful question. Frequently, merely rephrasing a question in terms of specified variables suggests the form that an experiment could take that would examine the question. Thus, when wondering how to do an experiment to answer a question, it is usually best to begin by thinking of how to rephrase the question so that the implicit variables are overtly specified.

Look at the following examples of researchable questions:

1. Is increased crowding associated with increased anxiety?
2. Is exposure to greater amounts of TV violence associated with more aggressive behavior in children?
3. Is increased stress associated with increased absenteeism on the job?

As a contrast, the same three issues could be verbalized in lay person's terms:

1. Joe: "I hate these crowded conditions." Mary: "I wonder if it is bad for us?"
2. "Wife: I wish I could get junior to stop watching all those violent TV shows." Husband: "Do you think that it affects him in any way?"
3. Boss's assistant: "There is a lot of stress on that assembly line." Boss: "It probably keeps them awake. Seriously, are

you suggesting that it is having an effect that we should be concerned about?"

Note that the lay person's phrasing is more general, and asks broader questions. This is generally the result of not specifying the second variable. Specifying the second variable, although making it easier to answer the question, does result in a narrowing of the question. For example, the phrasing in the lay persons's version of Question 3 about assembly line stress, ". . . having an effect that we should be concerned about," asks whether stress has any effect at all, while the professional experimenter's form of the same question asks whether stress has the specific effect of increasing absenteeism. The narrowing of the question with specificity generally means that the question has to be asked repeatedly, introducing different variables each time, to get the full answer. For example, along with asking whether increased stress on the assembly line increases absenteeism, it would be important to also ask whether it is associated with greater work-force turnover and with lower quality of the product.

MANIPULATED VARIABLES (EXPERIMENTAL RESEARCH)

The classic form of a psychological experiment involves the manipulation of a variable, reasonably called a **manipulated variable**, and a second variable, which is observed to see if it covaries with the manipulated variable. The manipulation is part of the experimental procedure. When there are no manipulations in an investigation of relationships between variables, it is still considered research, but it is no longer referred to as experimental research.

The manipulated variable is a variable involving different treatment of subjects in the different conditions. Each such condition, receiving a different treatment, is called a **level**. For example, different amounts of shock could be the levels of one variable, or different instructions for solving some puzzles could be the levels of another variable, or different forms of psychotherapy could be the different levels of still another variable. The manipulated variable has some finite number of levels (manipulations), most frequently not more than 5, though as many as 10 or 20 levels could be defined.

The manipulated variable is tested for its effect on the second variable. The second variable involves measurement of some responses, with the measurements, or scores, being called the **data**.

Data are the measurements of observations reflecting the behavior of subjects (such as reaction times in some task, number of errors in some task, or number of visits before discharge from treatment). A single piece of information, such as a single reaction time, or the number of errors for one subject, is called a **datum**. A single datum is usually a numerical measurement with a potentially infinite range of values. (For example, a datum could be a reaction time for a particular subject of 150 msec, or a specific number of errors, say 7, in the course of completing some task). Under some conditions the data will be qualitative (nonquantitative) observations, that is, recording of categorized outcomes, such as noting for each subject that the subject agreed (or did not agree) to participate, or that the subject did (or did not) detect the stimulus. Sometimes it is convenient to refer to the variable represented by the data as the **criterion variable**, because the data are observed in order to determine whether the variables are related. The data are also referred to as the outcome variable or the outcome measure.

The variations in the manipulation must be the only difference between the levels. It would confuse matters if, in addition to manipulation differences, the subjects in the different levels were different kinds of people. For example, in a study with noise and no noise as the levels of the manipulated variable, and number of errors in some task as the data (as the criterion of whether noise makes a difference), having men in the noise condition and women in the no-noise condition would prevent the experimenter from reaching any clear conclusions. Any differences in errors could be a function of either noise versus no noise, or gender, with no way of knowing which is responsible. (In this example, gender would function as a confounding factor.)

Drawing Conclusions About Cause and Effect with Manipulated Variables

With a manipulated variable the experimenter controls the differences in the variable across conditions of the experiment. If the imposed variations in conditions are associated with differences in the data, it is reasonable to infer that the controlled manipulations are responsible for the data differences. Thus, it is possible to draw conclusions of cause and effect between a manipulated variable and a criterion variable.

It is common to speak of a manipulated variable as an **independent variable**. An independent variable is a variable used to distinguish or define different conditions in the experiment. When using a manipulated variable, the criterion variable is called a **dependent variable**. The dependent variable is the variable on which observations are made during the experiment. The reason the phrase *dependent variable* is used when the other variable is a manipulated variable, is that if the variables are related, the scores constituting the data will tend to be different, depending on the level of the manipulated variable. The independent-dependent variable distinction makes sense for manipulated variables, because cause and effect inferences can be drawn. The independent variable is varied, the dependent variable is observed, and if the dependent variable's values tend to covary with the levels of the independent variable, we conclude that changes in the independent variable affect the dependent variable. The alternative to a manipulated variable is a subject variable, which does not lend itself as easily to cause and effect conclusions. Subject variables are discussed in the following section.

SUBJECT VARIABLES

Sometimes research is done in which there is no manipulation of a variable. For example, suppose there is interest in the possibility of a relationship between socioeconomic status and education. The question is whether, on the average, people in different socioeconomic classes spend different numbers of years in school. Suppose that three socioeconomic classes are defined, lower, middle, and upper. It would not be possible to arrange for people to be placed in different socioeconomic classes; rather, it would be necessary to find people in the different socioeconomic classes, and then to determine the average number of years of education for each socioeconomic class in the sample. It would not have been possible to manipulate socioeconomic class, but only to classify people according to their prior status.

When subjects are differentiated on the basis of a classification scheme rather than manipulation, the differentiating variable is called a **subject variable**. Stated another way, a subject variable is a variable based on differences between the subjects, where the distinctions in the levels are based on a classification scheme for the subjects rather than on any differences in manipulation. Usually the classification refers to some enduring personal characteristic of the subjects, such as personality, psychological diagnosis, religiousness, or gender; or the classification can be based on life circumstances, such as type of neighborhood, married or not, or socioeconomic status. Thus, married and not married would be two different levels of the subject variable marital status. The same variable could be defined with four levels: married, not married, divorced, and widowed. Ideally, the subjects in each level should be randomly selected from all members of the subpopulation with the classification of that level.

In summary, when a manipulated variable defines the levels, the different levels refer to different conditions of the experiment. When a subject variable defines the levels, the different levels refer to different groups (different categories of subjects).

A subject variable does not always have to refer to an individual's long-term personal status. It can refer to a brief experience (people who have experimented once or twice with drugs, or people who have experienced disabling moods of depression). A subject variable can also refer to some behavioral categorization, as when an experimenter is interested in comparing those subjects who came late for the experiment, with those who arrived early. Finally, because the measurements constituting the data in psychological experiments are representations of subjects' characteristics, the variable on which data are gathered is a subject variable (e.g., reaction times, numbers of errors, number of trials to learn, etc.). Thus, by definition, all criterion variables are subject variables. Therefore, a subject variable experiment has at least two subject variables, one designating different groups, and the other being the criterion variable. Sometimes, as discussed next, it is hard to know which variable is which, and the distinction is not used.

Difficulty in Determining Causality with Subject Variables

With manipulated variables it is possible to test for a causal relationship; that is, an experiment with a manipulated variable is a test of whether or not the manipulated variable has an effect on the data (the dependent variable). However, subject variables are less likely to be examined with the hope of obtaining that information. When using subject variables to define the different groups in an experiment, the question is likely to be restricted to whether there is a relationship between the two subject variables (the subject variable defining the different groups, and the criterion variable). That is, the question with subject variables is frequently restricted to whether different status on one variable (say, socioeconomic status) has any relationship to status on another variable (say, educational level).

By contrast, causal relationships can be inferred with a manipulated variable, because, with proper use of manipulated variables, all of the subjects are obtained from the same population and are randomly assigned to conditions. If differences are then found in the dependent variable, the best explanation is the variations in the manipulation (across levels).

Direction of Causality with Subject Variables

Along with the difficulty of determining whether or not there is a causal relationship between subject variables, there is often a problem of determining the direction of a possibly causal relationship. For example, suppose that a psychologist is interested in the relationship between depression in children, and parental interaction with the children. Is there a relationship between these two variables (depression in the children and amount of parental interaction with the children)? Assume that the psychologist identified one set of parents as spending much time with their children, and another group as spending little time with their children, and then measured the children on some depression scale. If a relationship was found, with less parental interaction time being associated with more depression, would that mean that lack of time spent was responsible for the depression? Could it not be that parents are discouraged from spending time with children who are depressed? The experimenter, in planning the study, could have done it another way. The experimenter could have reversed the sequence in which the variables were examined, first dividing children up into those who are depressed versus those who are not, and then measuring each child's home for the amount of time the parents spent with the child, yielding two groups of scores, time spent with depressed children and time spent with nondepressed children.

Usually, when both variables are simply observations (measurements or classifications), rather than one being controlled by the experimenter, the direction of causality is not clear. In fact, which variable is the criterion variable and which is the grouping variable is not always clear. That is why the question being answered is often limited to whether the two variables are related. By contrast, when the experimenter controls the status of the subjects on one variable, manipulating one of the variables, the direction of causality can be inferred. For example, suppose one could arrange for some parents to consistently spend much time with their children, and for other parents to spend little time with their children, the assignments to the different time arrangements being random. Of course, this could not be done for ethical reasons, but assume that it had somehow been arranged in an authoritarian state. A difference in depression between the two groups of children could then be interpreted as having been caused by the different amounts of parental attention.

Correlational Research

It is fairly common, when analyzing the data in an experiment that only includes subject variables, to use the statistical technique of correlation. Although other statistical techniques are also used, and subject variable research is not the only place where correlational techniques are applied, it has nonetheless become commonplace for subject variable research to be called **correlational research**. When researchers hear the phrase *correlational research*, they generally make the assumption of limitations on conclusions concerning causality. (Further discussion contrasting correlational research with manipulated variable research is offered in chapter 4, where different research designs are examined. A discussion of when to use the statistical technique of correlation is offered in chapter 5, the chapter explicating statistical procedures.)

There are some techniques for determining the direction of causality in some subject variable situations, using some advanced statistical techniques. But in most instances with subject variables the knowledge gained from research is limited to whether or not the variables are related and whether it is a positive or negative relationship.

A *positive relationship* is one in which high scores on one variable are associated with high scores on the other variable, with similar correspondences for low scores, and for moderate scores. A *negative relationship* is one in which high scores on one variable are associated with low scores on the other. For example, depressed people tend to have low activity levels, and so higher scores on a depression index are likely to be associated with lower activity levels. Thus, one would say that there is a negative relationship (or a negative correlation) between depression and activity level.

Confounding Factors in Relationships Between Subject Variables

The point has been made that interpreting causality is a frequent limitation with subject variables. One problem, already discussed, is that often the direction of causality cannot be ascertained. A second problem is that when a relationship is uncovered between two subject variables in a study, it is possible that the true relationship is not between the variables overtly studied, but between each of these variables and some third variable, which operates as a confounding factor. For example, in a study of school achievement of children who live within the take off and landing patterns of airports (and are therefore exposed to frequent low-flying plane noises), it might be found that the children within these patterns do more poorly in school. But because the two variables are subject variables (living area and school performance), it is possible that they are related through some third variable. Specifically, the neighborhood situated close to the airport noises may be poorer (having less political power to keep the planes away, or paying lower rents because of the noise). Thus, exposure to airport noises could be related to socioeconomic status. There is evidence of a relationship between socioeconomic status and school achievement: elementary school children in poor neighborhoods have lower academic achievement (Garbarino & Asp, 1981, chap. 4). Thus, the variable of school achievement is also related to socioeconomic status. The existence of a third variable (socioeconomic status) that is related to both of the two overt variables (exposure to more noise from low flying planes and school achievement) has implications for interpreting any positive results in such a situation. The two variables, each being related to socioeconomic status, could each be, in part, an indirect measure of socioeconomic status. When two measures, in part, both measure the same thing, the two measures tend to be related to each other.

As a simple example, ability to draw (which could be measured) is related to age, as is size of hands. Thus, one could show that larger hands draw better (because larger hands tend to belong to older children, who draw better). In fact, hand size itself does not affect drawing ability, but nonetheless a measure of size of hands and a measure of ability to draw would appear to be related, because they are in fact both related to maturity. Analogously, conclusions of a direct relationship between airport noise and school performance might be incorrect, despite a difference in school performance in the two different noise-exposed groups, if it is true that both variables are related to socioeconomic status.

A third variable that is related to both variables will have different values in the different groups that have been defined by one of the variables. For example, a third variable of socioeconomic status would only be related to whether or not people live near an airport if there are, on the average, differences in socioeconomic status between the people who do and do not live near the airport. In this sense, socioeconomic status would be a confounding factor in a study of the relationship between living near an airport and school performance. Specifically, both socioeconomic status and where people lived would be different in the two groups being examined for differences in school performance.

When potential confounding factors are recognized in subject variable experiments, they are usually removed by converting them to control variables (keeping them constant in both groups). Thus, Cohen, Gary, Krantz, & Stokols (1980) went to the trouble of locating groups within and outside of the airport noise patterns that could meet approximately the same socioeconomic criteria, and so made the comparisons across those socioeconomically matched groups. However, it is not always possible to identify all of the potential confounding factors when studying subject variables; there are usually many confounding factors present.

As another example, assume a study of the relationship between intelligence and self-esteem (both of which are subject variables). Intelligence correlates with success in school, and success in school correlates with self-esteem. If a positive relationship were obtained between intelligence and self-esteem, it might actually reflect the two facts that both intelligence and self-esteem are related to success in school. The initial observed relationship, however, would be that intelligence and self-esteem are directly related to each other, rather than that they are both related to scholastic success. Which interpretation is correct is difficult to establish with research that only uses subject variables.

It is difficult to avoid the presence of other naturally occurring confounding factors that can act as alternative explanations for observed relationships between subject variables. With a subject variable the experimenter often has to take the situation as it exists, with unspecified differences between groups accompanying the specified ones. Thus, when doing research with subject variables it is difficult to know whether the subject variables that have been chosen for examination and found related are directly related, or whether they are only related through some third variable that has a common relationship to the two studied variables and so acts as a confounding factor. When subject variables are tested for relationships with each other, it is useful to recognize that such a study is often best seen as a first step in identifying relationships between variables, and that a larger chain of connections may exist than initially appears to be the case.

These limitations in interpretation of subject variable relationships do not make investigation of such relationships useless. Finding two subject variables related, it is then possible to search for additional variables related to these two. Eventually a pattern of relationships may emerge that is itself informative. For example, assume a finding of a relationship between time on welfare and poor school performance—that is, the longer a family is on welfare, the more poorly their children do in school. The correlation would not make particular sense, but it indicates a problem to be investigated. What would probably be discovered is that both variables are related to extent of poverty. One is directly related: The longer on welfare, the more abject the poverty. School performance would only be indirectly related to extent of poverty—that is, in extremely poor homes, there are more often crowded conditions, with multiple families sharing the same dwelling. Crowded conditions offer poorer conditions for studying. It is not only the lack of a place to study, but with multiple families, and unemployed people, late hours are kept, and there can be inadequate sleeping time for children. These children are thus less likely to do well in school. The result could be that poor school performance, like time on welfare, could be related to the depth of poverty. An initial finding of a relationship between time on welfare and poor school performance could lead to further observations of these other, more interesting relationships.

Studies with subject variables are usually easier to conduct than studies with manipulated variables. Thus, one sometimes begins with the study of subject variables and, finding interesting suggested relationships, is then encouraged to invest in the more expensive manipulated variable studies. For example, a social intervention offering better study conditions to the children in some families, and comparing their later school performance with children in otherwise similar circumstances (similarly encouraged to study but with no special facilities made available), would offer a test of whether or not conditions at home are in fact relevant. A manipulated variable would offer a more direct test of a relationship, although it clearly would involve much expense to the society. It would be reasonable to first test the possibilities with subject variable research, going to the more expensive, but inferentially stronger, manipulated variable research after some encouragement from the subject variable findings.

THE POSSIBILITY OF DEFINING THE SAME VARIABLE AS EITHER A SUBJECT VARIABLE OR A MANIPULATED VARIABLE

Sometimes it is possible to define the same variable as either a manipulated variable or a subject variable. An example is level of motivation to succeed on a job. It is possible to manipulate motivation by varying the promises of promotion or eventual income; it is also possible to manipulate motivation by altering attitudes, making a job more desirable in terms of status symbols; or embarrassment could be used, putting someone in a position of facing embarrassment if he or she fails. There are many ways to manipulate motivation to succeed on a job, so motivation can be introduced as a manipulated variable.

However, degree of motivation can also be used as a basis for classification of people prior to the experiment, and thus be a subject variable. For example, people normally come to a job with differing degrees of motivation. It would be possible to measure the new job applicants on their initial desire to succeed, or some related measure might be used, such as how badly they need the job, or how long they were previously unemployed, or how much they are in debt, etc. Any such measure would be a measure of some prior status, and so if used as a measure of motivation, motivation would be a subject variable.

It is useful to contrast an examination of the same question both as a subject variable experiment and a manipulated variable experiment. Assume some means of identifying people who are clearly experiencing frustration within their lives, and people who are not experiencing frustration. A random sample is obtained from each of these two populations. The two samples of people (frustrated and not frustrated) are compared on a measure of aggressiveness, so that the study is a test of whether there is a relationship between frustration and aggression. Suppose that it is discovered that the people classified as frustrated are in fact more often classified as aggressive than those who are not frustrated. This would suggest that frustration and aggression are in some way related. However, it would not be possible from this research to know whether frustration leads to aggression, or, conversely, whether people who are more aggressive in life find themselves more frustrated by life.

This can be contrasted with the interpretation if the relationship between frustration and aggression had been investigated with frustration as a manipulated variable. This would have been done by creating the frustration for one group of subjects within the experiment while being careful not to frustrate the control group subjects. If, again, a relationship had been found between frustration and aggression, it could be concluded that frustration leads to aggression. The classic research with frustration and aggression does treat frustration as a manipulated variable. (Barker, Dembo, & Lewin,1941; Berkowitz, 1989; Dollard, Doob, Miller, Mowrer, & Sears, 1939).

Research with a manipulated variable is, in a sense, like moving a wall switch and seeing the light go off. We can repeat the manipulation, again seeing the effect, that is, seeing that the light goes off if and only if we move the switch (the effect only being there when we institute the manipulation). In the manipulated frustration example, frustration is actively instituted (switch on) for a group of subjects, and aggression is observed to be high; frustration is carefully withheld (switch off) for a group of subjects, and aggression is observed to be low. By controlling the presence or absence of frustration, we can identify the fact that there is a difference in amount of aggression in conjunction with the presence or absence of frustration, the aggression literally following from the presence or absence of frustration. In identifying a relationship between the movement of a switch and a light, although the light on and switch movement are essentially simultaneous events, our control of one (the switch) lets us see which one follows from the other.

As a contrast, research with subject variables is like most attempts to draw conclusions from mere observation. For example, it was observed, years ago, that there was a positive relationship between working as a milkmaid, and freedom from smallpox. What one saw was women working outdoors, and it was assumed that outdoor work was healthy, and responsible for the low disease rate. What was observed together was assumed to have a causal relationship. The specific milking of the cows and their incidental inoculation effects were not recognized as factors that were related to both the life style and the absence of disease.

FACTORS

There are times when it is not necessary, or useful, to specify whether a variable is a manipulated or a subject variable; it is then called a **factor**. A factor is a variable that distinguishes a finite number of groups or conditions of an experiment, without regard to the manipulated/subject variable distinction. If neither variable is defined in such a way as to permit the clear delineation of a finite number of distinct levels (a few groups or conditions), the word factor would not be used. But if there are clearly distinguishable groups or treatments, the word *factor* is often employed in referring to the levels of the variable. Stated another way, the dimension along which groups or conditions are distinguished is called a factor.

Having learned the distinctions between a manipulated variable and a subject variable, it may seem strange to have to learn a word that blurs the distinction. However, it has the advantage of offering a term to use for the variable differentiating the groups in an experiment prior to the decision as to whether to use a manipulated or subject variable, or when this distinction is not at issue. The technical literature frequently refers to variables as factors.

Another common meaning for the word *factor*, outside of its use in discussing experimental designs, is that of an essential or influential component in a situation: for example, "What factors influenced the recent downturn in the stock market?" or, "I doubt that his father's influence was a factor in his promotion." *Factor* retains some of that meaning here, in that a factor is a variable being investigated for possible influence or relevance within an experiment. This is usually done by differentiating levels on the basis of some factor (different conditions or different groups), and seeing if differences in levels on the factor are associated with differences on some criterion variable.

At this juncture only single-factor experiments have been discussed. In later sections of the text multiple-factor experiments are discussed, with some of the factors being subject variables, and some being manipulated variables. For example, one might wish to study the effect of physical threat, say from electric shock, on ability to perform fine motor tasks (such as soldering very thin wires, all close together in a very small space, with only some subjects led to fear shock), and also distinguish the performance of men and women at this fine motor task. Thus two factors would be studied simultaneously in the same experimental situation, one being a subject variable (gender) and the other being a manipulated variable (physical threat). The criterion variable could be time to complete the task.

It is the fact that both manipulated variables and subject variables are often found in the same experiment, and that the same variables can sometimes be defined both ways, that makes it useful to include a thorough discussion of subject variables in a text concerned with experimental methods.

THE NEED FOR OPERATIONAL DEFINITIONS

In defining variables used in research, it is critical that the experimenter be specific in indicating what is meant by each variable. The highly specific definitions used in psychology, as well as in other sciences, are called operational definitions. In this section, reasons are given as to why such care is required when defining variables, and two types of operational definition are described.

Psychological variables have been defined previously as potentially variable events and characteristics such as abilities, responses, attitudes, cognitive states, or experiences. Some variables are easily defined, so that if used in an experiment there would be no doubt as to what was being studied. For example, in a study examining the relationship between gender and annual income, normally there would be no question as to whether or not a subject was male or female, and annual income could simply be taken from tax returns.

On the other hand, what if the study examined the relationship between gender and anxiety, to see whether there is a difference in anxiety level between men and women? How would one define anxiety? Suppose a questionnaire was used. One such questionnaire could consist of a list of typical symptoms experienced by anxious people, such as irritability, sleep disturbance, muscle tension, headaches, problems in concentrating, and so on. The subjects would be asked to check those that applied to them, and each subject's score would be the total number of symptoms checked. Another approach might be to simply ask the subjects to rate themselves on how anxious they are on an 11-point scale (with 0 for never anxious and 10 for anxious all the time). The problem is that the most anxious person as determined by one method might not be the most anxious person as determined by another, resulting in different relative rankings with different definitions of anxiety.

This point might be clearer when looking at the definition of a nonpsychological attribute. Suppose one wanted to test people on sailing skill. Would you get different results depending on whether you used the speed with which people carried out the different necessary maneuvers (jibe, reefing, etc.), as opposed to having them enter a race and comparing different finishing times? As another example, suppose you wished to rank order people as to how well they cooked, relative to each other. Assume that the definition was to be based on how well the different people prepared different recipes, using judges to decide who made the dishes best. Would you find different results depending on which dishes you asked them to make? Would you find different results depending on whether the judges were asked to rate the dishes on how closely the dishes resembled some preconceived best version of that dish versus looking for originality in what was produced? Would there be still different results in seeing how quickly and efficiently each person made the dish?

Efficiency at a task might be positively related to the psychological variable of compulsivity, but creativity at the same task might be negatively related to compulsivity. What all of this implies is that if there are different definitions of a variable, be it a response, a skill, a mood, an ability, and so on, it is conceivable that the same person would be placed higher or lower on the dimension, depending on the definition used. This in turn could result in different results from the research, with the results changing with different definitions. It might seem that the critical issue is what is the *correct* definition for any one variable. But it is not always possible to decide just which is the correct definition. Therefore, emphasis is placed on being very clear as to which definition has been used. Knowing the definitions used, people can more readily replicate the results. Further, if they disagree with the definitions used, they can redo the experiment with different definitions for one or more of the variables, and see if that changes the results.

Operational Definitions Defined

An **operational definition** is one that clearly specifies how the levels of a variable are to be defined or manipulated, or how scores on a variable are to be measured, in a particular study. The word *operational* refers to the fact that the specific operations are specified for identifying differences along the dimensions of a variable. For example, assume that an experimenter is looking at the effects of success versus failure on moods, and plans to manipulate success and failure. One question to ask is, what operations did the experimenter engage in to make one group of subjects believe they were successful and another group believe that they had failed? Or, if the independent variable in a study had been problem complexity, what had the experimenter done to make one set of problems more complex than another set?

The definition used for defining a manipulated variable is called an **experimental operational definition**. In an experimental operational definition the manipulations are specified in a way that permits other experimenters to duplicate the manipulations. For example, if fear of shock were manipulated to vary anxiety levels, the levels of shock to which subjects were exposed in the different groups, and what the shock apparatus looked like, would be detailed.

Dependent variables are defined simply by specification of the means of measurement and specification of criteria used for classification. This is equally true of most subject variables, whether or not they are dependent variables. That is, subject variables are not controlled by the experimenter; they are merely responses of subjects, or classifications of characteristics that already exist in the subjects. The basis for the classification, or precisely how the measurements are made, has to be specified. In these cases, the operational definition used can be called a **measured operational definition**.

Let us again use the example of anxiety, assuming that it is a subject variable in a study (groups being identified, for example, as high or low in anxiety). The experimenter would specify just how anxiety is measured. If a standard test is used, such as the Taylor Manifest Anxiety scale (Taylor, 1953), the name of the test is given. Were it a rarely used test, the test would be described. If instead of an already developed test the experimenter used a simple self-rating by subjects of their own anxiety levels, then the precise nature of the wording, the number of points in the scale, the instructions to subjects, and so on, would all be fully described. The criteria for high versus low anxiety that were used, that is, the scores, or ratings, that define the different levels of the anxiety variable, would be specified. The same descriptive process would be used if, for example, anxiety were the dependent variable in a study of how being accused of cheating affects anxiety.

More often than not, dependent variables are quantitative variables. However, this is not always the case, sometimes because good quantitative measures are not available, sometimes because they are too time consuming. An experiment could be done in which the dependent variable is classification of subjects as anxious or not, or, in a compliance study, whether or not they volunteer to contribute time or money to some cause. The main point is that it is always important to specify just what criteria were used to make the classifications.

In summary, an operational definition is a highly specific definition of a variable in that it details the precise means of measuring the variable to obtain scores or classifications (a measured operational definition), or specifies the exact operations involved in the manipulation which defines the presence or absence—or variations in intensity—at the different levels of the variable (an experimental operational definition).

Many texts, and some experimenters, do not make a self-conscious distinction between experimental and measured operational definitions. They note, simply and correctly, that an operational definition is always a highly specific definition of a variable, as it is used in an experiment, period. We have offered a more specific discussion as an aid to the neophyte researcher who might otherwise be confused by having the same term referring to both specificity in measurement and specificity in manipulation.

SUMMARY

Variables were defined, and the usefulness of restating questions in terms of relationships between variables was discussed. Identification of implicit variables in questions, for the purpose of specifying more than one variable in any question, was illustrated. Different kinds of variables were distinguished.

One distinction was between manipulated and subject variables. A manipulated variable involves different treatment of subjects, creating different conditions within the experiment. Subject variables involve group differentiation based on different classifications of the subjects. Both manipulated and subject variables are examined for their relationships to criterion variables (outcome variables), which are variables represented by the data. When the variable is manipulated, it is also called an independent variable, and the criterion variable is called a dependent variable.

With manipulated variables it is possible to infer causal links between the independent and the dependent variable. When a subject variable is used, it is often difficult to draw conclusions of cause and effect. In fact, it is sometimes sensible to avoid trying to identify which one is the criterion variable. When only using subject variables in an experiment, the question is likely to be restricted to whether there is a relationship between the variables, leaving the issue of causality to further research. When research is carried out with exclusively subject variables, the research is often referred to as correlational research.

When doing correlational research, and using just two subject variables that are found to be related, the relationship could be a function of a third (unidentified) variable, which could have the role of a confounding factor. This can occur when both of the subject variables in the experiment are related to a third variable.

The possibility of redefining a variable as either a subject variable or a manipulated variable was discussed. The absence of the manipulated variable/subject variable distinction in the word *factor* was discussed, the word *factor* being appropriate in reference to both manipulated and subject variables. The word *factor* retains the more general distinction of referring to variables which define the different conditions or groups of an experiment.

Finally, an operational definition was defined as a highly specific definition of a variable, as it is used in a particular research project. In addition, we distinguished two types of operational definition. One is a measured operational definition, which describes the precise means of measuring the variable to define the different values or levels (when measurement is used), or describes the exact basis for classification when classification is used. The other is an experimental operational definition, which specifies the exact operations involved in the manipulation that defines the presence or absence (or variations in intensity) of the variable, generally used in defining manipulated variables.

NEW WORDS AND PHRASES IN CHAPTER 2

correlational research
criterion variable
data
datum
dependent variable
experimental operational definition
factor
independent variable
level
manipulated variable
measured operational definition
operational definition
subject variable
variables

CHAPTER 3

Rules For Research: A Brief Checklist of Things to Consider for a Credible Experiment

In chapter 1 it was stated that one of the ways of minimizing incorrect conclusions from observations is to have two groups of differently treated people simultaneously compared with each other (as in the contrast of an experimental and control condition). Comparing two or more conditions then, is one of the features of good experimental design. There are a few other rules that are generally followed, along with procedures and constraints that are only appropriate under some conditions. The five most consistently followed rules are specified and discussed in this chapter. These rules can constitute a kind of checklist for proper procedures. Additional concerns that are only relevant in particular circumstances are discussed in appropriate contexts. The rules begin with the familiar requirement of more than one condition in an experiment.

RULE 1: MULTIPLE CONDITIONS RULE

There must be more than one condition in the experiment. There should be at least one condition which can be recognized as a control condition.

Discussion of Rule 1

The classic distinction between conditions is between an experimental and a control condition. A control condition can only be defined with reference to a specific experimental condition, because a control condition is the absence of the experimental manipulation (with no alternative manipulation taking its place). For example, a test can be made of whether caffeine before bedtime delays falling asleep. The experimental group would have a cup of regular coffee with supper, and the control group would have a cup of high-quality decaffeinated coffee (that could not be differentiated, by taste, from regular coffee). A pill containing caffeine and an identical-looking pill that does not contain caffeine could be used in place of the two types of coffee. Suppose that, instead of the effect of caffeine, the effect of prebedtime exercise was being examined. In this case, the control group would be sure not to exercise before bedtime.

Sometimes it is necessary to compare two different manipulations. For example, an experimenter compared two different interview techniques to see which one elicited more statements involving personal feeling (Levine, 1961). As a dependent measure, the number of statements of feeling uttered by a subject during a half-hour interview was counted (the interview having been recorded, and observers having been trained to recognize statements of feeling). Subjects were recruited from the dormitories of an all-male college in the heart of a big city. Each subject was interviewed in his dormitory room twice, and was told that the interviewer "is interested in what you are experiencing as a student." For one interview the interviewer (the experimenter) limited his responses to "mm-hmm," uttered every time the subject expressed some personal feeling. This could be called the attention only method (because it constituted selective attention to statements of feeling). During the other interview, the experimenter, immediately following a statement of feeling, paraphrased the statement, offering both attention to feeling statements, and some evidence of understanding. For example, if a subject said, "I like the feeling of having friends around that I can talk to when I get bored with schoolwork," the interviewer would say something like, "It feels good to take a break with the boys." The experimenter made no other kinds of comments during the half-hour interviews, other than the paraphrasing of overtly stated feelings. Facial expressions were also controlled, limited to smiling whenever the subject smiled, in both the attention-only and paraphrasing interviews. Half of the subjects had the attention-only method first, and half the paraphrasing method first.

The question being asked by the experiment was whether the evidence of understanding implicit in paraphrasing was necessary, or whether the mere attention supplied with the attentive responding to feelings (mm-hmm) was sufficient to produce an equal amount of feeling statements. (At the time, paraphrasing was a popular psychotherapy technique thought by some to have the ability to increase expression of feelings, [Rogers, 1942].) The experiment did not produce any evidence of a difference in effectiveness between the two methods.

Note that there was no control condition in this experiment, just a comparison of two different techniques. Therefore, it is reasonable to ask whether the lack of difference between methods reflects the fact that both of the methods were ineffective, or that both of the methods worked and that they were equally effective in their influence on expression of feelings. It is even possible that both methods tended to reduce frequency of statements of feeling, but both did so equally.

To better appreciate this point, suppose that the result of the experiment had been that the paraphrasing method was superior, showing larger numbers of statements of feelings. What could then be concluded? Did only the paraphrasing method work to increase statements of feelings, or, did both methods work, but the paraphrasing method worked better than the attention only method? A third possibility is that neither method worked to increase statements of feeling, but the attention-only method suppressed statements of feeling, making the noneffective paraphrasing method look effective by comparison. The design as given, with just a comparison of the two manipulations, could not have decided between these three possibilities.

To find the answer, a control condition would have to have been added to the experiment, a control condition in which neither manipulation was used. Thus another condition would have to have been included, during which the experimenter merely kept quiet, just looking at the subjects while they spoke (and, as in the other conditions, smiling whenever the subjects smiled). Then any effects of the attention-only method could have been discernible in comparison to the control condition where neither manipulation was present. The control condition, by offering information about frequency of statements of feeling in the absence of the manipulations being tested, would have enabled the experimenter to draw conclusions about the absolute value of the manipulations, along with their relative effectiveness.

In summary, in designing experiments, clear interpretations are only possible when the design includes a condition where the experimental treatment is not present, and no other treatment takes its place. Therefore experiments are designed with multiple conditions, with at least one treatment condition and a control condition.

RULE 2: AVOIDANCE OF CONFOUNDING FACTORS RULE

With one factor, there must be only one difference distinguishing different conditions of the experiment, that difference being variations in the factor.

Discussion of Rule 2

This is the most difficult rule to follow. It is easier to follow with manipulated rather than subject variables. But even with manipulated variables, which the experimenter controls, it is often difficult to avoid confounding factors. The reason is that the imposition of any single manipulation can often introduce additional differences that are not immediately apparent. A classic example of this potential problem is the provision of some medication or other clear treatment to human subjects, which gives the subjects expectations of effects along with the treatment itself. For example, the experimental subjects might receive the medication in pill form. By contrast, the control condition subjects not receiving the medication lack both the medication and the expectation. A similar confounding can occur when introducing chemicals through injections, to either animal or human subjects, where the injection procedure can itself have aversive or stimulating effects independent of the possible effects of the chemical substance. Here, again, the experimental condition is different from the control condition in more than one way. Having more than one treatment difference between the experimental and control conditions prevents any clear conclusions about the causes of any dependent variable differences between the groups.

When it is recognized that the experimental manipulation will add differences between the experimental and control conditions beyond those being tested, the usual procedure is to first try to introduce the experimental manipulation in a way that would avoid introducing these undesired potential influences. For example, sometimes subjects are deliberately given the incorrect impression that they are in the control condition. If a chemical substance is being tested in pill form, the label of the bottle of pills could be exposed, as though by accident, for the subjects in both the experimental and control groups. The label would say *control condition*. Of course, although both groups would see the same bottle label, the experimental condition subjects would receive the real pill, and the control condition subjects would receive an identical looking pill that lacked the substance being tested.

If it is not possible to remove the confounding factors (such as expectation of improvement), the confounding factors are added to the control group (but without adding the manipulation itself). Again, using the pill example, if the experimental group could not be made to believe that the pill is useless, then the control group is given a chemically inactive pill that looks identical to the real pill, and is given the same opportunity as the experimental group to believe that they are ingesting something that could have an effect. If a learning-enhancing drug were being tested on a group of rats, both the experimental and control groups would receive injections, but the control group would only receive an inert saline solution in the injection, and the experimental group would receive the hopefully active drug. That is, whatever procedures are created for the purpose of introducing the manipulation (in this case the injection procedure in order to introduce the chemical), the same procedures are duplicated in the control condition. Thus both groups, in this example, receive injections. Every attempt is always made to maintain an identity in overt aspects of the treatment of subjects in the experimental and control conditions. Similarly, all interactions between subjects and experimenters are made as similar as possible for the two groups. For example, when working with animals, it is important that animals in all groups receive the same amount of handling, including the handling that is necessary to implement the experimental manipulation.

Control conditions that are arranged so as to offer the same expectations and other potentially influential byproducts of the manipulations in the experimental conditions are called **placebo control conditions**. When an experimental manipulation involves giving an aware subject some chemically active substance (such as a drug in pill or liquid form), a matched, chemically inactive, lookalike, and often taste-alike pill or liquid is given to other subjects. This inactive substance is called a **placebo**.

In an experiment in which there is some interest in the influence of subjects' expectations, it is not unusual to have both a regular control condition with no implications of treatment, and a placebo control condition with a pseudotreatment, along with an experimental treatment condition. The word *placebo* was originally applied with human subjects receiving inert pills or other deliberately ineffective treatments, wherever it was recognized that expectations could play an important part in the outcome of the research. However, the phrase *placebo control condition* can be extended to drug research with animals where the injection procedures are duplicated in the control condition. The phrase *placebo control group* is also often used in the context of psychotherapy research where deliberately ineffective pseudotherapies are offered to one group, to create a placebo control group with the expectation of being helped, but lacking a specific treatment that could be helpful. This extended use of the word *placebo* is discussed in chapter 15.

The existence of a name for a type of control condition, a placebo control, indicates the widespread general recognition of the potential expectation problem when specifically testing chemicals administered in the form of pills or injections, or for that matter testing any health-promoting treatment, physical or psychological. However, new experimental manipulations in new experiments that have nothing to do with treatment are always being tested. In all such new experimental situations the possibility exists of new confounding factors being inadvertently introduced by new experimental manipulations. It is easy to be wise in the case of familiar situations long ago recognized by other experimenters (for example, introducing a placebo control condition when testing pills). But new experiments often introduce new procedural details where it is not yet apparent that the procedures might be introducing differences between groups in addition to those that are intended. Confounding factors are therefore most likely to be present and undetected when doing research with new variables, or when introducing familiar variables in new ways.

Often newly published research consists of slightly altered versions of old experiments in which confounding factors have been eliminated only after having been recognized subsequent to the publication of the old experiment. It is important for experimenters to search for possible confounding factors when setting up new experiments, but it should be recognized that even experienced researchers sometimes fail to recognize confounding factors that have been inadvertently introduced by the manipulation that is being tested.

In the case of subject variables the experimenter selects the subjects for some characteristic. In keeping with Rule 2, it is hoped that the selected subject difference is the only difference between levels. However, because the subject characteristic is not superimposed by the experimenter, it is likely to be associated with other characteristics (as discussed in chapter 2 with *third variables*). As an example, categorizing people as being self-confident or not self-confident could conceivably include a difference involving prior numbers of successful experiences. With subject variables, the complete absence of confounding factors is generally not achieved. Instead, the hope is to minimize them by keeping recognized control variables constant, or, when that is not possible, taking recognized confounding factors into account in the conclusions drawn from the experiment.

RULE 3: RANDOM SUBJECT SELECTION, ASSIGNMENT, AND RUNNING RULE

Subjects must be randomly selected from the population to which the experimenter intends to generalize the results.

The subjects must be randomly assigned to their respective conditions. (This of course only applies to manipulated variables.)

The various conditions must be run either simultaneously or in a random sequence.

The three components of this rule can be summarized as follows: Randomization must be used in all procedures (selection, assignment, and running of subjects), unless the particular design precludes it.

Discussion of Rule 3

The definition of a *random sample* and definitions of several other terms need to be discussed for Rule 3 to be understood. These terms are examined next.

Definitions of Populations and Samples.   After doing an experiment, it is appropriate to restrict one's conclusions to those people who have had an opportunity to be represented in the experiment. Thus, it is important to make sure that the **population** about which the experimenter wishes to learn is properly represented by the **sample** of individuals used as subjects in the experiment. For example, if an experimenter wished to learn whether reading a particular book on how to study had any effect on college grades, it would be important to use a typical cross section of college students as the subjects in the experiment. The complete set of individuals of interest is called the population, which in this example is the set of all college students. The sample is a subset of the population, that subset that participates in the study and that is used to represent the population (about which conclusions will be drawn).

Definition of a Random Sample.   A **random sample** of subjects from a population is one in which every member of the population has an equal probability of being in the sample. A second requirement is that every possible combination of the chosen sample size also must have an equal opportunity of being selected. For example, it would not be appropriate in seeking a random sample of 50 people to randomly select 5 subjects and have each of these 5 subjects bring 9 friends. This arrangement would exclude some potential combinations of unrelated people from the sample. In seeking 100 households for interviews in a community with 1000 households, a random sample could not be obtained by randomly selecting 1 household, and then repeatedly skipping the next 9 and moving to the 10th household. This would exclude various combinations of neighboring households.

A single random sample is not guaranteed to accurately represent the population, but the larger the random sample, the greater the probability that it does mirror the characteristics of the population. Although it is not likely that a small sample will accurately reflect the characteristics of the sampled population (Hsu, 1989), the use of a random sample, small or large, will permit proper statistical conclusions.

Identifying Random Samples.   A common means of identifying random samples is with the aid of a table of random numbers. A table of random numbers is found in Appendix B. As the name implies, a table of random numbers is a sequence of numbers in which the next number in the list is not predictable. Technically, at any point in the table, every possible number has an equal chance of appearing. To use a table of random numbers to randomly select a sample from a larger population, every member of the population would have to be identified with a number that could appear in the sequence. The people could initially be ordered on any basis, say alphabetically, as from a phone book, or other alphabetical directory. They could then be given numbers corresponding to their positions in the sequence. The fact that a person was first or last would not matter, because any number could appear at any point in a table of random numbers. The table should be randomly entered. (For example, averting your eyes from the page, you could allow a pencil point to touch a page of the table, and wherever it landed you would begin the process. If there were six pages in the table, you might toss a die to decide which page, or if there were two pages, you could toss a coin for this purpose.) If you were to collect a sample from a population with less than 10,000 people, but more than 999 people, you would have to use four-digit numbers. The first number encountered in the table would indicate which is the first person in your alphabetical list to be included in your sample. Assume that your first number is 0064. The 64th person in the alphabetical list would be included as a subject. You would proceed from that point in the table either down the columns, or up, or alternately down and up, or however you initially decided, until you had obtained all of the subjects you needed.

Definition of Random Assignment. Assuming a random sample of subjects, the next issue is assigning these subjects to the various experimental conditions. For example, if there are four levels of the variable (four experimental conditions), the sample of subjects has to be divided into four groups. Which subjects should be assigned to which conditions, and how should this be done? Rule 3 says there must be random assignment of subjects to the different conditions. **Random assignment** of subjects is similar to random sampling, in that every subject in the sample must have an equal chance of being in every condition, and every combination of subjects must have an equal chance of being in every condition. The exception to this part of Rule 3 is the case of subject variable research. Here subjects are assigned to groups based on some preexisting classification, so cannot be assigned randomly. However, it is important in these instances to try to select the subjects for each level randomly from their respective class populations.

Implementing Random Assignment. One means of arranging for random assignment of subjects to conditions is to associate different conditions with different numbers, placing the numbers on slips of paper dropped into a container, and blindly withdrawing the slips. For example, assume that there are four conditions, and that a particular subject is the 12th subject to arrive. Four slips of paper would have been previously placed in an opaque container, each slip having the number 1, 2, 3, or 4. The slip drawn out of the container for that subject would indicate into which condition the subject is to be placed. This could be done in advance for all subjects. A table of random numbers could be used for this same purpose, using a single digit column, ignoring any numbers other than 1 through 4. At the point at which you had enough subjects in one condition, say the third condition, you would then ignore the number 3 for the remaining subjects.

Implementing Random Running of Subjects.   The easiest way to satisfy the third component of Rule 3 (random running of subjects) is to avoid the issue by running all subjects simultaneously. This can occasionally be done. For example, if an experiment involved testing people, or obtaining written responses from people, where the independent variable was variations in task instructions, it might be possible to run all the subjects at the same time in the same room (different subjects having different sets of written instructions). When simultaneous running is not possible, the sequence in which the different conditions are applied to individual subjects is randomized, usually in advance. The procedure would be similar to the procedure suggested for random assignment of subjects. Again, for each subject, each of the conditions is represented with a slip of paper in a container, and the order in which they are removed would provide the order for the conditions. A table of random numbers can be similarly used to provide a sequence.

Difficulties in the Implementation of Rule 3.   The ideal is random selection from the general population, or from the population to which the results will be generalized. This ideal is realized when each person in the target population has an equal opportunity of being included in the sample, along with any possible combination of the number of people in the sample. Unfortunately, experimenters frequently lack access to the complete populations to which they would like to generalize their results. (How often does a psychologist have the opportunity to randomly select subjects from the world at large? Yet people throughout the world differ widely in terms of class, culture, genetic endowments, etc.) Realistically, experimenters usually have to settle for random sampling from populations that are not different, in relevant ways, than the target population. For example, the population of college students in a highly selective private university might reasonably be sampled for research on perception, and the findings generalized to the population at large. But the same generalization of results would not be appropriate for a study on abstract reasoning. Fortunately, the subject selection procedure is usually described in published research. The reader of the research has the opportunity to decide whether the sampling was from within the appropriate population, or at least from one that would not be different on relevant characteristics.

Although we can recognize realistic limits on true randomization for the general selection of subjects, assignment of subjects to different conditions can (and should) be strictly random. Violations of random assignment can be inadvertently created, when, for example, subjects who show up early are assigned to one condition, and later subjects to another. There can be different personality characteristics in such people, or different life circumstances operating; thus, different subpopulations could have been sampled for the different conditions. (Difference in when subjects arrive or volunteer is a subject variable, and so is likely to have many other variables associated with it.) Strict random assignment is the most practical way to avoid such unpredictable confounding factors and at the same time permit proper statistical conclusions.

Similar temptations involving procedural shortcuts can sometimes operate to violate the need for a random sequence of conditions. For example, it could be hard to set up each of the experimental conditions, so an experimenter might be tempted to first run all of the subjects in one condition, and then run all of the subjects in another condition. The kinds of problems that this could create include having potential differences associated with times of day (subjects can be more tired or more distracted at different times of day), or having different kinds of people associated with time of the semester (subjects who sign up for sessions later in the semester may be procrastinators). There can also be differences caused by the experimenter's fatigue, or because of the experimenter's preferences for working at various times of day (feeling more awake early in the day or late in the day). In this case, too, adherence to a random sequence is the best way to proceed.

RULE 4: STATISTICAL TESTS RULE *ex. humans*

When working with highly variable (somewhat unreliable) data, it is necessary to use statistical tests to determine whether the experimental and control conditions generate different data.

Discussion of Rule 4

The data obtained in psychological research are generally somewhat unreliable in that the same subject will tend to offer different scores

from one test session to another, even if there has been no intervening manipulation. Thus, looking at a single score from a subject
in a particular experimental situation, it is hard to take that one
number completely seriously. Therefore the group differences that
are sometimes observed in scores can sometimes merely reflect
chance fluctuations. It is then hard to know if observed differences
between groups are a function of chance variability, or differences in
the factor (differences in manipulation or classification at the different levels of the factor).

Statistical tests are procedures for deciding whether an observed
difference between groups represents chance, or an effective factor.
In an experiment a relatively small number of subjects are examined, and some generalizations are made about people. When are
results sufficiently clear to permit generalizations from the sample to
people in general? The use of random sampling and other randomized procedures, in the ways described in Rule 3, is critical for
generalization from a sample to the population. An additional critical
factor is the surpassing of some criterion, a criterion of a difference
between groups, that discredits chance as an explanation of any
observed differences. Assessing the observed differences with statistical procedures (Rule 4) tests the observed differences against such
a criterion. Surpassing the criterion signals that it is reasonable to
expect the same results in any further sampling from the population.

RULE 5: USE ALL THE DATA RULE

No data can be selectively omitted from the analysis as a function of
the resulting scores.

Discussion of Rule 5

Normally all of the data must be used. Occasionally, the experimental equipment can malfunction, or it can be clear that some
subject did not understand or follow the instructions, or a subject
could have been inadvertently given the wrong instructions. The
data of such subjects can be excluded, provided that the subjects'
scores were not seen by the experimenter and so could not have
influenced the experimenter's decision as to whether or not to keep
the scores. The decision to exclude must be based on procedural or
equipment problems, not subject performance. The concern here is
that it is often possible to rationalize the removal of selected subjects

who did not perform in accordance with the experimenter's expectations or hopes.

Note that there is no reliance on some assumed objectivity by the researcher. Rather, it is assumed that bias can exist and so rules and procedures have been developed that help to avoid the effects of bias.

SOME APPLICATIONS OF THE RULES OF RESEARCH

The rules of research are easier to follow in simple experiments involving just a single factor. Most experiments within the literature actually manipulate, or examine, two or three factors in the same experiment. These more complex designs are discussed in chapter 6, with examples offered throughout the text. However, at this point, illustrations are somewhat simplified by presenting experiments that simultaneously analyze several factors as several separate experiments, each manipulating just one factor. The examples used in this section come from two articles by Higgins and Marlatt (1973, 1975).

Higgins and Marlatt were interested in exploring some of the reasons for excessive drinking of alcohol. One possibility that they explored was that alcohol provides reinforcement through its tension- or anxiety-reducing properties. In their experimental situation, anxiety was created for some people by making them expect some strong electric shock (high threat condition), whereas others were led to expect no discomfort in an otherwise similar situation (called low threat by the authors, but also reasonably labeled as no threat). The people placed into these two situations were people who normally drank a great deal; more specifically, people who could be classed as alcoholics. The question was, would the people under the high threat condition drink more than those under the low threat condition? (If they did, it would constitute evidence in support of the idea that anxiety increases drinking. This might then be used to bolster a theory that alcoholics drink, at least at times, to reduce anxiety.)

The opportunity for drinking was created by asking subjects to rate three alcoholic beverages. Adjectives were presented, one at a time, and subjects were asked to indicate which of the three beverages was best described and least described by each adjective. An ample supply of the three beverages was supplied, and subjects were told to do as much tasting as they needed to answer the questions. There were 65 adjectives presented (e.g., sweet, bitter, strong). The subjects were led to believe that the adjective ratings were the critical responses being observed. In fact, without the subjects' knowledge, what was being measured was the amount of drinking.

The high-threat condition was created by informing subjects that they would later be exposed to painful shock from an imposing-looking shock box, from which wires were attached to their ankles. The rationale presented to the subjects for the use of shock was that the experimenter was testing the effect of the sense of touch on taste, and that a very high voltage was required for touch to have any effect on taste. Subjects were told that they would perform the adjective rating task first without the shock, and again later with the shock, to see what changes the shock created. The wires were placed on their ankles, and then they were given the adjective rating task without shock. After the adjective rating task all subjects were told that they had been assigned to a control group, so that the shock condition was not needed. The threat of impending shock, with the wires already around the ankles of the subjects, was expected to create the high threat condition.

The low (or zero) threat condition was created by having another group of subjects see a much less imposing box, clearly containing just two flashlight batteries, although the box also trailed two wires that were attached to the subjects' ankles, but with the assurance that "you will only feel a slight tingle in your skin." The rationale for the experiment, however, was similar, the subjects being told that "the main interest in this experiment is the effect of touch on taste." The use of electricity in the low threat condition was explained by saying that "We have decided to use electrical stimulation as the way to excite your sense of touch because then we can carefully control the amount of stimulation that you get." This reference to careful control of the amount of stimulation was part of the general attempt to reassure the subjects that they would not be hurt, and thus reduce the threat to zero, if possible.

In summary, currently drinking alcoholics were given an opportunity to drink as much of three alcoholic beverages as they wished, in the context of an adjective rating task and taste test (determining which of 65 adjectives was most applicable and which was most nonapplicable to each of the three beverages). The fact that amount being drunk was measured was not revealed to the subjects during the experiment. Threat of shock was strong for half of the subjects, and minimized for the other half, in an effort to differentiate the two groups on anxiety arousal. The question was, would anxiety arousal create increased drinking in this group of people who were accustomed to drinking heavily?

The Rules of Research in the Higgins and Marlatt Experiments

Rule 1: Multiple Conditions Rule. There were two conditions, anxiety arousal, and none or minimal anxiety, the latter being the control condition.

Rule 2: Avoidance of Confounding Factors Rule. The drinking conditions and instructions were the same in the two tasks. The only difference was the use of anxiety arousal, which was the independent variable being tested for its effect on amount of drinking (the dependent variable).

Rule 3: Random Subject Selection, Assignment, and Running Rule. Subjects were recruited, by letter, from among men who had been admitted five or more times to a local inpatient alcoholism treatment center; from sign-up sheets distributed among bartenders and hotel desk clerks in areas where alcoholics congregate; from pretrial interviews with persons going before the local municipal court on drunkenness charges; and through an ex-alcoholic who suggested peoples' names. (All subjects received 5 dollars for their participation.)

Ideally, a list of all alcoholics in the society should have been used, from which to select a random sample of alcoholics. The realities of subject recruitment are made apparent here, where just finding people who are in that category, and then getting them to participate, presents real problems. Those who did participate are probably not a perfect representation of all alcoholics, and this was not a true random sample. But those who participated did meet specific criteria for being designated as alcoholics in an interview inquiring about current drinking patterns and rates, with accepted subjects having at least one previous admission to a treatment program for alcoholics, or four or more arrests for drunken conduct. Thus, the population sampled is a population of alcoholics, although just how representative it is of all alcoholics is not known. (For example, alcoholics who get into trouble from their drinking might have been overrepresented.)

The procedure for assigning the subjects to either the experimental or control condition could be the use of a coin toss, or a table of random numbers using odd numbers to represent one condition, and even numbers to represent the other. In this way, both assignment and when the two different conditions were run could be randomized. In the Higgins and Marlatt (1973) article this detail was not specified, although normally some mention of random assignment is made. It would not be necessary to explain just how randomization was implemented, but the statement "random assignment to conditions" is frequently found in research articles to assure the scientific community that randomization was used in the particular study.

Rule 4: Statistical Tests Rule.   There were a number of possible dependent measures in this experiment. One was the amount of alcohol consumed, another was the amount of beverage consumed, and a third was number of sips. Because there were different kinds of beverage (brandy, wine, beer), amount of beverage consumed and amount of alcohol consumed did not give identical results. (One person could drink more beverage but less alcohol than a second person, if the first person drank much beer and little brandy, whereas the second person had the opposite preference.) Using the amount of alcohol as the dependent variable, the high anxiety condition yielded a little more alcohol consumption than the low anxiety condition (1.56 oz vs. 1.46 oz). But a test of statistical significance indicated that there was no evidence that this was anything other than a chance difference. In fact, looking at the amount of beverage (as opposed to pure alcohol) drunk, the low anxiety group drank more than the high anxiety group, although this too failed to reach statistical significance, so it too can be treated as random variation. Thus, statistical tests indicated that apparent differences between groups in the sample could not be taken as indicative of an effective independent variable. Stated another way, there was no evidence that alcoholics drink more under high anxiety (high threat) than under zero or minimal anxiety (low threat), where high anxiety is manipulated through expectation of impending strong electric shock. Thus, the hypothesis that alcoholics sometimes drink to reduce anxiety was not supported in this study.

Rule 5: Use of All the Data Rule.   No mention was made in this study (Higgins & Marlatt, 1973) of the omission of subjects' data. If any subjects had been omitted, it would normally be mentioned in the article, along with the reasons for omitting them. An example is given in further discussion from the later Higgins and Marlatt (1975) article.

A subject variable was also tested by Higgins and Marlatt in the 1973 paper. They wanted to see if alcoholics would drink more in the adjective rating situation than social drinkers. They therefore also recruited a sample of social drinkers. They were recruited from bar sign-up sheets, from sign-up sheets given to the staff of a local manufacturing firm, and from a newspaper ad. These social drinkers were put through precisely the same experience and pair of conditions as the alcoholics, again being randomly assigned to either the high or low threat condition. Note that this suggests two independent variables in the same experiment: alcoholic versus social drinker, and high versus low threat condition. Because discussion of multiple-factor designs is pursued in a later chapter, the experiment is examined here as two single-factor experiments: one study looking at the difference between alcoholics and social drinkers under conditions of anxiety (high threat), and another study looking at alcoholics versus social drinkers in a low anxiety (low threat) situation. The dependent variable again was amount of drinking, once more analyzed in terms of both amount of total beverage drunk and total amount of alcohol drunk. The results obtained were that alcoholics drank more than social drinkers, both when comparing the two groups under high threat, and also when comparing them under low threat—not a surprising finding.

Rule 1: Multiple Conditions Rule. There were two classes of subjects, alcoholics versus social drinkers. It is hard to say which is the control group, because there was no manipulation versus an absence of a manipulation. However, because the question concerns alcohol consumption, it might be reasonable to consider the social drinkers to be the control condition.

Rule 2: Avoidance of Confounding Factors Rule. The situations were identical for the two groups; only the categorization of subjects was different. However, with a subject variable, there is always the likelihood of other differences being included. In this experiment, Higgins and Marlatt attempted to match the subjects in the two groups on educational level and social class but were not able to do so for social class. That is, a statistical test of a measure of social class yielded a significant difference between the groups, with alcoholics scoring in a lower social class. Thus, the results have to be examined for the possibility that the difference in drinking during the adjective rating task was a function of social class. Some additional statistical work done in the study suggested that it would not be a good explanation. But with subject variables, there is always the possibility that there are other unrecognized variables that are the true bases for an apparent relationship.

Rule 3: Random Subject Selection, Assignment, and Running Rule. With a subject variable, subjects are not randomly assigned to groups. However, it is appropriate to run the two groups randomly, so that one group is not being run earlier or later in the day or on a different day. Furthermore, it would be desirable for the subjects assigned to each group (the alcoholics and social drinkers) to have been randomly sampled from the populations that they respectively represent. From the description of the methods used to recruit the two groups of subjects, this is clearly not the case in this study, but this is a common compromise.

Rule 4: Statistical Tests Rule. Statistical tests were used and showed that both the differences in amounts of beverage drunk and the differences in amounts of alcohol drunk were statistically significant. This means that the observed differences between alcoholics and social drinkers in amounts drunk during the adjective rating task were too large to be attributed to chance variation. This yielded the conclusion that alcoholics do drink more than social drinkers, in this context.

Rule 5: Use All the Data Rule.   As previously indicated, there was no mention of omitted data in the 1973 Higgins and Marlatt article.

Redoing an Experiment with a Changed Operational Definition

Higgins and Marlatt did not find confirmation of their most important hypothesis, that is, that heavy drinkers sometimes drink to reduce anxiety. However, an experimenter is sometimes correct about a hypothesis but, unfortunately, incorrect in the choice of just what to measure, or how to measure it, or incorrect in the choice of ways to instantiate and manipulate the independent variable. Higgins and Marlatt suspected that some such problem may have been responsible for disappointing results in their first experiment on this question. They decided to change their operational definition of anxiety, and redo the experiment. (Recall the discussion in chapter 2 of operational definitions).

Although fear of physical pain might not produce higher drinking, perhaps interpersonal anxiety might have that effect. They decided to change the cause of anxiety in the experiment from the possibility of electric shock to a form of evaluation anxiety—a concern with how others might evaluate them. Many heavy drinkers do report that they drink in order to feel more comfortable socially. Two years after the first experiment Higgins and Marlatt (1975) retested their hypothesis, using a different way of creating anxiety in the experiment. Their subjects were college students who rated themselves as heavy drinkers. They once again used the alcoholic beverage tasting situation with adjective ratings, but this time omitted the shock box. To set up the new definition of anxiety, explained next, they added a period prior to the rating of beverages, during which subjects had to talk about themselves, answering some personal questions (e.g., "When did you begin to exercise some independence from your parents and what happened?"). This was rationalized to the subjects as having the potential to affect mood, and the experiment was then explained as testing the effects of mood upon taste. Higgins and Marlatt also informed the male college student subjects participating in the experiment that they would be involved in another brief experiment immediately following the current one. This was told to the subjects in both the experimental and control conditions.

The New Operational Definition of Anxiety

As the single difference between the two groups, the subjects in the experimental group were told that the second experiment

> . . . will involve having you engage in a discussion on interpersonal attractiveness with a group of girls. At the end of the discussion, you will rate each other on a number of qualities that people think of as being desirable. For the purposes of that experiment it is necessary for the girls to have some idea of what kind of person you are so I will have them in the control room with me during this experiment so that they can listen to your answers (Higgins & Marlatt, 1975, pp. 646–647).

This constituted the high anxiety situation (and replaced the use of the shock box).

The low-anxiety situation was arranged by telling another group of subjects that, in the second experiment, they would have to "rate some pictures of girls according to how attractive you think they are . . . ." In this low- (or zero-) threat condition, no evaluation of the subjects was implied, although they did have to answer the same personal questions (ostensibly to induce moods). It was the assumption of interpersonal evaluation by the women while the male students were answering personal questions that was expected to create anxiety in the high-threat condition (the evaluation did not take place and they in fact did not have to engage in a later discussion with the women). The low-threat condition subjects were not told that women would be listening to their answers to the personal questions.

In summary, the same opportunity to unobtrusively measure amount of drinking was arranged for two groups of self-described heavy drinking male college students, one exposed to some interpersonal anxiety and the other not so exposed. This was the manipulated independent variable, with amount of drinking again the dependent variable.

The Rules of Research with the Second Operational Definition of Anxiety

The five rules for research apply here as in the first case: that is, there was a single manipulated difference as the independent variable in a situation with no other differences from the control condition (satisfying Rules 1 and 2). As to Rule 3, random sampling here was done in another way than in the previous experiments. In this case a group of college students in an introductory psychology course was recruited. On the basis of a questionnaire, they were divided into five classes of drinkers, ranging from abstinent to heavy drinkers, with only the heavy drinkers recruited for the experiment. Again, this is a clear compromise from random sampling of the general population of heavy drinkers. Random assignment to conditions and random running of the two conditions (Rule 3) should have been followed, and indeed may have been, although this is not mentioned in the article. As far as Rule 4 is concerned, again the statistical tests had to be made, to know whether the differences in amount drunk that were observed were sufficiently large to represent an effective independent variable and not just chance differences. In this experiment Higgins and Marlatt did succeed in finding a clear difference in amount of drinking, with the high threat condition producing higher amounts of drinking, both defined as amount of alcoholic beverage and defined as amount of alcohol, both measures yielding statistical significance. Thus, with the operational definition changed, they did find support for the hypothesis they previously tested, unsuccessfully, and reported in their 1973 paper.

Rule 5, which says that no data should be omitted as a function of the scores, can be looked at as it applies to this experiment. A question was asked after the experiment to see if subjects were aware of the deception. The question was phrased in the following way: "Sometimes subjects feel that they are being deceived by experimenters and it affects their performance during the experiment. Did you feel that you were being deceived?" (Higgins &

Marlatt, 1975, p. 647). The authors noted: "Subjects reporting doubts about the evaluation manipulation were replaced if they were more than 50% confident that they had been deceived (five subjects)" (Higgins & Marlatt, p. 647). Note that this elimination of five subjects was not as a function of how they performed. It would be improper for the experimenter to examine the scores of subjects (amount they had drunk) before deciding whether or not to eliminate them.

CONTROL CONDITIONS AND THE DEPENDENT VARIABLE

In the preceding discussion of the Higgins and Marlatt experiments two factors were examined: degree of threat (a manipulated variable), and alcoholics versus social drinkers (a subject variable). The control condition for the manipulated variable was low (or zero) threat, which is a reasonable control condition for testing high threat. There is another issue closely related to the choice of control conditions.

Recall that the dependent variable was one or another operationally defined measure of amount of drinking (total amount of the beverage drunk, and amount of alcohol ingested). The experimental question was whether the subjects under high threat would drink more alcoholic beverage than those under low threat. It is true that only alcoholic beverages were used in the experiment. But then, how does one know whether the subjects would not have also drunk more nonalcoholic beverages under high threat? (After all, anxiety can increase thirst.) In this experiment, being able to interpret the experiment as applying only to alcoholic beverages is important because the question being asked is whether anxiety is a relevant factor in the drinking of alcohol. However, in order to conclude that high interpersonal threat increases the drinking of alcoholic beverages, one would want to know that it would not increase drinking of nonalcoholic beverages, or else the conclusion would have to refer to drinking in general. The motivation for the study was to uncover factors responsible for alcoholism, not high intake of fluids.

When it is important to be able to interpret the experiment as applying only to a narrow range of some variable (e.g., alcoholic beverages), both the broad and narrow range needs to be tested (e.g., nonalcoholic as well as alcoholic beverages). Stated another way, whenever the intended dependent variable is a subset of some more general variable (for example, alcoholic beverages as a subset of beverages in general), the conclusions are not clearly restricted to the intended variable, unless the broader range of the variable is also tested.

For this example two other conditions would be needed. Subjects in a high threat condition as well as those in a low threat condition would have to be tested with a nonalcoholic beverage. Thus, in a sense, the same experiment would be done twice, once with alcoholic beverages and once with nonalcoholic beverages. One could think of the additional two conditions as being control conditions for the importance of the alcohol factor in the drinking behavior.

As another example, this time with a subject variable, research has been done on causes of pregnancy among unmarried teenagers. Assume the following study: Teenage girls from a representative sample of neighborhoods are divided up into those who have become pregnant and those who have not. Then they are tested to see whether they differ in regard to sex information. It is found that those teenagers who had become pregnant were less well informed about sex than those who had not become pregnant. Could it be concluded that lack of sex information is one of the causative factors in teenage pregnancy? Of course, the answer from just one such experiment would be no, in part because of the usual problems in inferring causality when using subject variables. But beyond the subject variable limitations on conclusions, there is another issue. Information about sex is just a subset of information in general. It is possible that teenagers who have become pregnant are less well informed in general, or less intelligent, and that it is this generally smaller amount of information, or lesser intelligence, that is being measured in this case through the test of sex information.

There are two ways to deal with this issue in this type of subject variable study. One is to try to match the subjects in the two groups on such things as IQ, which includes general information, or to specifically include a test of general information as the basis for matching subjects in the two groups. Another way is to broaden the dependent variable to a test of general information, with questions on sex information only included as a subtest. One could then observe if the difference between teenagers who did and did not become pregnant consists of a difference in information in general, or is restricted to just certain classes of information such as sex information.

The general rule then to be observed here is to examine the question that is being asked, looking closely at the dependent variable that is being measured in the study. Then ask whether the dependent variable is in fact a subset of some more general variable that is merely being narrowly represented in the study (alcoholic beverages as a subset of beverages in general, sex information as a subset of information in general). If that is the case, include a broader class of dependent measures in the study.

CHAPTER SUMMARY

Rule 1, the multiple conditions rule, was given: There must be more than one condition in the experiment. There should be at least one condition which can be recognized as a control condition.

When comparing two or more manipulations, it can sometimes seem that a control condition is not necessary, but that is not true. The absence of a control condition limits the conclusions. Without a control condition it is difficult to decide whether different effects from two treatments are due to one treatment lowering scores, or the other treatment raising scores, or both.

Rule 2, the avoidance of confounding factors rule, was given: With one factor there must be only one difference distinguishing different conditions of the experiment, that difference being variations in the factor.

A major difficulty in following Rule 2 is the inadvertent introduction of confounding factors when introducing manipulations. The experimenter has to be alert to this possibility and must try to eliminate such confounding factors. When this is not possible, the control group has the confounding factors (such as positive expectations) added to the control condition. The classic example of this is in testing medications in pill form. The experimental group has expectations of improvement that are not present in the control condition. To eliminate this difference between groups, a placebo is given to the control condition subjects, permitting equal expectations in both groups. The control condition is then called a placebo control condition. With subject variables confounding factors are even more common than with manipulated variables, and can be expected to limit the conclusions from experiments, unless relevant control variables have been kept constant in the different conditions.

Rule 3, the random selection, assignment, and running rule, was given. First, population, samples, and types of randomization were defined and discussed. Rule 3 states that randomization must be used in all procedures (selection, assignment, and running of subjects), unless the particular design precludes it (as when using a subject variable and group assignment follows from preexisting category membership). If using a subject variable, the subjects in each classification (level) should be randomly sampled from the broader population with that same classification. Random running of conditions is critical as a means of avoiding the running of different conditions at different times, and random assignment of subjects to conditions is important to avoid such things as having all of the eager volunteers in one condition, and the latecomers in another. The most important reason for the use of randomization is that it is necessary for valid statistical conclusions.

Problems in implementing randomization procedures were discussed. The difficulty in obtaining a truly random sample of subjects was compared with the more minor difficulties that are much easier to overcome, in the randomization of subject assignment and the running of conditions. When a completely random sample of subjects cannot be obtained, it is important either to limit the conclusions to the population that was sampled, or to use reason in selecting populations that are not different in ways that are relevant to the factors being studied.

Rule 4, the statistical tests rule, was given: When working with highly variable (somewhat unreliable) data it is necessary to use statistical tests to determine whether the experimental and control conditions generate different data.

Statistical procedures are necessary to distinguish chance differences between the means of conditions from differences that reflect the influence of the factors being tested. Experiments usually involve relatively small numbers of subjects. Statistical procedures offer criteria as to when the limited experimental situations can be used to draw more general conclusions. Statistical logic is further discussed in chapter 5.

Rule 5, the use of all of the data rule, was given: No data can be selectively omitted from the analysis as a function of the resulting scores.

The issue here is to be careful when things go wrong in the experiment, and there is some rational basis for throwing out some data due to malfunctioning equipment, or because some subject has been clearly uncooperative, or has misunderstood instructions. The data can only be thrown out if there has been no influence from the experimenter's hopes or expectations on the selection of data to be discarded. The usual way to avoid this problem is to make the decision to keep or throw out such data without seeing the actual experimental results for such subjects. That is, the person making the decision to throw out data must not know whether or not the removal of the specific data would or would not support the experimenter's predictions.

Examples of the application of the rules of research were given, using the research of Higgins and Marlatt (1973, 1975). Some care in the conclusions from a narrowly defined dependent measure were discussed. In summary, when it is important for the conclusions to refer to only a narrow subset of the dependent variable (drinking alcohol vs. drinking nonalcoholic beverages, sex information vs. information in general), the experiment should itself demonstrate that the relationship only refers to the narrowly defined definition. This would require the experiment to be run with both the narrow and broad definitions of the dependent variable.

NEW WORDS AND PHRASES IN CHAPTER 3

placebo
placebo control conditions
population
random assignment (of subjects)
random sample
Rule 1: multiple conditions rule
Rule 2: avoidance of confounding factors rule
Rule 3: random subject selection, assignment, and running rule
Rule 4: statistical tests rule
Rule 5: use all the data rule
sample

CHAPTER 4

Single-Factor Designs: Simple Experimental Designs That Incorporate the Rules for Research

In chapter 3's discussion of rules for designing research it was mentioned that avoiding confounding factors is a difficult task. The experimenter is greatly aided in this task by the existence of standard experimental designs, the use of which lessens the probability of confounding factors. This chapter discusses the most common of these designs. Their use minimizes confounding factors in both manipulated and subject variable experiments, although the probability of completely eliminating confounding factors is unlikely when using subject variables.

It helps to appreciate the advantages of the standard experimental designs if they are compared with an improper design that should not be used because of its high susceptibility to confounding factors. Unfortunately, as explained later, this improper design is informally used sometimes by people drawing conclusions from personal experiences. When people use it, they do not call it an experimental design, and it is certainly not being recommended here as an experimental design. Rather, it is a way in which people sometimes reason. But it is useful to see precisely how this informal way of thinking and drawing conclusions is both similar to and different from a standard experimental design. This will make it easier to understand in what ways standard experimental designs offer better ways of determining just what is related to what in our world.

Problems encountered in designing and implementing experiments are sometimes categorized as threats to internal and/or external validity. It can be useful, at times, to see potential problems in the light of these two constructs. Internal and external validity are explained and discussed in the later sections of this chapter. The designs presented here are each summarized in symbolic form, so a discussion of the symbols is necessary.

SYMBOLIZATION OF THE DESIGNS

The symbolization of designs used here is similar in most respects to the symbolization devised by Campbell and Stanley (1963). However, in place of their X as the symbol of a manipulation that is being tested for effectiveness, we use a T (standing for some unspecified *treatment* of a subject, or group of subjects). An O stands for an observation (or set of observations on a group of subjects). The symbols are read from left to right. Thus,

T   O

implies a manipulation followed by an observation (the observation being the point at which data is collected). Although the observations are notated as though taking place after a treatment, in some instances a treatment and observation take place simultaneously. Because there are not any theoretical differences between observations following a treatment and observations that are simultaneous with treatment, in this discussion there is not any symbolic differentiation of the two situations.

The idea of many subjects receiving each treatment is usually implicit in the symbolization. Thus, in

T   O

many subjects are assumed to have been exposed to manipulation T and observation O. If there is more than one observation of each individual subject in the design, then the O's would be numbered, so that

O_1 T O_2

would mean that each subject was observed (measured), exposed to treatment T, and then observed (measured) a second time.

If there are to be different groups of subjects experiencing different conditions, then each set of subjects is represented on a different line. Thus, a situation in which a group of subjects receives a treatment and then an observation, and another group of subjects

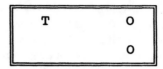

FIG. 4.1. Two sets of subjects, one group (with the T) receiving a treatment, and the other not receiving the treatment. Both groups of subjects are similarly measured (observed), as indicated by the O.

receives just the observation (is not exposed to the treatment), would require two lines and would be symbolized as in Fig. 4.1.

If the two sets of subjects are randomly assigned to their respective conditions (one receiving treatment and being observed, the other being similarly observed but without the preceding or accompanying treatment), the random assignment is indicated with an upper-case R, as in Fig. 4.2.

AN IMPROPER DESIGN (ONE-GROUP DESIGN)

Before looking at the first proper experimental design, it is helpful to examine a design that does invite confounding factors. We label this particular improper design the *one-group design*. It is symbolically summarized in Fig. 4.3.

The one-group design is barely recognizable as a design, yet it is an example of a situation from which people occasionally attempt to draw conclusions about the effectiveness of a manipulation (or some sort of intervention). For example, assume that a person has an idea of how to influence people, the method being to act self-certain. This person then tries out this new way of acting on the next few people that she encounters in some type of situation. This informal experimenter then decides whether or not the new approach has been effective. The T is the new way of behaving (appearing self-certain)

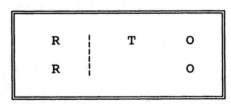

FIG. 4.2. Two sets of subjects, randomly assigned to their respective conditions. One group (with the T) receives a treatment, which is absent for the other set of subjects. Both sets of subjects are similarly measured (observed), as indicated for both groups by the presence of an O.

FIG. 4.3. One group design. The T would be applied to every subject, with the observation O made either simultaneously or following the treatment (the manipulation).

and the informal observation of the results is the O. Although there is no planned control condition, an informal experimenter, in reaching conclusions (about the effectiveness of being self-certain), is probably comparing the effects of the introduction of T with prior situations where T was absent. Thus, the one-group design could be symbolized in the manner shown in Fig. 4.4.

One problem with this way of reaching conclusions is that the situation reviewed in memory is probably different in many ways from the current situation in which T is introduced, not just on the dimension of self-certainty. For example, the informal experimenter could have been tired, or distracted, or busier at those times when T was not present. It is also possible that the informal experimenter could have been bored or unenthused about the old methods used prior to the introduction of T, and enthused when introducing T, or pessimistic with the old and optimistic with the new behavior. In a true experiment the experimenter would identify control variables to be monitored and maintained as identical in the two conditions. The identity of the two conditions, with the exception of the manipulation being tested, is one of the key features of a properly designed experiment. This identity is unlikely with the one-group design. The passage of time from the old to the new situations could make a difference, the difference stemming from changes in related circumstances and attitudes. Further, it is unlikely that memory for past situations is perfect. An experimenter could be in error in recalling a past situation as identical to a current one. Thus, potential differ-

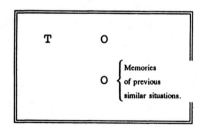

FIG. 4.4. One-group design, with an implicit comparison with memories of previous similar situations.

ences in the two situations offer the opportunities for potential confounding factors, violating Rule 2. Such problems are less likely to arise if Rule 1 (the multiple conditions rule) is followed, by incorporating a control condition.

An additional problem in the one-group design is that the informal experimenter is forced to violate Rule 3, that is, there would not be any provision for randomly ordering the sequence of conditions or for randomly assigning people to the experimental and control conditions. This of course follows from having run the informal memory control condition in some past time period. Additionally, nonrandom assignment to conditions raises the possibility of introducing subject differences as confounding factors. The population currently being encountered in the situation could be different than the population that was seen prior to the introduction of T. It is even possible that the informal experimenter might inadvertently utilize different approaches with different people in such informal experimentation. For example, he or she might act with greater self-certainty (if that is what is being tested) only with people who appear to be easily intimidated. Such people might be more easily influenced regardless of the approach, thus not offering a good test of the effectiveness of acting in a self-certain manner.

In summary, in the one-group design any apparent effects of the intervention of T are as likely to be a function of confounding factors (e.g., subject differences and situational differences) as of the intervention itself. Fortunately, the one-group design is rarely used by researchers, though it often constitutes a part of the procedures for drawing conclusions that people use in day-to-day reasoning, as discussed in the next two paragraphs. It is also used sometimes in making clinical inferences, which is also discussed later.

A factor that sometimes gives this undesirable approach a subjective sense of validity is the observer being the one to control the introduction of T. The personal introduction of T by the observer, followed by the observation O, yields a subjective sense of a causal relationship, like pushing a button and seeing something happen. If a light bulb burned out and at the same moment, by coincidence, you had banged on the wall, you would feel as though you had turned off the light.

Occasionally this conclusion of causal relationships is seen without the personal introduction of T, so that we lack the personal sense of having pushed the button. The subjective impression of a causal relationship can still be there if T is a dramatic event—being bitten by a dog, for example, or being thrown into the water before you could swim. Such events might then be cited, in later years, as the cause for a fear or dislike of dogs, or a fear or dislike of water. When a psychoanalyst asks a patient to search back in time for some possible cause T of later observed behavior O, there is a possible conclusion of cause and effect from sequential events, some dramatic event T followed by some observation of new behavior O. The presumption that T is the only relevant difference from earlier time periods when O was absent, that the factors influencing behavior before and after T are essentially the same except for the occurrence of T, is usually difficult to verify, leaving the issue open to the possibility of situational confounding. (Dramatic events that are often cited as causally related to feelings as an adult are early childhood instances of physical or sexual abuse, being a witness to abuse of someone else, death of a parent or sibling, etc. Although such experiences are likely to have impact, they may not be related to the specific future behaviors or moods that are attributed to them.)

COMPLETELY RANDOMIZED DESIGN

A control condition can be added to the undesirable one-group design, satisfying Rule 1. In addition, subjects can be randomly sampled and randomly assigned to either the experimental or control condition, with conditions randomly run, satisfying Rule 3. This would yield the proper and useful **completely randomized design**. This design is symbolically summarized in Fig. 4.5, where the R is used to indicate random assignment of subjects to either the experimental or control condition. (Figure 4.5 was previously presented as Fig. 4.2 when discussing the symbols being used.)

Figure 4.5 offers the simplest version of the completely randomized design, in which there are just two conditions (experimental with the T and control without it). We can return to a previous example for our illustration. Again, assume that the question is whether acting in a self-certain manner results in greater influence. The two conditions are the presence and absence of the appearance of self-certainty.

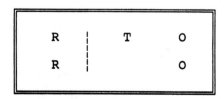

FIG. 4.5. Completely randomized design. The R indicates that the individual subjects are randomly assigned to conditions.

In describing the experiment, where we have previously identified the two variables (self-certainty or its absence as the independent variable, extent of influence as the dependent variable), we want to briefly delineate the experimental situation. Assume that subjects are exposed to some sort of puzzle, which, it appears, can be solved in a number of different ways. The subjects are permitted to use any way they please, but there is another person in the room, a bystander whose presence there is explained as being for some other purpose and who volunteers some suggestions about ways to solve the puzzle. For one set of subjects (those in the control condition), the bystander merely suggests a way to proceed. For other subjects (those in the experimental condition), the bystander additionally expresses certainty as to the advantages of the suggested procedure. The dependent measure is whether the subjects follow the suggestion of the bystander.

Note that in the one-group design the only condition would have been the certainty condition. In the completely randomized design there is the additional condition in which certainty is absent. This offers a baseline of performance against which to compare the certainty condition. Because subjects are randomly assigned to the two conditions, any clear difference in influence between the two conditions could reasonably be attributed to the manipulated difference of certainty versus its absence. In the schematic presented in Fig. 4.5, T is the presence of certainty, and O is the measurement of compliance with the suggestion. The conditions for both groups are identical, other than the presence or absence of T. Random sampling, random condition assignment, and random running of the sequence of conditions all help to avoid confounding factors that could offer alternative explanations for any observed differences between the conditions.

The completely randomized design can be expanded so that there are several different versions or values of T (more than two levels of the independent variable). For example, it might be desirable to compare several different ways of influencing people. Or, using a different example, an experiment could compare the effectiveness of different drugs for anxiety reduction, or different amounts of the same drug, including zero (the control condition); or several different forms of psychotherapy might be compared, or the same therapy carried on for different lengths of time (including zero exposure). This expanded version of the design is symbolized in Fig. 4.6, where each T (T versus T' versus T″) represents a different level or value of the experimental manipulation.

The name *completely randomized design* is a common name for

R	T	O
R	T'	O
R	T''	O
R		O

FIG. 4.6. Completely randomized design with several conditions.

this design in the literature (although Campbell and Stanley [1963] label it differently). Given the names used here for the other designs, one might prefer to call the completely randomized design the multiple-condition design. However, *completely randomized* refers to the assignment of the subjects. The concept of random assignment of subjects to the different conditions is a critical part of this design. Stating that there must be random assignment means that a study using a subject variable would not meet the criterion for being labeled as a completely randomized design.

The two critical aspects of this design are the random assignment of subjects to levels of the independent variable, and distinction of the levels through manipulations. Fig. 4.7 suggests how the data for this type of design might be recorded. When the dependent variable is a quantitative score, the means of the different conditions are compared, and are tested for evidence of statistically significant differences.

A SECOND IMPROPER DESIGN (ONE-GROUP PRETEST–POSTTEST DESIGN)

There is a second improper design that is sometimes encountered, which also employs a single condition, but which is occasionally

No T	T	T'	T''
score	score	score	score
.	.	.	.
.	.	.	.
.	.	.	.

FIG. 4.7. Form in which data would normally be listed in a completely randomized design with a quantitative dependent variable.

used by professional researchers. There are some practical reasons why this sometimes takes place. The reasons for this are briefly discussed, along with the problems that this creates in reaching conclusions.

In Fig. 4.8 this problematic design, which Campbell and Stanley call the **one-group pretest-posttest design**, is symbolically summarized.

The one-group pretest-posttest design differs from the totally inadequate one-group design in the increased amount of measurement. In the one-group pretest-posttest design there is formal measurement of events prior to the introduction of T as well as subsequent to T (pretesting and posttesting). This design does offer some limited improvement in possible conclusions from the simpler one-group design. Having both a pre- and postmeasurement permits the experimenter to see if the subjects are scoring higher or lower after the intervention than before. If alternative explanations (discussed later) can be eliminated, this opportunity for measured change can permit some conclusions from the research.

The one-group pretest-posttest design is most likely to be used when some new treatment or new manufacturing method needs to be examined, but economic, ethical, or political considerations do not permit omitting any subjects from the new treatment or procedure. If all of the subjects must receive the experimental treatment or be a part of the new procedure, it is not possible to have a control condition. For example, in industry the productivity of a factory might be measured (O_1) prior to the introduction of a new system (T). Production is then measured again (O_2) after the introduction of T. The problem of the disease of acquired immune deficiency syndrome (AIDS) offers an interesting example of the potential use of the one-group pretest-posttest design. When a new drug for AIDS is developed, patients who expect to die without a miracle drug all want to try it, even if its efficacy is not yet established; nobody wants to be in the control condition. Assume then that there was no control condition. All patients in the experiment would receive the drug, and would be measured before and after on several physical state variables to see if there is improvement. (In fact, there would probably be repeated measurements at several points.) The implicit use of this

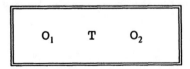

FIG. 4.8.   The one-group pretest-posttest design.

design is also seen in published presentations of case studies. A patient is assessed as having some problem, then given therapy, and then reassessed. Such case study reports sometimes include summaries of the results with several patients all evaluated both before and after being treated.

A clear decrease in symptoms, or any other clear change from pre- to postmeasurement that follows an intervention has strong intuitive appeal, giving an informal impression of effectiveness. Indeed, it is far better than simply eyeballing the postintervention behavior and concluding that it is better than what is remembered from some previous time where the intervention was lacking, as is done in the one-group design with its single measurement. The problems that still exist given the two measurements in a one-group pretest-posttest design (that lacks a control condition) concern the many alternative factors that could be operating between the two observation periods, in addition to the intervention.

The Problems in Interpreting Changes in a One-Group Pretest–Posttest Design

There are a number of potential sources of confounding factors that can flow from the use of pre-post measurements in the absence of a control condition. These potential sources of confounding can be usefully placed under four labels: **personal change, situational change, test familiarity**, and **test dimension awareness**. The time that passes from the first to the second observation can provide or permit confounding factors following from personal or situational change.

Personal change (called *maturation* by Campbell & Stanley, 1963) is a change in individual subjects that takes place in common among most of the subjects, as a function of time from the first to the second measurement. As examples of personal change, if the two observations take place during the same session, or same day, the subjects can become bored, tired, or fatigued between the two measurements. If this effect is fairly uniform for all subjects, this can be responsible for a difference between the first and second observations that can then compete with T as an explanation.

Situational change (called *history* by Campbell & Stanley, 1963) is a change in the external situation from the first to the second measurement. If the time factor was sufficiently long (say, 1 or 2 weeks), environmental events could intervene as influences on performance. For example, a teacher could try some new responses to control unruly behavior, with number of disruptions during class as her dependent variable. But such a new technique might take time to become effective, so she might record the number of interruptions before the new technique, and then 2 months later. During the intervening 2 months there could be some bad weather, or general rejoicing over sports victories for the school team, or quarrels could occur between groups of students, and so on. Such intervening events could affect the students' attitudes, possibly being responsible for a difference between the first and second measurement period.

Whereas time can help to create the first two problems (personal and situational change) with the one-group pretest-posttest design, the introduction of preliminary testing can be a factor in creating the two other problems (test familiarity and test dimension awareness). Test familiarity can affect test performance, and the preliminary testing affords this familiarity when the subject is being tested for the second time. Although test familiarity does not necessarily affect test scores, it often does. For example, the second time people take an IQ test they are likely to score 3 to 5 points higher (Campbell & Stanley, 1963, p. 9). There are also expected changes in scores in the second taking of some personality tests. Thus changes from the first to second observation could give the impression of an effective intervening T, although T itself might not have any effect.

Test dimension awareness, the fourth potential confounding factor, involves attitudinal changes that can take place as a result of the pretest. Test dimension awareness causes changes in performance that follow specifically from the first test giving an impression of what it is that the experimenter is interested in measuring, or what the experimenter is looking for. When people receive a pretest involving measurement of errors, they may assume that this is more important than speed, or vice versa if a pretest involving obvious monitoring of speed was given. They are likely to alter their behavior in terms of what the pretest suggests is critical. A pretest can often implicitly inform the subjects of the dimension that is relevant to the people doing the testing. The result can be a change in performance from the pretest where subjects are learning what is relevant, to the posttest where this information can influence performance. This offers one more way in which a change from pretest to posttest can occur without any intervening T, so that an ineffective T can then appear to be effective (or an effective T can have its influence obscured).

In summary then, having a pretest–posttest arrangement allows for at least four possibilities for confounding. The intervening time factor can permit two of these: (a) consistent changes among the subjects involving boredom or fatigue or nervousness (personal change), or (b) external events occuring that are relevant to most or all of the subjects, such as deteriorating or improving relationships between groups of students over time, or changes in other social conditions (situational change). The initial measurement process can be responsible for the other two possibilities: (c) prior exposure to the pretest can offer familiarity with the test, which can affect the second testing (test familiarity), or (d) the initial testing can simply create self-consciousness in regard to what is to be measured, possibly affecting performance on the posttest (test dimension awareness).

There are additional potential sources of confounding other than personal change, situational change, test familiarity, and test dimension awareness. They are discussed by Campbell and Stanley (1963) and Cook and Campbell (1979).

PRETEST–POSTTEST COMPLETELY RANDOMIZED DESIGN

When at least two conditions are included in a pretest–posttest design with random assignment to conditions, it is called a **pretest–posttest completely randomized design** in this text. (Campbell and Stanley identify it as the pretest–posttest control group design.) It is symbolized in Figs. 4.9 and 4.10, where, once again, the R indicates that the subjects are randomly assigned to conditions, with Fig. 4.9 offering the simplest case for this design, in which there is just one experimental and one control condition.

In the pretest–posttest completely randomized design the intervening time factor, which can be responsible for personal and/or situational change, is shared by subjects in all conditions. Any changes over time due to personal or situational factors should occur in all groups, but with differences between experimental and control

$$R \mid O_1 \quad T \quad O_2$$
$$R \mid O_1 \qquad O_2$$

FIG. 4.9. Pretest–posttest completely randomized design with just one experimental and one control condition.

R	O_1	T	O_2
R	O_1	T '	O_2
R	O_1	T ' '	O_2
R	O_1		O_2

FIG. 4.10. Pretest–posttest completely randomized design with several treatment conditions and a control condition.

conditions superimposed on any such changes. For example, suppose a new drug is offered that is expected to delay the onset of some AIDS symptoms. Assume that one group of AIDS patients receives a placebo, and the other receives the actual drug. Assume that the two groups are treated in their respective ways for 6 months. It is possible that both groups of subjects (the experimental and the control) will have increases in the targeted symptoms over the time period, because the course of the disease is such that an increase of symptoms is expected over time. However, if the drug, given only to the subjects in the experimental condition, is at least partially effective, the increase in symptoms will be greater for the control group. If the control condition had been omitted, then from seeing the treatment group subjects increase their symptoms, it might have been concluded that the drug is not useful.

It is possible that the passage of time between measurements can be coincidental with changes in the environmental situation (unusually hot weather, a local riot, power outages, school ending or beginning). Such things can have psychological effects. If impactful events that could affect all of the subjects occur during the period between testing, the use of a control condition that is equally exposed to the social changes permits the comparison of the pre to post differences for both groups, with the control group offering a baseline for the comparison.

The pretest–posttest completely randomized design is very similar to the completely randomized design. It does, however, have some special uses. For example, the initial scores for subjects might vary widely, and there might be concern about a possible lack of similarity of the scores in the different groups. There would be no way to know this without pretesting. If subjects start from different places (being high or low in scores), this might make a difference in how they would be affected by the manipulation. For some subjects there might be no room for improvement (called **ceiling effects**), or no possibility of getting worse (called **floor effects**, as when some subjects begin with a test's lowest score). Pretesting would alert the experimenter to these possibilities. Furthermore, as discussed more fully in chapters 5 and 6, great variability in scores makes the statistical tests less sensitive. With pretesting and posttesting, we usually use **change scores** (the difference between pretest and posttest scores for each subject) as the dependent variable. This usually reduces the variability. The reason is that if subjects begin with very different scores, and are then changed some more or less constant amount by the manipulation, their posttest scores will still be very different, given different starting scores. On the other hand, when using change scores, a more or less consistent change will result in very similar change scores, regardless of the initial (pretesting) scores (unless there are strong ceiling or floor effects).

Another important use for pre–post measurement is when there are multiple groups but none is a clear control condition. In this case, the use of pre-post measures can offer some help in still permitting useful conclusions.

Completely Randomized Pretest–Posttest Design with No Control

In chapter 3, in discussing Rule 1, it was stated that when comparing two or more different manipulations it is necessary to include a control condition. Yet there are occasionally practical situations where a control condition simply cannot be implemented. When there are two or more conditions but none of these are control conditions, the use of pre–post measures can sometimes serve to preserve a good deal of interpretability. To see how and why this is so, it is necessary to recall the problems in reaching valid conclusions when comparing two different manipulations without a specific control condition.

When there are two manipulations and no specific control condition, an outcome that indicates that one condition is more effective than the other could be the result of both conditions being effective, though one more than the other; or the result of one condition being effective, and the other not; or the result of one condition having a depressive effect on responding, whereas the other has neither a depressive nor a stimulating effect on responding. There are additional outcomes and interpretations possible. The large number of potential interpretations is a function of not knowing the absolute nature of the effects, but only the scores of one condition relative to the scores of other conditions.

If pre- as well as postmeasures are available, the absolute nature of the effects in each of the conditions is sometimes discernible. To see why this is so, we examine a hypothetical example of the comparison of two manipulations with no control condition, but pre–post measurement. Assume that an experimenter wanted to determine whether ridicule or sympathy would be more effective in reducing the anxiety of a person who complained about how anxious he or she was. The experimenter could obtain a group of highly anxious subjects and randomly assign half of them to a ridicule condition and the other half to a sympathy condition. The situation in which the intervention took place could be a companion-like interaction, or a more formal therapist–patient interaction, but would be the same for both interventions. The experimenter would measure the anxiety of each person just prior to the intervention, and then again after the intervention (which would involve either ridicule or sympathy). The dependent variable, rather than being the postintervention measurement, would be the change score (the difference between the pretest and posttest anxiety scores), with negative scores suggesting effectiveness in this example (reduced anxiety from pretest to posttest). If both techniques resulted in decreased anxiety, but one more than the other, this would be apparent because of the use of change scores. Similarly, it would be clear if only one condition resulted in a decrease in anxiety. If both conditions yielded approximately the same change score, the question of whether they were both equally effective, or equally ineffective, could be answered by looking at the average change score in each group, to see whether it was negative or positive. (But see further discussion for a persistent problem.)

The preceding paragraph suggests that an experiment comparing two manipulations, neither specifically identifiable as a control condition, is still interpretable if it includes pre-postmeasurement. A more accurate view would be that such an experiment is more likely to be interpretable than one without both pretest and posttest scores, so if no control condition is available, pretest and posttest scores should be obtained. There is still a problem, even with these scores, if there is no control condition. This is the general problem with the use of pre–post measurements, discussed at the beginning of this section on pre–post designs: There is the passage of time between the pre- and postmeasures.

What is the effect of that time? It is possible that anxiety will decrease naturally in that time, or possibly anxiety will increase in that time. If the natural course of anxiety (or any dependent variable) over the time period between the pretesting and posttesting is not known, then the absolute effects of the manipulations can not be known. For example, assume that anxiety normally declines over periods of time such as that intervening between the pre- and postmeasures. Also assume that it was found, in the experiment, that anxiety did not decrease for either manipulation. This could mean that both manipulations tend to increase anxiety (or prolong it), although it would have appeared from the scores remaining the same from pretesting to posttesting that both manipulations are merely ineffective. Thus knowledge of the natural pre–post course of events—that is, potential changes in the absence of a manipulation—can affect the interpretation of change scores. It is the role of a control condition to give this information about the natural course of events for the dependent variable values, in the absence of the manipulation. When a control condition is not available, if there is some prior information on the natural course of possible changes in the dependent variable over time, this can offer some ability to still interpret the results usefully (though a control condition is much better). For example, it might be known that people, on the average, score 5 points higher the second time that they take a particular test that is to be used as a pre–post measure. A pre–post increase of 5 points would then be considered to be a case of no change in the variable being measured. Unfortunately, such general knowledge about a test usually does not have the quantitative specificity that would be needed for statistical tests of differences.

THE SOLOMON FOUR-GROUP DESIGN

Although the pretest-posttest completely randomized design avoids most of the problems in interpretation that can result from doing experiments, there are some that we have not yet discussed. One of these problems is nicely illustrated by a hypothetical example offered by Campbell and Stanley (1963). A movie, titled *A Gentlemen's Agreement* (a classic, starring Gregory Peck), is shown to an audience. The movie has an antiprejudice message, but it is presented in the context of an effective and interesting love story. Assume that the people seeing the film were tested for prejudice before the film, and again after (using some paper and pencil test). Assume further that another group was similarly tested for prejudice before and after a film, but instead saw a different love story not containing an antiprejudice message. We might find that the group seeing the Gregory Peck movie would show reduced prejudice in the testing administered after the film, but that this would not be observed in the group shown the other film. It would be tempting to draw the conclusion that the film was effective in reducing prejudice, at least as reflected in a paper and pencil test. The film might then, in the future, be used in attempts to reduce prejudice.

What Campbell and Stanley pointed out (in this hypothetical example) is that the pretesting itself could have sensitized subjects in the treatment group to the antiprejudice message. The important point to be made here is that any effect of the antiprejudice message on reducing prejudice might depend on the sensitizing effect of the prior testing for prejudice. If the subjects had not been tested before seeing the film, they might have not noticed the antiprejudice message, and might just have reacted to the film as to any love story. The same experiment without any pretesting might not show a difference between the two groups.

There are other situations where the pretesting can have a sensitizing effect of its own, or react in conjunction with the treatment. There is a standard experimental design that can be used to identify this effect. It does this by including both presence and absence of pretesting. This is called the **Solomon four-group design**. It is summarized in symbolic form in Fig. 4.11. Note the use of various numerical subscripts for the observations, which will help in discussing the design.

The effect of the treatment can be assessed with a number of different comparisons: First there is the obvious one, $O_2 - O_1$, using $O_4 - O_3$ as a control in a pretest-posttest completely randomized design. Assume we found the treatment effective, that is, $(O_2 - O_1)$ is greater than $(O_4 - O_3)$. Then we test $O_5 - O_6$, as though this was a completely randomized design involving just two groups, then $O_2 - O_4$ as though this was a completely randomized design, except that subjects were given the opportunity of sensitization to the treatment by pretesting. If we obtained a reliable difference with this

R	O_1	T	O_2
R	O_3		O_4
R		T	O_5
R			O_6

FIG. 4.11.   Solomon four-group design.

latter test ($O_2 - O_4$) but not with the former test ($O_5 - O_6$), then we would have evidence that the treatment is only effective when it has been preceded by the pretest.

Effects of pretesting on test familiarity can be assessed through comparisons of O_4 with O_6, and there are many other analyses possible (see Campbell & Stanley, 1963, p. 25). This is a complex design and requires sophistication to use properly.

It is often possible to think about the nature of the pretesting and see if it contains clues to the nature of the manipulation. Pretesting procedures do not always give away the purpose of the planned manipulation to the subjects. For example, people are often measured without the knowledge that this is happening, or can be misled as to the nature of the measurements. (Recall in chapter 3, in the Higgins and Marlatt research, where subjects thought they were rating adjectives that were used to describe beverages, whereas in fact what was being measured was the amount that they were drinking in the course of making the ratings.) Thus, although we should consider the possibility of the effectiveness of treatments depending on pretesting, we do not always have to incorporate controls for this in our experiments. The Solomon four-group design, though often cited in the literature, is not used frequently, perhaps because of the number of subjects it requires.

REPEATED-MEASURES DESIGN

It is frequently convenient to use the same subjects in all conditions of an experiment. This is called a **repeated-measures design**. The repeated-measures design has some similarities to the pre–post completely randomized design in that both involve repeated measures (observations) of the same subjects. However, the repeated-measures design additionally involves repeated manipulations of the same subjects.

In a repeated-measures design, instead of, for example, having one group of subjects solving problems while exposed to noise, and a different group of subjects solving problems without noise, the same subjects are given the opportunity to solve some problems with and some problems without noise. The principle advantage of the repeated-measures design is that it increases the power of the statistical test. Greater statistical power means that weaker effects of independent variables can be detected. Stated another way, it is possible to use less subjects and still have the ability to detect effective independent variables. The concept of statistical power is discussed in chapter 5.

A variable that has the same subjects at all levels of the variable is called a repeated-measures variable. It is also called a "**within-subjects variable**," or within-subjects factor. When different subjects are used at each level of a variable, as in the case of completely randomized designs, the variable is called a "**between-subjects variable**," or between-subjects factor. Thus, noise would be a between-subjects variable in a completely randomized version of a noise and problem-solving experiment, and a within-subjects variable in a repeated-measures version of the same experiment.

As another example of a repeated-measures design, an experimenter might wish to determine the physiological reactions of people to a horror movie as a function of the number of times they have seen the movie. Would the results indicate that given more viewing the subjects would begin to anticipate the frightening scenes with increasing physiological responsiveness, or would the increased exposure reduce the subjects' responsiveness to each frightening scene? Suppose the subjects were exposed to the movie four times, and while they viewed the film they were continuously monitored on some physiological variables, from which a stress score was obtained, for each subject, for each of the four viewings. There would probably be an additional stress measurement prior to the showing of the movie, as a control condition. This would be a repeated-measures design with five levels of the independent variable (number of exposures to the movie, including zero).

When the independent variable is number of exposures to the experimental situation and there is a great deal of subject variability, the repeated-measures design is usually the design of choice. The subjects need to be observed at each of several exposures to the same experimental manipulation. Because the manipulations (or conditions of stimulus exposure) are always the same, there is no problem of order of presentation of manipulations. There is simply a first exposure, a second exposure, and so on. This is least complicated when the measures are observations (such as physiological recordings).

When the dependent variable is a verbal response, subjects' earlier responses can affect their later responses, because people often like to be verbally consistent. For example, assume that various methods for influencing people in an ambiguous situation are being compared. The ambiguous situation involves the presentation of a point of light, which is actually stationary, but gives the appearance of movement (the *auto-kinetic effect*). Several methods of influencing the subjects to see greater movement are being compared in the different conditions (levels). It is possible that a subject's prior response might influence later responses. Having seen a great deal of movement once, the subject might be discouraged from later reporting complete absence of movement. On the other hand, this situation, to the subject, might appear to be an objective situation (simply calling for what the subject has seen). But if the responses were clearly opinions, each time on the same topic, the early responses would certainly influence later responses (assuming that the subjects, like most people, wish to appear to be consistent). In such cases it is best to avoid the repeated- measures design, instead using different subjects in the different conditions, with the completely randomized design.

The repeated measures design most typically runs into difficulties when the sequence of the experimental conditions is not implicit in the nature of the independent variable. That is, suppose there were three levels of noise as the independent variable. There would be no natural order of exposures to the different levels. As another example, suppose that an experimenter tested the effects of different types of instruction for a problem-solving task on the time required for problem solution. A complication that might arise is that the first problem-solving task, regardless of the instructions, might be the one approached with the most enthusiasm, getting it solved most quickly, making the first instruction appear superior. If boredom or fatigue set in with task repetition, the last type of instruction might erroneously appear to yield inferior results (longer solution times). Thus, where a treatment condition appears in the sequence can affect the way in which a subject responds to that treatment, possibly obscuring the actual treatment effect. Differences in responding that follow from where the treatment conditions appear in the sequence of exposures are called **order effects**.

A more complex order effect is the one where a particular level, at a particular point in the sequence, has a special effect on the other conditions (levels) in the experiment. For example, the presentation of a relatively difficult condition as the first condition might overwhelm the subjects, and due to ensuing nervousness or lack of confidence cause problems with the subjects' encounters with subsequent conditions of the experiment. But if the subjects experienced a relatively easy condition as the first encounter with the experiment, they might perform well on the easy condition, gain confidence, and then do well in a later encounter with a more difficult condition. If the different conditions (different levels of the factor) involve different sets of instructions, one set of instructions might better prepare subjects for another type of instruction, which might otherwise be more difficult. Such order effects, like all order effects, can be weak or powerful. Order effects have to be considered as a potential problem when using repeated measures.

As the major solution to the potential problem of order effects, whenever the sequence of exposures does not define the levels of the independent variable, the sequence of exposures to the individual conditions must be arranged randomly for each subject. This is done quite easily with a table of random numbers. Randomization avoids one potential source of bias in the statistical test of a repeated measures design, and is the preferred way of proceeding.

Experimenters are occasionally tempted to try to avoid the problem of order effects in another way. They counterbalance the order of conditions. A **counterbalanced order** is one in which every possible order occurs equally often. If there are only two conditions, there are only two possible orders (1,2, and 2,1). If there are three conditions, there are six possible orders (1,2,3; 1,3,2; 2,1,3; 2,3,1; 3,1,2; 3,2,1). In general, for any number n, there are n! (n factorial) possible orders.

$$n! = n \times (n-1) \times (n-2) \times (n-3) \times \ldots \times 2 \times 1$$

The problem with counterbalancing is a statistical one. It creates something called negative bias, which reduces the power of the statistical test (makes it less likely that real but weak effects will be recognized). The use of randomization of exposure to the levels of the independent variable avoids the negative bias. If counterbalancing is used and a relationship between the variables is found despite the negative bias, the results are interpretable, because it suggests that the relationship is strong enough to overcome the obscuring potential of negative bias.

When there is reason to believe that the order of exposure has a strong influence on the dependent variable, but there are adequate reasons for using a repeated-measures design, a design is often used that combines repeated and nonrepeated measures (both within- and between-subjects variables). This solution is discussed in the context of multifactor designs (in chapter 6).

The repeated measures design is symbolized in Figure 4.12 where the randomization of the *sequence of conditions* for each subject is symbolized by $|Rs_i|$, the subscript i referring to some i^{th} subject. An O is juxtaposed with each T, T', and T'' to indicate that the observations (measurements) are repeated at each level of an experimental condition, while an isolated O is used to represent a control condition (because no manipulation, no T, would be present in a control condition). Note that in a repeated-measures design, if there is a

$|Rs_1|$	O	TO	T'O	T''O
$|Rs_2|$	O	TO	T'O	T''O
•				
•				
•				
$|Rs_i|$	O	TO	T'O	T''O
•				
•				
•				
$|Rs_n|$	O	TO	T'O	T''O

FIG. 4.12. Repeated-measures design. The $|Rs_i|$ indicate that the sequence of conditions is individually randomized for each subject. (Randomization would not be required if the sequence were a natural one.) The juxtaposed upper-case T's and O's, in TO, T'O, and T''O, indicate that the observations (measurements) are repeated at each level of the independent variable, including the control condition where there is no manipulation present.

control condition, each subject is exposed to the control condition as well as all of the manipulations.

It should be clear that a repeated-measures design, like the completely randomized design and the pre–post completely randomized design, requires the use of a manipulated variable. The reason is that a person's preexisting classification (on a subject variable) cannot be reassigned during an experiment.

MATCHED-PAIRS DESIGN

There is a design lying somewhere between a one-factor completely randomized design (with different subjects in each condition) and a repeated-measures design (with the same subjects in each condition). In this intermediate design different subjects are used in each group, but the subjects are pairwise matched before being assigned to the different groups. The matching is on some variable that is related to the dependent variable. For example, if the dependent variable was the score on an abstract reasoning task, the matching variable could be IQ. The result would be subjects in the different groups that are very similar on at least one dimension. When there are just two groups, and subjects are pairwise matched in the two groups on some third variable *that is related to the dependent variable*, the design is called a **matched-pairs design**.

When subjects can be matched on some variable that is related to the dependent variable, the power of the statistical test is increased, for reasons identical to those that increase the statistical power of a repeated-measures design. (The reason is a reduction in random variability, which is discussed in chapters 5 and 6.) In a sense, a repeated measure (using the same subjects in the different conditions) is a case of perfect matching of the subjects in the different conditions. An advantage of matching over repeated measures is that the problems of order effects do not arise (because each subject experiences only one condition).

Grade-point averages are often used as the matching variable when the dependent variable is classroom or exam performance, which would be typical in a test of different teaching methods. IQ is often used as a matching variable when the dependent variable is an intellectual task, because of IQ's close relationship to (high correlation with) specific intellectual tasks. Any variable that has a close relationship to (reasonably high correlation with) the dependent variable can be used as a matching variable.

Often, some pretesting is done as the basis of matching. For example, assume a study in which the dependent variable is the reaction time in some task, and the independent variable is praise, or absence of praise, for responding quickly. The subjects who volunteered for the experiment can be initially tested on their reaction times in a reaction-time task that is physically similar to the one that will be used in the experiment, then ranked according to their reaction times. Subjects who are adjacent in the ranks would be placed into pairs, and within each pair randomly assigned to one or the other group (praise or no praise). The two groups would then have approximately equal pretest reaction times. This would increase the power of the statistical test, more readily permitting the detection of weak but reliable effects of the independent variable (praise vs. no praise).

The matched-pairs design is symbolically summarized below in Fig. 4.13, where $|M_{s,s}|$ refers to the pairwise matching of the subjects, and O and OT represent the control and experimental conditions, respectively. $|R_{s,s}|$ refers to random assignment of conditions, in this case random assignment between members of a pair to either the experimental or control condition.

CORRELATIONAL RESEARCH

In the preceding sections, legitimate designs (completely randomized designs with or without pretesting, repeated-measures designs, and matched-pairs designs) were described as all sharing the char-

FIG. 4.13. Matched-pairs design. $|M_{s,s}|$ symbolizes matching of each pair of subjects, and $|R_{s,s}|$ symbolizes random assignment of the members of each pair, one assigned to the control condition (O) and the other to the experimental condition (TO).

acteristic of having two or more conditions that are distinguished on the independent variable by variations in the manipulation. In addition there is random assignment of subjects to the different conditions (with the exception of repeated-measures designs, in which all subjects are exposed to all conditions).

There are times when the differences being investigated are not manipulated differences, but instead are differences in the nature of the groups—that is, differently performing, or differently classified, or otherwise differently categorized subjects, are used to form the different levels of the variable which distinguishes groups of subjects. This is recognized as a different design, or class of designs, called *correlational research* (previously discussed in chapter 2 where limitations on conclusions with subject variables are examined). Some might not consider these to be legitimate designs, in that there is no experimental manipulation. But such designs are nonetheless commonly encountered in the literature, and can be used to broaden our understanding of relationships between variables. It is just more critical to be sophisticated about the limits to the inferences that can be made with these designs.

Let us look at an example of a psychological question, concerning memory, that could be explored with correlational research.

"Would people who have more trouble committing things to memory, also have greater trouble retaining things that they have committed to memory?" Our first step might be to classify subjects in terms of their ability to commit things to memory. Specifically, suppose that the subjects are asked to learn a long list of nonsense syllables. They are given several trials, and the trials are repeated until they have successfully recalled the entire list without error, for two successive trials. This is done for several such lists, after which subjects are classified in terms of the average number of trials they required to learn a list to this criterion.

Assume that a relatively small number of subjects take 5 or 6 trials, a much larger number require between 7 and 8, an equally large number between 9 and 10 and a few others require 11 or 12. Suppose that four groups are then identified, according to their performance (5 or 6 trials, 7 or 8 trials, 9 or 10 trials, and 11 or 12 trials). Assume further that they are given a new list of nonsense syllables to memorize, to the same high criterion used previously (so that it is clear that they have successfully learned all the items). They are then given some intervening arithmetic task for a few minutes.

For the experimental test (the critical observations), the subjects, after spending a few minutes at the arithmetic task, are asked to repeat the last memorized list of nonsense syllables. Each subject would receive a score, the score being the number of nonsense syllables correctly recalled.

The basic question being asked by these procedures is the following: Assuming that the subjects are first classified as to differences in ease of learning (number of trials needed for perfect performance), are there differences in retention among the different groups? Stated another way (remembering that all subjects learned their material to the same criterion), is retention related to ease of initial learning?

In this experiment there would not be any manipulation differences, and there would not be random assignment to groups. The differences in the groups would be the result of classification of the subjects on some prior status (in this case their measured performance, the number of trials each subject required for errorless immediate recall on previous lists). This is analogous to measuring people on their IQ in order to assign them to groups. This is a design with a subject variable as the factor.

In chapter 2 it was pointed out that experiments with subject variables are generally identified as examples of correlational research, from which it is difficult to draw causal inferences. One can conclude, following statistical significance, that the variables are related, but without knowing whether such an apparent relationship is actually mediated by some third variable.

The symbolization of this example of correlational research would not include T's, because there are no treatments or manipulations introduced, just observations. We can use a subscripted G to represent each different group, as illustrated in Fig. 4.14.

Another example would be a study comparing differences in annual

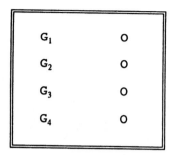

FIG. 4.14. Correlational research design with four groups.

income for the members of different religious groups. There would be as many groups as there are religions that have been identified in the population. Another example would involve comparing quantitative measurements of anxiety among three different groups of students: those who studied for an exam with at least one other classmate, those who studied alone, and those who did not study.

Although in each of these examples we have defined specific groups, it is possible to do **correlational research with no groups defined**. For example, is there a relationship between the number of days absent from work during the year, and the average amount of alcohol (in ounces) the person drinks in an average week? Here the variety of responses from subjects, on either variable, would not permit practical assignment to groups (unless people were grouped together into numerical intervals). However, it is still clear that we are using the performance of subjects to classify them (quantitatively). That is, the experimenter has not arranged for people to be in different conditions, but has taken them as they come. Subjects are merely measured, and their scores on two variables are recorded.

In this type of research, it is hoped that we can determine the degree to which a subject's relative position on one set of scores is predictive of the subject's relative position on the other set of scores. This in turn is used to obtain a quantitative statement of the extent to which the variables are related. The statistical technique of correlation is used for this purpose, and is in fact the source of the term *correlational research*. (The statistical procedure is described in chapter 5, where statistical issues are discussed.)

Figure 4.15 offers a symbolic picture of the correlational design when both variables have wide-ranging scores and no groups have been defined.

Note that the symbols used in Fig. 4.15 are only O_1 and O_2. There is no T, because there is no manipulation, only observations. This is

Subjects	A set of scores on one variable	A set of scores on a second variable
1	O_1	O_2
2	O_1	O_2
2	O_1	O_2
.	.	.
.	.	.
.	.	.
n	O_1	O_2

FIG. 4.15. Correlational research design with no groups defined (two wide-ranging quantitative subject variables, O_1 and O_2). Note that O_1 and O_2 represent a pair of scores from each subject. Each set of quantitative scores is on a dimension of a different variable. If the two sets of scores tend to be pair-wise related in the sense of both being high, or moderate, or low, or tend to be opposite to each other, then the two variables are related. If the scores on one variable are not predictive of the scores on the other variable, then the two variables are not related.

a common design and is frequently used with data that are readily available, or easily acquired, from shopping mall surveys, campus surveys, census data, hospital records, and so forth. Three examples of issues that could be explored with this type of data are the following: Is there a relationship between number of stressful events and physical complaints in the course of a year? Or between IQ and income? Or between number of hours of study for a course and final exam grade?

BRIEF REVIEW OF TYPES OF DESIGNS

The completely randomized design, with its random assignment of subjects to levels of the independent variable, and use of manipulations to distinguish the levels of the independent variable, is the classic experimental design.

The pretest–posttest completely randomized design is similar to the completely randomized design, except that it includes prior measurement in both the experimental and control conditions. When there are several conditions, but none are properly seen as control conditions, the use of pretesting helps in the interpretation of the results, by helping to identify the direction of change in the different groups. Pretesting helps either recognize or avoid the problems that are sometimes encountered when there is great variability in the initial scores. It helps us to recognize when subjects have begun at very different points prior to the manipulation. Second, through the use of change scores, it sometimes enables us to reduce variability in the dependent variable. Thus, when various manipulations are compared with each other, pretesting is often desirable. On the other hand, problems of sensitizing subjects to the manipulations by pretesting can create problems in interpreting the results of the experiment. The use of the Solomon four-group design was suggested as one way of exploring and dealing with this kind of situation.

As can be seen from the discussions in this chapter on both advantages of and problems with the use of pretesting, avoiding one problem sometimes can lead to another. Further, it is not always possible to arrange for subjects to be available in precisely the way we need them for correct experimental procedures. Outside of experimental laboratories, in factories and clinics trying out new programs, the acceptance of compromises in the design of research is often necessary. The previously cited works of Campbell and Stanley (1963) and Cook and Campbell (1979) discuss in great detail the topic of limited interpretability given compromises in design.

The repeated-measures design involves both repeated manipulations and repeated measurements. It is the case of the same subjects being used in every condition (every level) of the manipulation. When there is a great deal of subject variability, it is a good idea to use repeated-measures designs, if possible.

Matched-pairs designs are very similar to repeated-measures designs. However, instead of using the same subjects in each group, the subjects are matched on a variable that is related to the dependent variable. It has the advantage, compared to the repeated-measures design, of not creating problems with order effects. On the other hand it is important with this design that the matching variable be highly related to the dependent measure.

When there is no manipulated variable in the experiment and when subjects are placed into groups on the basis of some prior classification, the research is called correlational research. Correlational research obtains its name from the case in which the study is done with two widely ranging quantitative variables, which precludes the use of groups. In this case the correlation between the two sets of scores is obtained and then tested for statistical significance, as the test of a relationship between the variables. However, when finite sets of groups can be defined, permitting the use of statistics other than correlation, but the distinctions between groups are based on subject classification, we still call it correlational research.

INTERNAL AND EXTERNAL VALIDITY

In the Campbell and Stanley (1963) monograph, cited so frequently in the literature as well as in this chapter, threats to the validity of experiments are categorized and described. Campbell and Stanley distinguished two types of validity, **internal validity** and **external validity**. The rules for research suggested in chapter 3 can be seen as aids in avoiding threats to these two types of validity. Although additional types of validity have been named by Cook and Campbell (1979), the two broadly defined original notions of internal and external validity offer a simpler and possibly more useful distinction, when used in conjunction with the rules for research. The designs described in this chapter all have the advantage of maximizing internal validity. The Solomon four-group design is the only one among them that is designed to deal, to some degree, with threats to external validity.

Internal Validity

Internal validity refers to the likelihood of reaching correct conclusions about the role of the independent variable in an experiment. For example, were confounding factors absent? Was the attempted experimental manipulation successful? Internal validity is threatened by the difficulties of avoiding confounding factors, and by the occasional difficulties in actually implementing an intended manipulation. For example, if subjects were instructed to rehearse items in memory, or form mental images in some groups but not others, did the subjects behave as instructed? An experiment is usually done to see if some difference between experimental conditions (the independent variable) has an effect on some dependent measure. The minimum requirement for this to be a fair test is that the intended difference be present and that there be no competing explanations for any observed differences. Thus, internal validity depends not only on whether or not the experiment itself was properly designed, but also on whether it was carried out as intended. Following Rules 1, 2, and 5—that is, having multiple conditions including a control group, avoiding confounding factors, and not arbitrarily omitting data—are some obvious ways to avoid threats to internal validity. In addition, two parts of Rule 3, the random assignment of subjects to conditions and the use of a random order for the running of the subjects in the different conditions, are aids in avoiding confounding factors, and so help to safeguard internal validity. Finally, it is critical that the intended manipulations (the variations in treatment, the differences with regard to the independent variable) have been successfully introduced into the experiment. If different subjects were instructed to use different strategies to solve problems but many of the subjects did not follow the instructions, there would not have been a valid test of the relationship between the variables. Ways of assuring that the manipulations were effectively introduced are discussed in chapter 13 under the heading of Manipulation Checks.

Most of the threats to interpretations of experiments previously described in this chapter are threats to internal validity (including the possibilities of personal change and situational change between pre- and postmeasurements, and potential problems arising from test familiarity and test dimension awareness). The issue of internal validity has to be faced for each study. The mere fact that a study has been published does not guarantee that it is internally valid. In fact, since potential confounding factors are one of the primary threats to internal validity, and one can never be sure that confounding factors are completely absent, confidence in internal validity has to be a relative rather than an absolute thing. However, one can be reasonably certain that internal validity has been compromised when there are violations of the rules for research, particularly when there are not adequate control conditions, or treatment order has not been randomized, or data have been selectively discarded without the care recommended in the discussion of Rule 5.

External Validity

"External validity asks the question of generalizability: To what population, settings, . . . can this effect be generalized?" (Campbell & Stanley, 1963, p. 5). To appreciate how conclusions are limited when there are threats to external validity, it is helpful to recognize that an experiment always involves a sample of a population. The experiment, generally through the use of a statistical test, asks the question of whether any difference that is observed in the sample can be expected to also be present in the sampled population. A statistically significant statistical test indicates that an observed sample difference can be generalized to the population. But which population? Was the sample taken from the population to which generalization is planned? Here judicious use of part of Rule 3 is important, the part concerning random selection from the population. If a study about depression used depressed people as subjects, the question would have to be asked as to whether the subjects represented all types of depressives about whom conclusions were intended. Thus, Rule 3 is important for external validity, as is Rule 4, the application of a statistical test.

We discussed the possibility that the effect of a manipulation might depend on pretesting (in the example of the antiprejudice movie that might not have been seen as containing any message, without the sensitizing effects of pretesting). If pretesting were in fact necessary for an effect, we would have a limit on the generalizability of the observed effect. It would work given pretesting, but not without it. Thus, there would be an important limit on the generalizability of the finding. This is an example of a problem in external validity.

There are other, more obvious examples of questionable generalizability. One such example is in the use of animal subjects for conclusions about humans. Great care must be taken in the species selected, for the particular question. If studying ulcers in animals, it would be important, for example, to select animals with similar stomachs and similar gastric juices to humans.

Even when human subjects are used, they are not always obtained from the target population. This is seen in the frequent use of college students as subjects for psychological experiments. College students are in many respects like any other people, but in some respects they are different than the general population. An experiment might be seen as generalizable to all college students, but would the results be generalizable to senior citizens? Thus external validity is not an all-or-none issue. An experiment can be externally valid for some part of a population, but not other parts.

There is another issue concerning external validity: What operational definitions were used for the variables? Suppose that prolonged noise was investigated for its effect on levels of tension. Assume that it was found to increase tension. Could the results apply to noise in general, or only the types used in the study? This is a question of external validity. Thus, external validity refers to generalizability concerning not only populations and settings, but also stimuli, treatment, and criteria, which may differ in parts of the real world from those used in the experiment.

A related issue that can be seen as being relevant to external validity is the realistic or unrealistic nature of laboratory experiments. Sometimes critics claim that laboratory research with human subjects is not sufficiently realistic. For example, if doing experiments where levels of motivation are being manipulated, or physical threat is being manipulated, are the levels of motivation and the levels of fear from physical threat sufficiently high to apply to real-world analogues? Thus the levels of the variables have to be examined, as well as the realistic nature of the experiments, to determine whether the generalizability is as broad as the experimenter would like to claim after the experiment.

The answer to these questions is not that one can or cannot generalize from laboratory experiments. Rather, questions of external validity have to be answered for each experiment. The experimenter, or reader of research, should always ask about the limits of generalizability for the particular study. The most obvious threats to external validity come from the following:

1. Violations of Rule 3 concerning random selection of subjects.
2. The appropriateness of the population from which the random selection occurred.
3. The similarity of the stimuli, the situations, and the tension and involvement levels found in the experimental situations to the world outside the laboratory.

CHAPTER SUMMARY

The classic experimental designs have the form of one or another version of the completely randomized design. The two critical aspects of this design are the random assignment of subjects to levels of the independent variable, and the use of manipulations to distinguish the levels of the independent variable. The independent variable will always have some finite number of levels, usually just a few, with a minimum of two. One of these should be a control condition. Limitations on interpretability when no condition can be clearly identified as a control condition were discussed.

When there is no condition that can be clearly identified as a control condition, it is useful to include prior measurement on the dependent variable. This permits conclusions about the absolute effects of the independent variable, even without a control condition, providing that there is some prior knowledge about the normal effects of time and repeated measurement on the dependent variable. If there is a control condition, with pre- and postmeasurement, we then have the very strong pretest–posttest completely randomized design. This design offers the ability to use change scores as the dependent variable, as well as the opportunity of identifying possible problems from ceiling or floor effects.

These completely randomized designs were contrasted with two improper designs: the one-group design and the one-group pretest–posttest design. The inability to implement the rules of research with these designs makes it difficult to reach useful conclusions with them. The one-group design was presented more as an illustration of flawed informal reasoning. On the other hand, the one-group pretest–posttest design is sometimes used when practical considerations preclude the use of a control condition. Many of the alternative explanations for apparent effects that have to be faced (time passing between the two measurements, permitting confounding factors due to personal or situational changes; the use of the pretest that can be responsible for both test familiarity and test dimension awareness) were described in detail. Recognizing these sources of confounding factors can sometimes permit limited conclusions to be drawn. The Solomon four-group design was also introduced, offering a means of helping to both become aware of problems unseen without pretest-ing, and providing possible ways of coping with these problems, once recognized through the complex analyses required by this design.

The repeated-measures design was introduced. In a repeated-measures design the same subjects are used at all levels of the independent variable. The independent variable in a repeated-measures design is called a within-subjects variable, whereas in a completely randomized design the independent variable is called a between-subjects variable. A repeated-measures design has greater power, that is, can recognize weaker effects or, alternatively, can permit the use of smaller numbers of subjects in the experiment. In repeated-measures designs, when there is no natural sequence for the levels, the order of the levels is randomized for each subject.

The matched-pairs design was introduced. In this design subjects are pairwise matched in the two groups on some third variable that is related to the dependent variable. It has some increased power as a result of the matching, and avoids the problem of order effects in the closely related repeated-measures design, because, in the matched-pairs design, each subject is used at only one level.

We define research as correlational research when there are no manipulated variables in the research. If groups of subjects are being compared, they are defined on the basis of classification of subjects. Thus each level is verbally categorized (e.g., as low, middle, or upper class). When both variables are quantitative and wide-ranging (as with IQ and income), rather than arbitrarily dividing subjects into groups on the basis of numerical intervals, the data consist of two sets of scores that have been paired on the basis of other variables. Then statistical correlation can be used to determine the extent to which the scores in one set are predictive of their associated scores in the other set.

Whether or not groups are defined, when doing correlational research causal inferences are usually avoided, and the basic question is simply whether the variables are related. If they are found to be related (through statistical significance), the possibility remains that the relationship is only an indirect one, mediated by a third (unrecognized) variable that is related to both of the studied variables. However, correlational research can be done with survey and questionnaire data, with organizational records, and so forth, and can be used to detect relationships among variables in large social systems, and social forces. It can sometimes provide relatively cheap initial studies.

The concepts of internal validity and external validity were introduced. Internal validity refers to the likelihood of reaching correct conclusions about the role of the independent variable in an experiment. Internal validity is threatened to the degree that there are other explanations for the results, other than the effectiveness (or lack of effectiveness) of the independent variable. If it appears that procedural errors, or the presence of confounding factors, or failure of the intended experimental manipulation has been responsible for the outcome, then we have an example of lack of, or threatened, internal validity.

External validity refers to the generalizability of the outcome. To what populations, settings, levels of the variables, and operational definitions of the variables can the experimental results be generalized? Like internal validity, external validity should be questioned for each experiment, recognizing that confidence in validity is usually a matter of degree. It is sometimes reasonable to restrict our conclusions to limited populations or limited circumstances.

NEW WORDS AND PHRASES IN CHAPTER 4

between-subjects variable
change score
ceiling effects
completely randomized design
correlational research with no groups defined
counterbalanced order
external validity

floor effects
internal validity
matched-pairs design
one-group pretest–posttest design
order effects
personal change
pretest–posttest completely randomized design
repeated-measures design
situational change
Solomon four-group design
test familiarity
test dimension awareness
within-subjects variable

CHAPTER 5

Statistical Logic and Choosing a
Statistic: An Overview of the
Role of Statistics in
Psychological Research

The need for statistical tests arises when the data are less than perfectly reliable and are highly variable. As a possibly familar example, suppose that you had a bathroom scale that was unreliable. If you got on and off it a few times in succession, you might find that sometimes you were a pound above or a pound below the last reading. If you only got on it once, read the weight, changed your diet for a week, then got on the scale again and found that you had gained or lost a pound, you would not know whether the random variations in the scale's readings were responsible or whether you had actually changed in weight.

As mentioned in the preceding chapter, most psychological tests have reliability problems. Assume a person is seen in a psychological clinic, is given a test, and is diagnosed as depressed. The individual is treated with a new form of therapy, retested, and is found to be less depressed. Has the new treatment been effective, or is this a case of random variation in the scores?

The numbers produced by psychological tests give us a general idea of people's relative standing, but they do not identify exact *true* scores. **Random variability** in the measurement process adds to or subtracts from the true score. Random variability is unpredictable variability caused by chance factors, or caused by such a multiplicity of varied and changing influences that the precise contribution of random variability to the scores cannot be determined. This is why statistical techniques have to be introduced. Statistical techniques are procedures that permit researchers to draw conclusions from research when dealing with data that varies, at least in part, randomly. Statistical tests offer ways of distinguishing random variations from effective factors.

LETTING THE PROBLEM OF RANDOM VARIABILITY SUGGEST A SOLUTION

How do statistical tests enable researchers to draw conclusions despite the presence of random variability in the scores? Statistical tests include, in their calculations, an estimate of the extent of the random variability in the particular measurement situation. This estimate is used as a standard of comparison, to see if the difference between the means of, say, an experimental and a control group is greater than would be expected on the basis of random variability. If the difference is much larger than what is expected from random variability, random variability is considered to be an insufficient explanation. What is the alternative if random variablility is an insufficient explanation? The answer is the carefully built in difference between the experimental and control groups, the experimental manipulation. Thus, it is possible to confirm an effective independent variable. The way that this is done is to first assume that only chance (random variability) is operating, and then show that this is not reasonable, using criteria discussed later in this chapter.

Before discussing random variability and just how it is shown to be an insufficient explanation when an independent variable is effective, we need to define some terms: a statistic, a mean, a variance, a standard deviation, and a standard error.

THE MEAN

A mean, a variance, a standard deviation, and a standard error are all statistics. A **statistic** is a quantitative descriptor offering information about a sample of scores. Thus, the mean, which is one definition of the average of a sample, identifies a central point within the set of scores. The variance tells you how widely the scores are dispersed.

The mean is incorporated in the defining formula for the variance, and is the most frequently used definition of the average. It is centrally placed in the sample of scores in the sense that the sum of the differences between each of the scores and the mean is zero (the plus values and minus values canceling each other). Its formal definition, most likely already familiar to the reader, is the sum of all of the scores divided by the number of scores, $\mu = \Sigma X/n$, where μ is the symbol for the mean, ΣX instructs you to sum all of the scores, and n is the number of scores.

MEASURING VARIABILITY

The estimate of random variability that is needed in a statistical test is usually obtained from the individual scores within a sample. Each such estimate is made from the scores of subjects that are all within the same condition of the experiment (to avoid the influence of variations in psychological manipulations on the estimate of variability). There are two closely related measures that are most frequently used. One is the **variance**, σ^2, which is the average squared difference from the mean of a set of scores. The other is the **standard deviation**, σ, which is simply the square root of the variance. The formula for computing the *estimate* of the variance from a sample, s^2, is given in the appendix to this chapter.

Variability of Means

The average squared difference from the mean of a set of scores, the variance, is one measure of the extent of the variability among individual scores. However, experimenters are often interested in the variability of the means of groups of scores (rather than the variability among individual scores), for example, the variability in the average (mean) level of anxiety in some group. It can be shown that the means of sets of scores tend to vary less than individual scores. This is known as the law of large numbers. The law of large numbers can be appreciated intuitively, through the use of an example.

Think of a college campus where there are 20,000 students and the mean-grade point average (GPA) is 2.5. Individual people are randomly sampled and questioned as to their GPAs. One might find an individual with a GPA of 4, another with a GPA of 2, another unhappy individual with a GPA of 1.5, and so on. Virtually any GPA that occurs on campus could be found as one of the scores in the sample. The computed variance of all of the GPA scores on campus would give a numerical label for the extent of the variability among individual GPAs on campus.

Suppose that, instead of looking at individual GPAs, a random sample of 1,000 students was obtained, and the average GPA for this 1,000 students was computed. Given a campus average of 2.5, it is almost impossible for such a large sample to yield a mean of 4. Thus, a 4 is not a likely outcome as the sample mean, nor, for similar reasons, is a sample mean of 1.5. Whatever the sample mean actually turns out to be in any one random sample, it is a lot more likely to be close to the actual campus average of 2.5 than would be the case with an individual randomly sampled score; an individual score can more readily vary over the entire range. If an investigator repeatedly sampled 1,000 students at a time, took the mean GPA of each such sample, and then computed the variance of these means (each mean calculated from 1,000 scores), the variance of means would be smaller than the variance of individual scores.

If an investigator obtained the means of even larger samples, each time selecting a random sample of half of the 20,000 students, the individual sample means are likely to be even closer to the population mean, resulting in an even smaller variance. If on the other hand, the sample size was small, say 10 people, there could be a good deal of variation from sample mean to sample mean, resulting in a larger computed variance (of means). In other words, the smaller the sample size used in repeated sampling, the more variable the sample means; the larger the sample size, the less variable the sample means. It is in this sense that the larger the sample size, the smaller the expected variance (of means).

A statistic, such as a mean, or a variance, or its square root the standard deviation, each of which describes some characteristic of a sample, can naturally vary from sample to sample. Its variability from sample to sample can be reflected in (or described by) the standard deviation of the particular statistic (each statistic having its own formula for its standard deviation). The variance of means has a formula that is similar in form to the formula for the variance of individual scores. The square root of the variance of means is the standard deviation of means. Whereas the standard deviation of a set of individual scores is simply called the standard deviation, the standard deviation of any statistic is called the standard error of that statistic. Thus, the square root of the variance of means, being the standard deviation of means, is called the **standard error of the mean** and is symbolized as $\sigma_{\overline{X}}$. A formula for estimating the standard error of the mean from estimates of the variance of individual scores is discussed in the appendix to this chapter. Additional formulas for other needed standard errors are also found there, in the sections illustrating computations of various t tests.

GRAPHS OF THE NORMAL DISTRIBUTION

It has been stated in the preceding discussion that when sets of numbers vary from sample to sample, a single number can be used to express the extent of that variability: either a variance (σ^2) or standard deviation (σ) for individual scores, or a standard error of the mean ($\sigma_{\overline{x}}$) for means of scores. It is also possible to express the extent of variability with a graph constructed from the relative frequencies of the scores. In such a graph, the X axis consists of values for the scores, and the Y axis indicates the relative frequencies. This would be a graph of the distribution of scores (a picture of how the scores are distributed).

In Fig. 5.1 a smooth curve version of such a graph is pictured. The X axis indicates the scores (implicitly including scores between and beyond those specified). The shape of the graph suggests that the scores near the center are the most frequently occurring (the height of the curve being greatest there), and the scores at the tails are the rarely occurring scores.

The mode of a distribution is the most frequently occurring value and a modal point is the highest point in a curve. In the particular distribution pictured in Fig. 5.1 the modal point is 72, which is also the mean and median. (The median is another measure of central tendency for a set of scores. It is the value with as many scores above it as below it.) The occurrence of scores that are higher and lower than the mean, for example 65 and 79 in Fig. 5.1,, are less frequent, and more extreme scores, for example 51 and 93, are still less frequent.

The curve in Fig. 5.1 describes a **normal distribution**. A set of

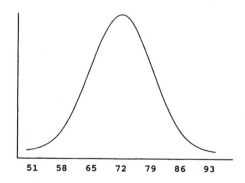

Individual scores in a population of scores.

FIG. 5.1. Distribution of scores in a population of scores. Height on the Y axis represents relative frequency. The mean of this distribution is 72, and the standard deviation is 7.

scores forms a normal distribution when the relative frequencies of the scores in the distribution present a bell-shaped curve that is perfectly symmetrical; the mean, median, and mode are the same centrally placed point on the curve; and the shape of the distribution follows a specific mathematical function (described in texts on mathematical statistics). A true normal distribution (one that precisely follows the mathematical function) is rarely encountered in data sets, but symmetrical bell-shaped curves that are approximations to it are frequently seen. Many biological data sets form normal distributions (e.g., people's heights). However, there are many other data sets that are not normally distributed. What makes the normal distribution an important one for statistics is the central limit theorem. The central limit theorem says that even when a particular distribution of individual scores is not normally distributed, a distribution of sample means from that distribution will tend to be normally distributed. It will more closely approximate a normal distribution as the sample size is increased.

Distributions of Means

Assume the same distribution as that pictured in Fig. 5.1, which is a distribution of individual scores. Assume that samples are taken from that distribution, but samples of size 12 instead of just individual scores. The mean of each sample is computed, and this is done endlessly. A collection of sampled means accumulates. A distribution of these means also forms a graphable distribution. According to the law of large numbers, this distribution should contain less variability than the original distribution of individual scores. The new distribution would have to be drawn so that it is less spread out (scores would tend to occur that are closer to the population mean), or else, if keeping the graph the same general size, the values on the X axis would have to change. Specifically, values that are numerically close to the mean would have to be placed further out on the tails of the X axis in this new distribution than they are in Fig. 5.1.

This has been done in Fig. 5.2, which offers a theoretical distribution of sampled means, where each of the sampled means is computed from 12 scores, taken from the same distribution as that pictured in Figure 5.1. The only difference between the two distributions is the position of specific values on the X axis.

Figure 5.1 offers a distribution of individual scores, and Fig. 5.2 offers a distribution of means. We will most often be interested in distributions of means. However, in a common use of statistical

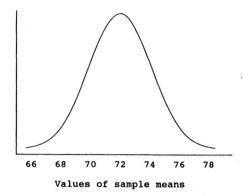

66   68   70   72   74   76   78

Values of sample means

FIG. 5.2. Theoretical distribution of sample means, $n = 12$, sampled from the distribution pictured in Fig. 5.1. The standard error of the mean is approximately 2.

tests, we would be interested in a third distribution, a distribution involving differences between two sampled means.

A Distribution of Differences Between Means

In a theoretical distribution of differences between sampled means, we would have a distribution constructed from a theoretically endless process of randomly sampling pairs of means. After each sampling the difference would be computed, and this would offer the data that was graphed. Of course, the inspiration for setting up this distribution would be an experiment. Specifically, there could be one mean from a control group and one from an experimental group. The question would be whether any observed difference between these two is sufficiently large to rule out random variability as the basis for the difference. We could only do this if we have a theoretical distribution of random differences between pairs of means. The purpose would be to distinguish differences that are common (would be expected to occur simply by chance) from those that are rare (unexpected). Common differences are more likely to reflect meaningless chance differences between the means from the experimental and control groups, whereas rare differences (differences on one of the tails of the theoretical distribution) are more likely to reflect an effective independent variable.

Assume two different groups that have been treated differently, in an effort to determine whether the difference in treatment will have some effect. As a specific example, assume that the subjects in both groups are given job interviews. The same interviewers are used for both groups, the members in both groups are asked identical questions, and every attempt is made to ask the questions in the same manner. However, for one group (the experimental group), the subjects are led to believe that the interviewer does not like the class of people to which the subject belongs (e.g., college students, or people who did not attend college, or people from a particular region of the country, etc.). The experimental question is whether the subjects who are led to believe that the interviewer is prejudiced against them will try harder to look their best, or whether they will be discouraged from doing their best. Judges who see tapes of the interviews but do not know the group conditions, nor the purposes of the experiment, are asked to rate the subjects in both groups on the extent to which they do or do not attempt to make a good impression on the interviewer. The judges use an 11-point rating scale for this purpose. The scores on this rating scale are used to obtain a mean score of attempt to make a good impression, for both the group with the belief of being the victims of prejudice and the group with no such belief. In other words, this is a study in which the independent variable is whether or not the subjects think that the inteviewer is prejudiced against them, and the dependent variable is the extent to which the interviewees (the subjects) make an effort to create a good impression.

The uses of statistical tests in this example would be typical of the use of statistical tests to draw conclusions from experiments. The average (mean) rating of effort to create a good impression is obtained for each group. Then these two average (mean) ratings are compared, to see if the obtained difference between the means is sufficiently large to suggest that something other than chance is responsible for the observed difference. What kind of distribution could be drawn to represent the potential outcomes from this experiment? Figure 5.3 offers such a distribution.

Figure 5.3 offers a picture of a random distribution of differences between randomly sampled pairs of means, that is, pairs of means that are randomly sampled from the same population. Note that the mean of the distribution is zero. It is zero because it pictures a distribution of differences between randomly paired samples of means. Because the two means in each pairing are both derived from the same population of scores, there is no reason to expect any consistent difference.

Assume that the two means are the mean ratings on the 11- point scale used to judge effort to make a good impression during an interview (discussed in the preceding paragraphs). One mean comes from the group of interviewees who believe that the person inter-

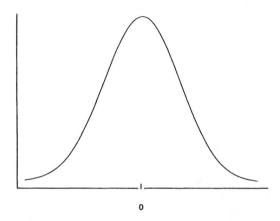

0

FIG. 5.3. Distribution of differences between two sampled means $\overline{X}_1 - \overline{X}_2$, with a null hypothesis mean difference of zero.

viewing them does not like them (is prejudiced), and the other mean comes from the control group. Assume further that the assumption of prejudice does not affect how hard they try to make an impression, and so the ratings of both groups are the same. Theoretically, if the experiment were done a thousand times, always subtracting, say, the control mean from the experimental mean, it would be expected that, on average, the difference in ratings should be zero, as seen in Fig. 5.3. The reason a distribution is shown, rather than just the average of zero, is because in any one instance in which the experiment is run, where the result is just a difference between a single pair of means, the difference will not necessarily be zero. In fact, it is unlikely to be exactly zero. What is most likely is that it would be close to zero. This is what forms a theoretical distribution. Most of the scores are close to zero, a few are far from zero, and still less are very far from zero, as the shape of the curve in Fig. 5.3 suggests.

In practice, a single pair of means is obtained in an experiment. The question is, just how close to zero is this empirical value? If chance could yield any value (any difference between means), how would we know when chance is an unlikely explanation?

The Logic of Statistics and the Null Hypothesis

We begin by computing a quantitative estimate of variability, which is a function of the variance, or standard deviation, previously discussed. It is derived from individual scores in the distribution, and gives an idea of just how variable the scores are that are being sampled in this experiment. High variability means we can expect great deviations from the mean (of zero difference), without that having too much meaning. On the other hand, with less variability, we can doubt that only chance is responsible when an experimental outcome yields a score very different than zero. What criteria are used are discussed next and just how the variance and standard deviation are used in computing statistics are discussed in the appendix to this chapter. What is important here is that the reader understand the logic that is used in most statistical tests.

The physical distribution seen in Fig. 5.3 offers a visual basis for understanding a statistical test. A sample difference that is very far out on the distribution (near either tail) suggests that something other than chance is operating, and confirms the experimental hypothesis that the independent variable affected the dependent variable. That is, on the basis of chance alone, we expect findings to be near the center of the distribution. Suppose that, in fact, a finding does occur that is near the right-hand tail of the distribution. The experimenter would then conclude that chance alone is not responsible, and the manipulation was effective (in the example, an assumption of prejudice by interviewees changes the extent to which they try to make a good impression).

An intelligent cynic could challenge this conclusion. After all, the distribution is a distribution of chance outcomes. Even when there is no difference, an extreme value could occur, even though it would be a very rare event. The answer is that the cynic is correct; though an unlikely occurrence, an extreme value, a very large difference, could occur. However, there is a more convincing explanation for the observation of a rare, extreme value. An experiment involves a carefully arranged difference between (at least) two conditions. After the manipulation, given the observation of a large difference in the scores of the different groups, the experiment (and its contrived differences) offers a more likely explanation of the resulting differences between the groups on the dependent variable. Remember, the alternative explanation is that something that is rare (unlikely) has occurred. We therefore conclude that the independent and the dependent variables are related, that the experimental manipulation was effective. At the same time, we also accept the possibility that our conclusion is incorrect; unlikely events can occur.

Recall that we follow statistical theory, for example, using a quantitative estimate of the variance to help in identifying what are likely and unlikely outcomes when only chance is operating. This means that instead of merely making the vague statement that we might or might not be wrong in our conclusion, we have the ability to state the probability that we are incorrect in our conclusion. Thus we can make the statement that the manipulation was successful (the variables are related), and at the same time state the probability that our conclusion is incorrect. Because our goal here is only to explain the general form of the logic that is used in reaching conclusions from experiments that involve statistical tests, we delay, till a later point, the explanation of how our probability estimate becomes mathematically specific.

When a distribution that is exclusively based on chance is used as the model of our expected experimental outcome, it is called the **null hypothesis distribution**. Figure 5.3 is a picture of a null hypothesis distribution. Our assumption of no effect of the independent variable is called our **null hypothesis**.

The word *null* in null hypothesis is easy to associate with a zero difference, which in most cases is what the null hypothesis assumes. However, a better association is with the word nullify, which means to negate or invalidate. The hope, usually, is to discredit the null hypothesis. As suggested earlier, the null hypothesis is a hypothesis that the experimenter assumes as a logical convenience, and then usually hopes to nullify. It is generally a working assumption that the levels of the factor are not relevant to the outcome of the experiment—that is, that the factor being tested has no relationship to the dependent variable. It is a feigned expectation of no statistical significance, with the experimenter most frequently hoping to discredit the assumption of only chance operating, by identifying the experimental outcome as a nonchance occurrence.

DISTRIBUTIONS OF z AND t

The shape of the null hypothesis distribution varies with the way in which the empirical score of interest (say, the difference between two means) is transformed for the statistical test. Why, the reader might ask, do scores have to be transformed for statistical tests? The reason is that when comparing sets of scores, we want to be able to use standard tables that are entered in the same way, regardless of whether we are working with large numbers, like IQ scores, or small numbers, like grade-point averages. This is accomplished by including, in our statistical formulas, transformations of sets of scores to some standard scale. One of these is a transformation to z scores (also called standard scores) and another is called t scores.

z Scores

In looking at a distribution of differences between means, each difference could be divided by the standard error of that distribution, as seen in Equation 5.1.

$$z = \frac{\overline{X}_e - \overline{X}_c}{\sigma_{\overline{X}_e - \overline{X}_c}} \tag{5.1}$$

In the numerator of Equation 5.1, $\overline{X}_e$ and $\overline{X}_c$ are the sample means, respectively, of the experimental and control groups. The standard error of the difference between two means, $\sigma_{\overline{X}_e - \overline{X}_c}$, is in the denominator. Like every standard error, this is the standard deviation of a statistic. The statistic here is the difference between pairs of means which in a theoretical distribution is assumed to be zero. The deviation of sampled pairs from that assumed zero difference (which reflects the extent of random variability) is what is expressed in the standard error of that statistic.

What Equation 5.1 does is convert the distribution of raw score differences between means to one in which the average score is zero and the standard error is one. This would be true regardless of the scale of the original scores. This new transformed distribution would be called a standard distribution, or a distribution of z scores. That is, each transformed difference between two means would itself be a z score. A distribution like that drawn for Fig. 5.3 would have zero as the mean, as currently drawn, but would also have the numbers 1, 2, and 3 placed at one, two, and three standard deviations away from the mean, on the right-hand side of the distribution, with 2 being close to the end of the tail, and 3 being quite a ways out on the tail. There would be identical minus values at the other side of the distribution. This same scale would describe the data, for any set of differences between means, whatever the original score values, and whatever the sizes of the original differences, as long as they were all transformed through division by the standard error of the difference between two means.

Putting that standard error in the denominator, and the difference between means in the numerator, transforms the difference between means into a scale based on random variability. The more variable the scores, the smaller the value resulting from the difference in the numerator means. The less variable the scores, the larger the value resulting from the difference in the numerator means. When the numerator is a sample difference, we can see how far out it is on the tail of the distribution, using the sample estimate version of Equation 5.1. The problems introduced by sample estimates are discussed in the next section. The use of the computational formula that is needed in practical situations is detailed in the appendix to this chapter.

t Distributions

A common problem in statistical applications is that the standard error is not known, but rather has to be estimated. In this case, the resulting distribution has a slightly changed shape. First assume that, because means, or differences between means, are being sampled, the distribution is approximately normal. Having to estimate the standard error that is placed into Equation 5.1 changes the distribution shape just a little bit. The center is slightly flatter, and the tails are slightly higher. This is only true with small samples. The larger the sample, the better the estimates of the standard error and consequently, the less that the distribution's shape is changed by the transformation.

The new distribution that is being discussed here is assumed to have been a normal (or approximately normal) distribution. It has been transformed with Equation 5.1, but using an estimated standard error. Under these conditions, the new distribution is called a **t distribution**. The formula for the t distribution is only different from the formula for the z distribution in regard to the use of an estimated standard error, $s_{\overline{X}_e - \overline{X}_c}$, in place of $\sigma_{\overline{X}_e - \overline{X}_c}$, as seen in Equation 5.2.

$$t = \frac{\overline{X}_e - \overline{X}_c}{s_{\overline{X}_e - \overline{X}_c}} \tag{5.2}$$

There are several forms of the t test. Equation 5.2 is used for the t test when it is applied to a difference between two means. Equation 5.2 is only appropriate when the scores in the two groups are unrelated in any pairwise fashion (that is, it is appropriate for completely randomized designs with two levels for the factor). This t test is called the **t test with independent samples**.

The t distribution obtained from an originally normal distribution itself approaches identity with the normal distribution, as sample size is increased. Therefore, Equations 5.1 and 5.2 produce the same values with large n, and only differ with small n. A t distribution has a mean of zero, with a standard error slightly larger than one; the exact value depends on the sample size (or, more precisely, on the degrees of freedom, which are closely related to sample size, and are discussed later). A transformation of a difference between two sampled means to a t score accomplishes a change in the difference from an arbitrary number, to something ranging, in most instances, between -3 and $+3$ (very much like a z score). Tables are available (discussed shortly), that suggest which values in that range would constitute reasonable criteria for deciding that the variables are related (or, if dealing with a manipulated variable, that the independent variable was effective).

When the difference between two means is divided by an estimated standard error, yielding a t score, the theoretical null hypothesis distribution has the shape of a **t distribution**. As stated earlier this is similar to a normal distribution, slightly flatter in the middle, and slightly higher at the tails, with the shape varying with sample size.

In the context of an experiment, sample experimental and control group means, $\overline{X}_e$ and $\overline{X}_c$, respectively, are obtained. The variance of individual scores is estimated within each group, and used to obtain $s_{\overline{X}_e - \overline{X}_c}$, as explained in the appendix to this chapter. The term $s_{\overline{X}_e - \overline{X}_c}$ is then divided into the empirically obtained difference $\overline{X}_e - \overline{X}_c$, as seen in Equation 5.2. This difference between the means, $\overline{X}_e - \overline{X}_c$, is then transformed into a version of a t score. In its transformed state as a t score, the (transformed) difference, $\overline{X}_e - \overline{X}_c$, can be used to reach conclusions about the experiment, as described later.

Figure 5.4 illustrates a t distribution of differences between two means. In the hypothetical example in Fig. 5.4, it is assumed that there are 16 subjects in each group, and that the estimated standard error of the difference between two means is 3. In Fig. 5.4 the upper row of the X axis offers the differences between means in terms of raw scores, and the lower row presents the differences in terms of t scores.

Criteria for Statistical Significance

The t statistic, in the context of a t test with independent samples, has $[(n_e - 1) + (n_c - 1)]$ **degrees of freedom**, or $2n - 2$ degrees of freedom if the sample sizes (n values) are equal in the two groups. Degrees of freedom reflect the number of freely varying scores that contribute to the statistic. The concept of degrees of freedom is discussed in greater detail in the appendix to this chapter. There are different degrees of freedom associated with different statistics.

A t table appears in Appendix B at the back of this text. Note that the table has two **levels of significance** at the top. A level of significance is the probability of a particular outcome (or one more

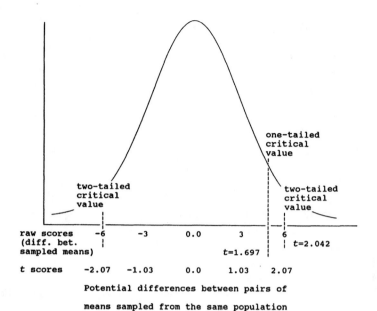

raw scores   -6   -3   0.0   3   6
(diff. bet.
sampled means) $t=1.697$ $t=2.042$

t scores   -2.07   -1.03   0.0   1.03   2.07

Potential differences between pairs of

means sampled from the same population

FIG. 5.4. A distribution of potential differences between randomly sampled pairs of means each computed from 16 scores, sampled from a population with an estimated standard error of the difference between two means of 3.00, as computed with Equation A2 in the appendix to this chapter. (The standard error for t, unlike z, is not exactly 1, but rather varies with the degrees of freedom. In this example it is approximately 1.03.)

extreme) being the result of only chance influences. The top line refers to one-tailed tests of significance, and the second line to two-tailed tests of significance. The distinction is discussed later. Looking for the moment at the first line (for one-tailed tests), locate the value .05. This column contains those computed t values that would only be surpassed 5% of the time, if only chance is operating. Thus if one were interested in maintaining a 5% level of significance (one-tailed), one would use that column.

The row to be used in the body of the t table is a function of the degrees of freedom. For the t test with two independent samples (Equation 5.2), the degrees of freedom are $[(n_e - 1) + (n_c - 1)]$. Thus, if there were 16 subjects in each condition ($n_e = n_c = 16$), the row used would be $(16 - 1) + (16 - 1) = 30$. At 30 df and a one-tailed .05 probability of an observed sample difference that is in fact only due to chance, the value 1.697 is found. This value is called a **critical value**. A critical value is that value that would be reached or surpassed the proportion of the time indicated at the top of the t table (in the level of significance row at the top, .05 in this example) when only random variability was operating (that is, when the null hypothesis was true).

The experiment is done, the data are gathered, and then, using Equation 5.2, the t statistic is computed. The computations yield the empirical value of t. The table is then consulted at the proper degrees of freedom, for the critical value. If the tabled critical value is reached or surpassed by the empirical value of t, it is then concluded that there is **statistical significance**.

Statistical significance is the term used when the sample difference between two means, transformed to a t value with the t statistic, equals or surpasses the tabled critical value. It implies, in the case of a t test of the difference between two (sample) means, that the difference is sufficiently large to conclude that the population means are different. Stated another way, statistical significance means that there is sufficient evidence to conclude that the experimental manipulation is effective. That is, statistical significance calls for rejection of the null hypothesis.

When, instead, the computed t value does not reach or surpass the tabled critical value, a less definitive statement is made. That is, the potential reverse conclusion, that the experimental manipulation is not effective, is avoided when the tabled critical value is not reached. Rather, the statement is made that "there is no evidence that the experimental manipulation is effective" or "there is no evidence that the variables are related," etc. Although it is sometimes stated that one then accepts the null hypothesis, it is more correct to say that there is no evidence available from the experiment to indicate that the null hypothesis should be rejected. Given statistical significance, a strong statement, a definite decision, is made. The null hypothesis is rejected. When statistical significance is not obtained, a more cautious conclusion is reached. The reason for this is discussed later, in the section on Type I and Type II errors. First, however, it is useful to distinguish one-tailed and two-tailed tests of statistical significance.

One-Tailed versus Two-Tailed Tests of Statistical Significance

In Fig. 5.4 a t distribution with 30 df is assumed. Looking at the t table in Appendix B, it can be seen that there are a number of different critical values at 30 df. Further, there are two different rows at the top of the table offering column headings, each representing a probability. In the preceding section the upper row, labeled One-Tailed, was used. The column headed .05 offers the critical values for one-tailed tests of statistical significance that have a .05 probability of being reached or surpassed if only chance is operating, and the null hypothesis is true. At the .05 level, and 30 df, the value 1.697 was found. This means that, using a one-tailed test of statistical significance, a value of +1.697 would only be expected to be reached or surpassed 5% of the time, when there are 30 df in the statistical test. This is illustrated in Fig. 5.4, in which the one-tailed critical value is marked with the highest vertical line, at the t value of 1.697. This can be restated in terms of raw scores (seen in the upper X axis row of Fig. 5.4). A raw score difference of 5.1 or larger would be needed for statistical significance. Even without Fig. 5.4, this would emerge in a test of empirical values, using Equation 5.2. For example, assume that an empirical difference of 5.1 had been obtained. Entering that value into the formula for the t statistic, Equation 5.2, would yield

$$t = \frac{\overline{X}_e - \overline{X}_c}{s_{\overline{X}_e - \overline{X}_c}}$$

$$= \frac{5.1}{3}$$

$$= 1.70$$

suggesting that this value was just barely significant (just surpassing the critical value). Thus, a difference between the means of 5.1 or larger would achieve statistical significance.

Assume that instead of using the top row in the t table, the second row of probabilities, labeled Two-Tailed, was used. In this case, the .05 probability would intersect 30 df at a point that suggests that 2.042 would be needed as the minimal value for statistical significance. Translated into raw scores, this would mean a minimal difference of 6.13, which produces a t value of 2.043, just barely surpassing the tabled t value of 2.042. That is,

$$t = \frac{\overline{X}_e - \overline{X}_c}{s_{\overline{X}_e - \overline{X}_c}}$$

$$= \frac{6.13}{3}$$

$$= 2.043$$

Figure 5.4 illustrates the placement of two critical values for a two-tailed test of statistical significance. The positioning of critical values at both tails of the distribution, using critical values from the t table of both +2.042 and −2.042, follows from the realization that if chance is operating, a rare event could occur at either tail of the distribution. The probability of chance events from both tails can then add to the probability of an outcome. To select a critical value that has only a 5% probability of being reached as a result of only random variability (chance), the probabilities from the two tails must be summed. Thus, with a .025 probability that a difference between the means, when transformed to a t value, will exceed $+2.042$, and a .025 probability that the t value will be less than -2.042, the probability of exceeding the critical value under chance conditions is .05. Stated another way, usually, with a **two-tailed test**, the test is one of whether some absolute value will be exceeded, the value being the critical value (in this example, $|2.042|$). The necessary summations were done in the preparation of the table, so all that the experimenter needs to do is the following: Compute the empirical t value with Equation 5.2. Look up the critical value in the t table, using $(n_e - 1) + (n_c - 1)$ df to select the correct row in the table. Use the two-tailed .05 probability to select the correct column. Find the critical value where the row and column intersect. If the empirical t computed with Equation 5.2 reaches or surpasses the tabled critical value (ignoring sign), you have statistical significance. (Appropriate variations in degrees of freedom, and different forms of the t test, are discussed later in the section titled Types of t Tests.)

There are times when experimenters elect to use **one-tailed tests**. With a one-tailed test the prediction is for only one tail of the distribution. Figure 5.4 includes a vertical line showing where a .05 one tailed test would be, on the right-hand tail of the distribution. The critical value in that distribution, for the one-tailed test, is $+1.697$, considerably closer to the mean than the two tailed value of ± 2.042.

Some researchers are liberal in their employment of one-tailed tests, suggesting their use any time it is possible to make a directional prediction, even if some other experimenter might see it as reasonable to make the prediction in the other direction. Other researchers, though also inclined to use one-tailed tests, are more conservative in their use. They only use them when when prior research, or theory, suggests that predictions of differences in only one direction are reasonable or realistic. They believe that well founded theory or prior research should suggest when one-tailed tests are appropriate, rather than the experimenter's own predictive inclinations.

It is reasonable, at this point, to ask what does one do if the prediction is in one direction, with expectation, say, of a positive value, and the results emerge with a negative value that could have achieved statistical significance were the prediction made in the opposite direction? Statistical theory says the experimenter must ignore the results, denying that there is statistical significance (otherwise the experimenter would have been using two tails, with the critical values closer to the mean than for a regular two-tailed test, doubling the probability of a Type I error). Would the experimenter believe that he or she has not found any evidence of a meaningful relationship when the finding turns out to be opposite to the one predicted, but far out on the opposite tail? Will that finding be treated as though no relationship was observed between the variables?

Science is full of surprises, and there are at least some instances in which people are certain that only one direction of difference or change is possible, but the experimental results turn out to be in the opposite direction. When researchers and statisticians compute statistical probabilities for experimental outcomes, should they include the personal beliefs of the experimenters doing the research in the theoretical models of chance? There is strong disagreement on this subject, so there are differences in how ready experimenters are to use one-tailed tests, ranging from using them any time that a unidirectional prediction is possible, to believing that they should never be used.

In the majority of instances in psychology, two-tailed tests are used. When one-tailed tests are used, it is critical that this decision be made before the data is collected, and that results in the opposite direction, no matter how extreme, are treated as not statistically significant.

TYPE I AND TYPE II ERRORS

In Fig. 5.4 the distribution assumes that the null hypothesis is true, as evidenced by the raw score mean value of a difference between means of zero. If the null hypothesis were not true, what would have to be different in Fig. 5.4? The difference would be a second distribution in the picture, with a nonzero mean, which would be the true distribution, often identified as the **alternative distribution**. The alternative distribution is a second distribution contrasted with the null hypothesis distribution, the alternative distribution stemming from the distribution of scores that would be expected when the manipulated variable is effective—that is, when the independent variable does have some effect on the scores. For example, if the experimental condition does result in higher scores, the distribution of potential outcomes would be shifted to the right, in Fig. 5.4, yielding the distribution on the right in Fig. 5.5.

Return now to the assumption that the null hypothesis is true, which means that Fig. 5.4 would be correct, rather than Fig. 5.5. If, when the null hypothesis is true, a difference between means occurs that surpasses a critical value at one of the tails, although it would be a rare event, it would be a rare chance event. It could not reflect an effective experimental manipulation, if the null hypothesis is true. As seen by the breadth of the X axis in Fig. 5.4, which includes values beyond the critical values, a rare but possible sample could produce an outcome beyond the critical values. In this case, the experimenter would have to conclude that there is statistical significance and that the experimental manipulation is effective. Such a conclusion would constitute an error, and would be called a **Type I error** (and also an **alpha error**).

A Type I error is the error made when the null hypothesis is true, but chance (random variability) produces a sample value that reaches or exceeds the critical value. The experimenter does not know whether Fig. 5.4, picturing the null hypothesis distribution, is correct or if, instead, the right-hand distribution in Fig. 5.5 is correct. That is the purpose of doing the experiment. All that the experimenter has to work with, in reaching a conclusion, is the actual difference between the two means obtained in the experiment, and the transformation of this difference into a t score. When the

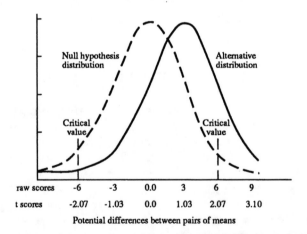

FIG. 5.5. A null hypothesis distribution of potential differences between two means, and an alternative distribution with a nonzero population mean. Each mean is computed from 16 scores, sampled from a population with an estimated standard error of the difference between two means of 3.00, as computed with Equation A2 in the appendix to this chapter.

transformed empirical difference between means surpasses the critical value, the conclusion of statistical significance is automatic. It is a good long-run decision, because when working with useless experimental manipulations the critical value will only be surpassed the percentage of times chosen in selecting the Type I error level.

Suppose that instead of a .05 Type I error level, the experimenter chooses a .10 Type I error level, increasing the probability of a Type I error from 5% to 10%. This would bring the two-tailed critical values closer to the center of the distribution, requiring a smaller absolute value to be reached (± 1.697 in the case of Fig. 5.4). On the other hand, the experimenter might decide to decrease the probability of a Type I error, say from .05 to .01, increasing the critical value that has to be reached, so that it is now a value way out on either tail (± 2.750 in the case of Fig. 5.4). The question that suggests itself is, why not always work with a smaller probability of a Type I error?

The reason is the possibility of another type of error, a **Type II error** (often called a **beta error**). Whereas a Type I error can only be made when the null hypothesis is true, a Type II error can only be made when the null hypothesis is false. That is, there has to be an alternative distribution that is true in order for the null hypothesis distribution of only chance differences between the means to be false. A Type II error is the error made when the null hypothesis is false, but chance (random variability) produces a sample value that does not reach or exceed the critical value. The possibility of this situation can be appreciated by studying Fig. 5.5.

The smaller the probability of a Type I error that is selected (the further the critical value is out on the tail of the null hypothesis distribution), the larger the critical value that the t table would show as being required for statistical significance. For example, going from a .05 to a .01 probability, a larger critical value would be required for statistical significance. As can be seen in Fig. 5.5, the larger the (positive) critical value (the further out on the distributions' X axis), the greater the amount of the alternative distribution that would be below that point. This would mean a greater probability of a Type II error. In general, when decreasing the Type I error probability by raising the critical value, the Type II error probabilty is increased. Thus, although a small Type I error value is highly desirable, making it too small can result in a very large Type II error probability.

It is important to keep in mind that the alternative distribution only exists when there is an effective independent variable (when the scores or observations have been changed in value by some experimental manipulation). That would mean the null hypothesis distribution is false and no longer expresses the probability of various outcomes. Instead, the alternative distribution is generating outcomes, as symbolized in Fig. 5.5. We would then hope that the experimental outcome would reveal this fact, by offering a value, a difference between means, that instead of being close to the center of the null hypothesis distribution, is as far out as possible on the alternative distribution (and beyond the critical value located at the tail of the null hypothesis distribution).

It should be clear from this discussion that the further apart the two distributions are, the more likely that the outcome would be beyond the critical value on the null hypothesis distribution. This is because it is the alternative distribution that is generating the outcomes, and the result of its being far apart from the null hypothesis distribution is that its outcomes are less likely to be within the expected range of the null hypothesis distribution.

An important determinant of the size of the Type II error probability is the size of the difference between the population means of the alternative and null hypothesis distributions—that is, how far apart the two distributions are. The distance between the two distributions is a function of the size of the effect of the experimental manipulation. The larger the effect, the further the mean of the alternative distribution is from the mean of the null hypothesis distribution.

Assume for the moment that the effect of the experimental manipulation was to increase the alternative distribution by 3 points, on the average, as illustrated in Fig. 5.5. However, the experimenter would not have this specific information. The experimenter usually hopes that there is some difference between the distributions (suggesting an effective independent variable), but does not know what the size of that difference is (if it exists). The experimenter, in a formal sense, assumes the null hypothesis distribution, and then relies on obtaining an empirical value that reaches or surpasses the critical value to suggest that an alternative distribution is generating the sample results.

If the particular alternative distribution in Fig. 5.5 is correct, what would be the probability of the experimenter recognizing that it is correct? Because the experimenter only makes the decision when the critical value is surpassed, this question can be restated in the following way: What is the probability that a sample difference from the alternative distribution in Fig. 5.5 would yield a value at or beyond the critical value? This is a function of the proportion of the alternative distribution that exceeds the critical value. That is, the proportion of the alternative distribution that lies beyond the critical value is equivalent to the probability that a sample will yield a value that exceeds the critical value. This in turn is the probability of recognizing that the null hypothesis distribution is false (and that an alternative distribution is true). This probability is called the **power of the statistical test**, which is simply the probability of recognizing an effective independent variable.

In the case of Fig. 5.5, the mean of the null hypothesis distribution is two standard errors below the critical value in that distribution. The mean of the alternative distribution is one standard error above the mean of the null hypothesis distribution, placing it one standard error below the critical value of the null hypothesis distribution. When the mean of an alternative distribution is itself below the critical value in the null hypothesis distribution, it means that more than half of the alternative distribution is below the critical value; that is, most outcomes will yield values that are too low to suggest statistical significance. In the illustration in Fig. 5.5, approximately 85% of the alternative distribution is below the critical value. This means that there is only a 15% chance of the alternative distribution producing a sample difference that reaches or exceeds the critical value; and so the experimenter has only a 15% chance of realizing that the alternative distribution is the correct one. Thus the power of the statistical test, in this instance, would be 15%. The complement of the power of a statistical test, which is one minus the power of the statistical test, is the probability of a Type II error. In this example then (the illustration in Fig. 5.5), there is an 85% probability that the alternative distribution will not generate a sufficiently large sample difference to permit the conclusion of statistical significance (an 85% probability of a Type II error). This is so little power that the experiment would not be worth doing. Experimenters generally do not know how much power they have, because power depends, in part, on the unknown difference between the null and alternative distributions. Usually, however, power is much greater than 15%, although it is not unusual, in clinical research, for it to be only 50% (Cohen, 1962).

The problem is that the Type II error probability could only be estimated when it could be assumed that the mean of the alternative distribution is a particular distance from the null hypothesis distribution's mean. Unfortunately, this knowledge is rarely available. The question being asked is whether there is an alternative distribution, and only occasionally can an informed guess be made as to where it would be located on the X axis, if it does exist.

The farther apart the two distributions, the greater the proportion of the alternative distribution that would be beyond the critical value, giving the statistical test more power, and decreasing the probability of a Type II error. Clearly, the actual (though generally unknown) difference between the null hypothesis mean and the alternative distribution mean is one factor that influences the probability of a Type II error. Another factor that is relevant is the size of the standard error.

The Standard Error and the Type II Error

If the standard error is very small, the two distributions (the null and the alternative) would also be further removed from each other (each distribution being narrowed, bringing the critical value in the null hypothesis distribution in Fig. 5.5 further to the left and putting a greater percentage of the alternative distribution above the critical value). As explained in the appendix to this chapter, the size of the standard error is a function of both the size of the estimated standard deviation of individual scores and the sample size. Therefore, both the size of the standard deviation and the size of the sample have an effect on the power of the statistical test (and conversely on the probability of a Type II error).

The smaller the standard deviation, and/or the larger the n (both of which produce a smaller standard error), the greater the statistical power (and the smaller the Type II error probability). Therefore, if the experimenter can find a way to reduce random variability (that is, to reduce the size of the estimated standard deviation of individual scores), the Type II error probabilty can be reduced. The same end can be accomplished in those instances in which it is possible for the experimenter to use a relatively large sample size. That is, both a reduced standard deviation and an increased sample size, serve to decrease the size of the standard error, increasing the power of the statistical test. Reducing random variability and increasing sample size decreases the probability of a Type II error (without increasing the probability of a Type I error). As stressed previously, the actual size of the Type II error probability is usually not known, because the potential size of the effect of an experimental manipulation is rarely known. (Ways to intelligently estimate these effects are discussed in the excellent text on power analysis by Jacob Cohen, 1988).

Summarizing Trade-Offs in Type I and Type II Error Probabilities

An important difference between Type I and Type II errors is that the experimenter sets the level (probability) of a potential Type I error (which then specifies a particular critical value). The probability of a Type II error, on the other hand, is generally not known. What is known is that decreasing the size of the Type I error probability by using a larger critical value (that is, simply selecting a smaller probability of a Type I error in the t table) increases the size of the Type II error probability. The importance of keeping the Type II error probability low is that Type II errors are synonymous with not recognizing effective independent variables. The only ways that the Type II error probability can be reduced without affecting the Type I error probability are if random variability can be reduced in the experiment, or if sample size (n) can be increased.

Using a Large Type I Error to Confirm a No-Difference Finding

In the psychological literature the convention has become the use of a .05 probability of a Type I error, using other probabilities only in special circumstances. We examine here an instance in which we might use a different Type I error probability. Assume, as a particular example, that an experiment was run in which subjects had been randomly assigned to two different groups. The experiment was completed, and the findings were statistically significant. A critic of the experiment claims that there was a potential confounding factor that might have been present and would explain the results. The critic says that the two groups might have differed, by the accidents of random sampling, on annual income, which is related to the dependent variable in the experiment. How could this be shown to not be true? If the experimenter did a t test using annual income as the dependent variable, contrasting the two groups, and there was no statistical significance, could the experimenter then conclude that she or he has demonstrated that the two groups do not differ on the basis of annual income? No, because you cannot accept the null hypothesis of no difference; the reason is the unknown Type II error probability. However, one approach to this problem is to make sure that the Type II error probability, although not specifically known, can be stated, with reasonable confidence, to be very small.

One way that this is sometimes done is testing the difference not at the usual Type I error probability of .05, but rather using a .25 probability of a Type I error. In this way, the critical value would be placed so centrally within the null hypothesis distribution (so close to the mean of the null hypothesis distribution, as opposed to being out on the tail) that one could have confidence that most of any potential alternative distribution would be above that critical value. Thus, it would have been detected in the statistical test, if it existed. In this way one would obtain large power, with a low Type II error probability, making it unlikely that we have missed an alternative distribution. One would do this with a potential confounding factor, because the important point is to clearly demonstrate that there is no alternative distribution. This is different from the usual test, where we want to have maximum confidence in the knowledge that we have not accepted a nonexistent alternative distribution.

TYPES OF *t* TESTS

Up to this point only one class of *t* test has been discussed, the *t* test with independent samples. This is used in the class of situations in which there are two sample means (e.g., one experimental and one control group), and different subjects in the two groups. Furthermore, when using the *t* test with independent samples, it is assumed that the subjects in the two groups are not in any way matched. This can be contrasted with situations in which the same subjects are used in both treatments, as when people's ability to solve problems under conditions of distraction versus no distraction are examined, using the same subjects in both conditions. In this type of situation a different formula would be used for the *t* test, as detailed in the appendix to this chapter. This second type of *t* test is called the **matched-pairs t test**, or the **t test with dependent samples.**

The matched-pairs *t* test is used either when the same subjects are used in both conditions, or when different people are used as subjects in the two groups, but they have been matched pairwise on some characteristic that is related to the dependent variable. For example, in testing the effect of distraction on solving problems, time to solve the problems might be used as the dependent variable. It is possible that IQ would be related to time to solve the problems, and so let us assume that this was in fact the case, and that different people were placed into the two conditions of the experiment (one condition with distraction while solving the problems, and one without the distraction). The subjects would have been matched pairwise for IQ. What this means is that for any individual in one group with an IQ of 110, there would be another person in the other group with the same IQ, all subjects in one group matched in this way with someone from the other group. When the same people are used in both groups, it is really a case of having perfectly matched the people in the two groups. The degrees of freedom when using the

t table for a matched-pair t test are $n-1$, where n is the number of paired observations. Thus, if using the same subjects in both conditions, n would be the total number of subjects.

There is a statistical test called a **test of statistical significance for a correlation**, which is also a form of a t test. A correlation is a statement of the degree of statistical association between two variables. As indicated in chapter 4 when discussing correlational research with no groups defined, an association can be tested between two continuous or wide-ranging quantitative variables. The degree of association is estimated using a measure of correlation. This is generally the Pearson r, the r representing the sampled estimate of the degree of relationship, ranging between -1 and $+1$. A correlation of zero would be equivalent to there being no relationship between the variables. However, even with a population correlation of zero, in a particular sample a nonzero correlation could be obtained. To determine, from the sample, whether the two variables are in fact related, the sampled correlation (the sampled value of the statistic r) is tested for its distance from $r = 0$, in terms of standard error units; that is, a t test of the sampled correlation is done. This is a test of whether the sampled correlation r is significantly different from zero. A finding of statistical signficance would suggest that the sampled correlation is so far from zero that the best bet is that the population correlation is nonzero, which is equivalent to saying that the two variables are related.

To test a sampled correlation for statistical significance it is generally not necessary to do any computations after the correlation (the value of r) has been obtained. Most introductory statistics texts have a table that can be consulted for determining whether the sampled correlation is significant. The table offers the value of the sampled correlation that has to be reached or exceeded for statistical significance, given the degrees of freedom (which are $n-2$, where n is the number of paired scores).

ONE-FACTOR ANALYSIS OF VARIANCE

The t test is only applicable when there are two groups (two conditions) in the study. When more than two groups are being compared, a single t test can no longer indicate whether the variables are related. The statistical test used in place of the t test is the **one-factor analysis of variance**, which is applicable with two or more groups in an experiment. The distribution used is an F distribution, in place of the t distribution. The statistic is a ratio, called the F ratio, or **F test**. The F test is the statistical test in analysis of variance that is analogous to the t test. Like the t test, the denominator in the F test is a measure of random variability. The numerator is an index of the differences between the means being compared that is a little more complex than the t test numerator (which is a simple difference between means). The complexity derives from the fact that the F ratio permits the simultaneous comparison of more than two means with each other.

The null hypothesis in the one-factor analysis of variance is that the group means are all sampled from the same population distribution. A statistically significant F test implies that the sampled group means do not all come from the same population distribution. This in turn leads to the conclusion that the independent variable that was used to differentiate the groups is probably related to the dependent variable. Just which groups are different from which other groups, that is, which population group means are different from which other population group means, is not answered by the F test. Other tests, including t tests or tests that are similar to t tests, are used to determine where the differences are, if the F test has been found to be statistically significant. The computation of a one-factor analysis of variance is illustrated in the appendix to this chapter.

THE CHI-SQUARE STATISTIC

When neither of two variables being measured for a relationship is a quantitative variable—that is, when both variables are categorized variables—we frequently use the **chi-square** statistic (χ^2). For example, we might wish to know whether men or women are more likely to be smokers. Male and female are categories, and people can be categorized as to whether or not they smoke. In a chi-square analysis the means are not compared as they would be when using t tests or an analysis of variance. Instead, the frequencies with which people fall into different combined categories are recorded.

As an example, look at the question of whether men or women are more likely to be smokers. A random sample of people would be obtained, and each person classified on the two variables: that is, male or female, smoker or nonsmoker. This would yield four categories, each jointly defined on two variables (gender and smoking). The four categories could readily be summarized in a two-by-two table as seen in Fig. 5.6.

Each subject in the study would be classified as belonging to one of the four cells in the table of Fig. 5.6. The number of subjects in each

	smoker	nonsmoker
male		
female		

FIG. 5.6. A contingency table suitable for a chi-square analysis.

cell would be summed, yielding four totals. If smoking were primarily a male habit, there would be a relatively large count both in the upper left-hand cell and in the lower right-hand cell (a relatively large number of male smokers and a relatively large number of female nonsmokers). There would be relatively small totals in the remaining two cells. That is, one diagonal would offer relatively large numbers, while the other diagonal would offer relatively small numbers. The table is called a **contingency table**, because it can reveal a contingent relationship between the variables. The word contingent has the conveniently broad meaning of either *dependent on* or *associated with*. If two categorized variables are related (dependent on each other, or associated with each other), a subject's classification on one variable is, to some degree, contingent on that person's classification on the other variable.

The chi-square value is inflated to the degree that the distribution of totals in the cells of the contingency table is not random. That is, randomness tends to yield uniformity among the cell totals. The chi-square statistic yields a large enough number for statistical significance when the totals clearly fall into a pattern such as the contrasting high and low diagonals described in the preceding paragraph.

The major restriction on the use of the chi-square statistic is that each contribution to the contingency table's totals must be independent of every other contribution. In research involving more than one subject, this means that each contribution to a cell total must come from a different subject. Because most psychological research involves more than one subject, in practice the need for each cell entry being independent of every other entry generally reduces to an absence of repeated measures.

An example is useful to illustrate and compare the correct and incorrect uses of the chi-square statistic. Assume a study of the relationship between gender and church attendance. A correct use would involve categorizing a random sample of people into those who do or do not attend church, and also categorizing them as male or female. An incorrect use would involve entering the same people into the analysis on each sabbath day, into a cell that indicated male or female, and having attended or not having attended church on that sabbath. In this second way of collecting the data each subject would appear repeatedly in the cells (the same subjects being repeatedly counted on each sabbath). There would be a relationship between the cell in which a person appeared in one entry (after one sabbath) and the cell in which the same person appeared in the next entry (assuming that there is some consistency in churchgoing behavior). This violates the rule that says that each entry must be independent of every other entry. Further, members of a family are likely to attend church together, influencing each other's attendance (or lack of attendance). Thus, there might be a violation of the assumption of independence by including more than one member of any household. It might therefore be more appropriate to randomly sample households, and then randomly sample just one adult member from each household.

Often, categorized variables are not dichotomous, but involve three or four or five categories (levels) for one, or both, of the variables. If the relationship between religious affiliation and being a college graduate was being investigated, the randomly obtained subjects could each be identified as to religious affiliation, and then further classified as to whether or not he or she is a college graduate. If five different religious groups had been identified in the sample, this would offer a five-by-two table. The chi-square statistic would also be used to analyze this example, or any other example with two variables, each of which is divided into a finite (and usually small) number of discrete categories (levels). The computation of the chi-square statistic is illustrated in the appendix to this chapter.

CHOOSING A STATISTIC

There are two related guides for choosing a statistic. One is classification of the variables as quantitative versus qualitative, and the other concerns the number of levels. On the issue of number of levels, it makes a difference if a quantitative variable has so many potential outcomes that it is not practical to define specific levels on that variable. We can speak of this condition as a widely ranging variable. The opposite extreme is the case of a variable with just two levels.

Assume an investigation of two variables that are both quantitative. If both are widely ranging, the difficulty of defining groups suggests the use of the Pearson r as the statistic. This sampled (estimated) correlation is then tested for statistical significance, using the test of statistical significance for a correlation. This is most conveniently done by using the degrees of freedom $(n-2)$, where n is the number of paired scores, to identify the critical value in a table of critical values for the Pearson r (found in most elementary statistics texts).

Assume now that one variable has just two levels (it does not matter whether it is qualitative or quantitative). Assume that the other is a widely ranging quantitative variable. This suggests the use of the t test. There are other technical requirements for the use of the t test, but the t test is reasonably robust to violations of these requirements, so the simple criteria suggested here will usually be sufficient. The next question is whether to use the t test for two independent samples, or the matched-pairs t test.

If different subjects are used in each group, and if there is no matching of subjects in the two groups, then the independent t test is the choice. If the two sets of scores are not independent (that is, the same subjects are used in both groups, or the subjects are matched across the two groups on a variable related to the dependent variable), then the matched-pairs t is used. Clearly, a matched-pairs design, and a repeated-measures design with just two levels for the independent variable, would be instances in which the matched-pairs t test would be considered. As a specific example, classifying people as to whether they drink alcoholic beverages or completely abstain offers a dichotomized (two-level) factor. If an experimenter was interested in whether there is a relationship between whether a person abstains from alcohol and the person's income, a t test would be appropriate. This would be a t test for two independent samples. If the experimenter then decided to increase the power of the statistical test by matching the subjects in the two groups (abstainers and drinkers of alcohol) on amount of education (which is a correlate of income), the matched-pairs t test would be used.

It would be possible to define the drinking/abstaining variable differently, so that instead of being categorized dichotomously, it could be treated as a quantitative variable. For example, one could ask about the relationship between the amount of alcohol drunk, and income. With two continous or wide-ranging quantitative variables the Pearson r would be considered, which would then be tested for statistical significance. (When and if the value of r is found to be statistically significant, the r is used as an estimate of the degree of relationship between the two variables. The squared Pearson r offers an estimate of the proportion of the variance in one variable that is associated with variability in the other variable.)

Given either a qualitative or a quantitative variable with just a few levels, if the other variable is quantitative, the one-factor analysis of variance is used in place of the t test. For example, the drinking variable could be used with four levels: abstainers, rare but occasional drinkers, moderate drinkers, and heavy drinkers. Health costs for these four different groups might be compared as the dependent variable.

With different subjects at all levels, as in the alcohol example, the one-factor completely randomized analysis of variance is used. With the same subjects used in all levels of the factor, a one-factor repeated-measures analysis of variance is used. In general, completely randomized designs, or correlational research designs, with one qualitative and one quantitative variable, suggest the use of t tests or analysis of variance. (The t test would usually be the choice when one variable is dichotomous and the other is quantitative.)

When both variables are qualitative, the chi-square statistic is the first to be considered. One of the reasons for this is that with two qualitative variables, there would not be any means that could be compared. Instead, observations would be jointly classified in the cells of a contingency table. The pattern of frequencies in the cells would be used to assess the possibility of statistical significance. In general, being aware of whether the variables are qualitative or quantitative, and the number of levels for each variable, is usually sufficient to guide the experimenter into the initial suggestions for relevant statistics. Once a relevant statistic is identified, then the finer issues should be considered. For example, the question might have to be asked as to whether or not the individual categorized observations are independent of each other (necessary for the use of chi-square), or whether the scores in two groups lack pairwise independence (suggesting they need to be treated as matched). Figure 5.7 summarizes the advice given in this section on choosing a statistic.

VARIABLE 1

		Qualitative		
		Levels = 2	Levels >2	Quantitative
V A R I A B L E 2	Qualitative Levels = 2	χ^2 *	χ^2 *	t test #
	Qualitative Levels > 2	▓▓▓▓	χ^2 *	Analysis of Variance †
	Quantitative	▓▓▓▓	▓▓▓▓	Pearson r, then test for statistical significance

*All outcomes must be independent of all others, when using chi-square.

If the same or matched subjects are in both groups, use the matched-pairs t test. If not, use the t test for two independent samples.

†If the same subjects are used in all groups, use the repeated measures analysis of variance instead of the one-factor completely randomized analysis of variance.

FIG. 5.7. How to make the statistical choices reviewed in this chapter.

Changes in Statistical Procedures with Changes in Definitions of Variables

As previously indicated, it is often possible to redefine variables so that they are qualitative instead of quantitatve, or vice versa. For example, in the gender and smoking example used earlier to illustrate the chi-square statistic, instead of categorizing people as smokers or nonsmokers, men and women might be compared on the amount of cigarettes they smoke each day, changing the qualitative variable into a quantitative variable. This would suggest abandoning the use of the chi-square statistic in favor of a t test. We also discussed alcohol abstention, illustrating its use as a dichotomous variable (do or do not abstain), as a four-level variable (four different levels of alcohol consumption), and as a continuous variable (amount of alcohol consumed). These different ways of defining the variable each suggested the use of a different statistic. This illustrates why the decisions about how to conduct the experiment, particularly with regard to the operational definition of variables, should be faced simultaneously with considerations as to the available statistical methods.

CHAPTER SUMMARY

Statistics were described as necessary when there is random variability in the data, as is the case with most psychological measurements. Random variability is unpredictable variability caused by chance factors, or caused by such a multiplicity of varied and changing influences that outcome prediction is not possible. Statistical techniques are procedures that permit researchers to draw conclusions despite the presence of random variability.

The mean and two measures of variability, the variance and its square root the standard deviation, were discussed. The standard deviation and the variance are measures of individual score variability around the mean of the distribution. The measure of variability for sample means is called the standard error of the mean, and is theoretically equivalent to the standard deviation constructed with sample means instead of individual scores, expressing the extent of variability of sample means. Distributions of sample means tend to form normal distributions, with the tendency increasing with increasing sample size. Distributions of differences between pairs of means also tend to form normal distributions.

For most sets of scores of interest the standard error is not known, but estimated. This use of an estimated standard error distorts the distribution, whether it is a distribution of means, or a distribution of differences between means. The distortion transforms the means (or differences between means), which were originally approximately normally distributed, into a distribution that approximates the t distribution. The t distribution is actually a family of distributions, varying with the degrees of freedom, which are closely related to sample size. The degrees of freedom for three different types of t tests were given. The degrees of freedom are used to determine where in the t table to look for critical values.

The logic of statistics was discussed, which involves the ways in which statistical procedures, such as the t test, are used to draw conclusions from experiments. The experimenter assumes the null hypothesis, as a logical ploy. The null hypothesis is a working assumption that the levels of the factor are not relevant to the outcome of the experiment; that is, it is assumed that the factor being tested has no relationship to the dependent variable. This is a feigned expectation of no statistical significance.

The advantage of this assumption is that it permits the selection of a particular critical value in the *t* table, which will only be surpassed some specified percentage of the time if the null hypothesis is true. Given a very small probability of this value being surpassed when the null hypothesis is true, on those occasions when it is surpassed the best bet is that the null hypothesis is not true. Thus the assumption of a null hypothesis, and the selection of a critical value that is rarely surpassed by chance, offers a specific means of rejecting the null hypothesis and declaring statistical significance. Statistical significance automatically leads to the conclusion that the variables are related.

Of course, although the experimenter realizes that the conclusion that the variables are related is the best conclusion from the evidence (given statistical significance), the experimenter knows that there is still a possibility that the conclusion is in error. The possibility would be realized during those rare times when the null hypothesis is true but, by chance, the critical value is surpassed. Under these circumstances an error will be made. The experimenter knows the percentage of the time when dealing with ineffective independent variables that the critical value will nonetheless be surpassed. The experimenter is forced to select the probability of that occurrence. By convention this value is usually 5%. This type of error is called the Type I error, or the alpha error, and the accepted probability of its occurrence is called the Type I error probability. The experimenter cannot know whether the Type I error has been made when the critical value is surpassed. When the critical value is surpassed, it is either by chance, or because the factor is indeed related to the dependent variable.

Given that the critical value is surpassed in a particular experiment, either a rare chance event has occurred, or the carefully arranged difference between the conditions, the experimental manipulation, is responsible. The conclusion is therefore always made, when the critical value is reached or surpassed, that the independent variable is responsible for the difference. This is equivalent to the rejection of the null hypothesis. This is what is meant by the term statistical significance. Statistical significance is concluded with the acknowledged possibility that a Type I error has been made. However, whether or not it has been made is not known in any one case.

The other type of error, a Type II error, was also discussed. This is the error that is made when the null hypothesis distribution is not true (when the null hypothesis is an incorrect assumption), and an alternative distribution is operating, but this fact is missed because the critical value was not surpassed. That is, this is the error that is made when there is in fact an effective factor in the experiment, but the obtained difference between the conditions is not sufficient to have reached statistical significance, and so the effectiveness of the factor is not recognized. Decreasing the Type I error probability by choosing a more extreme critical value from the table increases the Type II error probability; conversely, increasing the Type I error probability by choosing a less extreme critical value from the table decreases the Type II error probability. Thus, varying the choice of critical value to affect one type of error always influences the other type of error, in the opposite direction.

In order to decrease the Type II error probability without increasing the Type I error probability, it is necessary to either increase the size of the sample, or else somehow reduce random variability (or both). The complement of the Type II error is the power of the statistical test:

1 − Type II error probabilty = power

Thus, the power of the statistical test is the probability that a real difference between the null and alternative distributions will be detected. As suggested by the factors affecting the Type II error probability, increasing the size of the sample and/or reducing the amount of random variability will increase statistical power.

Two types of error have been identified, Type I and Type II. A Type I error can only be made when there is statistical significance, and a Type II error can only be made in the absence of statistical significance. Thus, an experimenter who finds statistical significance cannot be certain that the variables are related, knowing there is a possibility of a Type I error. An experimenter finding an absence of statistical significance cannot be certain that the variables are unrelated, knowing there is a possibilty of a Type II error. What then does the experimenter using statistical logic know?

If the experimenter always uses a particular Type I error probability, say 5%, that experimenter knows that when working with ineffective factors, in the long run of such decisions the experimenter will only incorrectly believe that variables are effective 5% of the time. The experimenter is actually interested in the broader question of what is the probability of being wrong, given statistical significance, not just the probability of being wrong when working with ineffective factors. To the extent that the experimenter is, at times, working with effective factors, she or he will be wrong less than 5% of the time when concluding that there is statistical significance (Pollard & Richardson, 1987). Thus, the chosen Type I error probability offers the maximum long-term probability of being wrong (about variables being related).

The percentage of times that the experimenter will be wrong in the absence of statistical significance is not known. It depends on three things: how strong or weak the effective factors are that the experimenter is working with (the distance between the null and alternative distributions), the extent of random variability in the data, and the sample sizes the experimenter uses. Because the probability of being wrong is not known when there is no statistical significance in a study, strong statements of conclusion are not appropriate. That is why such caution is shown in drawing conclusions with a lack of statistical significance. One merely states that there is no evidence of a relationship, avoiding the more specific statement that the variables are not related.

By contrast, given statistical significance, this same caution is not used. The experimenter states that the variables are related and gives the specific Type I error probability that was used in entering the statistical table (usually 5%). Being specific about the maximum probability of being wrong is what permits the experimenter to offer an unequivocal conclusion.

One-tailed versus two-tailed tests were also discussed. In two-tailed tests the critical values appear at both tails of the distribution, and the probability of a Type I error is the sum of the probabilities of exceeding either of the critical values. In one-tailed tests only one critical value, placed at a preselected tail of the distribution, is used. This results in greater statistical power (because the critical value is closer to the null hypothesis mean). Experimenters disagree about the conditions under which one-tailed tests can be used. Some think one-tailed tests should be used whenever the experimenter is able to make a one-tailed prediction. Some others think that one-tailed tests should not be used unless well-supported theory and prior research suggest that the outcome should be at only one tail. There are some who believe that one-tailed tests should never be used, in part because they doubt that researchers would in fact ignore positive results in the opposite direction, and science should not rule out the possibility of prior assumptions being upset by new findings. The disagreement is part of a larger philosophic issue in statistics about whether subjective probability estimates should be a part of statistical models of chance.

Three types of t tests were described: the t test with independent samples, the matched-pairs t test (the t test with dependent samples), and the test of statistical significance for a correlation. The Pearson r is calculated in this last case, and then tested for statistical significance. The Pearson r can be squared, yielding an estimate of the proportion of the variance in one variable that is associated with variability in the other variable. The one-factor analysis of variance and its F ratio were briefly described. It would be used with two or more levels of a qualitative variable, or even a quantitative variable if there were just a few levels of this variable, when the other variable is a quantitative variable. It can be used in place of a t test, and in fact has to be used when more than two groups are being compared in such a situation. A significant F test in the analysis of variance indicates that the means do not come from the same population, and in this way suggests that the two variables are related. The specific differences between the group means have to be tested with other statistics.

The chi-square test was discussed. It is used when both variables are qualitative. The importance of the individual observations each being independent of all others was stressed. Finally, the point was made that the ways in which the variables are defined dictate the type of statistic to be used. For this reason it is important to consider the possible statistics when designing the research and making decisions about how to define the variables. The two initial considerations in making decisions about which statistic to use concern whether the variables are qualitative or quantitative, and whether there are only two levels, just a few levels, or the variable is a widely ranging quantitative variable.

NEW WORDS AND PHRASES IN CHAPTER 5

alpha error
alternative distribution
analysis of variance, one factor
beta error
chi-square
contingency table
critical value
degrees of freedom
estimated standard error of the difference between two means
F test
levels of significance
matched-pairs t test
normal distribution
null hypothesis
null hypothesis distribution

APPENDIX

This appendix presents the formulas for t tests, one-factor analysis of variance, and chi-square, along with examples of their use. In addition, the formulas for the components of some of these formulas (the estimated variance and estimated standard error of the mean) are given. There is also a brief explanation of degrees of freedom.

Computing a t Test with Independent Samples, Equal n

The basic formula for the t test with independent samples is

$$t = \frac{\overline{X}_1 - \overline{X}_2}{s_{\overline{X}_1 - \overline{X}_2}} \tag{A1}$$

In Equation A1, $\overline{X}_1$ is the mean of one group, $\overline{X}_2$ is the mean of a second group (for example an experimental and a control group), and $s_{\overline{X}_1 - \overline{X}_2}$ is the estimated standard error of the difference between two means. Within chapter 5 the subscripts e and c were used in place of 1 and 2, because we usually specified an experimental versus a control group as the comparison.

The formula for the standard error of the difference between two means (with equal sample sizes) is

$$s_{\bar{x}_1 - \bar{x}_2} = \sqrt{\frac{s_1^2 + s_2^2}{n}} \qquad \text{(A2)}$$

In Equation A2 s_1^2 and s_2^2 are the estimated variances of the two groups, and n is the common sample size. To use Equation A2 the formula for computing s_1^2 and s_2^2 is needed. This computational formula for the estimated variance of a group is

$$s^2 = \frac{\Sigma X^2 - (\Sigma X)^2/n}{n - 1} \qquad \text{(A3)}$$

The two terms ΣX^2 and $(\Sigma X)^2$ are sometimes confused. The first is the sum of all of the individually squared scores. They are not summed until they are each individually squared. The second term, $(\Sigma X)^2$, is the square of the sum of all of the scores. That is, the scores are all summed first, and then that sum is squared. That squared sum has to be divided by the sample size, n, as implied by the denominator n in $(\Sigma X)^2/n$.

As a specific example, assume that we wished to obtain a sample estimate of the variance of a population of scores, but all that we had was the following random sample of four scores from that larger population of scores: 2, 8, 6, 5. We would use Equation A3 and the four sample scores to obtain an estimate of the variance of that larger population of scores. Two basic values are needed: the sum of all of the scores squared, $(\Sigma X)^2$, which is used to compute $(\Sigma X)^2/n$; and ΣX^2, which is the left-most term in the numerator of Equation A3. All of this is illustrated in Table A1.

Table A1 illustrates the computation of a variance estimate from one set of scores. Equation A2, the formula for the standard error, requires that two such estimates be made. Therefore, in using Equation A2, Equation A3 is simply used twice, once for each sample of scores. Table A2 illustrates the use of Equation A1 for a t test, in conjunction with Equations A2 and A3.

The degrees of freedom (df) used for entering the t table, are $2n - 2$, when there is equal n in a t test with independent samples. [It is $n - 1$ df for each sample, and $2(n - 1) = 2n - 2$.] In the example in Table A2, n is 5, so there are $2(5) - 2 = 8$ df.

TABLE A1.   Example of the Use of Equation A3, the Computational Formula for
the Estimated Variance

X	X^2
2	4
8	64
6	36
5	25
$21 = \Sigma X$	$129 = \Sigma X^2$

$(\Sigma X)^2/n = [(21)^2]/4 = 110.25$

$$s^2 = \frac{\Sigma X^2 - (\Sigma X)^2/n}{n-1}$$

$$= \frac{129 - 110.25}{3}$$

$$= 6.25$$

Computing a t Test with Independent Samples, Unequal n

When there is unequal n in a t test, the formula for the standard error is a little more complicated. The standard error for the difference between two means, when there is unequal n, is

$$s_{\overline{X}_1 - \overline{X}_2} = \sqrt{\frac{(n_1-1)\,s_1^2 + (n_2-1)\,s_2^2}{n_1+n_2-2}\left(\frac{1}{n_1}+\frac{1}{n_2}\right)} \qquad (A4)$$

In Equation A4 the two different n values are differentiated with the aid of subscripts. The use of this formula with a t test for two independent samples with unequal n is presented in Table A3.

The degrees of freedom with unequal n, for entering the t table, are $n_1-1 + n_2-1 = n_1 + n_2 - 2$. In the example in Table A3, the degrees of freedom are $5 + 3 - 2 = 6$.

TABLE A2. Computation of a t Test with Independent Samples, with Equal n.

Group 1		Group 2	
Scores	Scores Squared	Scores	Scores Squared
11	121	11	121
12	144	10	100
14	196	14	196
13	169	11	121
15	225	9	81
$\Sigma X_1 = 65$	$\Sigma X_1^2 = 855$	$\Sigma X_2 = 55$	$\Sigma X_2^2 = 619$

$$s_1^2 = \frac{\Sigma X_1^2 - (\Sigma X_1)^2/n}{n-1}$$

$$s_2^2 = \frac{\Sigma X_2^2 - (\Sigma X_2)^2/n}{n-1}$$

$$= \frac{855 - (65)^2/5}{4}$$

$$= \frac{619 - (55)^2/5}{4}$$

$$= 2.5$$

$$= 3.5$$

$$\overline{X}_1 = \frac{\Sigma X_1}{n} \quad \overline{X}_2 = \frac{\Sigma X_2}{n} \qquad s_{\overline{X}_1 - \overline{X}_2} = \sqrt{\frac{s_1^2 + s_2^2}{n}} \qquad t = \frac{\overline{X}_1 - \overline{X}_2}{s_{\overline{X}_1 - \overline{X}_2}}$$

$$= \frac{65}{5} \qquad = \frac{55}{5} \qquad = \sqrt{\frac{2.5 + 3.5}{5}} \qquad = \frac{13 - 11}{1.095}$$

$$= 13 \qquad = 11 \qquad = 1.095 \qquad = 1.826$$

Note. The t of 1.826 is not statistically significant. The critical value in the t table at $2n - 2 = 8$ df, for a two-tailed Type I error probability of .05, is 2.306. The small n used in this example would offer very little statistical power for detecting a difference between the population means.

SCORES

Group 1	Group 1 Squared		Group 2	Group 2 Squared
3	9		2	4
9	81		2	4.
5	25		5	25
8	64			
5	25			
$\Sigma X_1 = 30$	$\Sigma X_1^2 = 204$		$\Sigma X_2 = 9$	$\Sigma X_2^2 = 33$

$$\overline{X}_1 = 6 \qquad\qquad\qquad \overline{X}_2 = 3$$

$$s_1^2 = \frac{\Sigma X_1^2 - (\Sigma X_1)^2/n}{n-1} \qquad\qquad s_2^2 = \frac{\Sigma X_2^2 - (\Sigma X_2)^2/n}{n-1}$$

$$= \frac{204 - (30)^2/5}{4} = 6.0 \qquad\qquad = \frac{33 - (9)^2/3}{2} = 3.0$$

$$s_{\overline{X}_1 - \overline{X}_2} = \sqrt{\frac{(n_1-1)\,s_1^2 + (n_2-1)\,s_2^2}{n_1 + n_2 - 2}\left(\frac{1}{n_1} + \frac{1}{n_2}\right)} \qquad t = \frac{\overline{X}_1 - \overline{X}_2}{s_{\overline{X}_1 - \overline{X}_2}}$$

$$= \frac{6 - 3}{1.633}$$

$$= \sqrt{\frac{(4)6 + (2)3}{5 + 3 - 2}\left(\frac{1}{5} + \frac{1}{3}\right)} \qquad\qquad = 1.838$$

$$= 1.633$$

Note. The *t* of 1.838 is not statistically significant. The critical value in the *t* table at $n_1 + n_2 - 2 = 6$ df, for a two tailed Type I error probability of .05, is 2.447. The small *n* used in this example would offer very little statistical power.

Computing a t Test with Dependent Samples (The Matched-Pairs t Test)

Recall that for a matched-pairs t test, either the same subjects are used twice, or the subjects are paired through matching across groups. In the statistical analysis, instead of transforming the difference between the means of the two groups into a t score, a different approach is taken. Because the subjects are paired, it is possible to obtain a difference from each pair of scores. The average of these differences, $\overline{D}$, is then converted to a t score. Here is the rationale. If there is no difference between the two conditions of the experiment, sometimes a member of a pair from one condition will be higher, and sometimes a member from the other condition. Given an ineffective independent variable, these differences should average out to zero. In summary, the scores are paired, differences are taken, and a t test is done to see if the average difference $\overline{D}$ is different from zero at a statistically significant level. Therefore, it is the average difference $\overline{D}$ that is converted to a t score. A defining formula for t with dependent samples is

$$t = \frac{\overline{D}}{s_{\overline{D}}} \tag{A5}$$

The denominator in Equation A5, $s_{\overline{D}}$, is the estimated standard error of the mean difference. Equation A5, then, offers the usual form for a t test; it is a ratio with a numerator value that is transformed to a t score through division by an estimated standard error.

A specific computational formula for computing the matched-pairs t test that is more helpful than the equivalent but less specific statement of Equation A5 is

$$t = \frac{\Sigma D}{\sqrt{\dfrac{n\Sigma D^2 - (\Sigma D)^2}{n-1}}} \tag{A6}$$

It is important in using Equation A6 to note that the numerator is not the average D ($\overline{D}$), but rather is the sum of the differences, ΣD. The average D disappeared in an algebraic simplification of the formula. There will be n differences D, which will be algebraically added (including subtracting any differences in the opposite direction). Table A4 illustrates the use of Equation A6.

The degrees of freedom in a matched-pairs t test are $n - 1$, where n is the number of pairs. In the example in Table A4, where there are five paired scores, there are $5 - 1 = 4$ df.

Degrees of Freedom

The preceding section gave the formulas for degrees of freedom for using the t tables. Different degrees of freedom will be needed for the F table and the chi-square table. It may be useful at this point to offer

TABLE A4. **Computation of a t Test with Dependent Samples (the Matched-Pairs t Test).**

Subject	1	2	Difference	(Difference)^2
1	10	6	+4	16
2	12	4	+8	64
3	14	5	+9	81
4	8	10	−2	4
5	11	5	+6	36
			+27	$\Sigma D^2 = 201$
			−2	
			$\Sigma D = 25$	

$$t = \frac{\Sigma D}{\sqrt{\dfrac{n\Sigma D^2 - (\Sigma D)^2}{n - 1}}}$$

$$t = \frac{25}{\sqrt{\dfrac{5(201) - (25)^2}{4}}}$$

$$= 2.565$$

Note. The t of 2.565 is not statistically significant. The critical value in the t table at $n - 1 = 4$ df for a two-tailed Type I error probability of .05 is 2.776. The small n used in this example would offer very little statistical power for detecting a population difference between the two conditions.

a brief intuitive discussion of the concept of degrees of freedom, so that the formulas seem less arbitrary.

Degrees of freedom (df) are the numbers of scores that are free to vary when estimating a statistic. For example, in estimating the mean of a population with a random sample from that population, there is no way to know what the next score in the sample will be. Therefore, if there are n scores in the sample, that sample estimate of the mean has n df. On the other hand, suppose that we wish to estimate the variance of a population from a sample. The variance of a population is the average squared difference from the mean. Its defining formula is

$$\sigma^2 = \frac{\Sigma(X - \mu)^2}{n},$$ (A7)

where μ is the mean of the population of scores, n is the number of scores, X is any individual score, and the numerator,

$$\Sigma (X-\mu)^2$$

is the sum of the squared differences from the mean. However, if we want an estimate of this variance, taken from just a sample of scores, we are likely to have to estimate the mean of the population, μ, with a sample mean, $\overline{X}$, using the same sample of scores from which the variance is estimated. If we estimate the mean of a set of scores and then compute the average squared difference from that sampled mean, only $n - 1$ scores are free to vary. Thus, there are only $n - 1$ df in a sample estimate of a variance.

To see why this is so, assume that you already know that the mean of two scores, $\overline{X}$, is 9, and that one of the scores, X_1, is 8. Would you then know the value of the other score (X_2)?

$$\frac{X_1 + X_2}{n} = \overline{X}$$

$$\frac{8 + X_2}{2} = 9$$

Multiplying both sides by 2,

$$8 + X_2 = 18$$

and then subtracting 8 from both sides yields the value of X_2.

$$X_2 = 10.$$

Thus you can know X_2, if you know the other score and the mean. More generally, given the mean of a set of scores, the last score is predictable from all the preceding ones, and in this sense is not free to vary. This would be found regardless of the total number of scores in the sample. For this reason, the degrees of freedom in an estimate of a variance is stated to be $n-1$.

When statistics are estimated, the degrees of freedom are used in a number of ways. When estimating a variance, we want to obtain an unbiased estimate (one for which the long-run average of the estimates accurately reflects the population value). This is accomplished by using the degrees of freedom, $n-1$, rather than n in the denominator of the formula, to obtain the average squared difference from the mean:

$$s^2 = \frac{\Sigma(X - \overline{X})^2}{(n - 1)} \tag{A8}$$

In Equation A8 the sample mean is used in the numerator, along with n-1 in the denominator. Equation A8 is a defining formula for the sample estimate of a variance. Equation A3, the use of which was illustrated in Table A1, is the computational version of the sample estimate of a variance.

In the next section we discuss analysis of variance, which is used when there are more than two groups being compared. In that context, we need to estimate the variance of means, using the sample means. If there are g means (there being g groups in the experiment, that is, g levels of the factor), then the degrees of freedom for that estimate will be $g-1$.

Computing a One-Factor Analysis of Variance

This section presents the formula for the F ratio in a one-factor analysis of variance. The ratio given here can only be used for completely randomized designs. If repeated measures are used, a statistics text should be consulted for a different formula and cautions on its use and interpretation.

The F test in analysis of variance, like the t test, is a ratio, with a denominator that reflects random variance, and a numerator that is a function of the differences between the sample means. The null hypothesis is that the sample means have all been sampled from the same population. Statistical significance implies that the sampled means are not all from the same population, implying that the independent variable has some effect on the dependent variable.

The denominator of the F ratio is simply the average variance. The formula is equivalent to computing the sample variance in each condition of the experiment, summing these, and then dividing by the number of conditions. It will be symbolized here as MS_{rv}, verbalized as the mean square for random variance. Each estimate of the variance has $n-1$ df. Assuming g groups (g conditions of the experiment), this estimate of random variance has $g(n-1) = gn-g$ df, assuming equal n in all groups. If there is unequal n, gn is not defined. The equivalent number to gn is the sum total of the subjects in each group, that is,

$$n_1 + n_2 + \ldots + n_g = N$$

so the degrees of freedom with unequal n are $N-g$.

The numerator of the F ratio is the variance of the means, times the sample size (assuming equal n in the different conditions). It will be symbolized here as MS_t, verbalized as the mean square for treatments. With g groups it has $g-1$ df.

To provide the most generally useful formula, the equation that is given here is symbolized in a way that permits it to be used for unequal n, as well as equal n. Equation A9 presents the formula in very general terms.

$$F = \frac{MS_t}{MS_{rv}}$$

$$= \frac{SS_t/df_t}{SS_{rv}/df_{rv}} = \frac{SS_t/g-1}{ss_{rv}/N-g} \tag{A9}$$

In Equation A9 the symbols SS_t and SS_{rv} appear. These are, respectively, the sum of squares for treatments, and the sum of squares for random variance. Each is divided by its own degrees of freedom, df_t and df_{rv}. Remember that the F ratio is a ratio of variances. A variance is the average squared difference from the mean. When looking at the variance of a sample of individual scores, its numerator contains a sum of squares, where what are squared are differences of these individual scores from the mean of the scores. This is then divided by something close to the number of differences in the sample (the number of differences minus 1, because of a lost degree of freedom). (This is stated in the defining formula for the sample estimate of the variance, Equation A8.)

The numerator and denominator of the F ratio are two different (independent) estimates of the same random variability, but the denominator is obtained from the variances within sets of scores, and the numerator is obtained by computing a variance among the means of the groups. Equations A10 and A11 give the computational formulas for MS_t and MS_{rv}, respectively.

$$MS_t = \frac{\Sigma_j[(\Sigma X)^2/n_j] - (\Sigma\Sigma X)^2/N}{g - 1} \tag{A10}$$

$$MS_{rv} = \frac{\Sigma\Sigma X^2 - \Sigma_j[(\Sigma X)^2/n_j]}{N - g} \tag{A11}$$

There are three components in these two formulas, each involving a summation and a squaring operation. They are explained next, and then followed by an example.

The simplest component is $\Sigma\Sigma X^2$, which appears in Equation A11. It is simply each and every score individually squared, and then summed. If there were 3 groups, with 10 scores in each group, the 30 individual scores would each be squared, and then these squared scores would be added. The reason for having two summation signs is that one summation refers to summing the squared scores within a group, and the other summation sign refers to continuing this process over all the groups. Remember, the squaring process here is only with individual scores. When these are all added, no further squaring is done in this component.

The second component is also fairly straightforward. This component is $(\Sigma\Sigma X)^2/N$, which appears in Equation A10. For this component, no squaring is done until the summation is complete. That is, there are two summation signs within the parentheses, which suggests that the summation process precedes the squaring process. There are two summation signs, so the scores within any one group are all added, and then this process is continued over all groups. When all of the scores have been added up, then this grand total is squared. It is then divided by N, the total number of scores in the experiment.

The third component can cause some confusion, because one summation sign is within the parentheses and one is outside. This component is

$$\Sigma_j[(\Sigma X)^2/n_j],$$

seen in both Equations A10 and A11. It can also be printed as

$$\sum_j \frac{(\sum X)^2}{n_j} \, .$$

In this component, the summation within the parentheses begins first. That is, the scores in a particular group are summed, $\sum X$. Then this sum is squared, $(\sum X)^2$. Then this squared sum is divided by the number of scores in that particular group (n_j), where a subscripted j is used to symbolize any single group, yielding $(\sum X)^2/n_j$. Finally, as suggested by the other summation sign with the subscripted j, $\sum_j$, the same operation is repeated over all groups and added together. Symbolically, this is

$$\sum_j \frac{(\sum X)^2}{n_j} \, .$$

Thus, for any one group, the scores are added, squared, and divided by the sample size for that individual group. This is done for all groups and the results are added together. This procedure is illustrated in Table A5, where an F ratio is computed in a one-factor analysis of variance with unequal n.

In the example in Table A5, the numerator and denominator df for the F ratio are $(g - 1) = 2$, and $(N - g) = 10$, respectively. In an F table, such as the one given in Appendix A, the critical value at .05, with 2 and 10 df, is 4.10. At the .01 level it is 7.56. The obtained F value of 15.65 therefore clearly reaches statistical significance. Statistical significance is often indicated with a lower-case p, followed by an inequality sign, indicating that the probability value is less than some specific Type I error level. For example, if the critical value surpasses the .05 Type I error critical value, but not the .01 level, then significance is stated with $p < .05$. If it also surpasses the .01 level, as in this case, it is stated as $p < .01$.

Chi-Square Contingency Tables

The chi-square test is different than the statistics discussed previously. For the various t tests, and analysis of variance, means of groups are compared, requiring a quantitative dependent variable. The chi-square statistic is used for qualitative variables. For example, if people are categorized at one level of one variable (say, male, on the gender variable), would that mean that they are more likely to be categorized at a particular level of another variable (say, likely to accept physical risks)? Such a question could be answered if people

TABLE A5. Illustration of the Computation of a One-Factor Analysis of Variance, in a Completely Randomized Design.

G_1	G_2	G_3	G_1^2	G_2^2	G_3^2
1	2	8	1	4	64
1	2	6	1	4	36
4	4	10	16	16	100
	5	9	25	81	
	6	11		36	121
$\Sigma X = 6$	19	44	$\Sigma X^2 = 18$	85	402

$$\frac{(\Sigma X)^2}{n_j} = \frac{6^2}{3} \mid \frac{(19)^2}{5} \mid \frac{(44)^2}{5}$$

$$\Sigma\Sigma X^2 = 18 + 85 + 402 = 505$$

$$= 12.0 \mid 72.20 \mid 387.20$$

$$\Sigma_j \frac{(\Sigma X)^2}{n_j} = 12.0 + 72.20 + 387.20 = 471.40$$

$$\Sigma\Sigma X = 6 + 19 + 44 = 69 \qquad F = \frac{MS_t}{MS_{rv}} = \frac{52.5846}{3.36} = 15.65*$$

$$\frac{(\Sigma\Sigma X)^2}{N} = \frac{(69)^2}{13} = 366.2308$$

$$MS_t = \frac{\Sigma_j[(\Sigma X)^2/n_j] - (\Sigma\Sigma X)^2/N}{g - 1} = \frac{471.40 - 366.2308}{3 - 1} = 52.5846$$

$$MS_{rv} = \frac{\Sigma\Sigma X^2 - \Sigma_j[(\Sigma X)^2/n_j]}{N - g} = \frac{505 - 471.40}{13 - 3} = 3.36$$

Note. The critical F value, at 2, 10 df, is 4.10 at the .05 Type I error level, and 7.56 at the .01 level. The F value of 15.65 therefore achieves statistical significance.
   *$p < .01$.

```
              Risk │No Risk
              ┌──────┬──────┐
   Male       │  10  │  15  │ 25
              ├──────┼──────┤
   Female     │  10  │  15  │ 25
              └──────┴──────┘

                 20     30
```

FIG. A1. Illustration of a contingency table for a chi-square analysis, with no relationship between the variables.

have been divided into those willing and unwilling to take physical risks, and male or female.

Suppose that 50 people were randomly selected, and 25 of these people were males, and 25 were females. They would each be categorized as either risk taking or not (based on a questionnaire, or ratings by acquaintences, etc.). If the two variables are not related, we would expect the same proportions of risk takers among both males and females. Such a case is illustrated in Fig. A1. In Fig. A1, the proportion of risk takers is the same amongst both males and females. If this were the actual data, there would be no evidence of a relationship between the variables.

Assume now that there is such a relationship, and that men are more likely to be physical risk takers than women. If this were so, it is likely that in a sample of men and women, the proportions of risk takers would differ among the sexes. Fig. A2 illustrates how this might look.

Under conditions of statistical significance in a two-by-two table, the cell frequencies will include two relatively large values on diagonally opposite cells, and two relatively small values on the other diagonal. This is seen in Fig. A2. There are different patterns

```
              Risk │No Risk
              ┌──────┬──────┐
   Male       │  15  │  10  │ 25
              ├──────┼──────┤
   Female     │   5  │  20  │ 25
              └──────┴──────┘

                 20     30
```

FIG. A2. Illustration of a contingency table for a chi-square analysis, with a relationship between the variables.

when there is a lack of statistical significance. The existence of patterns that are associated with statistical significance can also be identified among larger contingency tables, for example, three by four or four by five. A general formula for detecting statistical significance in a contingency table is described next.

Frequencies, Marginals, and Expected Values

It is necessary to be able to distinguish the various numbers appearing in contingency tables, such as those seen in Figs. A1 and A2. The numbers in the cells are frequencies, numbers of subjects, not scores. That is, each subject in the study is assigned a cell, based on that subject's joint categorization on the two variables. In a two-by-two table there are only four possible assignments. The total number of subjects assigned to a cell is indicated by a number placed in the middle of that cell. Next, there are the numbers placed outside of the cells when beginning the computation of the statistic. These are called marginals, and appear at the bottom and sides of the contingency table. They are simply the totals in their particular rows or columns. The marginals are critical for determining the "expected values" for each cell. The expected values are an important part of the statistic. They are placed in the corners of the cells, but have not yet been shown in the two contingency tables seen in Figs. A1 and A2.

The marginals in a chi-square table are used to calculate what is expected in the individual cells, when the variables are not related (which is what is meant by *expected values*). For example, in Fig. A1, the row marginals indicate that there are equal numbers of females and males. The column marginals suggest that 40% are risk takers and 60% are not (20 out of 50 and 30 out of 50, respectively). If there is no relationship between the variables, the same proportion of risk takers to non-risk takers should be seen at every level of the gender variable (every row). This is seen in Fig. A1 (10 out of 25 in each row), but not in Fig. A2 (15 out of 25 in the top row and 5 out of 25 in the bottom row).

We use the row and column marginals for each cell to obtain the expected number for that cell. In addition to the marginals for each cell, the total number of subjects (N = total number of subjects) is also needed. This is obtained either by summing the row marginals, *or* by summing the column marginals (both yielding the same value). Figure A3 reproduces Fig. A2, but includes N, the total number of subjects, and includes the expected values (placed in the upper left of each cell).

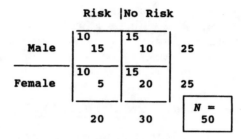

FIG. A3. Illustration of a contingency table for a chi-square analysis, including expected values, and N (number of subjects).

The formula for computing the expected value (E) for any one cell is

$$E = \frac{(R)\,(C)}{N} \tag{A12}$$

In Equation A12, R is the row marginal for that cell, C is the column marginal for that cell, and N is the total number of subjects (equivalent to the sum of all cell frequencies, *or* the sum of column marginals, *or* the sum of row marginals). For the upper left-hand cell in Fig. A3, Equation A12 yields the following:

$$E = \frac{(25)\,(20)}{50}$$

$$= 10$$

Thus, the expected number of subjects in that upper left-hand cell is 10. That number, or something close to it, should be empirically observed if there is *no* relationship between the variables. If there is a relationship between the variables, there should be a discrepancy between the expected cell values (E) and the observed cell values (O).

Computing the Chi-Square Statistic

The formula for the chi-square statistic is

$$\chi^2 = \Sigma\frac{(O - E)^2}{E} \tag{A13}$$

Note the upper-case sigma, Σ, in Equation A13. The sigma indicates that the discrepancies (after being squared and divided by the

VARIABLE A

		A1	A2	A3	
V A R I A B L E	B1	10 10	8 15	12 5	30
B	B2	15 15	12 5	18 25	45
		25	20	30	N = 75

FIG. A4. Hypothetical data for a three-by-two contingency table.

expected value) are all to be summed, to yield the chi-square statistic (symbolized by χ^2).

The use of Equation A13 for the hypothetical data in Fig. A3 is now illustrated.

$$\chi^2 = \Sigma \frac{(O - E)^2}{E}$$

$$= \frac{(15 - 10)^2}{10} + \frac{(10 - 15)^2}{15} + \frac{(5 - 10)^2}{10} + \frac{(20 - 15)^2}{15} = 8.33$$

The degrees of freedom are the number of rows minus 1, times the number of columns minus 1. In this example, it is $(2-1)(2-1) = 1$. In a chi-square table, such as the one given in Appendix B at the back of this text, the critical value at one degree of freedom would be found to be 3.84, with a .05 Type I error probability. The obtained value of 8.33 is therefore clearly statistically significant.

As another example, Fig. A4 offers a three-by-two contingency table.

Figure A5 illustrates the computation of the expected values for Fig. A4.

$\frac{(30)(25)}{75} = 10$	$\frac{(30)(20)}{75} = 8$	$\frac{(30)(30)}{75} = 12$
$\frac{(45)(25)}{75} = 15$	$\frac{(45)(20)}{75} = 12$	$\frac{(45)(30)}{75} = 18$

FIG. A5. Expected values for the hypothetical data in the contingency table illustrated in Fig. A4, computed with Equation A12. (Note that the computed expected values, 10, 8, etc., are in the upper left corner of the cells in Fig. A4.)

After the computation of the expected values (as illustrated in Fig. A5), the expected values are used with the observed values to compute the chi-square statistic. This step is illustrated in Fig. A6 for the hypothetical data in Fig. A4.

$$\chi^2 = \frac{(10 - 10)^2}{10} + \frac{(15 - 8)^2}{8} + \frac{(5 - 12)^2}{12}$$

$$+ \frac{(15 - 15)^2}{15} + \frac{(5 - 12)^2}{12} + \frac{(25 - 18)^2}{18}$$

$$\chi^2 = \frac{0}{10} + \frac{49}{8} + \frac{49}{12} + \frac{0}{15} + \frac{49}{12} + \frac{49}{18} = 17.01$$

FIG. A6.   Computation of the chi-square statistic for the hypothetical data in Fig. A4. The df are 2, and the critical value, at the .05 level, is 5.99. Thus, the computed chi-square of 17.01 is statistically significant.

CHAPTER 6

Multifactor Designs: Designing and Interpreting Experiments with Multiple Influences

The second rule for research states: With one factor there must be only one difference distinguishing different conditions of the experiment, that difference being variations in the factor. Most experiments actually contain two or three factors, and occasionally even more. Theorists realize that most behavior, and certainly most human behavior, is multiply determined. Factors, in the form of manipulated variables, are prospective influences on people's behavior (some dependent variable) that an experimenter wishes to examine. There are many influences on our decisions, and our preferences, and even on the speed or zest with which we do things. Therefore, psychological questions are more realistically inquiries about multiple influences, multiple factors. Designs examining the influence of more than one factor, and that can answer questions about interactive influences of factors, are called **multifactor designs**. In this chapter, multifactor designs are discussed, along with multifactor analysis of variance, which is a common statistical procedure used with multifactor designs.

Each factor in a multifactor design is a dimension along which experimental conditions (or subject qualities) are deliberately varied. Each subject must be exposed to (or classified according to) just one level of each of the factors. Thus, the second rule for research can be restated as, "All differences between conditions must be specified factor differences."

For example, assume an investigation, in a manufacturing plant, of the effects of two different factors on employees' attitudes. The two factors are each person's level of responsibility, and the basis for each person's bonus. The basis for the bonus factor has two levels. The bonus will be based either on company performance or, instead, on performance within the employee's own unit. The level of responsibility factor has three levels. The employees (the subjects) are all either division supervisors, foremen, or assembly line workers. The dependent variable is a specially constructed attitude measure. This is a behavioral measure of enthusiasm and general morale, which is measured without the knowledge of the employees. For example, coming early and staying late would be treated as a sign of high enthusiasm, as would volunteering for active roles in company-sponsored social events. A quantitative scale constructed from such evaluations is devised, and each subject is given a score on this scale at the conclusion of the evaluation period. This score is used as the criterion measure for appraising the effects of the two factors being examined in the study. Figure 6.1, which only expresses the factors but does not indicate the dependent variable, schematizes the design.

The group of subjects represented in the upper left-most cell in Fig. 6.1 would all be assembly line workers receiving a bonus based on company achievement; the group of subjects in the middle cell of the bottom row (second row, second column) would all be foremen receiving a bonus based on the achievements of their unit. Thus, each subject (employee in the study) is located within just one cell, where the cell is defined by both factors. All of the subjects in any one cell of the matrix have in common their classification on the factors in the study. Therefore, Rule 2 might be restated in the

RESPONSIBILITY LEVEL

		Assembly Line	Foreman	Unit Manager
BASIS	Company			
FOR				
BONUS	Unit			

FIG. 6.1. Schematic representation of a two-factor completely randomized design, in this example also called a 2 × 3 design because there are two and three levels of the two factors.

following way: Cells of the matrix can only differ along the dimensions of specified factors, and all subjects within the same cell must share the same levels of all specified factors.

FACTORS VERSUS LEVELS

People often confuse factors and levels. Different factors always refer to different manipulated or subject variables. Thus a three-factor manipulated variable design has three different independent variables plus one dependent variable. Most experiments contain anywhere from one to three factors, although occasionally four or five factors are used. Some of the results can be difficult to interpret when working with more than three factors.

Different levels always refer to the different conditions within a single factor. For example, a one-factor design comparing continuous noise to intermittent noise to no noise, as the single independent variable, has three levels of the single factor. (Assume number of errors in some task as the dependent variable.) If the variable of stress is introduced in addition to noise (where stress has two levels, present or absent), this two-factor design can be called a 2 × 3 design (stated as *a two by three design*) because the factors have two and three levels. A three-factor design, with 2, 3, and 3 levels in the different factors, could be called a 2 × 3 × 3 design (stated as *a two by three by three design*).

The first rule for research, that there must be more than one condition in an experiment, makes it clear that no factor can have less than two levels, but there is no theoretical upper limit to the number of levels. For example, socioeconomic class is sometimes expanded from the commonly used low, middle, and upper classes, to five levels, by adding lower lower and upper upper classes. Most examples in the literature contain factors that each involve no more than 3 or 4 levels, though in chapter 7 an example of an experiment with 10 levels of an independent variable is discussed.

Most frequently, multifactor designs are used to answer some theoretical question. To present a realistic example, it will be necessary to first offer some theoretical background for an issue. The newspapers have reported a few instances in which bystanders have watched an individual being assaulted (including cases of murder and rape), without calling the police or otherwise interfering. Social psychologists have examined this issue, attempting to find some explanations for this occasional absence of social responsibility.

EXPLORING REASONS FOR LAPSES IN SOCIAL RESPONSIBILITY

Latané and Darley (1970) conducted a series of investigations testing the relationship between number of people present (group size) and giving aid in an emergency. They construed giving aid in an emergency as equivalent to the socially responsible action of interfering or calling the police when seeing someone attacked. The kinds of emergencies that they and others have used include such things as a person in a public place suddenly appearing to be very ill, or a person appearing to have had an accident, or smoke suddenly entering under a door into the room. The two dependent variables used were time that passed until a subject offered help, or simply whether or not a subject offered to help (or otherwise took responsible action).

They found that the time that passed before an individual acted responsibly increased as the number of other witnesses present increased. Similarly, the likelihood of an individual helping at all decreased with the number of other people present. An individual witnessing an emergency alone was most likely to help, and helped most quickly. Thus, the number of people present appears to be a factor that is relevant to taking socially responsible action. Latané and Darley's explanation was that responsibility is diffused among a group of people, each person feeling less directly responsible to act in proportion to the number of people witnessing the event. A neighbor watching a noisily conducted crime from a window in a neighborhood with many windows and many neighbors might say, "I'm sure someone has called the police by now," rather than placing the call himself or herself.

Latané and Darley (1970) manipulated the number of witnesses as a variable, which was therefore the independent variable in their experiment. They defined their dependent variable, social responsibility, as willingness to help; they used slowness in the occurrence of the helping behavior as evidence of decreased willingness to help (which they took to imply decreased social responsibility). Amount of time passing before helping thus became the operational definition of degree of social responsibility. A person was defined as acting with less social responsibility as a direct function of the amount of time that passed before that individual offered help.

Latané and Darley's manipulations were successful in affecting socially responsible behavior. They showed that increasing the number of witnesses does have the effect of decreasing social responsibility, defined as slower, or less likely, helping behavior. This has been a consistent finding.

Rutkowski, Gruder, and Romer (1983) thought that the effect might be limited to groups of strangers. That is, they suspected that the relationship between number of witnesses and helping behavior might not exist among people who are in some degree familiar with each other. They reasoned that people are often wary of acting inappropriately. This concern might be increased among strangers, with people acquainted with each other feeling a greater willingness to take a chance and interfere. For example, people in large cities, being forever among strangers, learn to inhibit social responding. (How does one say good morning to everyone on a crowded subway car?) By contrast, in small groups, people do appear to get to know each other better. A sense of familiarity or group cohesiveness can develop, which may enhance not only social responding but also social responsibility. Rutkowski et al. (1983) explored the joint effects of group size and cohesiveness on socially helpful behavior. Their research offers a good example of the examination of the interactive influences of two independent variables (group cohesiveness and group size). A discussion of the rationale for their research follows, after which their experiment is described.

Rutkowski et al. (1983) pointed out that group cohesiveness (defined as people knowing and liking each other) has been shown to increase responsiveness to social norms. One social norm is helping people in trouble, so a socially cohesive group might evidence more willingness on the part of the individuals in the group to help than would be the case among a group of strangers. Thus, their postulated chain of causality is as follows: Social cohesion creates a tendency to be more responsive to social norms, and social norms include being socially responsible (e.g., helping people in trouble). The result should be that social cohesiveness leads to increased tendency for social responsibility. Rutkowski et al. (1983) also pointed out that most of the research on the tendency of people in groups to be less helpful has been with groups of strangers. The subjects did not know each other in the experiments where increasing numbers of witnesses depressed social responsibility. Rutkowski et al. wanted to see if this effect was lost, or even reversed, in a cohesive group.

What they did was to put together groups of people, manipulating the social aspects of the situation, getting the people in only some groups to know each other and keeping the people in other groups as total strangers. Then they reproduced the kinds of situations seen in previous experiments (some emergency suggesting the desirability of interference), to see if the decrease in helping with group size seen in prior research was removed or reversed if a cohesive group was present. That is, would the relationship previously observed between group size and helping behavior be changed by variations in social cohesion? This meant using a multifactor design. In a sense, this involved doing the classic experiment twice, manipulating group size among strangers, and also manipulating group size within a socially cohesive group.

More specifically, Rutkowski et al. (1983) brought 144 subjects to a laboratory as part of an experiment, which the subjects were told was concerned with group decision making. Subjects were initially gathered together in groups of six people, but for half of the subjects (72 people) the group members had no occasion to interact (they merely all listened together to a taped discussion). The remaining subjects in their interactive or cohesive groups were asked to introduce themselves "and say a few words about their major field of study." Then the experimenter introduced several topics to the subjects in the interactive groups and asked them to think about them. The experimenter then encouraged these subjects to talk with one another about these topics and share their feelings with one another. To summarize, they manipulated the independent variable of group cohesiveness by introducing a structured group discussion for half of the subjects.

The other independent variable was size of group. They had two-person groups and four-person groups, each split off from the groups of six people originally brought in together and permitted, or not, to become mutually acquainted. Group size was defined in terms of how many people would be jointly witnessing the emergency. Thus, the splitting up of the six-person groups into groups of two and four took place just prior to the emergency that was used as a test of social responsibility.

The subjects were told that there were several experiments being jointly conducted so that some subjects would have to be sent in different directions. They were aware, though, that they were going to one part of the building in the company of either one other person (those in the two-person groups) or three other people (those in the four-person groups). "They were informed that their experiment was on group decision making under conditions of limited communication and told that to create conditions of limited communication they would be separated from each other in rooms connected by an intercom system" (Rutkowski et al., 1983, p. 547). As detailed in the description later in this section, the emergency situation was made apparent through the intercom. Although the subjects were each alone in a room, half thought there was one other person besides themselves (sharing the same intercom) who was aware of the emergency calling for social action, and half thought there were three other people besides themselves (sharing the same intercom) who were aware of the emergency. This constituted the manipulation of number of witnesses.

Subjects were told that the intercom system was to be temporarily turned off, while the experimenter left for 15 minutes, and while the subjects worked on some problems. However, there was evidence for the subjects (in terms of sounds from an intercom speaker) that the microphone in the nearby control room had been inadvertently left on, so that they (and the other members of their two- or four-person group) could hear the events in the control room (which they had previously visited, and in which they had seen a maintenance man working on a ladder). The emergency consisted of a loud crash followed by someone being heard to scream (all this over the open microphone), "Oh, my god, my ankle . . . I . . . I can't move it. Oh . . . my . . . leg . . . I . . . can't get this . . . off me." The maintenance worker moaned for about 60 sec, gradually becoming quiet.

Both whether or not the subjects went to help the worker and the amount of time until they left their rooms to help (the latency data) were recorded as the dependent variables. Figure 6.2 offers a schematic summary of the experimental design and the average latencies within the four cells of the matrix. There is a column variable (group size) and a row variable (cohesiveness) that can each be tested for a relationship with the dependent variable (helping latency). They would be tested by comparing the marginals, which are the means for each column (74.3 and 75.6) and the means for each row (83.0 and 66.9), which are shown outside of the cells.

The variable found to be related to helping in previous studies is the size-of-group variable (larger size yielding slower helping, that is, longer latencies). Thus, the right-hand column of cells under the larger group size of four would be expected to have longer latencies. (This would be tested by comparing the marginals outside of the cells, at the bottom of Fig. 6.2.) The new variable in the Rutkowski et al. (1983) study is cohesiveness, differentiating the rows in Fig. 6.2. Their question is, does cohesiveness make a difference in the relationship between group size and latency of helpfulness? That is, is there a different relationship between group size and latency, depending upon which row in Fig. 6.2 is being examined? They anticipated that the usual difference between smaller and larger groups (the column difference in Fig. 6.2) would be found with low cohesiveness; that is, that longer latencies (more time to respond to

Group Size

	Two	Four	$\bar{X}$
Low Cohesive	71.3	94.7	83.0
High Cohesive	77.4	56.5	66.9
$\bar{X}$	74.3	75.6	

FIG. 6.2. Design of one of the studies by Rutkowski, Gruder, and Romer (1983), showing the averages for the latency data (in seconds), as a function of group cohesiveness and group size. Smaller cell values reflect quicker helping responses. The marginals, outside of the cells, are the means of individual columns and individual rows.

the emergency) would be found among those in the larger group, but just in the upper row of Figure 6.2. Note that this means that instead of comparing the two bottom marginals, the comparisons would be repeated, made separately at each row of the matrix.

The difference in the upper row of Fig. 6.2 (71.3 vs. 94.7) is consistent with this expectation, and does in fact yield statistical significance. Rutkowski et al. (1983) argued that the lower row (77.4 vs. 56.5) should have the reverse effect. Their rationale for this was that group cohesiveness normally increases adherence to social norms, and if the social norm here is to give aid, group cohesiveness should exaggerate the propensity of social norms to increase the need to give aid. They interpreted this to mean that aid would be given faster in larger socially cohesive groups than in smaller socially cohesive groups. They did obtain these results, as can be seen in the lower row of cells within Fig. 6.2. This difference is statistically significant.

INTERACTIONS IN MULTIFACTOR DESIGNS

The use of two independent variables (group size and group cohesiveness) permits the experimenter to ask about the relationship between each of these two independent variables and the dependent variable. Each of these tests are called **main effects**, referring to the relationships between each of the factors and the dependent variable. Main effects are tested by comparing the marginals of a matrix like that seen in Fig. 6.2. But as also can be seen in Fig. 6.2, a test for a relationship between a factor and the dependent variable, say the group size factor, can be done at each of the levels of a second factor (group cohesiveness). When one factor is tested separately at different levels of a second factor, these tests are each called **simple effects**, rather than tests of main effects.

In the Rutkowski et al. (1983) experiment, tests of simple effects were made at each level of the cohesiveness factor. One test was made at the level of low cohesiveness, and it was found that larger group size does inhibit helpfulness, as seen in previous research. Another simple effects test was made at the level of high cohesiveness, where, as their theorizing predicted, the results were reversed, and larger group size was found to enhance helpfulness.

Let us look at a larger, and more general, matrix, presented as Fig. 6.3, without any data in the cells.

In Fig. 6.3, we again assume just two factors (Factors A and B), but now there are several levels for each factor. Assume that Factor A represents four different religious groups, and Factor B three different levels of social class. Assume that the criterion variable is years of education (which could be shown as mean values, in the cells, but is not included in Fig. 6.3). As was done with the smaller matrix in Fig. 6.2, one could test the main effects of the individual factors. One could compare column marginals (appearing in Fig. 6.3 as three symbols for means, outside of the cells at the bottom of the figure), offering the main effects test of Factor B, asking whether

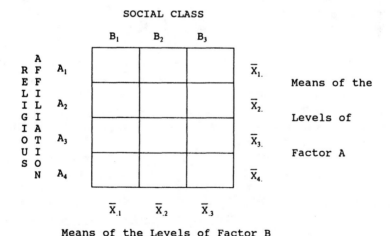

FIG. 6.3. Matrix of cells for a two-factor design with factors A and B (religious affiliation and social class, respectively).

there is a relationship between social class and years of education; and one could compare the row marginals (the four symbols for means outside of the cells at the far right of the figure), offering the basis for a main effects test of Factor A, asking whether there is a relationship between religious affiliation and years of education.

We could also examine the simple effects in Fig. 6.3 (assuming that it represented an actual study with data in the cells of the matrix). Here we could look at either four simple effects of Factor B (testing whether social class is related to years of education, but separately for four different religious groups, called the simple effects tests of social class), or we could look at three simple effects of Factor A (testing whether religious affiliation is related to years of education, but separately for three different social classes, called the simple effects tests of religious affiliation).

The more simple effects there are to test, the greater the probability that one of them will be significant just on the basis of chance (picking up a Type I error). It is normally considered proper to avoid interpreting simple effects tests, unless another very important test is found to be statistically significant; this is the **test of an interaction**. The test of an interaction is a test of whether the relationship between one of the factors and the dependent (or criterion) variable is different, depending upon the level of another factor at which the test is made. For example, if for some hypothetical data that were tabled in Fig. 6.3, religious affiliation (Factor A) were related to the criterion variable (years of education), but only at levels 1 and 2 of Factor B, then we would have to conclude that social class is a factor in the relationship between religious affiliation and education. We would say that there is an interaction between social class and religious affiliation. Before talking about the relationship between religion and education—say, some finding that one religious group is exposed to more education than another—the social classes of the people should be specified. Recall that in the Rutkowski at al. (1983) study shown in Fig. 6.2, Factor A, low versus high cohesiveness, reversed the relationship between Factor B (group size) and the dependent variable (latency in helping).

There are a number of ways to verbalize the important concept of an interaction. Our prior verbalization of an interaction was that the level of one factor makes a difference in the relationship between another factor and the dependent (or criterion) variable. We can also say that an interaction means that the nature or the pattern of the relationship between one factor and the dependent variable changes as a function of the level of another factor. Or, because the dependent variable is generally some behavioral measure, we can say that the way in which a factor affects a behavior varies with the presence or influence of particular levels of another factor.

We can also return to the specific issue of simple effects, noting that a statistically significant interaction implies that it is highly probable that some differences among the simple effects will be found. For example, some statistically significant simple effects are likely to be observed, along with other simple effect tests that are not statistically significant. Another possibility is that all simple effects are statistically significant, but some have different patterns of differences among the levels, or vary in the extremity of their differences between the levels. The least likely outcome, given a statistically significant interaction, is that no statistically significant simple effects will be found. Although a relatively rare event, it can occur, for example due to random variance obscuring differences. In practice, it is expected that a statistically significant interaction will reveal some interesting differences among the simple effects.

If an interaction is tested and not found to be statistically significant, there is no support for the idea that any observed simple effect differences reflect anything other than random variance. Thus, no simple effect tests should be done. If they had been done automatically as part of a statistical software package, they should not be interpreted (unless the test for an interaction was statistically significant).

In summary, the general rule is: *Simple effect tests should not be done, unless the test for an interaction has itself been found to be statistically significant.* If the interaction is statistically significant, the simple effects are usually more important, and more informative, than the main effects.

The different possible patterns of interaction effects, that is, the differences in simple effects that can lead to statistically significant interaction tests, can be described most clearly graphically. As an example, Fig. 6.4 illustrates a case in which only one simple effect would be statistically significant. Figure 6.5 illustrates a case where two levels would yield statistically significant simple effects, but with the direction of the effects reversed from one to the other (as in the Rutkowski et al. example).

A third possibility for a statistically significant interaction is one in which the patterns of the differences between levels of Factor B are all similar, for example, all having positive slopes, but with the differences between levels of Factor B producing steeper slopes at one level of Factor A than another. Figure 6.6 gives an example of this.

With many levels on the X axis, a significant simple effect can

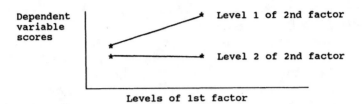

FIG. 6.4. Example of an interaction with only one statistically significant simple effect for the first factor (at Level 1 of the second factor).

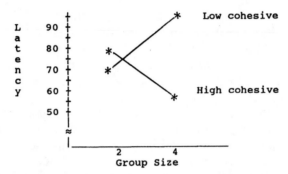

FIG. 6.5. Graph of results in Fig. 6.2. Both simple effect tests are statistically significant, although with the direction of the results reversed.

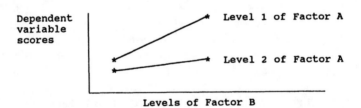

FIG. 6.6. Example of an interaction with patterns of differences between levels being similar, but differing in degree; Factor B has different slopes when examined at different levels of Factor A. Both simple effect tests are statistically significant. (An example of this type of interaction is discussed in chapter 11 and illustrated in Fig. 11.7.)

include alternating high and low values, or any other pattern of differences between groups. When the patterns of these simple effects differ from level to level of the second factor, a statistically significant interaction is expected. As previously suggested, such differences from level to level could include no significant simple effects (no pattern) at one or more levels, (as is the case at Level 3 of the second factor in Fig. 6.7), with statistically significant simple effects at one or more other levels.

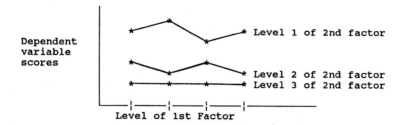

FIG. 6.7. Example of an interaction with different patterns at different levels, including one simple effect test that is not statistically significant (Level 3 of the second factor).

Portraying results graphically, as in Figs. 6.4–6.7, offers an intuitively clear way of revealing patterns in the data. However, exactly what effects are statistically significant in any experiment are determined numerically through the appropriate statistical tests.

In summary, a statistically significant interaction implies that the relationship between one factor and the dependent variable is different, depending on the level of the second factor at which the analysis is carried out. Therefore, after finding a significant interaction, simple effect tests are needed to see just which levels are, and which are not, statistically significant. If the statistical test for an interaction does not yield statistical significance, then no simple effect tests are done. Instead, the main effects of the factors are each individually tested for significance.

There are some instances in the use of multifactor designs in which it is not necessary to test for interactions. Rather, tests are conducted on differences between cells, when a specific pattern of differences between the means in a number of cells in a matrix is predicted. Examples of this are seen in the discussion of cognitive dissonance research in chapter 9. The more common procedure, however, is the one described in this section, which includes an analysis of variance, with a test for an interaction, followed by simple effect tests if (and only if) the interaction is statistically significant. The main effects are often ignored, and only the simple effects interpreted, when the interaction is significant. If the interaction is not significant, it is the main effects that are interpreted to yield the conclusions from the experiment.

Whether or not the main effects are statistically significant has no effect on whether or not the interaction is statistically significant. Figure 6.5 is an example in which there is a clear interaction, and there are statistically significant simple effects for the group size factor, yet the main effect for group size is not statistically significant. (In this example, the two simple effects with opposite linear slopes cancel out any potential main effect.)

MODERATOR VARIABLES

Sometimes both variables that are tested in an interaction are important. For example, both of the variables used in our hypothetical example, social class and religious affiliation, have some relationship to educational level. However, in many instances one factor is clearly the factor that is of major interest, and the other factor is only included in the experiment because it is expected to make a difference in the relationship between the major factor and the dependent variable. For example, in the Rutkowski experiment, the group size factor had already been shown to be related to helping behavior. The variable of group cohesion was not being examined because of interest in that variable, but rather it was specifically introduced to see if it would affect a previously observed relationship. Thus, we can think of the group size factor as the major variable, and the cohesion factor as a variable examined to see if it modifies the previously observed relationship.

It is sometimes helpful to refer to the newly introduced variable (the cohesion factor in our example) as a **moderator variable** (cf. Baron & Kenny, 1986). The moderator variable is the factor defining the different levels at which the major factor is tested for statistical significance. Another way of defining a moderator variable is as a factor that is not, itself, of interest. When a factor is only added to the experiment in order to test for a potential interaction, that is a factor that is described as a moderator variable. (The term *moderator variable* is used frequently in social and clinical research, but rarely in the experimental area.)

As another example, increased concern and interest by an individual in a subject's welfare would probably result in the subject liking the individual more. The dependent variable is the subject's liking for someone whom we will call the target person (liking measured with a rating scale). Increased interest and concern could be operationalized, and let us assume two levels of this independent variable, obvious interest in the subject (or a lack of interest) by the target person. Now we introduce another variable. We know that if a subject distrusts someone, we can say in advance that the subject is less likely to like that person, so that would not be a particularly interesting independent variable. On the other hand, as a moderator variable, it might be very interesting. We could see if the subject who normally likes a target person more when this target person shows interest in the subject, likes a distrusted target person less if that target person shows interest. This second variable, trust or distrust, would also be a two-level variable, but would be a moderator variable in this experiment. Having a person you distrust showing interest might cause a more negative reaction, rather than an increased positive reaction, reversing the relationship between evidence of interest and liking, seen when distrust is not present.

VARIABLES INTRODUCED TO INCREASE STATISTICAL POWER

There are times when a factor is introduced into an experiment although it is not a part of any question that is being asked, and is also not a moderator variable. It is introduced for statistical purposes, to make the statistical test more powerful. Several factors can be introduced into the same experiment for this purpose. In order to appreciate this special use of a second or even a third and fourth factor in an experiment, it is useful to pause for a brief discussion of the effects of variability in the F tests in analysis of variance.

The Role of Variability in F Tests in Analysis of Variance

Recall that in discussing t tests it was stated that decreased variability increases the power of a statistical test. This is because the denominator in the t test is a measure of variability within a condition. Decreasing the denominator increases the size of the t test ratio. In the F test of the analysis of variance the denominator is again a measure of within-cell variability, or of variability within some homogeneous conditions of the matrix. Thus, anything that could reduce variability within cells of the matrix should increase the size of the F ratio in the analysis of variance.

For example, assume a study examining the relationship between whether a person exercises, and physical strength. There will be a great deal of variability in the strength of people who all exercise, as there will be among those who do not exercise. Now suppose gender is added as a variable to the experiment. The two groups of the original design, people who exercise and those who do not, are turned into four groups, men who exercise, men who do not exercise, women who exercise, and women who do not exercise. The matrix representing this study is seen in Fig. 6.8.

EXERCISE

FIG. 6.8. Matrix representing a design testing effects of exercise on strength, with the added factor of gender. The nature of the dependent variable (strength) is not indicated within the matrix.

Each of the cells in the two-factor design will be less variable (in strength measures) than the two groups in the original single factor design. Note that the relationship of gender to strength does not have to be a question of interest. The purpose of introducing gender could be just to increase homogeneity of the dependent variable within cells of the matrix. Assume that there are a number of factors that are known to be related to the dependent variable. The larger the number of such factors on which subjects within a cell are similar, the less variability there will be among dependent variable scores within any one cell. This means a smaller value for the estimate of random variability (computed, for some designs, within each cell, and then averaged over cells). This smaller value is the denominator in the F ratio, producing a larger F value, resulting in greater power for the statistical test.

When groups are identified among the subjects (e.g., male and female), to reduce error variance in the cells by having cells that are homogeneous for this new factor, the groups that are defined by the levels of the new factor are called **blocks**, and the factor used in this way is called a **blocking variable**. Thus, in Fig. 6.8, the hypothetical subjects are blocked on gender, and gender is a blocking variable in the study of the relationship between exercise and strength.

RANDOMIZED BLOCK DESIGNS

When the major factor is a manipulated variable, and a blocking variable is introduced, the design is called a **randomized block design** (and sometimes a **treatment by blocks design**). Often the blocking variable is a quantitative variable. For example, there could be some prior measures of the subjects' performance on the dependent variable (e.g., reaction-time measures). Or there could be some other subject variable information, for example, the weights of the subjects, in a study of different diets and their effects on weight loss. It would probably be reasonable to block the subjects on their initial weights, or else on amount overweight. Whatever the blocking variable, subjects in the same block are randomly assigned to the different treatments (levels) on the major factor. This has the effect of matching subjects in the different treatments with regard to the blocking variable.

Assume that the dependent variable is reaction time, and that the subjects have been measured on reaction times before the experiment. The subjects could then be ranked on their reaction times, and then blocks of subjects would be formed based on the reaction time intervals into which they fit. As an example, all subjects with reaction times between 200 and 249 msec would be in one block, 250–299 in another, and so on, the interval sizes following from the range of scores and the number of blocks to be used. If there were 45 subjects, and three conditions of the independent variable (three different conditions under which reaction times were being measured), the subjects might be divided into five blocks, with 9 subjects in each block.

All of the interval sizes for the different blocks do not have to be the same. It is usually desirable to have the same number of subjects in each block, so this can influence interval size. The simplest way to do this is to take the subjects that are available for the study, and rank them on the blocking variable. If there are 45 subjects and five blocks are to be used, the 9 subjects with the smallest reaction times would be in one block, the 9 subjects with the next smallest reaction times would be in the second block, and so forth. The design is illustrated in Fig. 6.9, where within each block the 9 subjects would each be randomly assigned to one of the three conditions of the independent variable.

In summary, a blocking variable—call it B—is selected because it is related to the dependent variable, and groups are formed of subjects who are similar on the blocking variable, with these groups called blocks. The subjects in a block are randomly assigned to the levels of the major treatment variable; call this factor T. The result is that the subjects in the different levels of factor T are approximately equal on blocking variable B. A blocking variable therefore functions like a matching variable. In fact, the randomized block design is a multi-factor equivalent of the matched-pairs design discussed in the chapter on single-factor designs (chapter 4). In the example in Fig.

randomly assigned triplets	No Praise	Praise	Monetary Reward
s s s Block s s s 1 s s s	reaction- times		
. . . . . .	. . .		
s s s Block s s s 5 s s s			

FIG. 6.9. Randomized block design, with a blocking variable used to divide 45 subjects into five blocks, with 9 subjects in each block. The 9 subjects are randomly assigned to the three levels of the independent variable, with the restriction of equal numbers in each level.

6.9 it is assumed that reaction-time performance is the dependent variable. With preexperimental measurements of reaction times as a blocking variable, the subjects in the three levels of the independent variable would be approximately equal on reaction-time ability. It is in this sense that the blocking variable is a matching variable.

The higher the correlation between the blocking variable and the dependent variable, the larger the number of blocks that can be usefully defined. Given the range of empirically observed correlations among psychological variables, and the more common sizes of samples, the ideal number of blocks tends to vary between two and five. Pretesting (that is, additional measurements on the dependent variable) generally affords high correlates, as does the use of IQ as a blocking variable with a number of dependent variables (problem-solving ability, success at school or other intellectual tasks).

Sometimes many factors are used in an experiment, all of which are of interest, that is, all of which are included because the relationship to the dependent variable is not known. In such instances, when it turns out that the factors are all related to the dependent variable, within-cell variability is reduced in the same way as when factors are added exclusively for the purpose of reducing variance. In other words, using more factors means dividing up the experiment into more cells, each more homogeneous than otherwise, whenever the added factors are related to the dependent variable. The more factors in the experiment that are related to the dependent variable, the more homogeneous the cells, and so the smaller the denominator term in the F ratio. Thus, increased numbers of factors that are all related to the dependent variable mean a more powerful statistical test on any one of the factors. On the other hand, the more factors added that are not effective (not related to the dependent variable), the weaker the statistical test (assuming that the total number of subjects used is unchanged). Sometimes a factor is added to a study expressly for the purpose of reducing within-cell variability, under the expectation that it will be found to be related to the dependent variable. The study is done, and it is found that the factor lacks statistical significance in the F test of its main effect and is not involved in any statistically significant interactions. (Thus it is unexpectedly discovered to be unrelated to the dependent variable.) This is occasionally the case when gender is used in this way. When that happens, experimenters sometimes drop the unrelated factor from the statistical analysis. If it is a two-factor design, it is then treated as a one-factor design.

Sometimes variables that can be treated as blocking variables can instead be treated as control variables. Rather than differentiating subjects across levels of a blocking variable (e.g., with regard to gender, or how long since they have eaten, or level of anxiety), the level of the variable can be kept constant across all conditions of the experiment. Thus, the subjects can all be males, or all have been deprived of food for 24 hr, or all nonanxious, depending on what appears to be important to control for that experiment. Usually this limits the generalizability of the experiment, as when the subjects are all males or all females.

The use of either blocking variables or control variables in research is particularly important when sample sizes are small. Hsu (1989) demonstrated that the assumption of group equivalence through randomization is seldom justified in small sample studies, because of the likely presence of uncontrolled variables that are related to the dependent variable. These need to be controlled or used as blocking variables in order to maintain equivalence of the groups.

REMOVING ORDER AS A SOURCE OF VARIABILITY IN REPEATED MEASURES

In the discussion in chapter 4 of order effects in repeated-measures designs, it was suggested that if order effects are very strong, another design might be used, one combining both repeated and nonrepeated measures. The order in which the conditions of a repeated measures factor are applied is used as a second factor, a between-subjects factor, permitting each order to represent a different level of this second factor. Usually there would not be any interest in doing an F test on the order factor. The experiment would be run in this form to prevent strong order effects from obscuring the potential effects of the repeated measures factor. Subjects receiving the treatments on the independent variable in one order would be considered to be in one level of the order variable, and those receiving the treatments in another order would be considered to be the subjects in a second level of the order variable, and so forth. By using order as a separate factor in the design, it is removed as a source of variance from both the numerator and denominator in the statistical test of the repeated measures factor. Order is introduced in this way, and treated as a separate factor, in those cases where order effects are so large that they should be removed rather than handled with randomization of order. When order defines a second factor, every possible order should appear in the design. The order of administration of the treatments should be counterbalanced. As discussed in chapter 4, a counterbalanced order is one in which every possible order occurs equally often. This will work for independent variables with two or three levels. For example, if the independent variable being tested has three levels, there are 3! = 6 possible orders in which subjects can be exposed to the three conditions. With four levels the number of possible orders increases to 4! = 24, so the design is often not practical.

In summary, if order effects appear to be strong with a single repeated-measures factor, the design can be expanded to a two-factor design with order as a between-subjects factor. The major factor is still the repeated measure, which is the focus of the statistical analysis (examined for its main effect). If there are already two factors in the design, then the order factor can be introduced as a third factor. The major limitation concerns the number of levels in the repeated measures factor. With more than three levels, it is often difficult to include all of the orders needed for complete counterbalancing.

The psychological literature contains many examples of experiments with two or three factors. Usually, when more than three factors are involved, most of the factors are introduced to reduce within-cell variability, or to avoid order effects, or are used as blocking variables. That is, most often only two or three factors are targeted for an examination of effects on the dependent variable. For example, a study that is going to be statistically analyzed with the analysis of variance might be examining two independent variables, say Factors A and B, in a test of their relationships to a dependent variable, and the interaction of Factors A and B. However, the design of the study could include three other variables already known to be related to the dependent variable, in order to increase the statistical power. The data would be statistically analyzed as a five-factor analysis of variance design, but the F tests of interest would only include those for the two original factors, A and B, plus their possible interaction. Note that multifactor designs can include combinations of factors some or all of which are within-subjects (repeated measures) factors, and some or all of which are between-subjects (non-repeated measures) factors.

CHAPTER SUMMARY

The chapter opened with a rephrasing of the second rule for research so that it could encompass multifactor designs. Rule 2, restated, is: Cells of the matrix can only differ along the dimensions of specified factors, and all subjects within the same cell must share the same levels of specified factors. Factors refer to different manipulated or subject variables. They constitute the dimensions used to differentiate groups of subjects, or to differentiate conditions of the experiment. Levels refer to the different conditions (or classifications) within a single factor. Of course, as indicated by the first rule for research, every factor must have more than one level.

In multifactor research, statistical tests can be carried out on each of the factors. These tests are called main effects. A major feature of multifactor designs is the possibility of testing for interactions among factors. The research of Rutkowski et al. (1983) was discussed in order to provide an example of the interpretation of a statistically significant interaction. If a test of an interaction is statistically significant, it means that the relationship between one factor and the dependent variable is different, depending on the level of a second factor at which the analysis is carried out. A statistically significant interaction suggests that there are some differences among the simple effects. A test of a simple effect is a test of a relationship between one factor and the dependent variable, at just one level of a second factor. Note that, normally, in a single simple effects test of a factor, all levels of the first factor are compared with each other, but the test takes place only at one level of the second factor. This same test is repeated at different levels of the second factor, to determine what the relationship is between the first factor and the dependent variable, at each individual level of the second factor. The second factor, the one that is expected to modify the first factor's relationship to the dependent variable, is sometimes called a moderator variable. A simple effects test is only carried out when the test of an interaction has been found to be statistically significant.

Additional factors are sometimes introduced into an experiment simply to keep the scores within cells of the matrix more homogeneous. These factors are called blocking variables. Subjects who are similar on some dimension (some variable) that is closely related to the dependent variable are formed into blocks. Subjects within a block are equally dispersed within the levels of some factor that is of interest. If the factor of interest is a manipulated variable, then the subjects within a block are randomly assigned to the levels of the manipulated variable. This design arrangment is called a randomized block design (and also a treatment by blocks design). A blocking variable functions like a matching variable in a *t* test. It increases the power of the statistical test.

NEW WORDS AND PHRASES IN CHAPTER 6

blocking variable
blocks
interaction
main effects
moderator variable
multifactor designs
randomized block design
simple effects
test of an interaction
treatment by blocks design

CHAPTER 7

The Logic of Experimental
Psychology: The Problems
Encountered in Theorizing About
Internal Events

Experimental psychology could be described as the study of the basic processes of psychological functioning. Examples would include the details of how people think, solve problems, make decisions, convert impacting stimuli into perceptions, and store experiences in memory and then retrieve them. Psychologists develop explanations of how such things as thinking, problem solving, learning, and remembering take place and test their explanations. The major purpose of this chapter is to explain the logic that underlies much of contemporary research in experimental psychology and to offer examples of such research.

The chapter begins with definitions of some important words whose meanings are not always clear. This is followed by some examples of research by experimental psychologists. These examples are then used in a discussion of some logical difficulties that are often encountered in drawing conclusions from experiments.

HYPOTHESES AND THEORIES

The explanations of psychological phenomena that are developed by psychologists are sometimes called **hypotheses**, and sometimes

167

called **theories**.[1] Quite often these terms are used informally in the course of normal conversation. For example, assume that a friend of the reader had treated the reader badly. If a second friend tried to rationalize the unexpected treatment, tried to explain it, you might say something like, "Well, that's one theory." A psychologist might say exactly the same thing, or, with the same meaning, might say, "That's one hypothesis." It is in that sense that the words *theory* and *hypothesis* can be used to mean *explanation*.

Research psychologists use the terms theory and hypothesis to refer to the processes that can explain relationships between variables or events, particularly where one or more of the variables or events, or the process, is not directly observable.[2] An experimental psychologist might wonder whether the memory of breakfast is stored verbally (as a list of items), or visually (perhaps as a mental image of the breakfast table). Assume she postulated verbal rather than visual storage. She could refer to the assumed form of storage as a theory, or, equivalently, as a hypothesis. In this example, the explanation, the theory or hypothesis of verbal storage, would be an unobservable process. This unobservable process would be invoked in order to explain some observable phenomenon, such as accurate recall. More specifically, verbal storage would be used to explain

---

[1]The word *theory* as used in mathematics and the physical sciences has a more formal meaning. It refers to a set of axioms (assumptions), theorems (logical derivations from the axioms), and some terms that are either directly defined, or implicitly defined by the axioms. The axioms and theorems describe relationships among the terms. Thus, a theory in this formal sense involves a set of statements that describe relationships among terms and that permit the derivation of further relationships between the terms. Wilder (1965) offered an excellent discussion of formal theories. Although such complex theories have been developed in psychology (the most extreme example having been offered by Hull, 1943), for the most part psychologists tend to postulate very limited sets of relationships, often testing just a single relationship (a single statement) within a series of related experiments.

[2]For example, Madsen (1984), in an issue of the *Annals of Theoretical Psychology*, stated that "a hypothesis is a general proposition that formulates the relationship between two or more terms (variables) among which at least one term is hypothetical or transempirical (i.e., referring to an unobserved or unobservable intervening variable or to an explanatory construct)" (p. 187). Greenwald et al. (1986, p. 217), in an issue of the *Journal of Personality and Social Psychology*, defined theory similarly to the way in which Madsen defined a hypothesis. They stated that a theory refers to "statements that express relationships among concepts." They interpreted the word *concepts* very broadly, so that it can refer to both purely theoretical terms (what others would call an intervening variable or explanatory construct) and terms with varying levels of operational specificity (what would usually be called variables). Thus, *theory* and *hypothesis* are often used interchangeably in psychology, and usually include some reference to unobservable phenomena.

observable relationships between exposure to material and recall of that material.

A number of different terms are used, in the course of explanations, to suggest inferred but unobservable processes or events, the most common being **intervening variable**. A less frequently used term, with the same meaning, is *explanatory construct*. A term that has the added implication of a covert physical event, such as an unobservable biochemical or neurological change, is **hypothetical construct**.

The term *intervening variable* does not necessarily suggest a physical occurrence; it could refer to an unobservable relationship, or to an event or process without known physical referents, such as an intention. Most psychological theories do tend to invoke intervening variables or hypothetical constructs.

INDIRECTLY CONFIRMING UNOBSERVABLE EVENTS

This section begins with an experiment by Michael Posner and his colleagues and students (Posner, Boies, Eichelman, & Taylor, 1969). This is just one among a series of studies by Posner on the processes involved in recognizing that two stimuli are identical. They focus on the issue of how the stimuli are initially encoded, and then how these percepts are stored in memory. A second set of very different experiments on recognizing identity by two other experimenters is then introduced. All of these experiments offer illustrations of the common logical form of attempts to validate psychological theories.

Assume that you wished to know about initial encoding when subjects first confront a stimulus that is to be compared with another stimulus; specifically, you want to know the form in which the stimulus is first encoded (e.g., as a visual image or, alternatively, as a verbal label). A second question would be whether the form changes for storage. What variables that could be experimentally controlled, what events that could be monitored and measured, would be usefully examined to answer these questions? Posner and his colleagues (Posner et al., 1969) investigated the initial encoding processes, and the immediately following storage processes, in an interesting way. They measured the reaction times of subjects that were given the following task: Identify pairs of letters as having the same name or not. The pairs were, for example, AA, Aa, Ab, AB, aa, and bb, and subjects were instructed to make their decisions (about the paired letters having the same name or not) as quickly as possible after their appearance. Thus subjects were shown a pair of letters, such as AA, and asked to indicate whether the two letters have the same name. The decision reaction times of the subjects constituted the dependent variable.

When subjects are presented with physically identical letters (identical letters of the same case, such as AA, aa, and BB), they can use physical information when making their decision about the two letters being the same. That is, the two letters can be recognized as physically identical. By contrast, when they are given a pair of letters with mixed cases (Aa, Bb, etc.), they are forced to use verbal information (the name of the letters) to make the decision about letter identity.

The immediate question in the study was whether there is a difference in decision time for mixed versus identical cases. Individual subjects were exposed to both identical and mixed cases, and the reaction times were compared. This reaction time information was used (in a way that is explained later) to answer a larger question: whether people initially encode the paired stimuli visually or verbally. Thus, a question about unseen (internal) events was asked through the manipulation and measurement of easily observed and measured variables (stimuli differences and reaction times).

Some logical inferences are utilized to draw the connection between the manipulation and observation of overt variables and the conclusions about internal events. The logic in the Posner experiments begins with the reasonable assumption that if people have a consistent initial way of responding, permitting them to respond this way will yield the fastest response. Forcing them to respond differently than they normally would, should cause a time delay in responding. That is, if the response that the subjects are to make requires an encoding task that is different from the one they would normally use in that situation, they would have to switch codes, taking additional time. If two pairs both have letters with the same name, but only one pair is physically identical (e.g., AA and Aa), a quicker response to the physically identical pair (AA) would suggest that subjects characteristically use visual rather than verbal information, at least when initially confronting the stimulus. Stated another way, assume for the moment that when people first perceive a stimulus presented visually they normally encode it visually rather than initially registering the name. If this were true, they would be expected to respond more quickly with the word "same" to physically identical cases than to mixed cases (whose basis for identity is verbal).

This argument about an experimental outcome that would logically follow if internal events proceeded in a particular way is what permitted Posner and his colleagues to investigate how people initially encode letters. They did find that people responded more quickly with the word "same" to physically identical cases (physical matches) than to mixed cases (name matches), which is consistent with initial encoding being visual.

The other question that they asked is whether the information is maintained in a way that preserves the physical information, or whether it is transformed into a verbal code for retention. To obtain this information, Posner and his colleagues used sequential presentation of the two letters on a trial. The first letter of a pair was presented and the second letter was presented after delays of 0, .5, 1, 1.5, or 2 sec. Reaction times were measured from the time of appearance of the second member of a stimulus pair. Their results, shown in Fig. 7.1, indicate a rapid decline in the difference between physical and name identity matches as a function of the interval between presentation of the first and second letter of a stimulus pair.

When both letters were presented simultaneously (0 sec delay), physical identity matches were made approximately 90 msec faster than name identity matches. However, by 2 sec. the difference between physical and name identity matches was no longer statistically significant. The data are consistent with the idea that given 2 or more seconds between the appearance of the first and second letter to be matched, the subjects have converted their initial visual

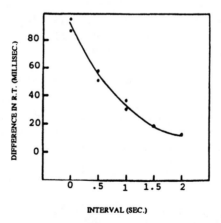

FIG. 7.1. Difference between physical and name identity matches as a function of the interval between presentation of the first and second letters of a stimulus pair. The two points at intervals of 0, 0.5, and 1 sec represent data from two different experiments. From Posner, Boies, Eichelman, and Taylor (1969). Copyright 1969 by the American Psychological Association. Adapted by permission.

encoding of the first stimulus to a verbal code (the name of the letter), for retention in memory.

Although each experimental result sheds some light, it also generally raises another question. For example, what produces the loss in relative efficiency of physical identity matches over time? Posner and his colleagues concluded that the switch to the verbal code probably follows from some instability in, or loss of, visually coded information over time, while verbal codes are more stable.

The stability of visual storage over time was investigated by Kroll, Parkinson, Parks, and colleagues. In a series of studies these investigators used a shadowing procedure to measure visual and auditory short-term memory processes (e.g., Kroll, Parks, Parkinson, Bieber, & Johnson, 1970; Parkinson, 1972; Parks, Kroll, Salzberg, & Parkinson, 1972). Shadowing is repeating aloud spoken stimuli as they are presented and has the effect of interfering selectively with retention of information maintained in an auditory-verbal code. Kroll, Parkinson, Parks, and colleagues reasoned on the basis of results from their previous studies that visual storage in the Posner letter-matching task might be maintained over a longer period of time if subjects were given an incentive not to translate the information to an auditory-verbal code. In the critical experiment, Parks et al. (1972) combined the Posner letter-matching task with shadowing. On each trial subjects were required to repeat aloud a series of spoken letters presented at a rate of two letters per second. While subjects were shadowing, two letters were presented visually and subjects were instructed to indicate whether the two letters had the same name or not. As in the previous experiments of Posner, the critical comparison was between physical identity and name identity matches. In the Parks et al. experiment the interval between the first and second letters of a stimulus pair was constant at 8 sec. Parks et al. reasoned that the auditory-linguistic activities involved in shadowing would encourage subjects to maintain visual storage as a basis for performing the memory version of the Posner letter-matching task. The results of the Parks et al. experiment, shown in Fig. 7.2, are consistent with their hypothesis. Physical identity matches were faster than name identity matches even at the 8 sec. interval tested.

The results shown in Fig. 7.2 suggest that when discouraged from using verbal storage by a concomitant verbal shadowing task, subjects give evidence for more durable visual storage. Thus the suggestion by Posner et al. that there is quicker loss of quality of the visual traces is not supported by the Parks et al. results. Some other research, discussed in chapter 9, is more supportive of the Posner et

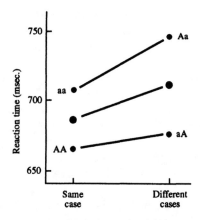

FIG. 7.2. Decision reaction times for physical identity (same case) and name identity (different case) matches. The interval between first and second letters of a stimulus pair was 8 sec. The top line shows data when the same-case condition was defined by two lower-case letters. The bottom line shows data for the condition when same case was defined by two upper-case letters. The line in the middle is the average of the two conditions. From Parks, Kroll, Salzberg, and Parkinson (1972). Copyright 1972 by the American Psychological Association. Reprinted by permission.

al. speculations, suggesting that there are some contexts where there is rapid decay of visually stored information.

Surrogate Variables

These examples offer illustrations of an important and challenging task faced by experimental psychologists in much of their research. They have to identify specific relevant variables over which they have some control and/or that they can measure; that is, they have to identify events and stimuli that are open to all observers, for the purpose of drawing conclusions about private internal events (such as the way in which some stimuli are intially encoded and the form in which they are stored). In the Posner experiments there were two overt, easily manipulated or identified independent variables: identical versus mixed cases in the pairings of the letters that were presented, and time between the presentation of the paired stimuli that were being compared by the subjects. The readily measured dependent variable was the reaction time in the decision (of "same" versus "different"). These overt variables that are manipulated and measured in the experiment can be called **surrogate variables**. The term "surrogate" means substitute, and surrogate variables are directly manipulable or measurable variables which are examined out of an interest in internal processes that are not directly observable. The definition of surrogate variables that we present has not been used before in psychology. We introduce it here because of the frequency with which experimental psychologists are forced to work with overt, observable external variables, while their interest lies in covert, unobservable internal events.

A theory, as defined in this chapter, expresses relationships between variables where, usually, one or more of the variables are not directly observable. Therefore, theory-driven research is usually forced to use surrogate variables to investigate the influence of internal processes. We further clarify our distinction between surrogate variables and those variables that are directly observed or directly manipulated, through two examples. One involves a direct examination of the variables of interest, without any concern for internal processes, and the other does ask questions about internal events that, uncharacteristically, can be directly controlled.

For the first case we look at a hypothetical experiment in which external variables similar to those in the letter-matching task would be used, but the external variables would not be treated as surrogate variables. Assume that a human factors psychologist is designing an instrument panel for an airplane, and that she is interested in seeing under what conditions a pilot can distinguish most easily between two different letters, deciding whether the letters are the same or different. The experiments would be conducted in a simulated airplane cockpit. Reaction time could be used as the measure of how easily the discrimination is made. Various characteristics of the letters could be varied, for example, line thickness, size, and placement in the visual field. One question would be, which line thickness yields the fastest reaction times for making the judgements. Another would concern placements in the visual field. A third question might concern the possible interactions between line thickness and placement in the field. In this example the independent variables (line thickness, placement in the visual field) would be manipulated because of a direct interest in their relevance for ease in making a visual discrimination.

The use of external manipulated variables in the letter-matching experiments of Posner and his colleagues differ in two important ways from those in the instrument panel experiment. First, the variables of interest in the Posner experiments, visual and verbal coding and storage processes, were internal and unobservable. The external variables that were manipulated, pure and mixed-case letters, were not of interest in their own right, but were selected to test the different hypothesized coding and storage processes. In the instrument panel experiment we would be interested in the external variables in their own right. We would be interested in the particular combinations of size, line thickness, and placement in the visual field that produce the fastest and most accurate responses. The characteristics of letters that produce the best performance in the instrument panel experiment would, undoubtedly, do so through their influence on internal and unobservable processes; but we would not be interested in specifying those internal processes in the instrument panel experiment.

This brings us to the second difference between the letter-matching and instrument panel experiments. Posner's letter-matching experiments were theory driven; the major interest was whether different coding processes exist, and which coding processes are used under different time constraints. In the instrument panel experiment we would not be testing a theory; rather, we would be interested in finding stimuli that would maximize performance when using the instrument panel. None of the variables would be surrogate variables.

Let us consider another example, one that *is* theory driven, to get a clearer sense of surrogate variables. An educational psychologist wants to test the common sense theory that motivation enhances learning. As with visual and verbal codes, motivation and learning are theoretical constructs and are internal and unobservable. The terms *motivation, incentive,* and *inducement* all concern factors moving people to action and increasing drive states. The educational psychologist decides to manipulate motivation by offering a financial incentive to one group for achieving a particular level of performance in a two week module on college algebra. Another group is not offered a financial incentive, just given the usual classroom instruction. Both groups receive the same type of instruction for the 2-week period, and both receive the same final examination at the end of the module.

Consider the relationships between external and internal variables in the Posner letter-matching experiment and in the motivation experiment. In the Posner letter-matching experiment, the external variables, pure and mixed case letters, do not define the internal constructs, visual and verbal codes. Rather, the relationship between external and internal variables is indirect; logic has to be used to tie the difference between pure and mixed-case letters, and the expected response differences, to the hypothesized internal coding events. In the motivation experiment, the relationship between external and internal variables is direct; the external event (financial incentive) can be accepted as an operational definition of a motivator.

Of course, as discussed at length in chapter 13, there is room for doubt and dispute in deciding which operational definition best represents a particular internal event. But the point here is that using an operational definition of an internal event to directly control an internal event involves a different kind of logical problem than we confront when we have to use surrogate variables. The surrogate variables used in the letter-matching experiment are tied to the internal events through a logical chain, whereas in the motivation experiment the connection between external manipulation and the internal event is merely in the use of an externally controllable operational definition of the event. If we can accept the operational definition as valid, we can assume that the variable of interest has been overtly manipulated. (For example, we have overtly created an internal motivated state.) If someone disagrees with the operational definition that was used, a different operational definition might be found. At least in principle, it would be possible for all observers to agree about the appropriateness of a particular operational definition, and thus to have consensus that the internal event did in fact take place.

Unfortunately, the use of operational definitions as just described is not frequent in experimental psychology. The variables of interest to experimental psychologists have not lent themselves to such definitions. They have been forced to use surrogate variables, and in fact have become quite ingenious in discovering ways to deal indirectly with internal events.

The experimental study of human cognitive processes (sensation, perception, memory, thinking, etc.) started out with a much more direct assessment of internal constructs. In the early days of experimental psychology subjects were shown various types of stimuli and were asked to describe the contents of their conscious experience when confronting these stimuli. This technique was called **introspection**, and subjects were highly trained in its use. Despite intensive training, findings proved to be unreliable from subject to subject. For example, in circumstances where some subjects reported vivid visual imagery, others reported no experience of imagery at all. This approach was abandoned at the turn of the century with the conclusion that the processes underlying human cognition are often not reliably accessible to consciousness. This view is still prevalent today.

We next review additional findings in contemporary experimental psychology in which internal processes have been identified that have durations of only a fraction of a second (in the Posner experiment the hypothesized translation to a name code was made in 80–90 msec). It is highly unlikely that human subjects have conscious access to these processes. Therefore, asking for verbal reports or descriptions of these processes is asking for information that subjects do not have available. As human cognition is the domain of experimental psychologists, and cognitive processes are internal and unobservable, it is the content area per se that determines the necessity for surrogate variables.

Another illustration of the use of surrogate variables to learn about internal events is now presented. This research was done by Roger Shepard and his student Jacqueline Metzler (Metzler, 1973; Metzler & Shepard, 1974; Shepard & Metzler, 1971; see also Shepard & Cooper, 1982, which contains closely related material).

Shepard and Metzler (1971) were interested in people's internal responses when comparing two visual images, when one object is rotated differently in space than the other. For example, assume that there are two rectangular pictures, hung side by side, one hung with the longer side vertical, and the other hung with the longer side horizontal. If a subject is asked to determine whether the two pictures are actually identical pictures, would the subject mentally rotate one of the pictures so that they are both identically oriented mentally, before deciding whether they are identical?

Shepard and Metzler (1971) did not use rectangular pictures. Rather, they used drawings of three dimensional geometric figures, as seen in Fig. 7.3, which shows the same figure in two different orientations.

Figure 7.3b is rotated 80 degrees clockwise from its orientation in Fig. 7.3a. Shepard & Metzler (1971) used these and other pairs of matched figures in comparisons where there were a variety of differences in rotation. The differences varied from 0 degrees to 180 degrees, in nine steps, each separated by 20 degrees, that is, 0, 20, 40, . . . , 180 degrees. There were also paired figures in these various orientations

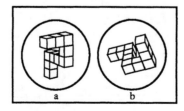

FIG. 7.3.   The same three-dimensional figure in two different orientations. From Metzler and Shepard (1974). Copyright 1974 Lawrence Erlbaum Associates. Reprinted by permission.

that were not identical. Subjects were exposed to all of these pairs, one pair at a time, and were asked to signal, as quickly as possible, whether or not each particular pair of figures was identical.

Shepard and Metzler reasoned that if mental rotation takes place under the specified conditions of the experiment, then paired figures with greater differences in orientation would require a greater degree of mental rotation before they are identically oriented. It is reasonable to assume that this mental rotation takes time, with larger rotations taking longer. It follows then that subjects would take longer to recognize identity in figures when comparing stimuli that had larger differences in orientation (because they would have to be rotated through larger angles). In fact, if the rate of rotation is constant, there should be a simple linear relationship between the differences in orientation and the reaction times (each additional 20-degree difference yielding the same additional increase in reaction time). This prediction of a linear relationship was their experimental hypothesis, and was confirmed, as can be seen in the graph of Fig. 7.4, which pictures the results from the experiment (Metzler & Shepard, 1974).

In this experiment, all subjects were exposed to all of the orientation disparities, tested on each disparity several times, with each subject yielding an average reaction time for a particular disparity. For each orientation disparity noted on the X axis of Fig. 7.4, the averages of all subjects at that disparity were averaged, to obtain the 10 points in the graph. From a design standpoint, this can be seen as a repeated-measures design, because the same subjects were mea-

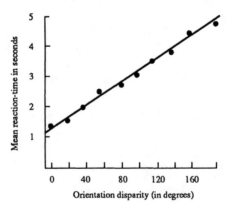

FIG. 7.4. Graph of the results for the experiment by Shepard and Metzler in 1971. From Metzler & Shepard (1974). Copyright 1974 Lawrence Erlbaum Associates. Adapted by permission.

sured at each level of the independent variable (orientation disparity). Because both variables are quantitative, but the independent variable has a modest number of levels, an analysis of variance would appear to be a reasonable statistical choice. There is a special type of analysis of variance, called a trend analysis, that can be used when the factor with several discrete levels is a quantitative variable (here degrees of orientation disparity in 20-degree steps). A trend analysis can be used to specifically test whether the increase with each additional 20 degrees of difference in orientation is linear. This was the statistic used to confirm that the predicted linear relationship was present. The procedural details of this first experiment by Shepard and Metzler have been summarized in Fig. 7.5.

In the Shepard and Metzler example it can be assumed that if internal rotation actually takes place, there is a relationship between amount of internal rotation and reaction time. The question being asked is whether internal rotation (the hypothesized internal event) takes place. Does disparity in stimulus orientation cause subjects to mentally rotate one of the stimuli till they are identically oriented? If

---

"The beginning of each trial was signaled by a warning tone followed, approximately one half second later, by the visual presentation of the pair of perspective drawings selected for that trial" (Metzler & Shepard, 1974, p. 160). The subject's instructions were to pull the right hand lever to indicate that the two drawings represented the same three dimensional objects, or to pull the left hand lever if the drawings appeared to represent two different three dimensional objects. They were told to respond as quickly as possible, keeping errors to a minimum. "The first slight deflection of either lever towards the subject actuated a microswitch that stopped the reaction-time clock" (Metzler & Shepard, 1974, p. 160).

"Each subject participated for a total of eight to nine hours in about as many sessions, completing on the average 200 trials per session for a total of 1600 trials. Prior to the first session the subject was verbally instructed as to the nature of his task. He then received 40 practice trials to familiarize him with the stimuli and general procedure" (Metzler & Shepard, 1974, p. 160).

In this text we have only discussed comparisons of drawings that were oriented differently from each other clockwise (or counterclockwise). In the study, they also included drawings that were oriented differently into the page, that is, into three dimensional space. This complicated the procedure and analysis somewhat, but did not change the fundamental nature of the findings.

Figure 7.5. Procedure for first experiment by Shepard and Metzler (1974).

mental rotation occurs, then the presumed relationship between mental rotation and reaction times should yield the pattern of reaction times that would confirm the hypothesis (greater reaction time with greater orientation disparity). The evidence as seen in Figure 7.4 is consistent with the occurrence of the hypothesized internal event. However, there is no direct evidence of mental rotation as the cause of the longer reaction times. Rather, there is simply a relationship between two surrogate variables (orientation disparity within the stimuli, and reaction times) that is consistent with the occurrence of the intervening event of mental rotation. One surrogate variable is manipulated (orientation disparity between the presented stimuli), and the other external variable (reaction time) is measured. Logical inferences are used to conclude that the unseen internal event (mental rotation of one of the figures) takes place.

When it is stated that direct evidence is lacking, and that the results are merely consistent with the hypothesis (of mental rotation of visual images), it is implied that the explanation for the results is not necessarily the only logical one, nor necessarily the correct one. The results do not rule out the possibility of satisfactory alternative explanations. For example, assume for the moment that subjects do not rotate the figures mentally. It is possible that it is more difficult to assess an identity between two figures when the two figures are differently oriented. Further, it is possible that the greater the disparity in orientation of the external stimuli being compared, the more difficult the task. Perhaps there is a linear increase in difficulty that accounts for the linear increase in reaction times. This offers an alternative explanation for the results.

The Logical Error of Affirming the Consequent

There is a general logical rule to be recognized here. When we theorize about an unseen event (such as mental rotation), and that unseen event has predictable consequences (such as a linear increase in reaction times), surprisingly, we can not use the occurrence of the predicted consequences to confirm that the unseen event has occurred. For any observed outcome, there are generally many alternative prior events that could bring about the same happening. By contrast, let us first look at a situation where the prior event is known to have taken place. If a man were to rob a bank, it could be assumed that he would be in a hurry to leave the bank. Thus, given that an important antecedent event is known, that is, a particular man has just robbed a bank, it can be correctly predicted that he will leave the bank in a hurry. However, seeing a man leave a bank in a hurry would not offer adequate justification for the assumption that he has just robbed the bank. Many other antecedent events could be responsible for a man's leaving the bank in a hurry. Even though if A were true it would offer a guarantee of the occurrence of B, if we were not sure whether A was true the occurrence of B would not tell us whether A was true.

What is being encountered here is a standard rule of logic. If A implies B (man robs bank implies man leaves bank in a hurry), finding that B is true (man leaves bank in a hurry) does not confirm A (that he has robbed the bank). From A implies B, what can be known is that, *given* A, then B is true. But, still assuming that A implies B, if all that we have observed is that B is true, the status of A is simply not known. Assume that a theory (A) implies a particular experimental outcome (B). We do the experiment and find B. If we draw the conclusion that the theory is true, we have made a logical error. Unfortunately, this is a frequent way of seeking support for theories in psychology.

It is the practice in science to discuss theories that have specific implications, so that ways can be found to validate or invalidate the theories. Experiments are most frequently done just for that purpose. Thus a theory A, whose truth is in question, implies some experimental outcome, B. An experimenter assumes that the theory is true, in order to be able to specify an outcome that should follow from the theory. In the case of the Shepard and Metzler theory about mental rotation (Shepard & Metzler, 1971), if mental rotation is assumed to take place, larger orientation discrepancies (between paired visual stimuli) should lead to larger mental rotations, which should take longer. Thus, if A (the theory that mental rotation is taking place) is true, then B (observed longer reaction times) should be true. It is in this sense that if A is true, then B is true. However, the important question is whether A is true, that is, does mental rotation take place? Unfortunately, sometimes all that can be tested is B, the experimental outcome. This is the case in the Shepard and Metzler example where what was tested were the reaction times. From longer reaction times for stimuli with greater orientation disparity (B), it would be improper to conclude that mental rotation takes place (A). At best, one can say that the finding of B is consistent with the truth of A[3].

---

[3]The same issue is present in the Posner experiments discussed earlier in this chapter. A theory of initial coding of visual stimuli is suggested (A), which predicts shorter reaction times for physically identical stimuli (B). The prediction holds (we find B). This finding is consistent with the theory, but it is certainly possible that something other than coding preferences were responsible for the shorter reaction times. The status of A (the theory) remains uncertain.

When A implies B, A is called the antecedent and B the consequent. Attempting to show that the antecedent (A) is true through affirming that B is true (trying to prove a theory A by correctly predicting the outcome B) is called the **logical error of affirming the consequent**. In summary, the major question is whether a theory, A, is true. It is reasoned that A implies B. B is confirmed as true, and this is used sometimes as evidence that A is true. This is indeed a logical error, but as will be explained in the sections that follow, the logical error of affirming the consequent can be difficult to avoid[4]. (A summary of arguments vulnerable to the logical error of affirming the consequent appears in Fig. 7.6. The arguments are presented in three forms: using abstract symbols, using a common sense example, and as an example involving empirical testing of a theory.)

Denying the Consequent (*Modus Tollens*)

What could have been concluded if Metzler and Shepard had not gotten their predicted results? Suppose that, instead of the neat constant slope seen in Fig. 7.4, they had simply obtained a horizontal line, indicating that additional differences in orientation did not increase the time to recognize identities. This would have been inconsistent with their hypothesis of larger orientation disparities leading to longer reaction times. It would have suggested that their picture of mental rotations was not valid. Logically, this takes the following form: A (the theory) implies B (a particular experimental

---

[4]It may be helpful to look at the logic when surrogate variables are not involved. In the instrument panel experiment, assume that paired letters centrally located in the visual field are more quickly reported as identical than those placed in the periphery. In this case, the experimenter provided the initial condition (location), which is A, and found faster reaction times, which is B. A leads to B in this set of instances (for a group of randomly selected subjects). We then have to be able to conclude that what has happened some finite number of observed times, will always happen. In a statistical science this inductive leap is accomplished through statistical tests, which in essence show (given statistical significance) that the phenomenon is reliable. *Reliability*, in this context, means that in future sampling we can expect to continue to obtain what was obtained during the experiment. This same logic applies in the case of the educational psychologist who predicted increased learning with financial incentives. If the motivation is externally controlled and therefore clearly instantiated, and the increased performance is then found, even though the increased motivation is an internal event, inductive logic is what applies. We prove that A leads to B within the experiment, and use statistical logic to specify a level of confidence in continuing to observe the same relationship. This is contrasted with the logical error of affirming the consequent, where we can assume A implies B, but try to use the observation of B to reach conclusions about the existence of, or validity of, A.

Premise: A implies B. (If A is true, then B is true.)

Observation: B is true.

Conclusion: *We do not know whether A is true.* More specifically, the observation of B is consistent with the truth of A, but it is certainly possible that A is not true.

Premise: Robbing a bank implies leaving the bank in a hurry.

Observation: A man leaves a bank in a hurry.

Conclusion: *We do not know whether the man robbed the bank.* More specifically, the observation of the man leaving the bank in a hurry is consistent with his having robbed the bank, but it is certainly possible that he has not robbed it.

Premise: The occurrence of mental rotation implies longer reaction times to paired figures with greater differences in orientation.

Observation: Longer reaction times to paired figures with greater differences in orientation.

Conclusion: *We do not know whether mental rotation occurred.* More specifically, the observation of longer reaction-times to paired figures with greater differences in rotation, is consistent with the occurrence of mental rotation, but it is certainly possible that mental rotation did not occur.

FIG. 7.6. Parallel arguments vulnerable to the logical error of affirming the consequent, using abstract symbols (top), a commonsense example (middle), and an example involving empirical testing of a theory (bottom). In each case, we are initially uncertain about the truth of the antecedent, and have used observation of a consequent in an attempt to learn about the true status of the antecedent.

outcome). We find that B is not true (we observe a contrary outcome); therefore, A is not true. This standard (and proper) rule of inference is called **modus tollens**, or, **denying the consequent**. Let us look at a simple example. We know that the following implication is true: If a person gives birth to a child, then that person is a woman. Call giving birth to a child A, and being a woman B. Then, A implies B. Now what happens if B is false? In this example, B is false means the person is not a woman. But we then know that this person cannot give birth to a child, that is, we know A to be false. Thus, in this example, we have A implies B, but if B is false, then A is false. We would find that, whatever the example, if A implies B, then finding that B is false guarantees that A is also false. If the implication involves a theory as A, and the theory's predicted experimental outcome as B, then finding that the outcome is not as predicted means that the theory is false (assuming, for the moment, no problems with the experiment).

The use of modus tollens is widespread in science as a preferred form of logic. Because of the logical difficulties with affirming the consequent in order to validate a theory, scientists instead most often use denying the consequent (modus tollens) to invalidate theories. If we cannot increase knowledge by confirming theories, we can at least get rid of misleading ideas by falsifying untrue theories. We use a disconfirmation procedure instead of a confirmation procedure. By testing each theory, we can be left with those theories that have withstood their tests. Generally, theories that pass initial tests get used in further theorizing and in this way tend to be exposed to a number of experimental tests. A theory that stands up to this disconfirmation procedure in a variety of experiments, without being disconfirmed, then represents a current reasonable explanation. Of course, some future research project could find contradictory evidence, or uncover limited conditions of the theory's validity, so any currently favored theory is only seen as a temporary explanation. The body of scientific understanding that develops in this fashion is a cumulation of theories, or explanations, that include statements about unobservable events that have been tested, and to date have not been invalidated. Most theories are therefore only seen as temporary explanations. Even highly successful theories are not treated as immutable facts. There are theories in physics that are extremely useful, and have passed so many experimental tests that they are treated on a day-to-day basis as though they are unchallengeable assumptions. However, there is always the possibility of some new insights and new experimental results that will suggest that the most accepted theories need revision. When dealing with a new science like psychology, with new theories, some skepticism is always desirable.

Thus we have a disconfirmation procedure, a system of testing to see if a theory should be rejected. Whether this system eventually reveals "truth" in some permanent sense is a philosophic question still being debated. Clearly, having a valid logical procedure for dismissing unworthy theories, or disconfirming nonexistent hypothesized internal events, is a good thing. Unfortunately, psychology's necessary use of statistical methods creates a logical problem for the disconfirmation procedure. We next discuss this logical problem, and indicate the kinds of things that good experimenters like Shepard and Metzler do to minimize it.

Statistical Tests of Theories and Modus Tollens. The problem that arises in disconfirming theories concerns the limitations on reaching conclusions when experimental results are not statistically significant. There are two major reasons why, given lack of statistical significance in a test of a relationship between a pair of variables, we refrain from concluding that the variables are not related: First, there is the usual lack of knowledge of the Type II error probability. (The Type II error probability is the probability that we have missed obtaining statistical significance when the two variables are in fact related. This lack of knowledge of the probability of an error can be contrasted with the Type I error probability, which is always known if the statistical assumptions are met, and gives the "license" for drawing specific conclusions from statistically significant results.) Second, there is the ease with which we can obtain a lack of statistical significance. For example, simply increasing random variability by careless or inconsistent procedures could yield a lack of statistical significance, even when the variables are related. Thus, from a lack of statistical significance, we generally conclude only that we have not obtained any evidence of a relationship from the study. Clearly, this is not the same as concluding that there is no relationship.

To use the logic of *modus tollens* in testing a theory (A) that implies some experimental outcome (B), we would have to show that B is false. B usually takes the form of a predicted relationship between variables (e.g., orientation disparity and reaction time, in the Metzler and Shepard study), where we attempt to confirm the relationship through statistical significance. We would therefore have to prove no relationship between the variables to invalidate a theory using *modus tollens*. But, as we have just indicated, when we have a lack of statistical significance in an experiment, we avoid concluding that there is no relationship between the variables. We limit ourselves to the weaker conclusion that there is no evidence that there is a relationship. If we have A implies B (a theory implies a relationship between the variables), we cannot disconfirm the theory by showing a lack of evidence that the variables are related; we would need to be able to show that we know that they are not related. Let us examine this issue in the context of the example of the relationship between gender and having given birth. We know that a person having given birth (A), implies that the person is a woman (B). If we could show that the person is not a woman (denying the consequent), we could conclude that the person did not give birth. But if all that we can determine is that there is a lack of evidence that the person is a woman, we can neither deny nor assert that the person has given birth. If B is in doubt, we do not know the status of A.

In summary, given a theory and its prediction of a relationship between variables, we cannot disconfirm the theory through disconfirmation of its prediction, if the disconfirmation is based on a lack of statistical significance. In addition, because of the error of affirming the consequent, we cannot reach the opposite conclusion, that a theory is correct, when we do obtain statistical significance. This is a dilemma frequently faced by psychologists researching theoretical questions.

Though these difficulties exist, and standard research approaches can be interpreted as ways of minimizing these difficulties, these problems are seldom expressed or directly confronted by psychologists engaged in research. In this text the underlying logic that keeps many of our conclusions tentative is made explicit. This has been done because those experimenters who understand this logic are in a better position to design research that offers less reason for doubts about conclusions. It is in the improved design of research programs that this knowledge will be of benefit. The reason that these logical issues are often obscured is that, in doing research, there are other problems, familiar to all experimenters, that also provide reasons for tentativeness in conclusions after most experiments. Obvious examples are the probabilities of Type I or Type II errors, one of which is always greater than zero. Add to that the fact that although researchers probably have been careful in trying to avoid confounding factors, they can never be sure that they have succeeded. Thus, all researchers share the bottom line that when they experimentally confirm a theoretical statement, or fail to find support for a theory, they rarely, if ever, can be confident that they have removed all reasonable doubt. This, along with being able to specify one or another basis for doubt, is what motivates them to continue to do additional research on the same issue even after experimental confirmations or disconfirmations of their hypotheses.

Circumventing the Logical Difficulties

We have identified two logical problems in evaluating theories concerning some postulated unobservable events: trying to draw conclusions about the confirmation of a theory (or some internal event) in the face of having committed the logical error of affirming the consequent, and trying to reject a theory using lack of statistical significance. The first is a general one affecting most of science, and is handled by a long-term process of tentative acceptance of theories that have successfully run an experimental gauntlet. When a theory's prediction is affirmed, although the theory is not proven to be true, it can be said that the theory is consistent with the evidence. As more and more predictions from the theory are made, if they are all affirmed, the theory begins to look like a good basis for making predictions. If there are many predictive successes, and no failures, the theory begins to be used in discussions as though it is true. However, most researchers keep their eyes on the research literature for any new evidence that casts some doubt on the theory, or that suggests limits on its applications. In summary, long-term accumulation of evidence through affirming the consequent in each study can give a theory tentative credibility as a useful predictor, though the same logic of affirming the consequent would not permit confidence in the theory as a result of a single experiment.

The tentative use of a generally supported theory is maintained even in the face of a small percentage of failures of prediction. The reason is that there can be occasional experimental errors, or chance findings that appear otherwise. For example, a theory can predict a relationship between variables, the relationship can exist, but a Type II statistical error could result in the relationship not being evident in a particular study. Similarly, a Type I error could produce apparent confirmation of a relationship that the theory says should not exist. One use of theories is to tell us when experimental results are suspect. A set of results consistent with a theory might be obtained, along with one inconsistent finding. Before attempting to alter or abandon the otherwise supported theory, an attempt should be made to replicate a single inconsistent finding. (Generally, the danger is in the other direction. That is, enthusiastic supporters of a theory are sometimes too slow in the acceptance of increasing amounts of contrary evidence.)

The second difficulty we identified in evaluating theories is specific to predominantly statistical sciences such as psychology. The problem with statistical sciences is that we are unable to proceed along the lines of simply exposing each theory to the possibility of disconfirmation in each study, and then eliminating from consideration those theories that have their predictions disconfirmed. Most of the more critical predictions from theories are predictions of relationships. To reject a theory it is usually necessary to show that a predicted relationship does not exist. This generally means drawing conclusions from a lack of statistical significance. But we previously discussed the major reasons why we are usually reluctant to take lack of statistical significance as evidence that variables are not related. For these reasons it is usually difficult to use failure of a prediction as a basis for concluding that a theory is false.

The usual way out of this dilemma is to find some conditions under which a theory would predict a relationship, along with minimally altered experimental conditions under which the same theory about an internal event would predict no relationship. Often a number of independent predictions, generated from a single theory, are made for specific variations within the same experimental context. A series of experiments are done, with the experimenter hoping to find the predicted pattern of both statistical significance and lack of statistical significance. Obtaining a different pattern of results could allow a rejection of the theory; obtaining the predicted pattern would offer more articulated support than is obtained with confirmation of a single prediction. To see how this is done, we return to the work of Shepard and Metzler.

Shepard and Metzler's theory states that the increase in reaction time (with increases in orientation disparity between paired figures) is a function of the time taken by mental rotation. This rotation was presumed to take place prior to the subject attempting a match between paired figures. Metzler (1973) decided to control the hypothesized rotation. Instead of presenting both figures simultaneously, she first presented just one figure, and asked the subject to mentally rotate it either clockwise or counterclockwise (in keeping with the experimenter's knowledge of the paired figure to follow).

If the experimenter knew how long it should take the subject to mentally rotate the first figure into agreement with the second figure, the experimenter could delay the appearance of the second figure accordingly. Then, because both figures (the rotated mental image and the physically present second figure) would be identically oriented, the subject's comparison between the figures should begin immediately upon the appearance of the second figure. (The subject would not have to spend any additional time rotating one of the figures.) This should be true no matter what the original orientation disparity, if the correct mental rotation time was allowed. Figure 7.7 illustrates this procedure.

If measured from the appearance of the second figure, the time required to compare the two figures should be the same for all pairs. Thus, a prediction in the altered set of circumstances pictured in Fig. 7.7 would be that there would not be any relationship between initial orientation disparity and reaction time (when reaction time is measured from the appearance of the second stimulus).

This altered experimental context then offers a situation in which the theory now predicts the absence of a relationship between reaction time and original disparity in orientation of paired figures. But there are two important issues to be dealt with before this situation could be practical, and meaningful. To be practical, the experimenter would need some way of determining, or at least reasonably estimating, the time that it would take for a subject to

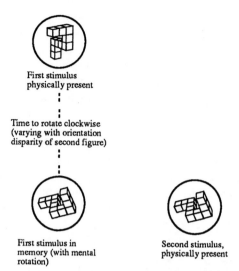

First stimulus
physically present

Time to rotate clockwise
(varying with orientation
disparity of second figure)

First stimulus in
memory (with mental
rotation)

Second stimulus,
physically present

FIG. 7.7.   Steps in Metzler's procedure for removing reaction time differences
in the presence of orientation differences.

mentally rotate a stimulus through a specific number of degrees.
Only then could the second figure be made to appear at the point in
time when the two figures were identically oriented. Second, to be
meaningful here, there needs to be some way of tying this changed
set of experimental conditions to the original experimental situation.
Otherwise, it would appear that in this new situation the subjects are
merely doing what they are told (mentally rotating a figure before
comparing the figures), rather than revealing whether subjects
spontaneously rotate figures mentally.

Both of these issues were dealt with by the device of estimating
each subject's personal slope of increased reaction time for increased
orientation disparity from the first experiment, and then using this
personal slope to determine the delay time for the second stimulus in
the second experiment. Figure 7.4 offered the average slope of all the
subjects. It was possible to construct individual graphs for each
subject, showing the increases in reaction time with increases in
orientation disparity. Although the average slope was about a third
of a second per 20-degree increase in orientation disparity, there
were wide individual differences.

By using each subject's personal slope from the first experiment,
the experimenter made use of what was, theoretically, each subject's
personal rotation-time requirements. The use of these times should
have resulted in the second stimulus being at the same orientation as
the first. This in turn would yield the prediction, in this second

experiment, of no relationship between reaction time and orientation difference. However, there is one factor that could yield a slight relationship. Subjects in the first experiment were not perfectly consistent in their reaction times to each orientation disparity, and larger orientation differences yielded greater trial-to-trial variability in reaction times. Larger variability means that estimates of rotation times for individual subjects were less likely to be accurate for larger orientation differences. As a result, in the second experiment, when the second stimulus appeared, for larger orientation differences the time allowed for rotating the stimulus was likely to be less accurate (than for smaller orientation differences). This in turn meant that the two figures being compared would be less likely to be identically oriented for large orientation disparities, so the subject would spend more time in further mental rotation after the second stimulus appeared. More time for larger orientation differences than for smaller orientation differences would mean that there would still be a slope, although the prediction would be that it would be slight in comparison to the one from the original experiment. In summary, by using each subject's slope from the first experiment to time the delay of the second stimulus, the slope seen in Fig. 7.4 from the first experiment should be replaced in the second experiment with either a zero slope, or at most a slight slope.

On the other hand, if the original slopes were not reflecting spontaneous mental rotation time during the first experiment, they should not be useful in estimating each subject's individual requirements for mental rotation time under instructions to rotate during the second experiment. In fact, if subjects do not need to mentally rotate before making their judgements, it is unlikely that giving them advanced opportunities to rotate would affect their reaction times. Thus, if spontaneous mental rotation did not take place in the original experiment, a reasonably large slope would still be expected in the modified experiment where subjects were instructed to rotate the image. The second, modified, experiment then offered a test of Shepard and Metzler's hypothesis of spontaneous mental rotation in the first (original) experiment.

The results were in line with Shepard and Metzler's predictions: Only a slight slope resulted when the subjects were given rotation times in accordance with their individual slopes. Because these rotation times came from the responses of the subjects in the first experiment where there were no instructions to mentally rotate, there is support here for the idea that the subjects were mentally rotating in the first experiment, even without instructions to do so.

Again, however, the support involves the logical error of affirming the consequent.

A brief summary is presented in Fig. 7.8 of the changes made in the procedures when subjects were given the instructions for mental rotation before seeing the second figure.

Using Interactions to Test Altered Experimental Conditions

There was a design flaw in the second experiment by Metzler, in terms of its relationship to the original experiment by Shepard and Metzler (1971). This design problem offers a precept for research design, when altering experimental conditions in order to produce a varied set of predictions from the theory. When incorporating variations in an experimental paradigm in order to test a theory's predictions of both relationships and lack of relationships, it is desirable to arrange the experiment as a multifactor design with a test of an interaction. In order to comprehend this useful working rule, we need to look more closely at the details of the two Shepard and Metzler experiments.

In the first Shepard and Metzler experiment:

> The beginning of each trial was signaled by a warning tone followed, approximately one half second later, by the visual presentation of the

---

First, one of the two perspective views was presented until the subject actuated a foot switch to signal that he would be able to maintain an adequate mental image of its shape. Thereupon that first perspective view vanished, to be immediately replaced by a uniformly colored field that, according to a predetermined random sequence, was either red or blue. The subject had previously been trained to imagine a clockwise or a counterclockwise rotation of the object depending upon this color. Then after a delay that was predetermined but unknown to the subject, the second perspective view appeared in place of the colored field. The subject was then to actuate a right- or a left-hand switch as rapidly as possible to indicate whether the second object was the same as, or different from, the first.

For each subject and for each angle of rotation, the delay was chosen to be identical to the mean rotation time estimated for that subject and angle from the preceding experiment (in which the stimuli had been presented simultaneously).

FIG. 7.8. Change in procedure in the mental rotation experiment (Metzler, 1973), incorporating instructions for prior mental rotation.

pair of perspective drawings selected for that trial. The subject's instructions were to pull the appropriate lever as quickly as possible to indicate whether the two drawings represented objects of the same or different three-dimensional shape, while keeping errors to a minimum. (Metzler & Shepard, 1974, p. 160)

In the second experiment:

First one of the two perspective views was presented until the subject actuated a foot switch to signal that he would be able to maintain an adequate mental image of its shape. Thereupon that first perspective view vanished . . . . The subject had previously been trained to imagine a clockwise or counterclockwise rotation of the object . . . . Then, after a delay that was predetermined but unknown to the subject, the second perspective view appeared . . . . As before, the subject was then to actuate a right or a left-hand switch as rapidly as possible to indicate whether the second object was the same or different from the first. (Metzler & Shepard, 1974, p. 184)

The flaw in the design is the instruction, in only the second experiment, to stare at the first figure until the subjects could maintain an image of that figure in their minds. Though this was necessary to the task that was to follow, it was a level of experience with one of the stimuli that simply did not exist in the first experiment. The difference in results between the first and second experiment could conceivably be the result not of the mental rotation preceding the appearance of the second figure, but rather of the subjects' more thoroughgoing acquaintence with the first figure as a result of having an initial period of staring at it. This greater acquaintance with the first figure could have permitted immediate comparisons with the second figure, regardless of any orientation disparity. Thus, there is another interpretation possible for the results of the second experiment.

This additional difference between the two experiments then constitutes a confounding factor, an additional difference beyond that desired for the two conditions being compared. One way to handle this would be to do the first experiment with a similar period of staring at the first stimulus, with each subject being given the same instruction to inform the experimenter when an image of the figure's shape could be maintained. At that point the second stimulus could be added, and the reaction time measured from that point, without any intervening instruction for mental rotation. The second experiment could then be done in the same way, with only the intervening mental rotation instruction as the difference.

The rule to be learned from the flaw in this example is to always attempt to maintain only a single difference between two sets of conditions that are being compared. This is generally understood, but the error does occasionally occur when the two sets of conditions are labeled as different experiments. It is usually preferable to combine the conditions as two levels of the same variable, within one experiment. In our example the new variable would have been presence versus absence of rotation instruction. The influence of the new independent variable would be examined in the context of a statistical interaction. That is, we would see if the first independent variable (orientation disparity) is related differently to reaction time, depending on the level of the new variable (presence versus absence of rotation instruction). We now summarize our recommendations and further specify how these two experiments could be combined as a single experiment including a test for an interaction.

The second experiment by Metzler (1973) should have repeated the first experiment by Shepard and Metzler (1971) as part of the second experiment, but with the suggested addition to the first experimental design of a period of staring at the first stimulus of a pair, as described earlier. Then when the new instructions (of the second experiment) requesting mental rotations were added, the rotation instructions would be the only difference between the two conditions. This single difference, a request to mentally rotate or not before the second stimulus appears, would define a second independent variable, the presence or absence of mental rotation instructions. The other independent variable is the set of orientation differences in the stimuli (from 0 to 180 degrees, in nine 20-degree steps), and the dependent variable is still reaction time.

The subjects would be randomly assigned to the two different conditions (rotation request or not). Both groups of subjects would participate in an initial condition with no mental rotation instructions. One group would simply repeat this initial condition. The other group, as its second condition, would be exposed to the variation of the experiment that includes mental rotation instructions. The second condition for both groups of subjects would yield slopes of reaction times over orientation disparities. There would be a single difference between the conditions generating the two slopes, subjects in just one group having been instructed to mentally rotate the first stimulus in memory while waiting for the second stimulus. However, subjects in both conditions would have stared at the first stimulus and been able to "maintain an adequate mental image of its shape" (Metzler & Shepard, 1974, p. 184). The two slopes would be compared (using a test for an interaction of trends, that is, asking if the linear trends for the two slopes are different).

We can be certain that Shepard and Metzler were not unaware of the design problem discussed here. Compromises in perfection of experimental design are often made in response to limitations on subject availability, time constraints, etc. The experiments described here are only part of the series on which the two experimenters collaborated, as well as part of the larger series Shepard conducted with some of his other students. What are seen in this series of experiments are ingenious examples of the most general way of attempting to deal with the logical error of affirming the consequent (although the experimenters may not have described their research program in these terms). In this approach the form of affirming the consequent is maintained in individual experiments, but for many predictions. When results are seen that are in keeping with large numbers of predictions from the theory, it is established as a strong predictor. It becomes subjectively harder to believe that there is a different theory that could make precisely the same predictions. There is thus a subjective experience of being more and more convinced of the validity of the theory, though the weak logical link of affirming the consequent is still there, precluding confidence in the supported explanation.

If there were only one theory possible that could make the successful predictions, the logical problem in affirming the consequent would be bypassed. The reason is that the problem with affirming the consequent is the potential for alternative antecedents leading to the same consequent. If alternative antecedents could somehow be ruled out, affirmation of the consequent would be sufficient for supporting a theory. Of course, it is not possible to rule out all alternative antecedents. The fact that current theorists cannot come up with an alternative explanation does not mean that some future theorist would also fail. But what we have in this approach of numerous successful predictions is an attempt to reduce the expectation that reasonable alternative explanations will be found.

There is another approach to confirming theories that is highly desirable from a logical point of view. It is frequently encountered in the physical sciences, but only rarely used in psychology. This is the making of a quantitative prediction that is so specific that there is usually little probability of an alternative theory predicting precisely the same outcome, and there is only an infinitely small probability of a confirmation stemming from chance. In such a case, confirmation of the theory could be accepted as strong support for the theory, even when it takes the form of affirming the consequent. Metzler's (1973) dissertation offers a rare psychological example of this approach, so we next discuss her use of a quantitative prediction.

Quantitative Predictions

If the theory of mental rotations is correct, larger differences in orientation between paired figures lead to longer reaction times because of the added time taken up by the larger rotations. However, if one figure of an identical pair was oriented 225° clockwise from the other figure, this same figure would be 135° counterclockwise from the other. The time required to make the comparison should then vary with whether the person mentally rotated clockwise or counterclockwise. This issue did not arise in previous experiments because it could reasonably be assumed that people would normally rotate in the shortest direction. What Metzler realized is that the two possible directions of rotation offered another test of the theory.

Metzler decided to arrange the experimental conditions so that if mental rotation was taking place, subjects would, at times, be subtly induced to rotate in the longer direction, thus increasing the reaction time. But such an increase in reaction time would only occur if mental rotation were taking place. (If the reaction time were, for example, a function of the difficulty of viewing two differently oriented figures, the attempted manipulation of a mental rotation that did not even take place would have no effect.) She set up an experiment that was similar to the original experiment where there were no instructions to rotate. The subjects were merely asked to indicate, as quickly as possible, whether the two figures were identical. The important manipulation in this new experiment was the consistent appearance in a block of trials of figures that always had the right-hand figure rotated in one direction from the figure on the left (consistently clockwise or consistently counterclockwise). Thus, if mental rotation was taking place, the subject would find himself (only male subjects were used) consistently rotating a figure in one direction to get the two figures identically oriented.

Specifically, an individual subject saw several right-hand figures all consistently rotated clockwise from the left-hand figure, in the sense of the left-hand figure requiring a smaller angle of travel clockwise (less than 180°) as compared to counterclockwise to align the two figures. It was hoped that this created a set to rotate the left hand figure clockwise only[5]. Then, on one trial, the right hand figure was oriented 225° clockwise from the left hand figure (equivalent to 135° counterclockwise). If the subject followed the induced set, the

---

[5]We are assuming, for simplicity in exposition, that if a subject rotated a figure mentally, it would be the left-hand figure. Of course, everything being said here applies equally well with direction of mental rotation reversed, if the right-hand figure was mentally rotated.

subject would treat this as a pair of figures with a 225-degree disparity, and rotate the left-hand figure 225° clockwise (assuming mental rotation). At other times, under conditions with no induced set to rotate in one direction, the same pair of figures should yield the shorter reaction times of a 135° difference in orientation (the subject rotating the left-hand figure counterclockwise). Of course, if the theory is incorrect, that is, if no mental rotation was spontaneously taking place, no set for unidirectional rotation would be established by the procedure. The stimuli should then be responded to similarly with or without the attempt to induce a unidirectional set.

In summary, there were the two different conditions of presentation of a 135° orientation disparity: one series of trials defined by a set for directional consistency inducing a 225-degree rotation, though a 135° rotation was possible, and one set of trials where no directional consistency was induced, so use of the shorter rotation (135°) was assumed. If mental rotation was taking place, these two conditions should yield two distinctly different reaction times. If the subject were not mentally rotating, no set for a particular direction of rotation could be established by the consistency manipulation, so the two figures, being equally disparate under both set and no set conditions, should result in a more or less consistent reaction time without regard to the condition.

Thus, the experimental procedure was expanded to include sometimes having a set to rotate in one direction. If the instances when subjects were set to rotate the long way yielded longer reaction times than when not so set, then the actual occurrence of rotation would be implied. (Recall there were no instructions to rotate in this experiment.) But the most important part of this experiment was the possibility of making a specific quantitative prediction about the reaction times with the induced set. This prediction and its importance are discussed next.

It is possible to extrapolate the reaction times to a point for a 225° disparity, using the average times observed at 0°, 45°, 90°, 135°, and 180° of disparity between paired figures. Assuming a linear increase in reaction-time from 0° to 225°, the empirical slope from 0° to 180° could be used to project the expected reaction times at 225°. In this way one could determine what the expected reaction times would be when people mentally rotated the long way. This value offered a specific predicted average reaction time. Metzler combined the data of all of the eight subjects in this experiment, normalizing the data (transforming it so that the reaction-time distributions for the different subjects would all fit on the same graph with a common intercept and slope). Transformed to a common slope that summarized the data for all eight subjects up through 180°, the slope was extended to see where the average reaction time for 225° should be. However, there was a complication in using this point on the graph as the predicted reaction time for all subjects in the condition with the induced set.

It is difficult to know whether or not a set has been successfully established. A reasonable assumption is that on some trials there has been a set induced to go the long way, and that on others the subject simply went the shortest way. If this were the case, the distribution of reaction times for those trials on which the experimenter attempted to induce a set would have a bimodal distribution, with modes appropriate to both 135° and 225°. This could be contrasted with the distribution of reaction times for the same orientation disparity when no attempt was made to induce a set, which should yield a unimodal distribution at the point appropriate for 135°. Using the transformed data so that all of the data could be placed on the same graph, Metzler and Shepard (1974) drew up the graph shown here as Fig. 7.9, which pictures the various distributions.

The X axis in Fig. 7.9 indicates the degree of orientation discrepancy between paired figures, varying from 0° to 180° in 45° steps,

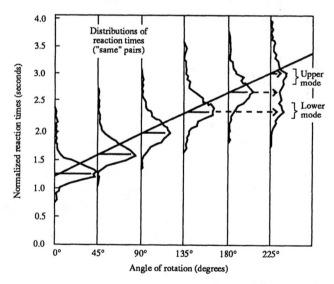

FIG. 7.9. Distributions of reaction times at various disparities in rotation for paired stimuli. Data are normalized and averaged over subjects. The diagonal line cutting across the distributions connects the means of the different distributions through 180°, but is a projection at 225°. From Metzler and Shepard (1974). Copyright 1974 Lawrence Erlbaum Associates. Reprinted by permission.

and including the theoretical 225° difference (which is physically identical to a 135° difference). To understand Fig. 7.9, it is helpful to turn one of the distributions so that its X axis is horizontal, as has been done in Fig. 7.10, which offers the distribution above the 90-degree point on the X axis in Fig. 7.9.

Fig. 7.10 offers the distribution of reaction times when there was a 90° disparity in orientation. However, the distribution has been turned for Fig. 7.10 so that it is upright, as in most such displays. Figure 7.10 shows a mode (point of greatest frequency) at approximately 2 sec. That is, 2 sec. was the most frequently occurring reaction time to a 90° orientation disparity. The distribution in Fig. 7.10 is drawn so that the reaction times increase to the left. (The same distribution in Fig. 7.9 increases upward.) Note that the distribution is skewed to the left—that is, instead of being perfectly symmetrical, it slants to the left, with a slightly extended (and higher) tail on the left side. When a distribution is skewed in the direction of higher scores, the mean is higher than the mode. (In this drawing, then, the mean is to the left of the mode.) The approximate mean is marked in Fig. 7.10 by a brief diagonal line cutting through the curve. This brief diagonal line is in approximately the same position as the line that has been extended in Fig. 7.9 so that it connects the means of all of the distributions.

Return now to Fig. 7.9. Each point on the X axis in Fig. 7.9 has a single mode, just like the distribution in Fig. 7.10, with the exception of the 225° point, which is the test case. The location of two modes at the 225° point offers a test of the theory. The two modes suggest two overlapping distributions. The means of the other points have all been connected to produce a theoretical point for the mean of the 225-degree distribution. The question is whether one of the two implicit distributions at the X axis point of 225° does have a mean appropriate to a mental rotation of 225°. Visual inspection suggests that this is the case for the upper distribution. The lower distribution in the bimodal distribution is located at about the same point as the 135-degree distribution, as can be seen by comparing the actual

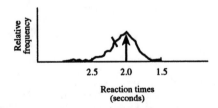

FIG. 7.10. Distribution above 90° on the X axis in Fig. 7.9.

distribution of responses at the X axis point of 135°, which is connected by a dotted arrow to the lower bimodal distribution at the X axis point of 225°.

Another way of looking at the bimodal distribution above the 225° point on the X axis is to recognize an actual mean value for the complete bimodal distribution. This appears to be at that point on the X axis that is close to that found for the 180-degree rotation (at the middle arrow between the two modal points). But that area in the bimodal distribution shows a minimum between two modes rather than a maximum point for the distribution. That is, relatively few reaction times were at the point appropriate for a 180° rotation. Most reaction times (as seen by the two modal points) were either close to the mode for a 225° rotation, or close to the mode for a 135° rotation. This suggests that a directional set for rotation was at times operating, but was not always operating.

The fact that a bimodal distribution was created is consistent with the idea of a set to rotate that was only effective at times. The finding that the two modal points of the distribution are at the values expected for 135° and 225° disparity in rotation is further support for this interpretation. It would be hard to justify this finding of a bimodal distribution with one mode at 225° as coincidence, and it would not be easy to come up with an alternative theory predicting these highly specific results. With numerical outcomes, there are usually so many possibilities that any one outcome has a low probability on a purely chance basis. When a theory successfully predicts a low-probability outcome (such as one numerical value among an infinity of possible values), it is interpreted as strong support for the theory.

By contrast, if a theory successfully predicts a highly probable outcome, the success can be attributed to a lucky guess. One does not have to have special powers to predict rain in Seattle. One can say that one's dream gave the information, or one's aching toe. The theory can be sublimely irrelevant, and the prediction correct, with a highly probable event. But when a theory successfully predicts an otherwise unexpected (rare) event, there is adequate reason to attend to the theory and take it seriously. The less likely a specific outcome (without the implications of the theory), the more impressive is the theory that can predict the specific outcome.

Quantitative predictions generally involve many alternative outcomes, sometimes infinitely many alternatives. Any one outcome is then, by definition, unlikely. It is like predicting the winner of a lottery. If a person could predict the one winner, this would offer good indirect evidence that the person had some useful predictive information. In the Metzler example the prediction of one of two modes at the extrapolated position for 225° was not one prediction from an infinity of alternative outcomes, because the measurement was not planned to be so exacting as to allow highly specific different alternative outcomes to be recognized. In fact, confirmation was by visual inspection, not by some highly accurate measurement procedure. But even allowing for only approximate measurement, the successful quantitative prediction in this example offered what would otherwise have had to have been amazing coincidence, were it not for the theory.

Shepard and Metzler advanced a theory of mental rotation that generated predictions of relationships between surrogate variables (orientation disparity and reaction times). They offered successful manipulations of conditions that affected the relationships in ways that are consistent with their theory. Such related predictions in support of hypothesized internal events are common in good psychological research. Metzler's (1973) prediction of a modal point at the 225° orientation offers an unusual example (for psychology) of the successful testing of a prediction of a quantitative outcome. Though uncommon in psychology, quantitative predictions are desirable because they reduce the concerns about alternative theories that could predict the same outcomes, blunting the criticism for the use of the logic of affirming the consequent.

CHAPTER SUMMARY

The words *theory* and *hypothesis* were discussed in regard to their common meaning as an explanation. Research psychologists use these terms when offering explanations for relationships between variables. Most psychological theories refer to unobservable processes or events, which have been inferred from what can be directly observed. A common term for these inferred unobservable events is intervening variable. Sometimes the term explanatory construct is used, with an identical meaning. Any unseen event that is used to make sense out of observed behavior can be called an intervening variable or explanatory construct. Another term frequently encountered is hypothetical construct, which has the added meaning of some unobservable physical change. For example, the theory might suggest a particular neurological or biochemical change that underlies forgetting. If it has not been successfully recorded, but merely hypothesized as existing, it would be called a hypothetical construct. On the other hand, if the explanation involved, say, a loss of interest in the topic as the basis of forgetting, this would be an intervening variable or an explanatory construct. The explanation of a loss of interest, or any other suggested intervening variable, offers some mechanism for the observed phenomenon (of forgetting), but it is an explanation that is clearly speculative and requires some strong, well-articulated inferences from controlled observation, before it becomes more than speculation. This latter point is equally true of hypothetical constructs.

Two examples were given of experiments in which variables were manipulated and measured for the purpose of learning about internal psychological events (the work of Posner and colleagues, and of Shepard and Metzler). The overt variables used to learn about events that can not be directly observed were identified as surrogate variables. The point was made that theory-driven research most often requires the use of surrogate variables. This was contrasted with research where the variables that are manipulated are of interest in themselves. This is usually the case in applied research, where in the pursuit of learning what works best, we merely wish to know how one variable influences another, but not necessarily the principles underlying the relationship. To this end we discussed an example of airplane instrument panel research, looking at what features of letters would make them easier to identify, and compared this research with the Posner et al. (1969) study of internal coding processes, where letters were again used as the experimental stimuli, with aspects of the letters varied, but this time clearly as surrogate variables.

We briefly mentioned that early in psychology's history introspection was used, with subjects who were usually carefully trained to become sensitive to internal processes, in an attempt to deal with the difficult problem of learning what takes place within human beings when perceiving, or problem solving, or making decisions. This approach was abandoned with the conclusion that much of human cognition is not reliably accessible to consciousness. In its place we have inference through research relying on surrogate variables.

We then discussed the logic of the inferential processes that are most often encountered in doing research in experimental psychology. We identified a logical error in the process, called affirming the consequent. In the context of attempts at experimental confirmations, affirming the consequent involves first showing that the theory would predict a particular experimental outcome, then doing the experiment and showing that the theory successfully predicted the outcome. In bare logical form, this involves the assumption that A (a theory) implies B (an experimental outcome), and then attempting to validate the truth of A (the theory) by affirming B (producing the predicted experimental outcome). In fact, B can be true, without A being true. A implies B, does not mean that the truth of B implies the truth of A. What we have, after using the logic of affirming the consequent to bolster a theory, is the conclusion that the experimental results are consistent with the theory, not proof of the theory's validity.

We then discussed a logically correct avenue to at least disconfirming theories, called *modus tollens*, which involves the opposite of the procedure with affirming the consequent. With *modus tollens*, instead of affirming the consequent (showing that the consequent is true), we deny the consequent, disconfirm it, show that it is not true. This in turn, when it can be done, logically implies that the antecedent is not true. If the antecedent is the theory A, and the consequent is the predicted experimental outcome B, then we show the prediction to be false (B is not true), and this, logically, proves that the theory which made the prediction (A), is not true.

Theories are put through this filter, tested in this way, and theories that survive many tests begin to appear to be reliable predictors. They take on the status of theories that are treated as true, although we always understand that any one such theory could fail some future test and be replaced by a subsequent, better theory.

There is a special problem in the use of denying the consequent in statistical sciences, like psychology. The problem, discussed at length in this chapter, stems from the difficulty of using the results of statistical tests to show that a prediction from a theory is false. Most predictions from theories are predictions of relationships (between variables). We usually have to discover that a predicted relationship is not supported by the evidence, through a lack of statistical significance. A lack of statistical significance usually cannot convince us that something is not true. We merely conclude that there is no evidence of a relationship. Lack of statistical significance is not sufficiently strong to permit us to say we have denied the consequent. Thus, we usually cannot disprove a theory by failing to obtain a theoretical prediction.

All of this would appear to suggest a very pessimistic conclusion, that one cannot determine the truth or falsity of theories. This is a true picture when all we have is a single instance of affirming the consequent (obtaining the predicted result), or a single instance of not obtaining the predicted result. A single finding does not take us very far. However, an accumulation of supportive findings can give a theory some status that is short of certification as to its truth, but permits us to speak of the theory as well supported. This would involve many predictions from the theory being affirmed, few or no contrary findings, and competing theories failing by comparison.

We have also discussed the importance of testing interactions where there are both predictions of relationships and predictions of no relationships, with both types of predictions being confirmed. This too adds support to a theory. It was suggested that, in general, variations in experimental procedures are often best done in the context of tests for statistical interactions, rather than as separate experiments.

Finally, we discussed the importance of making quantitative predictions, where this is possible. The advantage is the likely elimination of alternative theories as explanations, when one prediction out of an infinity of possible predictions is successfully made. If alternative explanations can be eliminated, the major problem with affirming the consequent (using successful prediction to prove a theory) is overcome. Quantitative predictions in psychology are infrequent. Metzler's successful quantitative prediction was discussed. Although she did not provide one out of an infinity of outcomes for the prediction, it was nonetheless an impressive example of a quantitative prediction, with an outcome that would be highly unlikely and very difficult to predict without the theory of mental rotation.

NEW WORDS AND PHRASES IN CHAPTER 7

affirming the consequent
denying the consequent
hypotheses
hypothetical construct
intervening variable
introspection
modus tollens
surrogate variables
theories

CHAPTER 8

Detection, Discrimination, and the Theory of Signal Detection

There are many situations in which it is important to identify conditions that aid in the successful detection of stimuli. One example is the design of radar screens. Another is the design of instrument panels on airplanes, which are usually crowded, and so have to be designed so that some critical signals stand out. Psychologists and human factors engineers are employed to test conditions that maximize successful detection. Psychologists are also interested in the more general questions about what conditions are good and bad for detection, and what are the quantitative relationships between stimulus changes and detectability (suggesting laws of perception).

An early detection question that was asked, which gave birth to a classic form of research, is the question of how weak a stimulus can be and still be detected. A similar question, concerning discrimination, is, how slight a difference between two stimuli can permit the two stimuli to be distinguished? Questions about **detection** and **discrimination** have become somewhat more sophisticated with time, but the two basic forms of research the initial questions suggested are still recognizable in current research designs.

Questions of detectability are generally examined in a large series of trials, in which a specified stimulus is either present or absent on each trial. On each trial a subject is asked to decide whether or not the stimulus is present. The question is how much of the stimulus is required for the subject to hear it, or see it, or taste it, etc. The minimal amount of energy required for detection is called the **absolute threshold**. One of the classical psychophysical procedures for measuring the absolute threshold is the **method of limits.**

In the method of limits the experimenter presents a series of stimuli that vary in intensity, to establish the absolute threshold for that stimulus dimension, under specified conditions. For example, a spot of light might be presented on a screen, or a tone over earphones, in either case with intensity varied over trials. The stimuli could begin with a level of intensity clearly above threshold, with each following presentation being lower in intensity, until the subject said that it was no longer present. This would define the limit of that series. If the series began that way, that is, with an above-threshold stimulus, the next series would begin with a stimulus that was clearly below threshold, with the stimulus intensity increased at each trial until it was detected. This would define the limit of that series. The two different sets, descending and ascending, would alternate for several trials. The first series could be either ascending or descending. Table 8.1 illustrates the procedure, with the minus signs representing the subject saying no (not detected) and the plus signs saying that it was detected.

The threshold for a series is defined as the point between the two values involving a shift from detected to not detected, or vice versa. Thus in series 1, 2, and 4 in Table 8.1, the threshold was 9.5. Clearly, though, it was not always 9.5. The average thresholds for the ascending series, and also for the descending series, are each calculated, and then these two values are averaged to yield the absolute threshold.

The use of both ascending and descending series is incorporated in the method of limits as a control for two different types of errors, habituation and anticipation. Consider what happens in a descending series. The series starts with a signal that is clearly above threshold and signal intensity is decreased each time the observer makes a "yes" response. On any descending series, then, the observer makes a number of "yes" responses in a row. Habituation stems from habit, and an error of habituation in a descending series is one in which the observer does not detect the signal but makes a "yes" response because he has made the same response several times in succession. The observer might have to fail to detect the signal twice before changing the oft-repeated "yes" response to a "no" response. Errors of habituation in a descending series would tend to produce values that underestimate the true threshold; habituation errors would tend to overestimate the true threshold in an ascending series.

TABLE 8.1.   **Determination of the Absolute Threshold with the Method of Limits**[a]

Intensity of the Stimulus (Scale Units)	Series					
	Down 1	Up 2	Down 3	Up 4	Down 5	Up 6
15	+					
14	+					
13	+		+		+	
12	+		+		+	
11	+	+	+	+	+	+
10	+	+	−	+	+	+
9	−	−	−	−	+	+
8	−	−		−	−	−
7	−				−	−
6		−				−
5		−				
4						
Threshold for series	9.5	9.5	10.5	9.5	8.5	8.5

Mean descending threshold $\dfrac{9.5 + 10.5 + 8.5}{3} = 9.5$

Mean ascending threshold $\dfrac{9.5 + 9.5 + 8.5}{3} = 9.17$

Mean absolute threshold = 9.3 units

[a] A plus means the subject said the stimulus was present, and minus implies absent. The units would refer to the dimension being varied, such as decibels.

Anticipation errors are the exact opposite of habituation errors. Having made the same "yes" response several times in a row, an observer anticipates a change and makes a "no" response in a descending series even though he detects the signal. The effects of anticipation errors work in the opposite direction to that of habituation errors, underestimating thresholds in ascending series and overestimating in descending series.

The two types of errors just described are equated by using ascending and descending series and defining the threshold as the average of the two types of series. Note that in Table 8.1 the ascending series did not always begin at the same low point, and the descending series did not always begin at the same high point. This is used to discourage the subject from anticipating when the stimulus will change from detectable to not detectable.

Another design method for controlling anticipation and habituation errors is randomization, and that is the technique used in another classic psychophysical method for measuring absolute thresholds, the **method of constant stimuli**. The procedure in the method of constant stimuli starts off in a manner similar to that of the method of limits, that is, some ascending and descending trials to obtain a rough initial approximation of threshold. Once this is done, a number of stimuli slightly above threshold and slightly below threshold are selected for further testing. An important criterion in selecting the stimuli is that none are included that are detected or not detected correctly 100% of the time. All of the stimuli selected are in the range of uncertainty, sometimes receiving a "yes" response and sometimes a "no" response. These stimuli that bracket the true threshold are then presented in random order for a large number of trials, and threshold is defined as the stimulus value that is detected 50% of the time.

We have noted earlier that the absolute threshold is used to determine the level of intensity required for a stimulus to be detected, and we showed how this can be done with either the method of limits or the method of constant stimuli. When we wish to determine just how small a difference between two levels of intensity can be detected, we obtain a **difference threshold**. The question being asked when obtaining a difference threshold, is whether or not two specific stimuli on a single dimension can be distinguished. That is, can one stimulus be discriminated from the other? The psychophysical question is how small a difference on some dimension can be discerned by the subject. In the classic tests of the difference threshold, the subject views (or hears, or feels) two stimuli, one a **standard**, and the other a **comparison stimulus** in which intensity is systematically varied. The subject is asked to state whether the comparison stimulus is brighter or duller, or louder or softer, or heavier or lighter, etc. than the standard. The smallest difference between the standard and the comparison that permits correct responding at better than a chance level is called the difference threshold. The difference threshold is also called the **just noticeable difference**, which is usually abbreviated as the **JND**.

WEBER'S LAW

The JND is generally measured for a variety of levels of the standard stimulus. A consistent mathematical function, called **Weber's law**, has been obtained in experiments of this type. The mathematical function describes the relationship between the level of the standard stimulus, and the smallest increase in the comparison stimulus that can be discriminated by a subject as different than the standard.

The different JND values for the different levels of standard stimuli are all identified, and usually graphed, with the JND values on the Y axis and the standard stimulus values on the X axis. A typical set of JND values, graphed in this fashion, is seen in Fig. 8.1.

The mathematical law is stated in Equation 1, which offers a concise way of stating that the minimum value for a noticeable change in the stimulus, ΔI, is a proportional constant of the stimulus.

$$\Delta I = KI \tag{8.1}$$

In Equation 8.1, Δ is the Greek letter delta, I is the magnitude (intensity) of the standard stimulus (in decibels, if sound intensity is being examined, or foot-candles if light, etc.), and ΔI is the size of the JND. The most important term in Equation 8.1 is the constant K, constant that is, for any one type of stimulus. It varies with the type of stimulus, for example, being different for sound than for light. From Equation 8.1 K can be seen to be equal to $\Delta I/I$, and is known as the Weber fraction. Weber's law states that K is a constant proportion (a constant fraction) of any standard stimulus (the intensity of which is symbolized as I). Thus, KI in Equation 8.1 refers to a constant proportion of the particular standard stimulus, which is the amount by which an equivalent stimulus must be increased in order for its difference from the standard to be detected. The fact that the same proportionate increase is needed as the intensity I of the standard stimulus is changed is the heart of Weber's law.

A more succinct verbal statement of Weber's law is the following: *For every level of intensity of a particular stimulus (called the standard stimulus), the same proportionate increase in intensity in a comparison stimulus is required for the comparison stimulus to be perceived as just noticeably more intense than the standard.* If speaking of a stimulus dimension other than intensity, say the

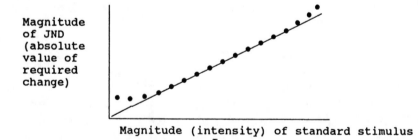

FIG. 8.1. Illustration of Weber's law, and slight deviations from the theoretical function. The straight line is the theoretical function, and the points are the usually observed values. The deviations from the theoretical function are generally found only at the extremes of the standard stimulus.

frequency of a tone, the statement would be the following: *For every frequency level of a standard tone, the same proportionate increase in frequency in a comparison tone is required for the comparison tone to be perceived as just noticeably higher than the standard.* The theoretical form of the law is seen in the straight line in Fig. 8.1. The dots in Fig. 8.1, which represent typical experimental results, suggest where some divergence from the equation is generally found. Specifically, the mathematical predictions understate the magnitude of the JND at the extremes of the standard stimulus, the discrepancies being greatest at the low end, but the predictions tend to be accurate for the middle range of many stimulus dimensions.

Let us look at an example. Tone frequency (psychologically, pitch) is measured in hertz (Hz). Assume that there is an interest in the smallest increase in tone frequency that can be discriminated. This value will differ with the particular tone frequency being tested, but Weber's law states that the proportion by which a comparison stimulus needs to be increased for detection of a difference in tone can be expected to remain constant. To test this, standard tones of varying frequencies would be used. Comparison stimuli would be systematically compared with each standard stimulus, to find the smallest fractional change above the standard that could be recognized as different. For example, we could use a 500 Hz tone as the standard. We might find that a difference would not be detected until the comparison was changed to at least 515 Hz. The absolute difference of 15 Hz is 3% of 500—that is, $KI = .03(500) = 15$—so that .03 is the Weber fraction for tone frequency, when a 500 Hz tone is being used as the standard stimulus. If instead we used a standard stimulus of 1000 Hz, Weber's law of a constant fraction (proportion) of needed increase implies that we would find that the comparison stimulus would have to be at least 1030 Hz, in order to be recognized as different. The reason is that K is a constant, still .03, so we would have $KI = .03(1000) = 30$. Thus an increase of at least 30 Hz would be needed.

We now summarize our hypothetical case. With the particular source of a tone that was used, a JND at 500 Hz was 15, and at 1000 Hz was 30. In Fig. 8.1, above 500 Hz on the X axis, there would be a dot placed 15 units high on the Y axis. At 1000 Hz on the X axis, there would be a dot placed 30 units high on the Y axis. The JND was seen to increase with the level of the standard (in the example from 15 to 30), but the proportionate increase (the Weber fraction of .03 in the example) remained the same. The theoretical straight line in Fig. 8.1 is a graphic expression of the constancy of the Weber fraction.

Empirically, we find that for most of the range of a stimulus dimension the same proportionate increase is required for a just noticeable difference in the stimulus.

NONSENSORY FACTORS AND BIAS

It is important to realize that a response in a simple detection task is a function of both the observer's sensitivity and other nonsensory factors such as habituation and anticipation. Classical psychophysical methods like the method of limits and the method of constant stimuli attempt to deal with nonsensory factors by experimental design techniques such as equating ascending and descending series and randomization. However, such classic psychophysical methods provide no means for separating the contributions of sensory and nonsensory factors from performance data.

For example, one subject might be inclined to state that there is a difference between two stimuli when less than certain, whereas another might wait until absolutely certain to state that there is a difference. Similarly, in detection experiments, a particular subject might be more inclined to say that a stimulus is present when he or she is uncertain, but another subject might be more inclined to say the stimulus was not present when uncertain.

In the early years of this research such personality or motivational factors were assumed to be nuisance factors. Various corrections were introduced for personal differences in tendencies to say "yes" or "no," but motivational factors did not receive critical scrutiny, because it was assumed that, primarily, what was being measured was individual sensitivity to a particular stimulus. It was believed that for any stimulus dimension, and an individual subject, an absolute threshold could be defined.

Increasingly, psychologists have become aware of the importance of nonsensory factors in determining when a subject is willing to state that a particular stimulus is present (or absent), and that this could change the apparent absolute threshold. That is, with the usual measurement procedures, the obtained absolute threshold probably reflects both sensory and nonsensory factors. Errors of habituation and anticipation mentioned earlier are examples of nonsensory factors. Personality and motivational factors are other examples of nonsensory influences in detection experiments. Regarding motivational influences, compare the likelihood of a radar operator awakening the commanding officer to report an unidentified object on the screen, under two different conditions: (a) The soldier is on night duty in a busy war zone with frequent attacks, and (b) the soldier is on night duty on a post where there have not been any attacks in the last year, and no enemy forces are assumed to be in the area. Let us call a stimulus that warrants sounding an alarm a *signal*. The question confronting the soldier observer is whether the blip on the screen should be reported as a signal.

In Condition (a) the soldier would have reason to assume that the probability of an attack is high, and in Condition (b) that it is low. It is reasonable to assume that the soldier's willingness to state that he has detected a signal will depend in part on the probability of the signal. Second, in reporting a signal, or failing to report a signal, there can be different costs. In the example, the assumption was made that the commanding officer had to be awakened. This is a situation in which the cost of a false alarm (reporting that a signal was present when no signal was presented) could be considered, by the individual soldier, to be high, but so could his having missed a true presence of the enemy. Suppose instead that the soldier had to alert some spotter planes that were already in the sky. Here the cost of a false alarm would be less, and so the observer might more readily report seeing a signal. In other words, the different costs and benefits of reporting and not reporting a signal could play a part in an observer's willingness to report having detected a signal. Research has now clearly established the importance of the costs and benefits of incorrect and correct responses, as well as the importance of signal probability, in an observer's willingness to report a signal.

These examples assume important decisions with high potential costs for errors. However, research has shown that even in less dramatic experimental situations of the investigation of detection thresholds, a subject's willingness to say that a signal is present varies with the subject's assumption that the signal will be present frequently or rarely. Willingness to report the presence of the signal has also been shown to decrease if the subject believes that falsely reporting a signal will be considered foolish. Willingness to report the signal increases if a subject believes that the critical thing is never to miss a signal when present, even if it means sometimes erroneously reporting the signal as present. Thus, the subject's assumptions, beliefs, and attitudes could change the apparent absolute threshold.

A subject's tendency to be more willing to report presence, or more willing to report absence, of the signal is called **bias**. In the early 1950s mathematical techniques were developed that permitted differentiating the subject's bias from the subject's physiological sensitivity to the stimulus. The techniques for separately estimating bias and the subjective strength of a stimulus were developed in the context of the theory of signal detection (Green & Swets, 1974; Swets, 1973; Swets, Tanner & Birdsall, 1961). The theory of signal detection is briefly outlined here, along with the method for the computation of subjective strength of the stimulus, independent of the influence of bias. When we discuss bias in signal detection we refer to it as the response criterion or more succinctly as the **criterion** because it is a value of internal stimulation that the observer selects for separating "yes" and "no" responses. The criterion is affected by variables such as probability of a signal and expected gains and losses from decisions. The criterion is not affected by signal strength.

Signal detection theory is described here in the context of a detection task. It is useful to precede these discussions with a description of the four types of outcome that are possible in a detection task.

TYPES OF OUTCOME IN THE DETECTION SITUATION

Given a simple detection task (a signal is sometimes present, and sometimes not present), there are two possible conditions, signal present, or not present, and two possible responses, "yes" (the signal is present) or "no" (the signal is not present). There are consequently four different possibilities, summarized in the two-by-two table presented here as Fig. 8.2.

SIGNAL DETECTION THEORY

In **signal detection theory** the intended dependent variable is the subject's internal level of subjective stimulation, given a particular

RESPONSE

		Yes	No
S I G N	Present	Hit	Miss
A L	Absent	False alarm	Correct rejection

FIG. 8.2. Potential outcomes of a trial in a signal detection experiment. There are four possible outcomes within the table: A **hit**, a **false alarm**, a **miss**, and a **correct rejection**. The two outcomes that are used in computing a measure of subjective sensitivity to the signal are the hit rate and the false alarm rate.

stimulus. What are actually measured are the relative frequencies of two of the outcomes pictured in Fig. 8.2. Then the mathematical model of signal detection uses the relative frequencies (of hits and false alarms) to yield a value that, theoretically, is identified as each subject's subjective level of stimulation. This internal level of stimulation is called **d prime (d')**. An important point about d', is that the theory suggests a way in which d' can be assessed independently of criterion, where the criterion is symbolized as β (the Greek letter **beta**). In the case of studies of detection, the value of d' has become a frequent dependent variable, with variations in stimulus level as one of the independent variables.

Assume that an experimenter wishes to determine the subjective strength of a signal, a brief flash of light, presented in the center of a screen that is otherwise uniformly illuminated. In practice, this is a case of determining the value of d' for a specific signal intensity. On each of a long series of trials the subject is asked whether the signal is present. It is only present on some of the trials. In signal detection research, it is common to let the subjects know the percentage of times that the signal will be present. (Changes in expectation of signal frequency lead to changes in criterion. Controlling the subject's expectation is a way of applying some degree of control to the subject's criterion.)

The observer's visual nervous system is always active, with neural firings occurring all of the time, at some relatively low level, even without the addition of an external signal. These internal neural firings are random, so there are random changes in the level of internal stimulation. Of course, external stimulation has a critical effect on internal neural firings. Within an experiment, to keep internal random firings as similar as possible for all subjects, the screen on which the signal is to appear is itself always lit at some constant level. This offers a constant source of light that continuously affects internal random firings. Some spontaneous internal firing still occurs, however, resulting in some variation in the internal subjective state, even with the constant external stimulus. Thus the internal state will vary, but to some small degree, around some mean value that is primarily determined by the level of constant external stimulation. The level of stimulation, without the presence of the signal, is called *noise*. In this context, noise consists of the constant level of light in the room and on the screen, plus internal random firings. When the signal is added, there should be a momentary increase in the level of internal stimulation. The question is whether this increase is large enough to be detected by the subject.

The lack of a truly constant internal state, that is, the expected presence of some variation in the level of noise from internal random firings, makes it necessary to think of the level of internal stimulation under the noise condition as a distribution (rather than a single value). Fig. 8.3 offers a theoretical picture of the noise distribution, with the mean symbolized as μ_n and the standard deviation symbolized as σ_n.

Recall that a standard deviation σ is simply the square root of the average squared difference from the mean. The standard deviation σ briefly discussed in chapter 5, offers a measure of the degree to which the relative frequencies of values on an X axis vary (among a set of n observations). A defining formula is:

$$\sigma = \sqrt{\frac{\Sigma(X - \mu)^2}{n}} \tag{8.2}$$

The use of standard deviations to mark off the points on the X axis in Fig. 8.3 suggests the use of z scores in discussing levels of noise, or levels of signal plus noise. As seen later, it is the use of z scores that makes it possible to determine the distance between the signal and noise distributions, and from this to establish a measure of d', the subjective intensity of a stimulus. This is accomplished by the use of tables of normal probabilities, which, given an assumption of

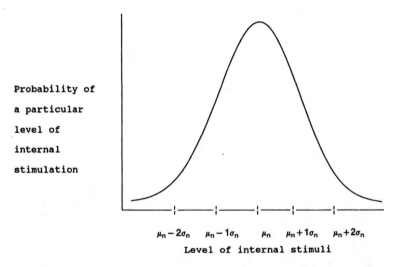

FIG. 8.3. Distribution of internal stimulation under the noise condition; μ_n and σ_n are the mean and standard deviation of the noise distribution, respectively.

a normal distribution of the scores, permits converting relative frequencies (interpreted as probabilities) to z scores. To understand how this is done, it is helpful to pause and illustrate the way in which the table of normal probabilities is used in conjunction with z scores.

z scores and the Table of Normal Probabilities

In chapter 5 the formula for a z-score transformation of a difference between two means was given in Equation 5.1. Here, the formula for a z-score transformation of an individual score is presented as Equation 8.3.

$$z = \frac{X - \mu}{\sigma} \tag{8.3}$$

As suggested by Equation 8.3, a z score, also called a standard score, reexpresses a score X in terms of its distance from the mean of the scores, μ, using the standard deviation, σ, as the unit of measurement. When z scores are used in conjunction with the table of normal probabilities, the mean of the distribution is assumed to be zero (the mean of a distribution where all the scores have been transformed to z scores is always zero). Given a mean of zero, a score's z-score equivalent is precisely its distance from the mean in terms of numbers of standard deviations. Thus a z score indicates a score's distance from the mean of the distribution in numbers of standard deviations (as suggested by the units on the X axis in Fig. 8.3).

Appendix B contains a table of probabilities under the normal curve. It is important to be able to use that table in order to understand how the value of d' is obtained. For any z score listed in the first column of the table, column 2 indicates the probability of occurrence for any value between the mean and that particular z score. The table begins with a z score of zero, so the first z score offers the distance from the mean to itself, yielding a second column that also begins with a zero. If a z score of 0.50 (which is half a standard deviation from the mean) is selected from column 1 of the table, the adjacent probability value, in column two, is found to be .1915, which means that approximately 19% of the scores in the distribution are within the interval from the mean of the distribution to a z score of .50. We can also ask about the percentage of *all* the scores that are surpassed by individual z scores. The mean of the distribution, in the exact center of the distribution, where $z = 0$, represents a value surpassing 50% of all the scores. A z score of 0.5

represents a value surpassing approximately 69% of all the scores
(.50 + .1915 = .6915).

No negative values are listed in the table, so, for example, one
would not find a -0.50 in the first column. Because the normal
distribution is symmetrical, the positive values are all that are
needed. For example, assume that there was a z score of − 1, and one
wished to know the probability of obtaining a score between the
mean and a z score of − 1. Looking at z = 1 in the first column, one
would find .3413 in the second column. Because the distribution is
symmetric, the area between the mean and + 1 also gives the area
between the mean and − 1.

In computing d′, it is usually necessary to go from a probability to
a z score. For example, suppose you were told that there is a z score
that marks an area under the curve, such that scores between the
mean and that point only occur 37% of the time. You would look
through the second column, locate the closest value to .37, which
would be .3708, and then on the same row you would shift to the first
column, and recognize that the answer is z = 1.13. However, from
the question, you would not know whether the answer should be z =
+ 1.13 or z = − 1.13, because there was no indication of whether this
value was to be found above or below the mean.

Suppose that you were told that the value that was desired was the
z score equivalent to a score that is only surpassed 10% of the time
(the point dividing the top .10 from the rest). The upper half (.50) of
the normal probability distribution would contain this z value.
Subtracting the top .10 from the rest of the upper half (.50 − .10)
yields .40 as the proportion between the mean and the upper .10 of
the distribution. Thus, .40 is the value to be sought in the second
column. The closest four-place value is .3997, with an adjacent
z-score value of 1.28.

If you were looking for the z-score equivalent of a value that
surpasses 22% of the scores, this would be found in the bottom half
of the distribution, and thus would be a minus z score. Look at Fig.
8.4 to make it easier to follow the remainder of the discussion in this
paragraph.

The bottom half of the distribution contains 50% of the scores, and
the lowest 22% of these scores would end (have its highest value) at
the point where the upper 28% of the bottom half begins
(50−22=28). That is, the point on the X axis that is equivalent to the
top of the lowest 22% is also equivalent to the point on the X axis
dividing 28% of the highest scores in the bottom half of the distribution from the lowest 22%. Thus the score topping the lowest 22%
is separated from the center of the distribution (the mean) by 28% of

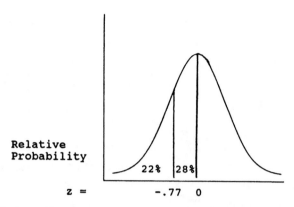

Relative
Probability

22% 28%

z =   -.77 0

FIG. 8.4. Illustration of the identification of a minus z score.

the scores. To find that point in the table of normal probabilities, one would search for .28 in the second column, where it would be found adjacent to 0.77. The answer to the question of which z score is equivalent to the value that surpasses 22% of the scores is z = −.77.

Picturing the Noise and Signal-Plus-Noise Distributions on the Same Axis

Assume for the moment that the presence of a very brief signal raises the level of subjective internal stimulation by some small amount. If the level of internal stimulation is defined by a distribution, the presence of a momentary signal briefly displaces the whole noise distribution slightly to the right. The two distributions, one for noise and one for signal plus noise, are seen in Fig. 8.5.

The theory of signal detection assumes that the subject selects

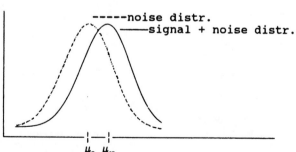

-----noise distr.
———signal + noise distr.

Probability of a

particular level of

internal stimulation

μ_n μ_{sn}
Level of internal stimulation

FIG. 8.5. The two juxtaposed distributions of internal stimulation under the conditions of noise, and signal plus noise.

some value on the continuum of subjective internal stimulation such that values below that point are considered by the observer to be only noise, whereas values above that value are considered to indicate the presence of the signal. This value is called the *criterion*, and is identified in Fig. 8.6, where it is centrally located between the two distributions.

The criterion value (in Fig. 8.6) changes with the factors that influence bias, though the distance between the two means remains the same, even if the criterion point is moved. The theory offers ways to compute the subject's criterion, β, and we show how that is done later in this chapter. The distance between the means of the noise and signal plus noise distributions is the measure of subjective stimulation, d'.

Using the Proportions of Hits and False Alarms to Compute d'

Assume a series of detection trials, with a single signal that is sometimes present and sometimes not present. As seen in Fig. 8.2,

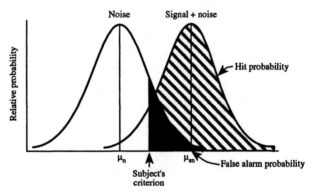

FIG. 8.6. Two theoretical distributions of subjective internal stimulation in response to just noise (the left-hand distribution) and to signal plus noise (the right-hand distribution). The hit probabilities are the proportion of times that a signal is presented and recognized as present. This is the area within the signal-plus-noise distribution that is above the point of the subject's criterion (mostly filled with downward sloping parallel diagonal lines, plus a small dark area). The false alarms are the times that only noise is presented, but the subject indicates that a signal is present. The proportion of the times that this occurs in the absence of a signal is signified by a dark area. It is located under the noise curve in the area to the right of the subject's criterion. Relative probability on the Y axis is interpreted in terms of relative frequency.

presented earlier in this chapter, there are four possible trial outcomes. The hits and false alarms are used to compute d'.

The curves in Fig. 8.6 are filled in with diagonal lines and a shaded area to respectively represent the hit and false alarm probabilities. The proportion of the trials on which a signal is detected offers the proportion of hits. The proportion of the trials on which no signal is present but is nonetheless reported as present offers the proportion of false alarms. (The proportion of the time that an event occurs is a definition of the event's probability.) Assume that, in the particular experiment, for a particular subject, the subject scored 92% hits. (For example, the signal could have been presented 500 times, and reported as present 460 of those times.) Assume further that the subject had 14% false alarms. (For example, noise alone could have been presented 500 times, but mistaken for a signal 70 of those times.) These areas are approximately represented in the drawing in Fig. 8.6. The purpose of the drawing is to give some intuitive understanding of the theory. However, the actual computations require the use of the table of normal probabilites, rather than the use of a graph.

The distance between the mean of the noise distribution and the mean of the signal-plus-noise distributon is computed in terms of z score units. Notice that in Fig. 8.6, the subject's criterion is somewhere between the two means. If the distance of each distribution's mean from the criterion value could be computed, the two distances could be added together to offer d', the distance between the two means. Because one mean is above the criterion and the other is below it (in this illustration), one of the z scores will be a minus. The formula that is used takes this into account, as seen in Equation 8.4, where the two z scores appear to be subtracted one from the other, but the double minus results in addition.

$$d' = z_n - z_{sn} \qquad (8.4)$$

In calculating d', the first thing that is done is that the table of normal probabilites is consulted to obtain the z score value for the point in Fig. 8.6 identified as the subject's criterion. For example, assume that the subject's false alarm rate was found to be 14%. Assuming these errors all occurred at the highest values of noise, this means that the top 14% of the noise distribution was misidentified as a signal. Thus, the subject's criterion would appear to have been placed at the point on the noise distribution dividing the top 14% from the rest of the distribution. The second column of the table of normal probabilities offers percentages (probabilities) between the mean and particular z scores, so only concerns 50% of the distribution. Removing 14% from 50 leaves 36% between the mean and the z score. Looking for the closest value to .36 in column 2, the value .3599 can be identified with an adjacent z score of 1.08. It identifies the position of the subject's criterion value on the noise distribution. This implies that the criterion value is 1.08 standard deviations above the mean of the noise distribution.

Next, the location of the signal-plus-noise distribution's mean is obtained. Assume that the hit probability was found to be 92%. This means that the criterion value extends 92% of the way down through the signal plus noise distribution. That is, 92% of the sampled events in the signal-plus-noise distribution surpassed the critical value. Recognizing that we only deal with half the distribution when using the table of normal probabilities, we subtract .50 from .92, yielding .42. This suggests that the criterion value is at a point below the mean of the signal-plus-noise distribution that is separated from the mean by 42% of the scores. The closest value to 42% in column 2 is .4207, adjacent to a z score of 1.41. However, because this z score is below the mean of its distribution, the answer is $z = -1.41$.

It is now possible to compute d' for this situation, using Equation 8.4.

$$d' = 1.08 - (-1.41)$$

$$d' = 2.49$$

Looking at Equation 8.4 for this situation in terms of Fig. 8.6, one mean is 1.08 standard deviations below the criterion value, and the other mean is 1.41 standard deviations above the criterion value, yielding a distance between the two means of $d' = 2.49$ standard deviations.

It is also possible for the value of d' to be zero, implying that the subject is not sensitive to the signal, and cannot differentiate it from noise. Like most z scores, d' is not expected to be greater than 3, and in practical situations where detection can be difficult, d' varies between 0 and slightly over 1, approaching 2 only rarely.

The Criterion

The criterion is the value of internal stimulation that the observer selects for saying that she or he detected a signal. Values of internal stimulation greater than the criterion (to the right in Fig. 8.6) receive "yes" responses (hits and false alarms), and values less than the criterion (to the left) receive "no" responses (correct rejections and misses). How does the observer adopt a particular criterion? According to the theory of signal detection, if signals are presented half the time, and there is no difference in payoffs for hits versus costs for false alarms, an observer sets the criterion to maximize the number of correct responses. Note that the criterion in Fig. 8.6 cuts through both signal-plus-noise and noise distributions. A way of expressing the criterion is in terms of a likelihood ratio: Given a particular level of internal stimulation, what is the likelihood that it is derived from a signal plus noise trial or from a noise-only trial? The actual values used in the likelihood ratio are the ordinates (Y axes) of the signal-plus-noise and noise distributions at the point of the criterion. This ratio is symbolized as

$$\beta = \frac{f(SN)}{f(N)} \tag{8.5}$$

The value of the ordinate of the distribution varies with z, being greatest with a z score of 0 (the center of the distribution) and smaller with larger values of z (positive or negative). Appendix B contains ordinate values for given values of z, as Column 3 in the table of normal probabilities.

Figure 8.7 shows three graphs representing three different criterion settings for the same signal (the distance between the means of the noise and signal plus noise distributions, d', is the same for all three graphs). The dark areas in Fig. 8.7 represent the false alarm probabilities, the left side of the dark edge demarcating the criterion. Given that signals are presented on half of the trials and that there is no difference between the benefit of a hit and the cost of a false alarm, observers are likely to set the criterion at the point where the two distributions intersect. This case is shown in the top graph, Criterion 1. At the point of intersection the ordinates of the two distributions have the same value. A criterion placed there has equal ordinates in both distributions. Equation 8.5, with equal values in the numerator and denominator, yields a beta value (a criterion value) of 1.

Criterion 2 depicts a case in which there is bias favoring the noise distribution. The criterion value is moved to the left. Its ordinate, in the middle of the noise distribution, is higher than in the signal-plus-noise distribution where it lies in the left tail. With $f(N)$ higher than $f(SN)$ (in Equation 8.5), the value of beta (the criterion) is less than 1. Note that with Criterion 2 the observer is responding "yes" a lot more than with Criterion 1. Consequently, the observer makes more hits than with Criterion 1 but also makes many more false

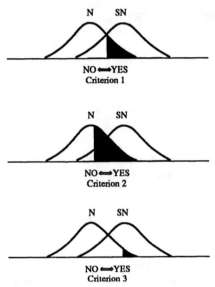

FIG. 8.7. Illustration of three different criteria, where the dark area shows false alarm probabilities, its left-hand edge demarcating the criterion. Figure from *Woodworth & Schlossberg's Experimental Psychology*, Third Edition, edited by J. W. Kling and Lorrin A. Riggs, copyright 1971 by Holt, Rinehart and Winston, Inc., reprinted by permission of the publisher.

alarms. This is seen in the large dark area in Criterion 2 of Fig. 8.7. A situation resulting in Criterion 2 would be one in which the signal was presented 90% of the time or where the benefit of a hit was much higher than the cost of a false alarm.

Criterion 3 shows a case where the ordinate of the criterion in the signal-plus-noise distribution has a higher value than the ordinate in the noise distribution, producing a criterion value greater than unity. It takes a more intense signal (a stimulus value higher on the X axis) to obtain a "yes" response. In this case the observer is making more "no" responses, which leads to both fewer hits and fewer false alarms (the latter represented by the relatively small dark area). Criterion 3 corresponds to a situation in which the signal was presented on only 10% of the trials or in which the cost of a false alarm was much higher than the benefit of a hit.

Now let us do an actual calculation. In the example used for calculating d', Fig. 8.6, the probability of a false alarm was .14 and the probability of a hit .92. In our calculation of d' we found that the criterion was 1.08 standard deviation units above the mean of the noise distribution and 1.41 standard deviations below the mean of the signal plus noise distribution. Now consult Appendix B for determining the values of the ordinates for z scores of 1.08 and

−1.41. Remember that the normal distribution is symmetrical so that the ordinate for a z score of 1.41 is the same as that for a z score of −1.41. Looking in Appendix B we find that the ordinate for a z score of 1.08 is .2227 and for a z score of −1.41 is .1476. It is now possible to compute beta for this situation using Equation 8.5. Dividing .1476 [f(SN)] by .2227 [f(N)], we identify a criterion (a beta value) of 0.663. This criterion, being less than 1, lies to the left of the point of intersection of the two distributions. In our example the observer is making more "yes" responses. That is, there is bias in favor of "yes" responses. If the probability of a signal was .50, then the theory suggests that the observer is valuing "yes" responses over "no" responses.

An Alternative Measure of the Criterion

Beta is the standard measure of criterion, and most studies using signal detection report criterion in terms of β. In a recent paper, MacMillan and Creelman (1990) compared several different measures of criterion and concluded that a criterion location measure, **c**, is favored on a number of practical and theoretical grounds. A major practical advantage is that the calculation of c uses the same information required for computing d', and does not require reading ordinate values. The value of c is calculated as the average of the transformed hit and false alarm rates, using the same z-score values that are used to calculate d'. However we add the two z scores in calculating c, whereas we subtracted them in calculating d'. The formula for c is given in Equation 8.6.[6]

$$c = .5(z_n + z_{sn}) \tag{8.6}$$

We next use the same data to calculate c as we used for calculating d' and β, that is, $z_{sn} = -1.41$ and $z_n = 1.08$.

$$
\begin{aligned}
c &= .5[1.08 + (-1.41)] \\
&= .5(1.08 - 1.41) \\
&= .5(-0.33) \\
&= -0.165
\end{aligned}
$$

---

[6]MacMillan and Creelman (1991), in a new text on Signal Detection Theory, reverse the usual definition of z, calling minus values plus values and plus values minus values. This forces them to make the small change in Equation 8.6 of using -0.5 as a coefficient rather than 0.5. It also forces them to reverse the order of z_n and z_{sn} in Equation 8.4 for the computation of d'. (Their z value reversal has been identified in the literature by Irwin [1992].)

At this point it helps to refer back to Fig. 8.7 which shows three criterion values. Remember that β was 1 at the intersection of the two distributions, less than 1 when to the left of the point of intersection, and greater than 1 in locations to the right of the intersection. Thus, c has a value of zero at the point of intersection, is negative at locations to the left of the point of intersection, and is positive at locations to the right of the point of intersection. The value of c in the example, -0.165, indicates that the criterion is to the left of the point of intersection. This was also indicated previously with a fractional value of β. An important property of c is that it is directly related to β, as seen in Equation 8.7.

$$\ln \beta = cd' \tag{8.7}$$

We can use Equation 8.7 (having first used Equation 8.6 to compute c) to calculate the value of β without using the ratio of normal ordinates. Equation 8.7 gives the natural logarithm of β as equal to c multiplied by d'. In the earlier example, d' was 2.49 and c was -0.165. Multiplying those two values gives $\ln \beta = -0.4109$. Therefore we can find β by taking the antilogarithm of 0.4109, which is 0.663, the same value of β that we found earlier by taking the ratio of the normal ordinates.

Discrimination

Discrimination performance is analyzed similarly to detection performance. Instead of a noise and a signal-plus-noise distribution, the theory posits two distributions, one for each stimulus. If the stimuli are similar (difficult to discriminate), the two distributions overlap a good deal. If they are dissimilar, the distributions are far apart, and d' is large. When we speak of similarity and dissimilarity of distributions, although we acknowledge that the objective features of the stimuli are relevant to extent of dissimilarity, we are at bottom dealing with the subject's awareness of these differences. We could have widely divergent stimuli, and an insensitive subject (leading to a relatively low d'), or slight differences and an acute observer (leading to a relatively high value of d'). Thus, in the final analysis, d' reflects the subject's awareness of similarity and difference. The other determinant of performance, for discrimination as for detection, is the criterion chosen by the observer. It is important to remember that d' is independent of criterion. However, in discrimination, as in detection, overall performance is a function of both sensory and nonsensory factors.

The Receiver Operating Characteristic, the ROC Curve

Performance data in detection experiments are typically plotted in graphs relating the probability of hits and the probability of false alarms. The data plotted in the graphs are called **receiver operating characteristic (ROC)** curves or **isosensitivity** curves. There are three theoretical curves and a diagonal plotted in Fig. 8.8. Note that probability of a hit is shown on the Y axis and probability of a false alarm on the X axis. Consider first the meaning of the diagonal. The diagonal represents no detection ($d' = 0$). Any points (data) on that line would imply zero sensitivity, so let us assume that the signal is too faint for detection. Then, only bias could influence variations in the proportions of hits and false alarms.

Assume a refusal to admit to any presence of a signal—that is, assume responses of "no signal" on each trial. In this situation there would be zero hits and zero false alarms. This would contribute a data point at the lower left of Fig. 8.8, the bottom left-hand end of the diagonal line.

Next, consider a situation in which there is a strong bias against saying the signal is present (a very high criterion with regard to internal stimuli), specifically, one in which there is a 10% chance of randomly occurring "yes" responses. Assume equal frequency of signal presence and signal absence in the situation. Remember again, in this example, that the subject cannot in fact perceive any external signals (zero detection). With these assumptions, approximately 10% of the time that external signals occur they will be reported as present (10% hits), and, similarly, 10% false alarms (saying "yes" in the absence of a signal). The diagonal is also the line on which the proportions of hits is equal to the proportions of false alarms. This point of 10% hits and 10% false alarms is located at the lower left of Fig. 8.8, on the diagonal, at .1 on both axes.

The middle point on the diagonal would represent the case in which the subject was as likely to emit a "yes" as a "no" response, but, because it is on the diagonal, we would still assume that there is no actual perception, no sensitivity to the signal.

The value of d' is greater than zero when performance is located above the diagonal, where the probability of a hit is greater than the probability of a false alarm. The distance from the diagonal to the particular receiver operating characteristic curve that represents actual performance in the situation is a measure of d'. As can be seen, the values of d' for the three curves shown in Fig. 8.8 increase with the distance from the diagonal. Each receiver operating char-

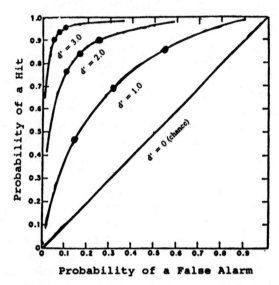

FIG. 8.8. Different isosensitivity functions associated with different stimulus magnitudes. Each curve represents a particular stimulus magnitude, and the distance from the diagonal represents d', an indication of sensitivity to the stimulus (increasing to the upper left). Different points on any one curve represent different criteria, and therefore different amounts of bias. The same three bias points are represented on each of the three curves: $\beta = 0.5$, 1.0, and 2.0, reading from the top down. The diagonal line, with $d' = 0$, represents zero sensitivity. Bias points taken from Figure 7 in Swets (1973). Copyright 1973 by the American Association for the Advancement of Science. Printed by permission.

acteristic curve is generated with one signal of a specific magnitude, and d' remains constant throughout the curve (hence the term isosensitivity curve). The different points on each of the curves represent different criterion settings manipulated by varying signal probability, or costs and benefits of different responses. The same three criterion settings (bias points) are shown on each curve: $\beta = 0.5$, 1.0, and 2.0, reading from the top down, on each curve.

The main advantage offered by signal detection theory over classic psychophysical methods lies in the separation of sensory and nonsensory contributions to performance. The ROC curves shown in Fig. 8.8 are theoretical curves predicted by signal detection theory for three signals of different strengths over a wide range of signal probabilities. What actually happens in signal detection experiments? Do observers adjust criteria according to signal probability even when the signal strength remains constant, so that d' would be expected to remain constant?

Data obtained in an auditory detection experiment are shown in Fig. 8.9.

The data for Fig. 8.9 were obtained with the same signal magnitude over a large number of trials, and d' was found to remain constant at 0.85. The solid line is a theoretical curve, and data are represented by open circles. Each open circle represents data from a block of trials with a different signal probability: .1, .3, .5, .7, and .9. The data points show that the observer adjusted the criterion according to signal probability and that sensitivity (d') remained constant over the range of signal probabilities investigated. The insert in Fig. 8.9 shows noise and signal-plus-noise distributions separated by 0.85 of a standard deviation (d' is constructed from z scores, which are standard deviation units, and in the example $d' = 0.85$). The dashed vertical lines represent the five criterion settings resulting in the five data points lying about the theoretical ROC curve. The variations in data points due to changes in criterion on any one ROC curve, and different curves caused by differences in sensitivity, illustrate the independence of criterion (β or c) and sensitivity (d').

Despite the major advantages to using d', a drawback is that it is

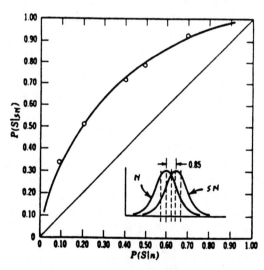

FIG. 8.9. ROC curve for detection of an auditory signal in noise. The empirical data points were obtained by varying the signal presentation probabilities: .1, .3, .5, .7, and .9. The theoretical curve is for $d' = 0.85$, and the data points can be seen to fit closely, suggesting that d' remained constant despite changes in criteria with changes in signal probability. From Green and Swets (1974). Reprinted by permission.

difficult to develop an intuitive understanding of d'. In an appendix to this chapter, we offer a measure, **percentage nonoverlap**, along with some practical examples, to help clarify the relationship between detection accuracy and d'.

Other Applications of Signal Detection Theory

The original applications of signal detection theory concerned either detection or discrimination of threshold stimuli, focusing on auditory or visual stimuli. However, the model can be, and has been, applied to other situations. Within the area of experimental psychology, signal detection has been used, for example, to analyze recognition memory (e.g., Kintsch, 1967; Parks, 1966). In recognition memory tasks, subjects receive a series of to-be-remembered items in a learning or acquisition phase. In a subsequent test phase these familiar items are presented along with items of the same class that were not presented in the acquisition phase, and subjects are asked to judge each item as "old" (seen in the first phase) or "new" (not shown in the first phase). The application of signal detection to this paradigm requires the assumption of a dimension of familiarity. The signal-plus-noise and noise distributions are conceived of as being positioned on that dimension. Old items are represented by the signal-plus-noise distribution, which is displaced upward on the familiarity dimension above the noise distribution (new items).

Signal detection theory has also been found to be useful as a guide or stimulus to interesting analyses and research in other areas of psychology. For example, clinical psychologists have used signal detection methodology in pain assessment (for reviews of this literature see Grossberg & Grant, 1978; Irwin & Whitehead, 1991). The advantage of signal detection over classical methods in this case stems from the ability to separate the influence of sensory and nonsensory factors. If a patient were to complain of heightened sensitivity to painful stimuli, signal detection analyses would permit us to distinguish between an actual increase in the patient's sensitivity (d')—increased pain—and an increase in the patient's willingness to report a stimulus as painful (β or c)—willingness to complain.

More generally, John Swets argued persuasively that signal detection theory offers an excellent system of analysis for evaluating the accuracy of diagnostic systems (Swets, 1986, 1988). This useage extends the range of application of signal detection theory far beyond the laboratory environment in which it was developed.

A diagnostic system is any system from which a diagnosis or decision is made after reviewing evidence or data. A radiologist looks at a mammogram (breast x-ray) and must diagnose (decide) whether a lesion is benign or malignant. Weather forecasters look at a variety of indices such as barometric pressure, temperature, and dew point and diagnose whether it will rain or not. Materials testers use an ultrasound technique on an airplane wing and diagnose whether the airplane wing has a crack in it or not. Many diagnostic systems, such as the ones just indicated, attempt to discriminate between one event or class of events and all other events or event classes (e.g., malignant or not; rain or not; crack or not). Swets argued that the performances of these diagnostic systems can be examined in the context of signal detection theory. The to-be-searched-for event (malignant, rain, crack) is called a signal, and other events (benign, no rain, no crack) are called noise. As with other detection and discrimination situations, both noise and signal-plus-noise can be characterized by normal distributions along a common axis.

Diagnostic systems are commonly evaluated with a simple measure of their accuracy, such as percent correct. As Swets pointed out, a simple percent correct measure reflects (a) the discriminability of the two event classes, (b) relative frequencies of the event classes (rain is common in Seattle, WA but rare in Phoenix, AZ), and (c) the tendency of the particular diagnostic system to choose one event class or the other. These three factors (discriminability, relative frequency, and choice tendency) cannot be separated out with a simple percent correct measure of accuracy. A preferable method for evaluating the accuracy of a diagnostic system would provide a measure of accuracy that is based on discriminability of the event classes and that is independent of the relative frequency of the events and the tendency of the system to choose one alternative over the other. This is exactly what signal detection theory accomplishes with the separate indices of sensitivity (d') and criterion (β or c). In the example of mammogram lesions, discriminability between the two events (malignant or benign) would be reflected in d', and any bias in choosing one alternative over the other would be reflected in c.

CHAPTER SUMMARY

The chapter opened with a discussion of thresholds for detection and discrimination. How faint a stimulus can be detected? The minimal stimulus permitting detection is called an absolute threshold. The method of limits was described for establishing an absolute threshold, along with the method of constant stimuli. The second question asked was, how slight a difference can exist between two stimuli that would still permit their being discriminated one from the other? The minimal difference between two stimuli permitting discrimination is called a difference threshold, which is also called a just noticable difference (a JND).

Weber's function describes the relationship between the level of a standard stimulus, and the smallest increase in a comparison stimulus that can be discriminated. Weber's law states that a constant percentage of increase is required in a comparison stimulus, whatever the intensity of the standard stimulus, in order for the difference in the intensity to be recognized. Weber's law tends to hold for all but extreme stimulus values, the largest discrepancies found at very low intensities.

It has been recognized that there are differences in a subject's willingness to report a faint stimulus. Within the theory of signal detection this is called bias. Bias can affect the apparent absolute threshold, suggesting that the absolute threshold is not strictly a measure of the subject's sensitivity. Signal detection theory provides a way of separately estimating bias (β) and the subjective strength of a stimulus (d'). A second, equivalent way of estimating bias, symbolized as c, was also described. The hit and false alarm rates are used in all these estimation procedures.

The theory assumes that the subjective strength of the stimulus is best represented by a distribution. It is further assumed that in the absence of the stimulus there is still some neural excitation, which has its own average level and variance. Thus, two distributions are assumed, one labeled noise, and the other labeled signal plus noise; the latter is displaced from the former, on the same X axis. The subject elects some criterion value on the X axis, and when the stimulus conditions exceed the criterion value, the subject reports the stimulus as present. The hits and false alarms (successful detections and erroneous reports that the signal is present) yield information on the location of the means of the noise and signal-plus-noise distributions, relative to the subject's criterion value. In conjunction with information in the table of normal probabilities, the hit and false alarm rates permit a determination of the distance between the two distributions in standard deviation units, identified as d'. A distance of zero implies no detectability ($d' = 0$).

The data in signal detection theory experiments are often summarized in ROC curves (receiver operating characteristics), which have false alarm probabilities (percentages) on the X axis, and hit probabilities on the Y axis. A straight-line curve takes the form of a diagonal through the graph when there is no success in detection. As the value of d' increases, indicating greater sensitivity to the stimulus, the ROC curves are placed further toward the upper left of the graph, with greater curvature. Bias is represented by specific points on the curves. Bias can be affected by a subject's assumptions about relative payoffs of hits, and costs of false alarms, as well as by expectation about the relative frequency of trials containing a signal. To control bias in experiments it is common for the subjects to be told the relative frequency with which the signal will occur. Payoffs and costs are often manipulated in experiments.

The theory of signal detection has been invoked for explanatory purposes in a wide variety of paradigms in psychology, including recognition memory, pain assessment, and diagnostic success. A diagnostic system is any system in which a diagnosis or decision is made following a review of evidence or data. An example was offered of radiologists examining mammograms and diagnosing whether lesions are malignant or benign. The advantage of a signal detection analysis over other measures of accuracy in evaluation of diagnostic systems is that d' is affected by the discriminability of the two events (malignant or benign lesions), but not by the relative probabilities of the two events or the tendency or willingness of the decision maker to respond one way or the other.

NEW WORDS, PHRASES, AND SYMBOLS IN CHAPTER 8

absolute threshold
beta (β)
bias
c
comparison stimulus
criterion
cumulative frequency distribution
d'
difference threshold
isosensitivity curve
just noticeable difference (jnd)
method of constant stimuli
method of limits
percentage nonoverlap
receiver operating characteristics (ROC curves)
standard stimulus
Weber's law

APPENDIX

Percent Nonoverlap: A Way of Thinking About Detection and Discrimination Accuracy and the Value of d'

We defined d' as the distance between the means of the noise and signal plus noise distributions. We also indicated that the distance from an ROC curve to the diagonal was another measure of d'. The advantage of d' over other measures of accuracy is that it is a pure measure of detectibility or discriminability. Other measures, such as the probability of a hit, are not independent of decision criteria. Although this presents a strong advantage to using d', there is also a drawback. We all have a good intuitive understanding of percentage measures. When we say that an observer detected 95% of the signals, we know that, given 100 signals, the observer detected 95 of them. We can also relate this value meaningfully to other percentages of accuracy. We don't have as good an intuitive understanding of d'. If $d' = 1.0$, we know that one standard deviation unit separates the means of the signal-plus-noise and noise distributions. But how large is a difference of 1 standard deviation? Is it a modest difference or a huge difference? How can we think about it?

Jacob Cohen (1988) introduced the use of **percentage nonoverlap** to increase our understanding of the magnitude of the difference between means of two normal distributions in standard deviation units. We use percentage nonoverlap to help clarify our understanding of d'.

As was stated previously, when $d' = 0$ there is no detection. When $d' = 0$ there is no distance between the means of the signal-plus-noise and noise distributions. Another way of saying this is that the two distributions are 100% overlapped; there is 0% nonoverlap. As d' takes on values greater than zero, some portion of the area covered by both distributions combined will not be overlapped. The percentage nonoverlap provides us with a way of thinking about discriminability and values of d'.

Consider a d' value of 0.50. The means of the signal-plus-noise and noise distributions are separated by 0.50 standard deviation. This means that a portion of the area covered by both distributions does not overlap. Cohen (1988, Table 2.2.1) listed the percentage nonoverlap between two normal distributions separated by distances from 0 to 4 standard deviation units. Referring to his table, we find that 33% of the combined area is nonoverlapped when $d' = 0.50$. That is, 33% of the area covered by the signal-plus-noise and noise distributions combined is either noise or signal plus noise, but not both. For a d' of 1, the percentage of nonoverlap is 55.4%, and for a d'

of 2, the value is 81.1%. As stated in the section on the computation of d', in the majority of difficult detection and discrimination situations, obtained d' values will range from 0 to slightly over 1. So for practical purposes we want to develop an intuitive understanding of d' values within that range.

Cohen (1988) listed some practical examples of differences between two normally distributed populations in terms of standard deviation units, and we use these to clarify the value of d'. Cohen suggested that a difference of 0.50 standard deviation unit is one that is "visible to the naked eye." By that, he meant that in the course of normal experience, we would notice this difference. For $d' = 0.50$ we found that there was 33% nonoverlap in the area covered by the two distributions combined. How large is this difference? Consider the heights of American females aged 14 and 18. Some girls stop growing by age 14 whereas others continue to grow for a few years. On the average, then, 18-year-old females are taller than 14-year-old females. If we consider 14-year-old and 18-year-old females as two normally distributed populations, what would be the average difference in height between the two populations? The actual average difference in height between 14- and 18-year-old females is 1 inch, with a population standard deviation of 2 inches. Therefore, the distance between the means of the two distributions is 0.50 standard deviation unit. Detection or discrimination performance yielding a d' value of 0.50 is equivalent to what you would find if you tried to distinguish between random groups of 14-year-old and 18-year-old females, having only their heights as the basis for deciding which group was which. Even though a d' value of 0.50 sounds small, there is a discriminable difference between the average heights of 14- and 18-year-old females. This gives us a reference point with which to consider a d' value of 0.50.

Now consider an example where $d' = 0.80$, where the percentage nonoverlap in the area covered by the two distributions combined is approaching 50%. A value of 0.80 is the d' difference associated with the mean difference in height between 13- and 18-year-old females. Successful discrimination between the two groups, just on the basis of height, would not be difficult. Consider one other example with a difference of 0.80 standard deviation units. Imagine trying to discriminate between two sets of IQ scores, one from people with PhDs, and the other from an unselected group of first-year college students.

These examples give us some concrete ways to think about d'. Even though d' values below 1 sound very small, d' values of 0.50 and above represent clearly discriminable differences generating performance that is well above chance. Discrimination and detection accuracy is expected to be very high when d' exceeds a value of 1.

CHAPTER 9

Evolution of a Theoretical Construct: Changes in the Construct of Iconic Memory over 30 Years of Research

This chapter's main focus is the very first half second or so after a visual stimulus is presented to a subject. There is some sort of visual persistence beyond the duration of the physically present stimulus. Neisser (1967) was the first to apply the term **icon** or **iconic memory** to visual persistence. His initial description of the icon as a transient visual memory is as follows:

> . . . visual input can be briefly stored in some medium which is subject to very rapid decay. Before it has decayed, information can be read from this medium just as if the stimulus were still active. We can be equally certain that this storage is in some sense a "visual image." (pp. 18–19)

The development of the notion of iconic memory offers an instructive example of the research-driven evolution of a psychological construct.

That the effects of a visual stimulus can persist beyond the duration of the physical stimulus is easily demonstrated with the phenomena of afterimages. The initial theoretical construct of iconic memory bore a strong resemblance to a visual afterimage. Afterimages are images that occur in response to a visual stimulus. They commence after the offset of the visual stimulus, often last for several seconds, and, given high-energy stimulation, can continue for several minutes.

An afterimage can retain the colors of the original stimulus (**positive afterimage,**) or the colors might be reversed in the afterimage, like in a photographic negative (**negative afterimage**). The conditions favoring the production of afterimages are either brief exposures to intense or very bright stimuli, in otherwise dark conditions (a quick glance at the setting sun), or prolonged exposures to colored stimuli in well-lighted conditions (fixating steadily on a colored object for 60 sec and then averting the eyes to a gray or white background). With brief stimuli the first afterimage is generally positive (same colors as the visual stimulus), and when only a single stimulus is presented, the positive afterimage is difficult to distinguish from the initial image or sensation (Sperling, 1960).

Afterimages offer an analogue for the construct of iconic memory in demonstrating a type of visual persistence that endures beyond the duration of the physical stimulus and that fades over time. The question asked in this chapter on iconic memory is not whether visual persistence occurs, since such persistence is well documented through the phenomena of afterimages. Rather, the question is, does visual persistence occur in the absence of intense stimulation or prolonged exposure, under conditions in which there is no subjective experience of afterimages? It is precisely under these conditions that the persistence of iconic memory has been inferred. The indirect evidence from perceptual research has continued to support the notion of poststimulus persistence with ordinary visual stimuli. Attempting to understand precisely what iconic memory is, what is stored, and in what form, has been a major goal of this research. Some of this research is reviewed in the following sections.

THE SPERLING PARADIGM

George Sperling (1960), in a now classic experiment, asked the question, how many things can we comprehend in a single glance? He presented arrays of letters and numbers (alphanumeric arrays) such as shown in Fig. 9.1, which contains 12 items, for very brief durations (e.g., 50 msec). Achieving such precise control over stim-

$$7 \; I \; V \; F$$
$$X \; L \; 5 \; 3$$
$$B \; 4 \; W \; 7$$

FIG. 9.1. Stimulus display in the Sperling experiment. From Sperling (1960). Reprinted by permission.

ulus duration requires a special apparatus called a **tachistoscope**, which permits the cycled presentation of visual fields with millisecond exposures. Sperling manipulated number of items in the array and found that performance was perfect when the number of items was equal to or less than four. Further increases in the number of items led to an average recall of around 4.3 items. This condition is called **whole report**, as subjects attempted recall of the whole array.

Sperling's subjects reported that they seemed to have a lot of information available immediately after the array, but that the information was lost rapidly in the course of recall (writing down letters and numbers in blank grids). This gave Sperling the notion of a rapidly decaying visual trace. He decided to investigate this possibility using a **partial report** technique. Array presentation was as before but one of three tones (high, middle, or low pitch) was presented immediately after array offset. Subjects were instructed to report only the items in the row of the array designated by the tone: high pitch—report top row; middle pitch—report middle row; low pitch—report bottom row. Remember that the array was not present when the tone cue was presented.

Sperling found that subjects recalled an average of around 3.04 items in this partial report procedure. The row on each trial was randomly selected, and as subjects reported an average of 3.04 items for the row selected, Sperling inferred that subjects actually had 3.04 items × 3 rows or 9.1 items available. The logic of Sperling's inference is dependent on an *equal attention* observing response by subjects. This is a method in which subjects attend to all stimuli in the array equally, rather than focusing on a specific row. The subjects in these experiments were highly trained, and equal attention observing was encouraged by using larger arrays and by first training with tone cues that preceded the array. Training with early tone cues that alternately focused on different rows encouraged the development of an equal attention strategy for the later trials when the tones only occurred after the array was no longer present on the screen. The use of these techniques resulted in a relatively equal distribution of errors among the three rows during the actual test trials, suggesting equal attention.

The increase in average number of items available, from 4.3 in whole report to 9.1 in partial report, is called the **partial report advantage**. The partial report advantage is the evidence for iconic storage in the Sperling task. Absence of a partial report advantage implies an absence of iconic storage. Sperling next attempted to determine the time course of iconic storage by varying the time between array offset and tone cue onset. The results of this experiment are shown in Fig. 9.2.

As can be seen in Fig. 9.2, the partial report advantage (evidence for the icon) decreases rapidly over the first 250 msec. By 300 msec the loss function is almost level, with the number of items available just slightly above the number found in whole report. No statistical tests were conducted on these results so it is not possible to determine whether performance at the longer intervals, say at 1 sec, is significantly greater than for whole report.

Sperling's research supports the view that large capacity and brief duration are properties of iconic memory. What is the type of code used for information storage in iconic memory? Another way of asking this question is, at what level is the information processed? Imagine that information can be processed in a series of levels or stages. Imagine an initial level in which alphanumeric information consists of an array of features, for example, horizontal, vertical, and diagonal lines and various arcs and curves. Imagine further a second level in which combinations of features activate representations of

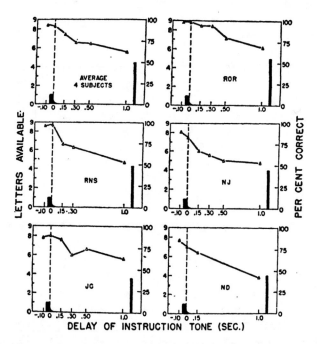

FIG. 9.2. Decay of available information: 12 (4/4/4) letters and numbers. Light flash is shown on same time scale at lower left. Height of bar at right indicates immediate whole report memory for this material. From Sperling (1960). Reprinted by permission.

letters and numbers in long-term memory. The output of this second level would be identification and categorization of all alphabetical and numeric characters in the array. A clue to the level of processing in the icon comes from the types of cues that can be used to direct partial report. Remember that Sperling used the tones to indicate different spatial locations—top, middle, or bottom row. In another condition in his experiments Sperling attempted to use category of item, digit or letter, to direct partial report. In this version of the task, a cue following stimulus presentation instructed the subjects to report either all of the letters in the array or all of the numbers in the array. In this condition no partial report advantage was obtained. Other experimenters using variants of the Sperling procedure found a partial report advantage when size, shape, and color differences were introduced into the matrix and were then used as the selection criteria. Spatial location, size, shape, and color all can be determined by a preliminary level of analysis of physical features. On the other hand, determination that a particular combination of features is an *A* or a *9* is thought to occur at a higher level of analysis and, as stated earlier, item category was not found to yield a partial report advantage. These results are consistent with the hypothesis that information in iconic memory is stored at the level of physical feature analysis. A similar conclusion follows from a study conducted by Coltheart, Lea, and Thompson (1974). In one of their partial report conditions subjects were required to select letters for partial report based on whether the letter names did or did not contain the phoneme *e*. No partial report advantage was obtained in this condition. This result is consistent with the hypothesis that phonemic information is not available in iconic memory. Phonemic information would be expected only after letters and numbers are verbally coded.

THE AVERBACH AND CORIELL PARADIGM

Averbach and Coriell (1961) tested partial report with a slightly different procedure. In their task subjects were shown 16 letters presented in two rows of eight and recall was tested after various delays. Only a single letter was tested on each trial, and two types of indicators were used to indicate which letter was to be recalled. In one condition a marker was placed above a letter in the top row or below a letter in the bottom row and subjects were asked to report the letter that was in the position designated by the marker. Results using this bar marker technique provided estimates of iconic memory duration very similar to those found by Sperling, 250–300 msec. In the second type of indicator condition a circle was shown in the same spatial location as one of the letters in a row and the subject was asked to report the letter that had occupied that position. Performance in this condition was much worse than in the marker condition when the circle was presented within 500 msec following the offset of the array. This procedure has come to be called backward masking, and the degradation of performance is thought to result from erasure of the to-be-recalled letter by the circle. Backward masking has come to be a main research area in its own right, and there are different interpretations of how backward masking works (e.g., Turvey, 1973), that is, whether the mask terminates processing of information in the icon (interruption) or whether the mask decreases legibility of the icon by being superimposed on the same spatial location (integration). (There are several different kinds of backward masking, and the one described here is called **metacontrast**. For a recent review of backward masking phenomena, see chapter 3 in Uttal [1988].) The main point to be made here is that information stored in the icon is vulnerable to interference from subsequent visual stimulation. No degradation of performance relative to control is found when the mask is presented at intervals of 500 msec or longer following the array. This is consistent with the hypothesis that information in the icon persists for only 250–300 msec and that recall at long delays is based on another form of storage, which is not susceptible to interference from masking.

SUMMARY AND CRITICISMS OF THE ICON AS INFERRED THROUGH PARTIAL REPORTS

So far we have a picture of a large-capacity store that persists for a very short time, on the order of 250 msec. Furthermore, information in the icon is vulnerable to interference from subsequent visual stimulation, and information in the icon is stored at the level of physical feature analysis.

Although the existence of the icon is consistent with data from the partial report procedure, several criticisms have been directed toward the partial report task that bear on the characteristics of the icon as inferred from that method. Many of these criticisms have been summarized in two reviews (Coltheart, 1980; Long, 1980). The criticisms of the partial report task can be roughly divided into iconic and aniconic interpretations of the partial report advantage, iconic meaning *image-based* and aniconic meaning *other than image-based*. Iconic criticisms do not challenge the basic findings and logic of the experimental procedures, but rather point to limitations inherent in the experimental tasks, or limitations in specific ways in which investigators have chosen to test various aspects of persistence. They challenge the specificity of some of the findings, offering questions such as: Is storage capacity larger than seen in the partial report advantage? Just what is it that decays during sensory storage over time? Aniconic criticisms attack the existence of the icon, offering alternative explanations for the findings. Aniconic criticisms have taken several forms, interpreting partial report data in terms of guessing strategies (Holding, 1970), differential output interference (Holding, 1975), and grouping strategies (Merikle, 1980). Although each of these aniconic interpretations offered a plausible account of partial report data, subsequent research has shown that none of these provides a strong competing alternative to an iconic or image-based interpretation. In the sections that follow, we discuss a few of the existent iconic criticisms of the partial report task and then present findings obtained with procedures other than partial report that bear on visual persistence.

Iconic Criticisms

In Sperling's version of the partial report procedure, a tone is sounded following the array, indicating which row to report. The subject must observe the array, hear the tone, interpret the tone (e.g., high tone, report top row), and report items from the designated row. It has been pointed out (Crowder, 1976) that the interpretation of the tone requires a mental transformation (high pitch, report top row), which in turn takes time. Partial report studies suggest that the icon is a very brief memory. Perhaps the time required to transform the tone to a useful cue could have been used to produce a report from an icon that, during the transformation, had decayed; that is, the transformation could result in an underestimate of the number of items available. A similar conclusion is reached from an analysis of number of letters available and display size. In the 3 × 4 array mentioned earlier, subjects reported 76% of the 4 letters in a row with partial report, and thus subjects had 9.1 items available. In a later study (Sperling, 1963) with 18-item arrays, the estimate of the number of items available was between 16 and 17. As the number of items available increases with display size, even the estimate of 16–17 items could be considered a lower bound of the estimate of iconic capacity. Larger displays might result in larger estimates of capacity, but eventually there would be a resolution problem as too many items are crowded into the display.

Most studies of partial report phenomena have used alphanumeric displays. Another criticism of this procedure is that properties of the icon determined by this method might be idiosyncratic to this stimulus set. It would seem that this would be easy to verify, but one of the properties of alphanumeric characters is that they are readily translated into a verbal code and therefore are appropriate for a recall task. What other large set of commonly recognized stimuli could be used in place of them, in a recall task? Suppose we used simple visual forms as stimuli instead of alphanumeric characters. How would subjects output them? We could ask subjects to draw them but that would take even more time than outputting alphanumeric characters. In addition it would add a source of subjective bias (judging drawing accuracy). Yet another way of testing would be to change the measure of retention to recognition rather than recall. In this method an array of simple forms would be followed by another array of simple forms, and subjects would be asked if the two arrays were "same" or "different". This is certainly an acceptable method but it involves two changes at once (stimulus materials and measure of retention), which can complicate interpretation.

A final criticism of the iconic variety concerns the type of information that is decaying in a delayed partial report experiment. Townsend (1973) pointed out that identity and spatial location information are confounded in the Sperling task. Consider the usual experiment where subjects are given a tone cue indicating the row of stimuli to be reported. Failure to report correctly could result from loss of identity information (failing to recall "A" when an A was in the row) or position information (recalling "A" when it was in the wrong row, suggesting that location information was lost). From an analysis of error data Townsend concluded that the rapid drop over such brief intervals in partial report performance reflects primarily a loss of spatial location information. This suggests that there may be less, or slower, decay of the identity information than Sperling thought. Neither the distinction between nor the confounding of the two types of information is unique to iconic memory. The importance of this distinction in serial recall of sequentially presented materials has been emphasised by Estes and his colleagues (e.g., Estes, 1980).

Despite all these criticisms, it is clear that there has been consistency in the partial report results. Iconic memory lasts approximately 250 msec, and is stored at the level of feature analysis. These results were replicated in different laboratories, and with some variations in procedures. Where the data are less secure and more dependent on the stimuli used is in the question of the capacity of the iconic store, and precisely what is lost in the milliseconds following removal of the physical stimulus.

Iconic memory is a theoretical construct, and up to this point in the discussion the properties attributed to the icon have been based soley on research with the Sperling procedure, the Averbach and Coriell paradigm, and the partial report advantage. Indeed, the partial report advantage stands as the operational definition of the icon. Experimental psychologists realize that there are multiple interpretations available for the results of any single experiment and that each experimental paradigm brings its own peculiarities in terms of what subjects are required to do and how they go about accomplishing their task. We have just discussed some of the peculiarities of the partial report task in the section on iconic criticisms. A theoretical construct gains much wider acceptance when the evidence for that construct comes from different experimental paradigms, from manipulations of different variables, and from the use of a variety of operational definitions of key variables. The studies reviewed here have all involved partial reports. There have been a number of additional studies of the internal persistence of visual images using different procedures than those reviewed thus far, which we examine in the following section.

ADDITIONAL MEASURES OF ICON-RELATED VISUAL STORAGE

Haber and Standing (1969) attempted to provide a more direct measure of iconic memory by having subjects judge the apparent continuity or discontinuity of a test stimulus. Subjects were given repeated presentations of a circle followed by a blank adapting field. The cycle time was defined as the interval between onsets of consecutive test circles, and it was varied over a number of values in 20-msec steps using the method of limits (see chapter 8). Haber and Standing reasoned that cycle time could provide a direct measure of the duration of iconic memory. Consider two consecutive test circles, C1 followed by C2. If C2 were presented during the persistence phase of C1, then C2 should be seen as continuous with C1. However, if C2 were presented after the persistence phase of C1, then subjects should see discontinuity, that is, C1, blank field, and then C2. Haber and Standing gave the following instructions to their subjects:

Say C if the circle appears continuous and D if it appears discontinuous in time. The perceived continuity of the circle need not be perfect: it may appear to fluctuate somewhat without losing the appearance of being present continuously. However, you should rate the stimulus as discontinuous if you can perceive a blank interval, however brief, between presentations of the circle. (p. 46)

Haber and Standing found that the duration of visual persistence was approximately 250 msec. Despite the use of a very different procedure (judgment of continuity), the estimate of duration of visual persistence was very similar to that found by Sperling (who had used partial report of letters and numbers from an array). There was another important difference between methods used by these investigators. Remember that Sperling used highly trained observers because it takes a large number of trials to develop an equal attention observing response. (In a more recent study, Chow, 1985, compared partial and whole report over 400 trials, administered in four blocks of 100 trials each. There was no partial report advantage in the first block of 100 trials. More items were available in partial than whole report only in trial blocks 2–4.) Haber and Standing were able to use untrained subjects in their experimental paradigm. Each subject participated in four experiments on persistence with a total participation time of 2 hr.

Another and very creative measure of iconic memory was provided by Eriksen and Collins (1967). The stimuli in their study consisted of **consonant-vowel-consonant (CVC) trigrams**. The letters in the trigrams were made up of dotted lines so that if all the dots were presented together, the CVC was identifiable (see Fig. 9.3).

They reasoned that visual persistence could be measured by dividing the CVC into two stimuli, one presented first and the other delayed. If the second stimulus were presented during the persistence phase of the first stimulus, the CVC would still be identifiable. The way they divided the CVC was to randomly assign the dots making up the lines to the first and second stimulus. Neither stimulus alone then contained sufficient letter information to permit identification of the CVC. Only when the stimuli were superimposed was CVC identification possible. Eriksen and Collins found that CVC identification was still above chance when the second stimulus was presented 100 msec after the offset of the first. The only longer interstimulus intervals that they used were 300 and 500 msec. The performance dropped at that point to about 40% correct and seemed to have stabilized.

Guessing was possible during the experiment (there were a list of

FIG. 9.3. The upper two dot patterns, when superimposed, result in the bottom stimulus pattern in which the nonsense syllable VOH can be read. From Eriksen and Collins (1967). Copyright 1967 by the American Psychological Association. Reprinted by permission.

20 nonsense syllables that were being used, and the list was always in front of the subjects). The experimenters assumed that partial visual cues aided guessing beyond the 1 in 20 implied on a purely numerical basis. They assumed that the point of stabilized performance was the guessing point. This in turn suggested that 40% was the guessing level, and that the information from the first stimulus, after its offset, endured as useful information for longer than 100 msec but less than 300. The temporal estimate of persistence obtained with this procedure fits within the time domains discussed earlier.

An important methodological advantage of the Eriksen and Collins study is that the subjects' responses were specific nonsense syllables that they either could or could not identify. This can be contrasted with the Haber and Standing (1969) paradigm where subjects had to state when a stimulus (a circle) was no longer present. The measurement of persistence within the Eriksen and Collins paradigm is less vulnerable to criticisms concerning the lumping together of presence of an internal image and willingness to report it.

Another procedure offering support for visual persistence, and roughly similar duration, involves the presentation of stereograms. Engel (1970) tested **stereoscopic persistence** using pairs of Julesz random-brightness fields (Julesz, 1971) as stimuli. Each member of a pair consists of 10,000 brightness elements, and each element is assigned one of seven brightness values. The brightness distributions for the two fields of a pair were identical with the exception of a central square area which was displaced laterally in one field relative to the other. No contours are visible when looking at only one of the fields; rather, only a gray speckled surface is seen. However, when the fields are stereoscopically fused (that is, when one field is presented to the right eye and the other simultaneously to the left eye), depth is perceived in the central area where the elements have been displaced in the two fields. Because the central area is only seen at a different depth than the surround when the two fields are fused, the procedure can be used to study the time course of persistence by varying the onsets of the two fields of a pair. That is, one of the fields can be presented, say to the right eye, and the onset of the second field to the left eye can be delayed so that the perception of depth would be dependent on persistence of the field presented in this case to the right eye.

Engel actually measured two types of persistence: monocular and stereoscopic. **Monocular persistence** is what is measured with the method described earlier; that is, a field is presented to one eye with the second field to the other eye delayed until after the offset of the first field. *Stereoscopic persistence* was measured by presenting both fields simultaneously for a brief period and then presenting them again after brief intervals. The maximum temporal interval for a second presentation of both fields that would not produce an interruption of the stereoscopic sensation can be taken as a measure of the duration of stereoscopic persistence. (This latter procedure is similar to Haber and Standing, 1969, in requiring a subjective report of discontinuity in the stimulus.) Two different time estimates were obtained for monocular and stereoscopic persistence, monocular being on the order of 80 msec and stereoscopic around 300 msec.

In many of the direct tests of visual persistence it was the time interval between the test stimulus and its reinstatement that was manipulated. The time intervals used were not all the same in the different studies, so it was not possible to always arrive at precisely the same conclusions about duration. However, the general picture provided by these studies is consistent with the conclusions found with partial reports: visual persistence tends to endure, and be useable, for no more than approximately 250 msec.

Contradictory Results with Variations in Exposure Duration

The implication from the studies just reviewed is that all of the tasks measuring visual persistence, partial report and direct, are measuring the same store or process. However, we have not examined some other studies, and some aspects of the previously discussed studies, in which exposure time of the initial stimulus was varied.

Here for the first time we find some consistent differences, suggesting different conclusions about the nature of that brief primitive storage process and what affects it. Does this mean we should recognize two different sensory stores? Different types of icons? Assume different characteristics for the icon under varying circumstances? Or question the value of the construct? We return to these questions after reviewing the research.

Until this point our discussion has focused on time after, or time between, stimulus exposures. Sperling (1960, Experiment 3) manipulated stimulus exposure duration itself, in the partial report task, and found no systematic changes in whole report accuracy over exposure durations ranging from 15 to 500 msec. In a later experiment in the same paper (Experiment 5), no systematic changes in partial report accuracy were obtained with exposure durations of 15 and 50 msec. In the partial report task, then, persistence, as measured by whole and partial report accuracy, is invariant over a wide range of exposure durations.

Exposure duration has also been manipulated in some of the more direct measures of icon-related storage, and these studies have indicated some very surprising results. Efron (1970) presented subjects with two small circular discs of light. The lights were presented side by side on a black background. First one light would be turned on (briefly), and for one set of trials the other light would flash while the first was still on. On other trials the first light would go off before the second light was flashed. Let us call the leading light the test flash and the following light the probe flash. Subjects were asked to judge whether the onset of the probe (second) flash occurred before or after the offset of the test (first) flash. Efron used a method of limits procedure (see chapter 8) for varying the interval between test and probe flashes. The mean of the ascending and descending series was defined as the mean point of **subjective similarity** of test offset and probe onset, and this provided the measure of persistence in the task. In addition to the interval between test and probe flashes, Efron manipulated the duration of the test stimulus with intervals ranging from 10 to 500 msec. When the duration of the test stimulus was 150 msec or greater, the results were similar to those found by Sperling: The duration of persistence did not vary with the exposure duration of the test stimulus. The duration of persistence in this task with test stimuli 150 msec and longer was 100 msec. What was found that was startlingly different was that when the test stimulus was less than 150 msec, the shorter the duration of the test stimulus, the longer the visual persistence. Specifically, test stimulus duration + persistence = 230 msec. For example, a 5-msec test stimulus would yield a persistence of 225 msec.

For another impressive demonstration of the inverse relationship between exposure duration and persistence consider the following experiment by DiLollo (1980). The stimulus display consisted of a 5 × 5 array of 25 dots. On each trial one of the dots, chosen randomly, was not plotted and the subjects' task was to name the coordinates of the missing dot. The 24 dots actually displayed on a trial were not all shown together. Rather, they were shown in two patterns of 12 dots, each separated by an interstimulus interval. Each experimental trial consisted of three phases: (a) an array of 12 dots chosen randomly from the 5 × 5 array, (b) an interstimulus interval of 10 msec, and (c) a second array consisting of the remaining 12 dots. The main independent variable was the exposure duration of the first field (10, 40, 80, 120, 160, or 200 msec). The results shown in Fig. 9.4 indicate virtually errorless performance for exposure durations up to 80 msec. However, performance deteriorated rapidly over longer exposure durations of the first array.

The data of DiLollo provide an important replication of Efron's major finding, that there is an inverse relationship between persistence and exposure duration when the duration of the first field is less than 160 msec.

CHANGES IN HOW THE ICON IS VIEWED

After our initial review of partial report and other measures of icon-related storage, we concluded that visual persistence on the

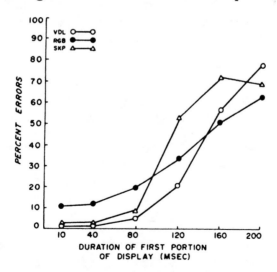

FIG. 9.4. Results of the DiLollo (1980) experiment. Copyright 1980 by the American Psychological Association. Reprinted by permission.

order of 250 msec was a consistent finding across all tasks reported. The implication of the consistency in the findings was that all tasks were measuring the same type of visual storage, which we have been referring to as iconic memory. In the last section, however, we found that exposure duration can have an effect on visual persistence. At very brief exposure durations there can be a negative relationship between exposure duration and visual persistence. With more extended durations of the presenting stimulus (150–160 msec or longer), there is no longer any effect of stimulus duration. How can we view the different effects of exposure duration? Coltheart (1980) maintained that the differential effects of exposure duration are indicative of two different types of persistence. The logic here is that if two tasks are measuring the same store or process, and a manipulated variable is identified as affecting that store or process, then the effects of that manipulated variable should be the same in both tasks. Stores or processes are differentiated when a manipulated variable shows an effect in one condition and no effect or a different effect in another condition. This form of reasoning is sometimes called **functional dissociation**.

In the present case we have different effects of exposure duration under two sets of conditions, no effect in the partial report task and an inverse effect in other tasks. On the basis of these different effects of exposure duration, Coltheart (1980) functionally dissociated the types of storage measured in the partial report task from other tasks reviewed in this chapter. He concluded that partial report tasks measure one type of store or process called **informational persistence** and that the other tasks measure a second type of store or process, which he termed **visible persistence**. Informational persistence refers to the fact that an observer still possesses a great deal of information about the visual properties of a visual signal following stimulus offset. Visible persistence refers to the fact that a visual stimulus continues to be phenomenally present, that it is in some sense visible for some time after the physical offset.

More current researchers have continued to emphasize a distinction between visible and informational persistence (e.g., DiLollo & Dixon, 1988; Loftus & Hogden, 1988; Loftus & Hanna, 1989). However, rather than defining visible and informational persistence in terms of different tasks, these researchers view visible and informational persistence as different stores or processes that contribute to performance in all iconic memory tasks. Rather than a single-process iconic memory, then, current theorists posit two processes or stores, which operate independently over the time course heretofore referred to as iconic memory.

We next outline the main features of the DiLollo and Dixon (1988) model to show how a two-process model can fit data from two different tasks, partial report and missing dot, which have been described as measuring informational and visible persistence, respectively. DiLollo and Dixon (1988) used the terms *visible persistence* and **visual analog representation** to refer to visible and informational persistence, respectively. As with Coltheart's (1980) definition, the salient characteristic of visible persistence is that it can be in some sense seen. It is assumed that visible persistence is operating when shorter stimuli yield longer periods of poststimulus readouts (within a narrow range of very short stimulus exposures). The duration of the readability of the poststimulus information is, in other words, a negative function of the duration of the original stimulus, when visible persistence is operating.

By contrast, when informational persistence is operating, the duration of the stimulus does not influence the duration of the poststimulus information. It is generally constant for a particular set of experimental conditions.

A major difference between visible and informational persistence is in the representation and rate of decay of spatial information. DiLollo and Dixon (1988) stated:

> We suggest that tasks requiring fine spatial alignment of sequential stimuli can be performed best on the basis of visible persistence, which maintains a faithful visible representation of the contents of the display. On the other hand, tasks with less stringent spatial demands can be performed on the basis of [informational persistence] in which there is rapid loss of spatial details but a more gradual decay of coarse spatial information and of more symbolic aspects of the display. (p. 672)

(These latter comments are based on the differential decay of spatial and identity information, presented earlier in the section detailing criticisms of the partial report task.)

Consider now performance on two tasks that make differential demands of the retention of spatial information, missing dot and partial report. The missing dot task requires precise alignment of spatial information between the two halves of a display. The dots are undifferentiable, so there is no information other than spatial information. According to DiLollo and Dixon, accurate performance on that task requires visible persistence, which means a negative relationship between stimulus duration and icon persistence. For the missing dot task performance does deteriorate with longer exposure durations. This can be contrasted with the Sperling partial report task, which is less dependent on precise spatial information. Performance in that task should be based primarily on informational persistence, which does not vary with exposure duration. For the partial report task, performance is invariant over a wide range of exposure durations. DiLollo and Dixon, in their 1988 paper, conclude both from their logic and from some additional experimentation that both types of poststimulus persistence (visible and informational) probably operate in all tasks, but that one or the other often predominates.

VISIBLE PERSISTENCE, INFORMATIONAL PERSISTENCE, AND AFTERIMAGES

We have traveled a long logical and empirical road in our discussion of the icon. It began with an assumption of some afterimage-like process as a brief preserving trace of visual stimuli. Studies of the effects of exposure duration on persistence indicated two different effects. In partial report experiments the apparent duration of persistence did not vary with exposure duration. With other experimental tasks that also suggested some sort of visual persistence, it was found that there was a negative relationship between the duration of the stimulus and the duration of the assumed trace, or icon (with very short stimulus presentations). These differential effects of exposure suggested two different kinds of stores, visible persistence, when the duration of persistence is an inverse function of exposure duration, and informational persistence, when persistence is invariant over different exposure durations.

It is now time to readdress the basis of the initial construct of iconic memory, that of an afterimage-like process. Do visible persistence and informational persistence behave like afterimages? Or must we now drop the afterimage analogy and find some other way of portraying persistence? We have two different types of persistence to consider, and we treat them separately. Let us start with visible persistence. In all of the more direct tasks measuring visual persistence, subjects were asked to describe what they saw following stimulus offset. In all cases subjects continued to see an image that was indistinguishable from the physical stimulus even when the physical stimulus was no longer present. This fits the definition of a positive afterimage. Remember that a positive afterimage appears as an extension of the physical stimulus. The positive afterimage has the same qualitative characteristics as the physical stimulus (same colors and same relative brightness relations), and, with a brief single stimulus, is difficult to distinguish from the physical stimulus. As a process or store, the duration of visible persistence is thought to vary as a negative function of the duration of the test stimulus when the test stimulus duration is less than 150–160 msec. If visible persistence is a positive afterimage, or if it behaves like a positive afterimage, we would expect to find the same negative relationship between exposure duration and the duration of positive visual afterimages. As a general rule, the relationship between stimulus duration and afterimage duration is positive, that is, the longer and brighter the stimulus, the longer the duration of the afterimage (e.g., Brown, 1965). However, there is an exception to this rule, and it is with brief exposure durations (less than 1/3 sec). In an important but rarely cited study, Helmholtz (1924; cited in Brown, 1965) found that with stimulus exposure durations less than one-third of a second, the duration of the positive afterimage was an inverse function of the duration of the stimulus—the shorter the stimulus, the longer the afterimage. The inverse function between exposure duration and positive afterimage duration parallels the inverse function between exposure duration and the duration of visible persistence found by Efron (1970) and DiLollo (1980). Thus, in terms of both phenomenal reports (persistence indistinguishable from physical stimulus) and effects of manipulated variables (inverse function of exposure duration), visible persistence acts like a positive afterimage. The conclusion we draw from these findings is that visible persistence is a positive afterimage.

What can we say about informational persistence? Subjects rarely report the experience of afterimages in the partial report task. Moreover, the duration of informational persistence in partial report tasks is constant over a wide range of exposure durations. This can be compared to the duration of visual afterimages, which vary with stimulus exposure. These differences suggest that informational persistence is not an afterimage. What can be said about informational persistence is that some type of internal representation outlasts the physical stimulus, because information continues to be available for 250 msec after the offset of the physical stimulus. This type of persistence is not visible.

In summary, positive afterimages were found to be a possible basis for visible persistence, but not for informational persistence. Thus, the original afterimage inspiration for iconic memory continues to be a productive way of thinking about one type of persistence, but not the other. We have, as yet, no clear analogy for portraying informational persistence. In some ways this persistence seems visual (it is maskable), and in other ways it does not (it does not vary with exposure duration). It appears that we are at a point at which we can show, convincingly, that information of some sort does persist beyond the duration of the physical stimulus. But it will be tomorrow's experimental psychologists who will clarify the nature of the process, or processes, that underlie informational persistence.

CHAPTER SUMMARY

We reviewed construct development, research findings, conclusions, doubts, and theoretical revisions of iconic memory. We started with a view in which iconic memory was a theoretical construct developed from studies using the partial report procedure. The properties of the construct thus developed were large capacity, rapid decay, maskable, and storage at the level of physical feature analysis. Next we looked for evidence supporting iconic memory from other experimental procedures. Results from the other experimental methods were broadly supportive of a rapidly decaying trace of large capacity. No single view of the construct of an icon was found to accommodate all the findings across the array of tasks. Specifically, the influence of exposure duration was not shown to be consistent across tasks. It had no appreciable effect on partial report, but had an inverse effect on duration of persistence in a number of other experimental procedures. This differential influence of a variable (functional dissociation) suggested the need for a revision of the view that all the tasks investigating poststimulus duration are measuring the decay of the same large capacity store. The varying effects of exposure duration gave rise to the hypothesis that there are two different types of persistence. Visible persistence appears to be operating in tasks that show a negative relationship between exposure duration and persistence (given relatively brief stimulus exposures). When informational persistence is operating there is no relationship between exposure duration and persistence. The theorists positing this new dichotomy have, for the moment, concluded that the two types of persistence make independent contributions to tasks using visual stimuli. The relative contributions of the two types of persistence are expected to vary with general level of exposure duration and other details of the experimental task.

The original model of an iconic store was that of a stimulus that simply has a persistent effect, not unlike that of a visual afterimage. Positive afterimages were found to be a possible basis for visible persistence, but not for informational persistence. We have as yet no analogy or model for portraying the store or process underlying informational persistence.

Iconic memory is no longer a single theoretical construct in the sense of referring to a single hypothesized internal store. The postulated icon refers to at least two processes that occur commencing with the onset of a visual stimulus, and continuing up to approximately 250 msec following stimulus offset.

NEW WORDS AND PHRASES IN CHAPTER 9

apparent continuity or discontinuity
consonant-vowel-consonant trigram
iconic memory
informational persistence
functional dissociation
masking
metacontrast
monocular persistence
negative afterimage
partial report
partial report advantage
physical feature analysis
positive afterimage
stereoscopic persistence
subjective similarity
tachistoscope
visible persistence
visual analog representation
whole report

CHAPTER 10

Testing Theory I: A Close Look at
the Methods and Logic Used in
Evaluating a Theory of
Short-Term Memory Search

A good theory makes many testable predictions, which in turn prompt many experimental tests of the theory. Saul Sternberg (1966, 1969, 1970) developed a theory of short-term memory that generated many predictions, and has been responsible for a good deal of research. It is a frequently cited model, and has been supported, at least in part, by much of the research. It offers an interesting example of theoretical work in experimental psychology. His theory, and the kinds of research it inspired, are described in this chapter. A brief history of some related early work on reaction-time measures precedes the description of Sternberg's model.

DONDER'S ASSUMPTION OF ADDITIVITY AND HIS USE OF REACTION TIME

F. C. Donders, a 19th century Dutch physiologist, developed a method that he believed would permit the measurement of the time required for some mental acts (Sternberg, 1969; Woodworth, 1938). First he defined a situation in which a simple reaction time could be measured. An electrical stimulus was applied to one foot, and the subject pressed a key with the hand on the same side as the foot, at the instant that the subject felt the stimulus. Donders called this an *a* reaction. It indicates the basic time required to react to a particular stimulus. As a second, more complex situation, he arranged for two electrical connections, one to each foot, and gave the subject two keys, one for each hand. The subject then had to press with whichever hand was on the side of the body that received the electrical impulse. Donders called this the *b* reaction. It measures the time required for the discrimination as to where the electrical impulse has occurred, along with the time required for the choice of which key to press, plus the basic time required to react to the stimulus (the *a* reaction).

Donders reasoned that if these were additive components, each adding its own time to the process, by subtracting the basic time required to react to the stimulus (the time of the *a* reaction), from the *b* reaction, he could learn the time required for the psychological processes of discrimination and choice. This is called the **subtraction method**. Furthermore, by adding a third type of reaction (which he called the *c* reaction), he could tease apart the time for discrimination of the impulse from the time required for making a choice of key.

The *c* reaction consisted of the same foot arrangement as for the *b* reaction, that is, either foot could get the stimulus. But the hand arrangement consisted of only one key, which the subject was always to press with the same hand, but only if a preselected foot was stimulated. If the other foot was stimulated, the subject was not to press the key. The *c* reaction measured the discrimination time (determining which foot was stimulated) plus the basic reaction time, though it excluded the choice response and its time requirements. Thus the *c* reaction (discrimination plus the basic reaction time), minus the *a* reaction (basic reaction time), gave the time required for discrimination. The *b* reaction (involving choice, plus discrimination, plus basic reaction time), minus the *c* reaction (involving discrimination plus the basic reaction time), gave the time required for choice, or so Donders believed. Reiterating the three tasks, they were the following: a simple reaction time—stimulus and one response; discrimination—having to deal with two stimuli; and choice—having to deal with two responses (along with two stimuli). Table 10.1 shows the three tasks and the processes thought to be involved in each.

The differences in latency to accomplish the three tasks were assumed to reflect the presence of different numbers of components in the reaction-time tasks, with a simple reaction (R1 if S1) embedded in all three (*a*, *b*, and *c*) reaction tasks (as seen in Table 10.1). A further, and critical, assumption was that the simple reaction process is constant in the three tasks. That is, it was assumed that

TABLE 10.1. Donder's Three Tasks and Associated Processes.

Task name	a reaction	b reaction	c reaction
Task diagram	S1 R1	S1 S2 R1 R2	S1 S2 R1
Task description	R1 if S1	R1 if S1 R2 if S2	R1 if S1 No R if S2
Processes measured	Simple RT	Simple RT Discrimination Choice	Simple RT Discrimination

Notation: S1 = Stimulus 1   S2 = Stimulus 2   No R = No Response
             RT = Reaction Time   R1 = Response 1   R2 = Response 2

the time required for the simple reaction process measured in the a reaction is the same as the time for the simple reaction process in the b and c reactions. It is only with this assumption that the differences in latency can be attributed to additional processes. That an addition to a task can add further processing steps without altering the other processes already present is called the assumption of **pure insertion** (Sternberg, 1970).

The logic of the subtraction method seemed reasonable, so Donders carried out this experiment in more than one form, using voice reaction times as well as hand reaction times. Others developed further variations on the subtraction method, attempting to take advantage of what appeared to be an interesting way to map the time course of inner events that could not be directly observed.

After many years of research using Donders' three types of reaction-time tasks, and additional types of reaction-time tasks developed by others, the conclusion of the profession was that the subtraction method did not give the hoped-for information. The various components did not appear to be additive. That is, the more complex reaction times were not simply a summation of the times required for the various components. There were times when a more complex reaction time was no longer than a simple reaction time, suggesting some interaction of the components that had been assumed to be additive, or else there were some parallel processes at work. Thus the approach was abandoned for some years.

Donders' general scheme for dividing some tasks into stages that each add their own components of time was taken up many years later, though in a different form, by Sternberg (1966, 1969, 1970). Two important modifications differentiate Sternberg's approach from that of Donders. First, Sternberg replaced the strong assumption of pure insertion with the weaker assumption of **selective**

influence. Rather than assuming that a task change resulted in the addition or deletion of a processing stage without altering others (pure insertion), Sternberg assumed that a change could influence the duration of one stage without altering others (selective influence). Second, rather than assuming **additivity**, he used statistical techniques to test for it. The importance of these differences is clarified in the sections that follow.

A TYPICAL SHORT-TERM MEMORY RECOGNITION TASK

Sternberg was interested in the processes of short-term memory. By short-term memory we usually mean the retention of items that are actively held in memory. Sternberg was interested in memory processes lasting only a few seconds. Most people can retain approximately seven items, plus or minus two, for such brief intervals (Miller, 1956). For example, phone numbers consist of seven numbers, and we can usually remember them long enough to write them down right after hearing them, without requiring that the numbers be repeated.

Sternberg was interested in recognition memory in a situation not unlike the following: Suppose you were asked to buy a few things at the store, and the person making the request stopped, and said, "Did I mention bread?" Sternberg wanted to understand the internal processes in such short-term memory tasks. One of his questions about the process was whether each item in memory was checked sequentially, or if all of the items were checked at once (assuming a small number of items). More specifically, assume that no more than six or seven items had been mentioned. You would probably be able to say whether bread had been one of the items. But would you have to sort through the items in the list one at a time to see if bread was among them, or would all of the items be simultaneously available for mental scrutiny? The former approach is called a **serial process**, or more specifically a **serial search** (examining each item in memory in sequence), and the latter approach is called a **parallel process**, or more specifically a **parallel search** (examining all of the items in memory simultaneously).

STERNBERG'S EXPERIMENTAL SITUATION

The kind of experimental situation that Sternberg had in mind is one in which subjects are given a set of digits that they are told to memorize. The digits are visually presented, usually one at a time, at a fixed exposure of, for example, 1.2 sec per digit. (This is not unlike the presentation of a list of grocery items, but successively presented on a screen.) Two seconds after the last digit in the set is displayed, a warning signal appears, followed by a test stimulus. The subject has to indicate, as quickly as possible, whether the test stimulus is a member of the memorized set ("Did I mention bread?"). The digits to be memorized are anywhere from one to six numbers, taken from a larger set that Sternberg called the stimulus ensemble. (In the basic experiment these are the numbers 0 through 9.) The subjects are told what the stimulus ensemble is, in advance. The numbers sequentially presented to be memorized Sternberg calls the positive set. The remaining numbers from the stimulus ensemble he calls the negative set. There are two levers available, and the subject uses one to indicate that the test stimulus is a member of the positive set, and the other to indicate that it is a member of the negative set. Subjects are paid in such a manner that errors are heavily penalized, so that, although subjects respond quickly, there are few errors.

The dependent variable in this situation is the reaction time (also called the latency), the time taken by the subject after appearance of the test stimulus to decide whether it is a member of the positive or negative set. The presentation of items from either the positive or negative set constitutes one independent variable. Reaction times to items that are in the set that were just memorized (the positive set) are compared to reaction times to items in the negative set. The most important independent variable is the size of the positive set (the number of items presented to be memorized in any one trial). As other independent variables, Sternberg used the relative frequency of positive and negative items during an experimental session, and the stimulus quality of the test stimulus (whether it was intact, or degraded so as to be somewhat unclear). Sternberg's choice of independent variables is related to his suggestions of stages in item recognition in this experimental situation. These stages, major components in Sternberg's theory of short-term memory, are presented graphically in Fig. 10.1.

Sternberg posited that four psychological stages occur between the moment that the test stimulus appears and the point at which the subject pulls one of the two levers (implicitly saying yes, it is a member of the positive set, or no, it is a member of the negative set). The stages are assumed to be sequential and nonoverlapping. A stage does not begin until its preceding stage has ended. The input to a stage, n, is the output from the preceding stage, $n-1$. The first stage is the stimulus encoding stage. It is the stage during which the subject first discerns the test stimulus, and goes through the process

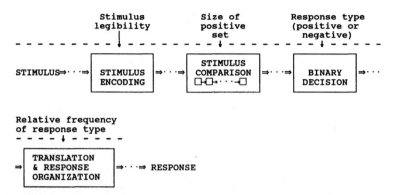

FIG. 10.1. Four hypothesized processing stages in item recognition, with four experimental factors believed to influence the respective stages. Vertical arrows show each factor influencing only one stage. Other factors, not shown, may also influence each of these stages, and dots between arrows indicate the possibility of additional stages, as yet unknown. From Sternberg (1969). Copyright by Elsevier Science Publishers. Reprinted by permission.

of identifying it. In some conditions, this would be equivalent to naming the stimulus. Different stimuli, under different conditions, would be expected to be encoded differently; for example, the form or color or sound is sometimes identified prior to naming.

The phrase *stimulus legibility* above the stimulus encoding stage in Fig. 10.1, is a statement about one of the factors that can affect the time it takes for the subject to pass through the stimulus encoding stage. Specifically, the quality of the test stimulus will have an effect on the time required for the stimulus encoding stage to be completed. This is what was referred to previously as the assumption of selective influence. That is, changes in legibility are assumed to influence the duration of the encoding stage, but not to affect any other stage.

Sternberg's second stage, the stimulus comparison stage, is the stage in which the encoded test stimulus is compared to the stimuli that have been memorized (those in the positive set), to see if it is identical to one of them. The little boxes within the stimulus comparison box in Fig. 10.1 are little substages, each consisting of a comparison of the test stimulus with another item in the positive set. This sequential presentation with arrows between substages is a pictorial summary of Sternberg's conclusion from the data that each such comparison is carried on separately, in an extremely rapid sequence, rather than being carried on in parallel. The evidence for this conclusion is discussed next. As indicated above the stimulus comparison stage in Fig. 10.1, an independent variable that will have an effect on the stimulus comparison stage is the size of the positive set, because of the serial comparison.

The next stage identified by Sternberg is the binary decision stage. That is, after the comparisons within the stimulus comparison stage are completed, a decision has to be made based on those comparisons. It has been found that it takes longer to determine that a test stimulus is a member of the negative set than to determine that it is a member of the positive set (if test stimuli from the positive and negative set occur equally often). Sternberg believed that this additional time accumulates in the binary decision stage, rather than in the stimulus comparison stage, as indicated by his having placed the words "response type (positive or negative)" above the binary decision stage.

The binary decision stage we have just discussed is the stage during which the subject makes a decision about which response to emit (yes it is part of the positive set, or no it is part of the negative set). But an inner decision is not the same as a response. The actual emission of the response occurs, according to Sternberg's model, in still another stage, the translation and response organization stage, Sternberg's last stage. The inner decision is translated into a response in this stage. One independent variable that can affect this late stage is the relative frequency of the response type, as indicated above that stage in Fig. 10.1. To understand this intuitively, it may be helpful to think of the extreme case where one type of response occurs repeatedly trial after trial, such as the test stimulus always being a member of the positive set. Then suddenly, on one trial, the test stimulus is a member of the negative set. The subject would have been set to respond with the lever for the positive set, and somehow have to stop and switch, and this would lengthen the reaction time. Sternberg found that he could get approximately equal reaction times to positive and negative set test stimuli by having positive items only occur about one-fourth of the time. When positive and negative test stimuli occurred equally often, responses to negative stimuli were approximately 40 msec longer.

In Fig. 10.1 the dots between the last stage and the word RESPONSE indicate that Sternberg was not certain that his last stage is really the final stage. Similarly, the dots between the arrows between the other stages in Fig. 10.1 indicate that Sternberg did not consider that the other stages that he identified are necessarily exhaustive. He merely presented those stages that he believed were justified by the data.

Ways of Testing Sternberg's Theory

When the total time for a response is a simple sum of the times required for each stage, we call it an **additive process**. Donders' stages in reaction-time tasks were questioned because of the issue of additivity. The time for the separate stages he had defined did not sum to the total time required. Sternberg therefore did not assume additivity for his stages, but rather wanted to test whether or not there was stage additivity. He was able to do this because he recognized that there was an interesting way to establish the presence or absence of additivity for the stages of his theory of item recognition.

Lack of a statistical interaction in an analysis of variance implies additivity for the factors that do not interact. Recall (from chapter 6) that in a statistically significant interaction, the effect of one independent variable on the dependent variable is different depending on the state of the other independent variable. As an example, suppose that we are measuring reaction times in Sternberg's task. Assume that we have decided to vary two factors in the experiment. As the first factor we vary the number of items in the positive set, giving the subject either one, two, or four items in the positive set, just prior to each appearance of a test stimulus. As the second factor, half the time the test stimulus is clearly presented, and half the time it is partially masked by a superimposed grid, made up of random dots, so that the test stimulus can be recognized, but not as easily. This then constitutes a two-factor analysis of variance design (with two repeated measures), each subject being in all six conditions. Figure 10.2 summarizes the design in a table into which data can be entered. Hypothetical means from data are summarized in matrix form in Fig. 10.3.

If we found that the effect on reaction time of having a degraded stimulus was different, depending on whether we had one, two, or four stimuli in the positive set, then we would have an interaction between positive set size and legibility. Suppose that, instead, there was no interaction. For example, suppose that, with just one stimulus in the positive set, the latency to an intact test stimulus

	One positive item		Two positive items		Four positive items	
	Intact stimulus	Degraded stimulus	Intact stimulus	Degraded stimulus	Intact stimulus	Degraded stimulus
Subj. 1						
Subj. 2						
.						
.						
Subj. n						

FIG. 10.2. Two-factor repeated-measures design, item recognition task.

CONDITION OF TEST STIMULUS

		intact	degraded
NUMBER OF	1	reaction times 360	420
STIMULI IN	2	410	470
POSITIVE			
SET	4	480	540

FIG. 10.3. Two factor design, repeated measures, item recognition task, pictured as a matrix. The numbers are average reaction times in each cell for a hypothetical experiment where there is no interaction.

averaged 360 msec, and to a degraded test stimulus it averaged 420 msec; with two stimuli in the positive set, an intact and degraded test stimulus respectively yielded 410 and 470 msec; and with four stimuli in the positive set, an intact and degraded test stimulus respectively yielded 480 and 540 msec. These are the numbers in Fig. 10.3. In the example in Fig. 10.3 there is the same increase in response time going from intact to degraded test stimuli, 60 msec, regardless of the number of items in the positive set; that is, the difference in seconds is the same in all rows. This would suggest that the stimulus degradation offers a specific influence, occurring in some part of the process that does not interact with the processes involved in dealing with additional stimuli in the positive set. This is in keeping with Sternberg's theory of additive stages, as schematized in Fig. 10.1.

The process of lack of interaction in analysis of variance is called additivity. The influence of one factor on reaction time simply adds to the influence of the other factor. If one more stimulus in the positive set adds a certain number of milliseconds to the latency, it does it in addition to any additions to latency caused by degradation of the test stimulus. If going from one to two stimuli adds 50 msec, and stimulus degradation adds 60 msec, doing both adds 110 msec. This is the case in Fig. 10.3 where going from Row 1 to Row 2 adds 50 msec, regardless of the column. Going from Column 1 to Column 2 adds 60 msec, regardless of the row. Combining the row and column increases of 50 and 60 msec to the cell in the first column and first row (360 + 50 + 60 = 470) yields the average reaction time found in the second row of the second column. It is in this sense that additivity and lack of interaction are equivalent. Proving lack of interactions yields support for additivity, which is necessary as evidence of separate stages.

Of course, in actual experiments, there is some variability from such perfect additivity, just because of stimulus sampling error. Normally, this would require some special criteria, because we usually only prove the presence of an interaction with our statistical tests. To show that an interaction does not exist, we would have to draw conclusions from a nonsignificant finding. To do this, we generally increase the Type I error probability (from .05 to say .25), so as to decrease the Type II error probability (which is the kind of error possibility we confront when drawing conclusions from lack of statistical significance). But in the case of Sternberg's research, variability around the parallel lines demonstrating lack of interaction was so small that the Type II error probability also had to be small. An example of the results from the particular case discussed here is seen in Fig. 10.4.

Our discussion thus far has focused on design and statistical issues. It might be helpful at this point to consider a psychological interpretation of potential additivity, as well as of its absence, again using stimulus degredation. Consider two possible results of the encoding process with a degraded stimulus, keeping in mind that the dependent variable is the time it takes to respond. It should take more time to encode the degraded stimulus. We would add this time

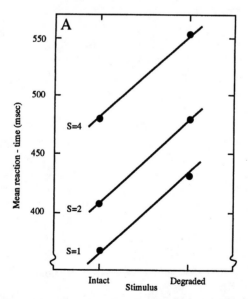

FIG. 10.4. Graph of results of an experiment by Sternberg testing for a lack of interaction between stimulus legibility and size of positive set. From Sternberg (1969). Copyright 1969 by Elsevier Science Publishers. Reprinted by permission.

to the encoding stage. The degrading of the stimulus would result in a poor copy. We could then match that poor copy to items stored in memory. We would also expect that matching a poor copy of the test stimulus to an item in memory would take longer for each comparison during the serial comparison stage. Thus, the effect of stimulus degradation would vary with the number of items in the memory set. In this case the poor legibility of the stimulus would affect both the first and second stages, the stimulus encoding and stimulus comparison stages. This would result in a statistically significant interaction, rather than additivity.

Now consider another possible result of encoding. In this case, though a degraded stimulus may take more time to initially encode, once encoded, it is a clear copy. Then we match our clear copy to items in the memory. The only additional processing time is the time required to produce a good copy from an initially degraded stimulus, and that time is added to the encoding stage. Once having clearly encoded the stimulus, no additional time should be required for matching the stimulus (or its clear copy) to items in memory. This is a possible interpretation of additivity in those instances in which stimulus degradation is found to affect encoding but not stimulus comparison. Some type of stimulus clean-up or preprocessing is suggested by, or at least consistent with, the results shown in Fig. 10.4.

Sternberg pursued this approach of testing for interactions between the four factors of stimulus legibility, size of positive set, response type, and relative frequency of response type. All of his experimental evidence confirmed the picture of separate additive stages for these four factors.

An additional variable that can be examined is the effect of variations in the relative frequency of the appearance of a particular number. This factor was found to interact with the stimulus legibility factor. Because the stimulus legibility factor is assumed to have its influence in the encoding stage, this interaction tells us that the stimulus frequency factor also has some of its influence in the encoding stage. This example illustrates how once particular experimental factors are identified exclusively with particular stages, the method of testing for interactions can yield some clues as to which stages are influenced by which additional factors.

Sternberg's stages are theoretical constructs, hypothetical entities that have no physical existence. There would not be any way of proving their existence through direct observation. What he did was use surrogate variables to find support for the existence of his stages. Therefore, as seen in chapter 7, his supportive evidence has to be taken as consistent with the existence of his stages, but not as proving their existence.

Recognizing Parts of a Task as Reflected in the Intercept, and Others in the Slope

There is an analytic device used by Sternberg that can be used to analyze many other situations. This is the use of the zero-point intercept on a graph to indicate the amount of time required for some components in a complex multistage task, and the slope to indicate the way in which other components affect the overall reaction time. The time required for completion of the complex task can be seen as a sum of the times required for each of the stages to be completed. Assume that a single stage could itself be divided into substages, with the experimental manipulation increasing the number of substages. This could result in a longer time requirement for completion of the stage, resulting in a general increase in reaction time to the task. But would the increase be reflected in a higher intercept, or would it be reflected in the slope of the curve? The example used by Sternberg is the stimulus comparison stage, which is assumed to increase with additional items in the positive set. Assuming that there is a serial search through these memorized items, each additional item could be seen as an additional substage within the stimulus comparison stage. Of course, these substages can not be seen, nor can the whole stage itself be seen. But support for the concept of substages within the stage was looked for through selective changes in the graph of the process. Rather than merely finding increases in reaction times to the overall task (which could reflect almost any underlying process), what was found was an increase in slope, the reaction times increasing with increased items in the positive set. This can be contrasted with an increase that could have occurred in the intercept, which would also have added to the overall reaction times. The idea here is to see if increases in reaction times would affect the parts of the graph that are consistent with the theory as implied in Fig. 10.1.

Placing the substages on the X axis in a graph of task reaction times, the slope of the curve for reaction times would indicate the rate at which additional items in the positive set (additional substages) would increase the reaction time for the task. Figure 10.5 uses some of Sternberg's data to illustrate this analysis. The open circles in Fig. 10.5 represent the reaction times when the test stimulus was a member of the negative set, and the filled circles when it was a member of the positive set.

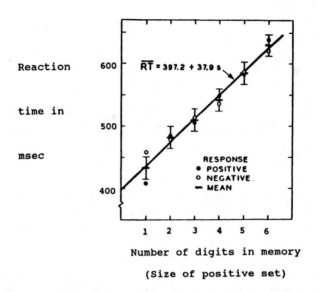

FIG. 10.5. Reaction time in msec; RT = 397.2 + 37.9 s

RESPONSE
• POSITIVE
○ NEGATIVE
— MEAN

Number of digits in memory

(Size of positive set)

FIG. 10.5. Relation between reaction time in a recognition task and number of digits in memory (size of the positive set). The subject must compare the test stimulus to the digits in memory, to determine if the test stimulus is among the memorized set. Filled circles indicate average reaction times for "yes" response (test stimulus in positive set), and the open circles average reaction times for a response of "no". Test stimuli from the positive set only occurred 27% of the time (which explains the approximately equal reaction times for positive and negative test stimuli). The zero intercept is at 400 msec. From Sternberg (1970), in *Cognition and Affect* edited by J. Antrobus. Copyright 1970 by Little, Brown and Company Inc. By permission of Little, Brown and Company.

The analysis in Fig. 10.5 is a dissection of just one of the stages, Sternberg's second stage, the stage of stimulus comparison. This stage would be prolonged (creating longer reaction times) if each item in the positive set was individually checked (a serial comparison). The upward-sloping straight-line function in Fig. 10.5 does suggest (is consistent with, but does not prove) such a serial process.

The zero intercept, at 400 msec, represents the time taken by all of the other stages: stimulus encoding, binary decision, etc., all stages other than comparison with the test stimulus. The time for the item recognition task, for each item, is reflected in the slope (the increased time of 35–40 msec per additional item). If the experimenter wished to burden one of the other stages analogously to burdening the comparison stage with more items, this could be done also. For example, by making it harder to identify the stimulus, the stimulus encoding stage is burdened, and this should cause a response time increase at that stage. If the analysis is correct, this time increase would only be reflected in the zero-point intercept of Fig. 10.5, and not in any changes in the slope. This is indeed the experimental result. This is good indirect evidence in support of the theory. If the theory is correct, these are the results we would expect; however, once again this is a case of affirming the consequent.

An interesting discovery from the analysis summarized in Fig. 10.5 is that the positive and negative responses have the same slope. The increase in reaction time (on the Y axis) is the same for each additional item added to the positive set (on the X axis), whether we are looking at a test item from the positive or negative set. The graph in Fig. 10.5 was drawn from data in an experiment in which the test stimulus was from the positive set only 27% of the time. When both positive and negative items appear equally often as the test stimulus, the curve for the negative stimulus is higher (by about 40 msec). However, both the negative and positive test items yield straight-line curves that have the same slopes (are parallel). This finding of equal slopes has been replicated in the vast majority of studies done with this paradigm, in a wide variety of laboratories.

As explained later, straight-line curves with equal slopes for positive and negative test stimuli imply that the recognition task involves a search through short-term memory that is serial and exhaustive, proceeding through all the items in short-term memory, even after the test stimulus has been previously encountered. In terms of events that we are normally familiar with, in which we usually stop looking when we have found something, this is coun- terintuitive. This process of scanning all items, even when the test item is encountered early in the process, is called an **exhaustive search**. We can contrast this with a process of scanning only until the test item is encountered, which is called a **self-terminating search**. We now explain why the equal slopes imply an exhaustive search.

Assume for the moment that the subject stops searching when she or he comes across the test stimulus in a mental search (a self- terminating search). In that case a test stimulus from the positive set (the memorized set) will, on some trials, be recognized early, yielding a relatively short reaction time. This would not be the case for a test stimulus from the negative set. The subject would always have to go through the entire memorized set if the test stimulus was from the negative set, because, by definition, a negative test stimulus would not be a member of the set in memory. Therefore, with a test item from the negative set the experimenter would not expect to find the occasional short reaction time from an early recognition; each additional item in memory means one more item to have to check on every negative trial. Thus, six items in memory should take longer than five, which should take longer then four, and so on, and the increased time requirements for additional items in memory should be influencing every trial. This means that for each item added to the positive set in the memory phase of the experiment, the reaction time to a negative test stimulus should be incremented by the full value of having to always go through one more item in the memory search, giving the slope in Fig. 10.5 its full increase for each item on the X axis. Thus the slope for negative test items offers a model of the slope for an exhaustive search.

By contrast, for test stimuli from the positive set, where we would rationally expect a self-terminating search, the added items on the X axis of Fig. 10.5 should not always represent a full additional item in the search. Occasional early recognitions would rob the added positive set members of their full impact, theoretically yielding a less steep slope for positive than negative test stimuli. Under the assumption that subjects search their memories only until they find the test item in memory, on average a positive test stimulus would be compared to only $(n+1)/2$ items, contrasted with the comparison with items for a negative test stimulus, which we can assume involves checking all n items. This means that for a positive test stimulus (a stimulus from the memorized set) the slope of increased time for additional items should be one half of the slope for a negative stimulus (assuming a self-terminating search for positive items and an exhaustive search for negative items).

The contrary finding of equal slopes suggests that perhaps the search for an item is an exhaustive search through all items in the positive set, continuing even after the item is encountered in the set. Although this is counter-intuitive for normally paced procedures, it may not be for high-speed processes. The rate of individual comparisons as suggested by the slope is between 35 and 40 msec per item, a scanning rate of about 30 items per second. (We can compare this with the number of items we scan when thinking or talking to ourselves, which is around 6 per second.) It is possible that it is more efficient when conducting such high-speed searches to forgo evaluations of the outcome at each check, to simply run at high speed through all items, and then give the decision as to whether or not the stimulus was present at the end of the search, rather than stopping the high-speed search for a decision at each item.

The logic here is interesting. Picture a graph, with numbers of items in the positive set on the X axis, and reaction times on the Y axis. Assume a self-terminating search (a search that terminates when the test item is found in memory). As already discussed, this predicts a slope that is less steep for reaction times to positive set test items than it is for negative set test items, because the average number of items examined would be $(n+1)/2$ when the test item is in the positive set, but would include all n items for a test item from the negative set. The sound line of reasoning that is then invoked is an example of *modus tollens*. Recall that *modus tollens* begins with the premise that A implies B, obtains the observation that B is false, and moves to the logically valid conclusion that A is false. In this example A is the assumption of a self-terminating search for positive test stimuli and an exhaustive search for negative test stimuli, which implies a predicted finding of a difference between the positive and negative reaction-time slopes. We call this predicted difference in slopes B. The experiment is done, and there is an absence of a statistically significant difference in the slopes for positive and negative reaction times. The assumption (of a self-terminating search among memorized positive set items) predicts a difference, and the difference is not found to exist. This is almost an instance of "not B" having been found in a *modus tollens* argument, which would normally imply that the assumption A (of a self-terminating search) is not valid (suggesting its alternative, an exhausive search).

There is a problem with the use of *modus tollens* here. As previously indicated in chapter 7, when evidence of lack of a difference between conditions (here a lack of difference between positive and negative slopes) is used to invalidate a consequent, the consequent has not really been invalidated. Rather, what has been found is lack of support for the consequent, but not proof that the predicted consequent is not true. If we have not actually invalidated the consequent, we have not succeeded in invalidating the antecedent (the theory predicting the consequent).

Although in general it is a good rule to be suspicious of denial of consequents through a lack of a statistically significant difference, in this case there has been so much evidence from so many experiments showing parallel lines for negative and positive test stimuli that we can reasonably conclude that the two types of test stimuli do, in most versions of the Sternberg paradigm, yield the same slopes. Because the predicted finding (the consequent) is different slopes, we can say that the accumulated evidence over many experiments has invalidated the consequent, so we can say that the antecedent has thus been invalidated, through *modus tollens*. Although a single experiment with lack of statistical significance offers weak support, a large number of experiments with similar results can constitute a convincing case.

Additional data corroborating the exhaustive search for the positive set items is that the minimum reaction time increases with set size.

The minimum reaction time is a subject's shortest reaction time. To see why an increase in the minimum reaction time with larger set sizes corroborates an exhaustive search, assume that there is not an exhaustive search—that instead the search terminates with a match, rather than being exhaustive. In that case the minimum reaction time should occur whenever the test item is the first item encountered in memory. This will occur less often when dealing with a large set size, but whether it is frequent or infrequent, that minimum reaction time should still be approximately the same value (the value associated with immediately encountering the target stimulus). For example, suppose there are just two items in the positive set in one series of trials, and four items in the positive set on another series of trials. If the search is not exhaustive, but terminates when there is recognition of the test stimulus in the positive set, this should sometimes occur on the first item searched. This would yield the minimum reaction time. If there are only two positive items, this minimum reaction time should occur about half the time. If there are four positive items, this same minimum reaction time should occur about one-fourth of the time. The more items in the positive set, the less frequent the minimum reaction times, if the search is not exhaustive. *But this minimum reaction time should always be around the same value*, the average reaction time for looking at one item in memory. To summarize, if the search is self-terminating, the average minimum reaction time for different numbers of items in the positive set should be around the same value (allowing for a good deal of trial-to-trial variability).

On the other hand, if the search is exhaustive, the minimum reaction time should be longer with more items in the positive set, because there would be no early termination of the search. The data do indicate that the more items, the longer the minimum reaction time in a series of trials. This adds more support for the picture of an exhaustive search, by providing evidence that is consistent with an exhaustive search but incompatible with a self-terminating search. The logic for drawing conclusions here is again *modus tollens*, but with more secure conclusions. A self-terminating search for positive items is assumed (A), which implies a constant minimum reaction time, (B). The experiment shows that the minimum reaction time is not constant, so B is false. In this case, we do not become mired in the problem of reaching conclusions with lack of statistical significance. Here we can show a statistically significant difference in minimum reaction times when comparing smaller to larger positive set sizes. (Statistical significance takes into account trial-to-trial variability.) Thus we can use a statistically significant finding to reject B, and thus properly reject A in a *modus tollens* argument. Once again then, the idea of a self-terminating search for positive test stimuli appears to have been invalidated.

Additional Findings

A prodigious amount of research was conducted during the 1970s with the memory scanning paradigm. Whereas much of the data now accumulated is consistent with Sternberg's theory, some reliable findings have appeared that are not explained by Sternberg's theory. There are some unexpected effects when items in the positive set are duplicated (so that, for example, the number 4 occurs twice in the positive set). A duplicated item in the positive set adds to the reaction time just as any other additional item would, as long as the test item is another item in the positive set. However, on the trials when the test item is the duplicated item itself, it has a briefer reaction time, which does not follow from Sternberg's theory. Although there were findings at odds with predictions from Sternberg's theory, the bottom line of the 1970s was that the serial and exhaustive search model provided a more complete description of the available data than competing models. Sternberg (1975) summarized his position with his last paper on the topic.

Current Status: Valuable Methods but Uncertain Interpretation

The coverage thus far provides a relatively complete treatment of the findings that have been consistently obtained with the memory scanning paradigm up through the mid 1970s. Given the methodological sophistication and the elegance of the model developed by Sternberg, it would be reasonable to expect that work has continued to flourish in the area, and that the construct of high-speed serial exhaustive search is now firmly entrenched in memory theory. In fact, quite the opposite is true: There has been a precipitous drop in empirical research with the memory scanning paradigm, and very little space is devoted to the topic in current textbooks on human memory (Ashcraft, 1989; Baddeley, 1990). In one of his final comments on the topic, Baddeley (1990) stated: "There is no doubt that the Sternberg technique is an elegant one that has the advantage of allowing two separate measures, the slope of the function and its intercept. It is, however, far from clear what these measures mean" (p. 279).

What happened in the late 1970s and in the 1980s? Why do we

seem to be less certain about conclusions now than before? The major reason for the uncertainty stems from more recent theoretical developments, which challenge the interpretations of research with this procedure and with other procedures (e.g., visual search), attempting to discriminate between serial and parallel searches and between exhaustive and self-terminating searches. The major thrust of these theoretical formulations is that there are classes of serial and classes of parallel searches, and that there are members of both classes that make the same predictions, for example, linear reaction times as a function of set size. That there are serial and parallel processes that mimic one another makes the problem of interpretation of empirical results much more difficult than was originally conceived. This recent theoretical work is highly specialized and technical, and a thorough treatment is beyond the scope of this textbook. Because of the importance of this work, however, we present a brief treatment of some of the issues and problems. The interested reader is referred to Luce (1986) and Townsend and Ashby (1983) for comprehensive coverage. A brief and up-to-date view of the status of the work in this area may be found in Townsend (1990).

Townsend and Ashby (1983) maintained that there are several independent theoretical dimensions that need to be considered when determining the nature of a processing system. Two of these dimensions, serial versus parallel, and exhaustive versus self-terminating, have been considered in depth earlier. A dimension that has not been mentioned, but that has been important in recent theorizing, is **system processing capacity**. A system can have limited or unlimited capacity to process stimuli. If the behavior of a system changes with processing load, it is said to have limited capacity. Unlimited capacity is indicated by invariance in system behavior with changes in processing load.

An important consideration about these theoretical dimensions is that they are independent. Thus, knowledge that a system processes in parallel tells us nothing about whether it is self-terminating or exhaustive, or whether it has limited or unlimited capacity. Systems can be realized with all combinations of these dimensions.

Sternberg (1970, 1975) argued that the empirical work supported the conclusion of a serial and exhaustive search and excluded the possibility of parallel search. Townsend and Ashby agreed that this finding disconfirms some types of unlimited-capacity parallel models. For example, in one such model, where search is exhaustive, the prediction for reaction time is an increasing, negatively accelerated function of the number of items in the memory set. In another unlimited-capacity parallel model, where search is self-terminating, the prediction for reaction time is a flat function regardless of the number of items in the memory set. Because the data provide neither negatively accelerated nor flat functions, the data disconfirm these models.

However, Townsend and Ashby also pointed out some limited-capacity parallel models that mimic the serial and exhaustive model and whose predictions are consistent with the data. One of these is called the **capacity reallocation** model. Its properties are parallel, exhaustive search, and limited capacity. According to this model, all items are searched simultaneously. The processing system is held to be of limited capacity, so processing rate varies with the size of the set. Even though all items are searched simultaneously, processing of some of the items will be completed before that of others. As soon as the processing of an item has been completed, the processing resources initially dedicated to that item are freed for the processing of the remaining items. This is capacity reallocation, using processing resources that were allocated to one item for processing other items when the processing of the first item has been completed. The prediction of this model is reaction-time set-size functions that are linear, and parallel functions for positive and negative set stimuli, the same as that for the serial and exhaustive model developed by Sternberg.

When two or more models yield the same predictions for experimental results, the experiments cannot be used to discriminate between the models. At the present time researchers are examining different classes of search models, and are testing predictions from these models with an expanded range of dependent variables. Accuracy measures are being considered in addition to latency, and analyses of the variances of reaction time distributions are being considered along with the more familiar analyses of arithmetic means.

Sternberg started a valuable and important line of investigation on memory search. The recent developments just outlined do not lead to the conclusion that Sternberg's interpretations are incorrect. Rather, theorists are now confronting the realization that there are other types of models in addition to those considered by Sternberg that could be consistent with the data.

The positive side of this situation is that the new research has drawn the attention of researchers to the dimension of system processing capacity. It is not unusual for a line of research to lead to concern for new dimensions, or new variables. Finding the most salient dimensions and variables for investigation is often a preliminary step, before gaining greater insight into an area being investigated.

Regardless of the final outcome of research on memory search processes, Sternberg's methodological innovations have provided valuable contributions to the arsenal of analytical techniques available for the investigation of mental processes. One example is his use of lack of interactions in analysis of variance paradigms to demonstrate additivity. Another is his use of the slope of a function and its intercept as measures of different mental processes. This latter method has seen increased application since Sternberg's successful use of it (e.g., Estes, 1980).

CHAPTER SUMMARY

F. C. Donders analyzed choice reaction times to stimuli as an additive process, consisting of three additive stages (time for discriminating one stimulus from another, time to choose a key for the response, plus time for reacting). He assumed that the addition of further tasks (moving from a simple reaction time to one requiring stimulus discrimination, and then to one that also requires choice of a response) merely adds time-consuming components, any one component's addition not affecting the time required by any other component. The approach was abandoned when it was concluded that the assumption of additivity of the components was incorrect. Years later, Sternberg suggested a loosely analogous additive process in searches through short-term memory, substituting an assumption of selective influence for pure insertion. That is, inserting a new component in the task, or changing stimulus conditions that affect one component in the task, might influence the time required for one or two other components, without disturbing the rest. He concluded that there were independent stages in his short-term memory task that were additive, but recognized that they were sometimes jointly responsive to a single influence. His analysis offered an interesting way to analyze internal processes in short-term memory.

In the typical experimental situation most often employed by Sternberg, the subjects were informed that the stimuli were the numbers 0–9, and were then told that a specified subset of the numbers (no more than six) were chosen as the positive set. Then the subjects were shown individual stimuli (numbers), which they had to identify either as members of the positive set, or as one of the remaining stimuli (not chosen for the positive set, and called the negative set). The dependent variable was reaction time, and the major independent variable was the size of the positive set. Whether the presented stimulus was a member of the positive or negative set affected the reaction times and turned out to have important theoretical implications, so this too was treated as an important independent variable.

Sternberg used the analysis of variance to try to detect any interactions between stages that he posited as contributing to the final reaction time. He concluded that his stages are passed through in a serial fashion, and that they are independent, any one stage being completed before the next stage begins. His four stages are stimulus encoding, stimulus comparison, binary decision, and translation and response organization. He specified some of the things that could influence response time— stimulus legibility, size of positive set, response type, and relative frequency of response type— each of these influences being specific to a particular stage, and not affecting any of the others. Other influences were identified that could affect more than one stage.

When the total time for a response is a simple sum of the time required for each stage, it is labeled an additive process. The presence of a statistically significant interaction in an analysis of variance is normally taken as evidence of lack of additivity, and the absence of a statistically significant interaction supports additivity. Sternberg took the absence of such an interaction as evidence of the presence of additivity, though there is always some question about drawing conclusions from a lack of statistical significance. However, a large amount of evidence has accumulated, most of which supports additivity for the stages identified by Sternberg. The data are also consistent with a serial process, and an exhaustive search through short-term memory in a recognition task, in that the reaction times increase linearly with numbers of stimuli in the positive set, and both negative and positive stimulus items produce the same slope. The notion of an exhaustive search is counter-intuitive, and thus its wide empirical support is of special interest. However, recognizing that the search process during the recognition task is assumed to be extremely rapid (measured in milliseconds), forgoing interspersed decision processes may in fact make intuitive sense.

Although there was considerable agreement in the 1970s regarding Sternberg's interpretation of performance in the memory scanning task, more recent theoretical developments have clouded the picture. The current position is that there are classes of serial and parallel searches and that some members of each class make many of the same predictions. Thus, the finding that reaction time is a linear function of set size rules out some types of parallel search models but allows others. Invoking the concept of system processing capacity has enabled some investigators to construct both parallel and serial models that make currently indistinguishable predictions, including those predictions that have already been empirically confirmed. System capacity now appears to be a dimension that cannot be ignored in modeling search processes.

The slope intercept was used by Sternberg to represent the time taken (in the reaction-time measures) by all of the stages other than the stimulus comparison stage. The stimulus comparison stage is the stage responsive to number of items in the positive set. Thus, presenting the number of items in the positive set on the X axis, and reaction time on the Y axis, the stimulus comparison stage is assumed to be accounting for the reaction-time differences found at different points on the X axis. Experimentally manipulating the other stages (through the manipulations assumed to affect the other stages) should only result in changes in the zero-point intercept, and not in the slope. The results were consistent with this prediction. This offered an interesting way to test some aspects of Sternberg's theory, and has since been found useful in the testing of some other theories. This identification of some stages or processes in a model with the intercept, and others with the slope, along with his use of analysis of variance to identify additivity or its lack among stages of the model, are enduring methodological contributions of his work, even though alternatives to his theory are still being considered.

NEW WORDS AND PHRASES IN CHAPTER 10

additive process (additivity)
capacity reallocation
exhaustive search
parallel search (or parallel process)
pure insertion
selective influence
self-terminating search
serial search (or serial process)
subtraction method
system processing capacity

CHAPTER 11

Testing Theory II: A Close Look at the Methods and Logic Used in Evaluating a Theory of Visual Search and Attention

In chapter 10 we dealt with the topic of memory search and showed how reaction times have been used to infer search types. The logic developed for inferring different types of memory search on the basis of reaction time has been used more recently by Treisman and her colleagues for measuring types of visual search. The issue here is how we search our environment. Treisman and her colleagues have developed a theory of visual information processing that they term *feature integration theory* (Treisman & Gelade, 1980; Treisman & Gormican, 1988; Treisman & Schmidt, 1982; Treisman & Souther, 1985). First, we outline the theory. Second, we consider experiments in visual search using the logic developed by Sternberg for inferring search types. Third, we examine additional predictions from feature integration theory examining the role of focal attention in visual information processing.

FEATURE INTEGRATION THEORY

According to **feature integration theory**, early visual information processing occurs in two stages. In the first stage, environmental stimuli are analyzed at a feature level. That is, complex stimuli are broken down into component features. The initial stage of **feature recording** is thought to be **preattentive**, and features are held to be

277

recorded in parallel. In the preattentive stage features are recorded independently. Features detected during that stage do not belong to an object and they are not tied to a specific location. Rather, features detected during that stage are free-floating. It is in the second stage of processing that the various features of an object are combined or integrated. The process of **feature integration** is thought to involve **focal attention**, and focal attention is held to be a serial process.

Now look at the display shown in Fig. 11.1, which consists of a variety of white, grey, or black letters. Feature integration theory maintains that initially the letters are not seen as letters as such, but rather as features: lines oriented vertically or horizontally, diagonals, curves, and shades or colors. The first stage following exposure to a visual stimulus display involves the determination of the features that are present in the display (noticing there was a curved line or the color grey, but not yet recognizing or retaining how these are combined). As already mentioned, this stage is thought to operate in parallel, with all features being recorded independently and simultaneously. If stimulus processing were terminated at this point we would be able to tell what features had been presented but not where particular features occurred in the display or what letters had been presented. The first stage is characterized very much in the same manner as was discussed in the chapter on iconic memory, with attention divided equally between all parts of the display. If we were looking at a natural scene in our environment, this first stage would be similar to a glance in which we take in the whole scene without attending to a specific object. Now let us say that we want to know if

FIG. 11.1.   Thirty item display with letters that are white, grey, or black.

a particular object is present in the scene. According to feature integration theory, we would need to search specific locations in the scene serially to determine whether the object is present or not.

Testing Visual Search Using Reaction Times

In one set of experiments, Treisman and Gelade (1980) measured reaction times in a visual search task to test whether feature recording is parallel and whether feature integration is serial. This can be restated as the question of whether searches for disjunctive features are parallel and whether searches involving a conjunction of features are serial. First, consider the meanings of the words **disjunctive** and **conjunctive,** as they come up many times in the following sections. Disjunctive means separate, and conjunctive means combined or conjoined. Imagine that a T printed in pink ink is the stimulus. The shape of the letter T and the color pink are both features. In the feature recording stage these features are considered to be separate or disjunctive and they can be searched for independently. In the feature integration stage these features combine to form a pink T. In this latter stage searches are conjunctive, pink and T.

The logic underlying the tests for types of searches is that developed by Sternberg using the slope and intercept of a function to measure different mental processes (see chapter 10). A major independent variable used by Treisman and Gelade in Experiment 1 was display size. Displays consisted of 1, 5, 15, or 30 letters. On each trial subjects were given a target and were told to search for the target in the display. Type of target was a second independent variable. A target could be a feature (a shape, designated by a letter name, or a color), or it could be a conjunction of features (a letter of a specific color). Examples of feature and conjunction targets are shown in Fig. 11.2, where in place of brown, green, or blue, used by Treisman and Gelade, we have used black, white, and grey.

In Fig. 11.2, distractor letters are black Ts and white Xs. Feature targets are a grey T and a black S. Note that the grey T (on the far right) has a unique feature (shade, or color), but has the same shape (T) as one-half of the distractors. (It is probably more difficult to detect the grey T in the midst of black and white letters than it was to detect a pink T in the midst of brown and green letters, which was the task during the actual experiment.) The black S (in the middle display) has a unique shape (S) and shared color with half of the distractors. Both feature targets are unique in regard to one feature (being grey, or the letter S), but are not unique in regard to the other

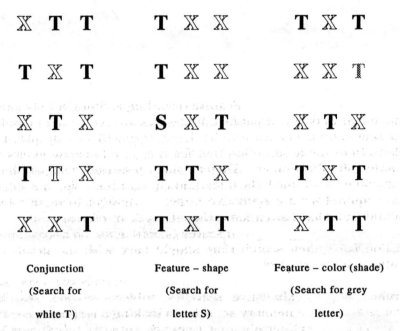

Conjunction　　　　　Feature – shape　　　　Feature – color (shade)

(Search for　　　　　　(Search for　　　　　　(Search for grey

white T)　　　　　　　letter S)　　　　　　　letter)

FIG. 11.2. Search targets analogous to those in Treisman and Gelade, who used different colors, rather than grey, black, and white, as pictured here. With conjunction targets, search was for a unique combination of single features that were discernible elsewhere in the array. With feature targets, search was for a new feature: in the middle example, a different shape, designated by a letter name; and in the far right example, a different color (or here, shade) of letter.

feature. This makes it possible to interpret the request to search for a grey *T* as the search for the single feature "grey," and the search for a black *S* as the search for the single feature "*S.*"

The conjunction target (in the far left display in Fig. 11.2) is white and *T*. It shares shape with half of the distractors and color with half of the distractors. The conjunction target is unique in its combination of features within the display, without being unique in regard to any one feature.

Six subjects participated in the Treisman and Gelade experiment. Throughout any single session the target was always either a unique feature target (like an *S*, or a pink letter), or else it was a conjunction target (like a pink *T*). On each trial of a session a target was identified (by being presented alone), and subjects were instructed to search for the target within a subsequent display. On half of the trials the target was present in the display, and on the other half it was absent. A fixation point was shown for 1 sec and was followed by the search display. Order of display size (number of distractor letters) and target present and target absent were randomized within a session. All variables (display size, type of feature, and target present/absent) were within-groups (repeated-measures) factors. The experimental design for this experiment is shown in Table 11.1.

Now let us consider the logic of the experiment and predictions of feature integration theory. Feature recording is thought to be preattentive and to occur in parallel. If features are recorded in parallel, then search time for a feature should not vary with display size. This follows from the assumption that features of all display letters are recorded simultaneously. Whereas single features (color or shape) are recorded in parallel, the integration of features (color and shape), as is required for a conjunctive target, is thought to require focal attention, and focal attention is thought to be a serial process. Again following Sternberg's logic, if search is conducted on a location-by-location basis then search time should vary with the number of locations (display size). Remember that Sternberg differentiated between two types of serial searches, exhaustive and self-terminating. In exhaustive searches subjects always searched through the entire memory set prior to making a response, positive or negative. In self-terminating searches subjects terminated the search when they found a match. Exhaustive and self-terminating searches are assessed through an analysis of the slopes of the

TABLE 11.1. Design of Treisman and Gelade (1980) experiment[a]

	Type of Target							
	Feature				Conjunction			
Size of Display	1	5	15	30	1	5	15	30
Target Present or Absent	T+ T−	T+ T−	T+T−	T+ T−	T+ T−	T+ T−	T+ T−	T+ T−

[a]The experiment contained three repeated-measures factors: type of target (feature or conjunction), size of display (1, 5, 15, or 30), and presence or absence of target (symbolized with T+ and T− in the table). Feature trials and conjunction trials were run in separate sessions. Within a session (feature or conjunction) there were 128 trials. Within the session each of the four display sizes was presented on 32 trials, 16 trials with the target present, and 16 trials with the target absent. The 128 trials were presented in random order. The order of sessions (feature or conjunction target) was counterbalanced in an ABBA sequence. An A in this sequence stands for feature for half of the subjects and conjunction for the other half.

functions relating display size and reaction time. Parallel slopes for positive and negative searches are indicative of exhaustive searches. Self-terminating searches are suggested by negative slopes that are twice as steep as those for positive searches.

A graph of the data from the Treisman and Gelade experiment is shown in Fig. 11.3. First consider the feature or disjunctive searches, shown in Fig. 11.3 with dashed lines. There is almost no change in reaction time over display size (going from 1 to 30 letters in a display), when subjects are searching for a feature such as the letter S or color blue when they are present in the display (a positive search). Data for positive feature searches (target present) are shown in the two dashed lines at the bottom of the graph. This is consistent with the hypothesis that feature search occurs in parallel. The subjective experience of subjects in the feature searches was that the target popped out of the display (look again at the feature targets in Fig. 11.2, and search for the S in the middle display).

Now consider conjunctive search data where the subject is

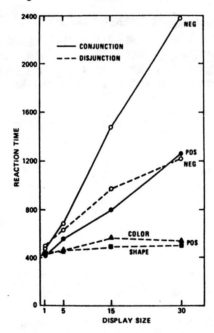

FIG. 11.3. A graph of the data from the first visual search experiment by Treisman and Gelade (1980). Search reaction times for feature (disjunctive) targets and conjunction targets are shown as a function of display size and reaction time. From Treisman and Gelade (1980). Copyright 1980 by Academic Press. Reprinted by permission.

searching for a green *T* among brown *T*s and green *X*s. (For the experience of this type of search, return to Fig. 11.2, and, in the left-most display above the word *conjunction*, search for a white *T*.) In this case reaction time increases linearly with both positive and negative searches, suggesting a serial search process (see unbroken lines in Fig. 11.3). The negative search function is much steeper than that of the positive search function, and indeed the slope ratio is very close to 2:1 (negative slope = 67.1 msec; positive slope = 28.7 msec). The finding that the slope for positive searches is approximately half that for negative searches suggests serial self-terminating searches. (In chapter 10 it was explained how both definition and logic implied that in serial exhaustive searches the subject searches through all n items, but, on average, only searches through $(n + 1)/2$ items in a self-terminating search.) Unlike the case for memory search, which Sternberg concluded was serial and exhaustive, the data suggest that search of a visual display appears to occur in parallel if the target is a unique feature, or is serial and self-terminating if the target is a conjunction of features.

Let us restate the tenets of feature integration theory and see what aspects of the theory have been addressed by the Treisman and Gelade experiment. An initial level of processing was hypothesized in which features are recorded in parallel. Processing at this level is said to be preattentive, and features in the display are recorded as present but they are not localized. When searching for a unique feature in an array, subjects' reaction times were very similar over display sizes ranging from 1 to 30 letters. This is indeed consistent with, but does not prove, the hypothesis that feature search occurs in parallel.

Searching for a conjunction of features is thought to involve focal attention. Attending to a specific spatial location results in the integration of features in that location. Attention-directed search is held to be a serial process. Reaction times increased linearly with display size when subjects searched for a conjunction of features. Moreover, slopes for negative searches were roughly twice those for positive searches. These findings are consistent with a serial and self-terminating search.

What about the preattentive-attention issue? A serial search for a conjunction of features is consistent with attentional requirements. However, there was no attentional manipulation in the Treisman and Gelade experiment so no direct test of attentional requirements. What about the issue of features existing in a free-floating state, not tied to a particular location prior to focal attention? Again, attention was not manipulated, and separate tests of location versus feature identity were not given, so this experiment does not address whether features are indeed free-floating or not.

Treisman's overall theory has several different aspects to it, and only some of the aspects are tested in any given experiment. In reading about this and other work we need to keep in mind what is being examined in each experiment. Having one variable show a predicted relationship does not mean that all aspects of the theory are supported. Only those aspects that are actually tested can receive support.

Free-Floating Features and Localized Conjunctions of Features

In the next experiment to be discussed, Treisman and Gelade investigated the relationship between feature and location information. According to the theory, in the first stage of processing, features are recorded but they are not tied to a particular location. Imagine a pink *T* in a specific location in the display. In feature detection the color and shape features are recorded independently and simultaneously. At this point our feature detectors tell us that a color feature (pink) and features in the shape of a *T* occur somewhere in the display. The features detected are not tied to a specific location and they are not integrated—that is, they exist as pink having been seen somewhere in the display, and *T* also having been observed. Therefore, if searching for a feature in a briefly exposed array, it should be possible to recognize the feature's presence, although having it mentally positioned in an incorrect location.

Searching for a conjunction of features is thought to involve focused serial search of locations. The features are integrated—for example, as a pink *T*—only when focal attention is directed at that location. In other words, correct identification of a pink T can only occur if location is also recognized. In summary, whereas features can be detected but mislocated, correct detection of conjunctions is tied to recognition of location.

Treisman and Gelade investigated these hypotheses by examining the conditional probability of correct identification of features, and conjunctions of features, given whether they were correctly located or not. According to their theory the probability of correct detection of individual features should be the same when the features are correctly located as when they are incorrectly located. By contrast, correctly locating a conjunction is a necessary by-product of its detection. Correct detection of a conjunction of features should only occur if the conjunction is located correctly. Detection should be at chance levels when a conjunction of features is incorrectly located.

The stimulus display for this experiment consisted of two rows of six colored letters, one above the other, yielding 12 positions. Distractor letters were pink Os and blue Xs. Targets (feature or conjunction of features) were located randomly in one of the eight internal positions. Feature targets were H (in pink or blue) or the color yellow (in the shape of an O or an X). Thus, a subject saw an array of 12 letters in two rows, which were all pink Os and blue Xs, with one exception. Somewhere within the inner 8 letters there was a letter H (in either pink or blue), or else there was a yellow letter (which could be either an X or an O). Thus, during a feature search trial, the subject was given a brief exposure to the array, and then had to state whether it was an H or whether it was a yellow letter that was present, and where this stimulus had appeared. The subject just had to identify a single discordant feature (a letter or a color), not an integrated percept (a letter of a specific color).

Conjunction targets were a pink X and a blue O (again in a distractor array of blue Xs and pink Os). The subjects had to report whether the discordant target item was the pink X or the blue O, and where it had appeared (its location).

Examples of feature and conjunction targets, using black, white, and grey in place of color, are shown in Fig. 11.4. Because targets only appeared in the eight internal positions of the displays only the eight internal positions are shown in the examples.

The distractor items in Fig. 11.4 are black Xs and white Os. The conjunction target shown, in the left-most array, is a white X. The feature target in the middle array is an H that is black. It could be a white H. The subject would merely have to report that an H was present, and where it was located in the display. The alternative feature target that subjects would see would be a grey letter, such as is seen in the far-right array, where there is a grey X. It could be a grey O, but the subject would merely have to report the color grey, along with its position in the display.

Each of six subjects participated in the actual experiment, with colored stimuli, for two sessions on two days. During each session

FIG. 11.4. Stimulus displays analogous to those for the second experiment by Treisman and Gelade. Left: Conjunction target, an X that is white. Middle: Feature target, H. Right: Feature target, grey letter.

subjects received three 32-trial blocks with feature targets and three 32-trial blocks with conjunction targets (192 total trials). Half of the subjects received feature blocks before conjunction blocks, and the other half started with conjunction blocks followed by feature blocks. Order of presentation of targets was reversed for each subject on the second day of testing.

On each trial subjects were shown a fixation point for 1 sec followed by the stimulus display. The stimulus display always contained a target: an H or the color yellow in feature trial blocks, and a pink X or blue O in conjunction trial blocks. The stimulus display was followed by a random noise mask made up of colored line segments. The duration of the stimulus display was adjusted individually to keep error rate constant across subjects. Following each stimulus presentation, subjects indicated the identity and location of the target by recording their response on a 2 x 4 cell matrix (the positions on the 2 x 4 matrix corresponded to the eight internal positions of the stimulus display). The dependent variable in the experiment was accuracy of report, rather than response time as in the previous experiment.

Consider again the predictions of feature integration theory for accuracy of report in this experiment. A target was presented on each trial in both feature and conjunction blocks. There were two possible targets on every trial (H or yellow for feature trials, and pink X or blue O for conjunction trials), so chance identification of the target is .50. The investigators were interested in probability of correct target identification given that a subject was or was not correct in target location. For this purpose Treisman and Gelade classified location responses into one of three categories: (1) correct, (2) incorrect but adjacent, or (3) incorrect but distant. In the adjacent and distant categories the target was identified correctly but was located in the wrong position. In the adjacent category the reported location of the target was displaced either one letter vertically or one letter horizontally from the actual position. In the distant category correctly identified targets were displaced more than one letter away from the actual location in either or both directions, vertical and/or horizontal.

Feature integration theory asserts that correct feature identification does not depend on knowing where within the stimulus display the feature is located. Therefore, success in feature identification should not vary as a function of whether a subject has located the feature correctly or not. Further, extent of mislocation of features (when mistaking feature placements both near and far from the correct location) should not be related to accuracy in identification.

On the other hand, correct identification of a conjunction of features is dependent on correct location (supposedly because features are not integrated unless focal attention is directed to the location where the features reside). The probability of correct identification of conjunction targets should be at above-chance levels when the location is correct and at chance levels when the target location is incorrect. The data for this experiment are shown in Table 11.2.

The data shown in Table 11.2 are the probabilities of reporting the identification of the target correctly, given whether the target was reported as in the correct or incorrect position. Incorrect locations are separated into adjacent and distant categories. Remember that chance target identification is .50.

If we initially restrict our examination of Table 11.2 to the correct and adjacent columns of data, we can see a close correspondence between the predictions and the results. Specifically, for feature targets we have correct detection that is far above chance (almost perfect), and that varies little with regard to whether the location report was correct or incorrect. Correct identification of conjunction targets did vary with location response, which was predicted by feature integration theory. Conjunction identification was well above chance when the target was located correctly, and close to chance when the target was incorrectly located in the adjacent cell.

Some deviation from the theory's predictions is found when we examine the incorrect location responses from the distant cells (more than one cell away from where the target was actually located). For the location of feature targets, we see that there is some drop in ability to report features when they have been mislocated by more than one cell away from the correct location. There is in fact a 20% difference in accuracy of feature identification between correct and distant locations. If, as the theory asserts, location is not a part of feature identification, the extent of location error should not be related to the probabilty of correct feature identification. Thus,

TABLE 11.2. Results of Second Treisman and Gelade Experiment[a]

	LOCATION RESPONSE			
	Correct	Adjacent	Distant	Overall
Conjunction	.840	.582	.453	.587
Feature	.979	.925	.748	.916

[a]The numbers in the table are the median probabilities (percentages) of reporting the target identity correctly, given different categories of location responses. Correct locations are those in which the target was actually in the selected location. *Adjacent* and *distant* are defined in the text.

contrary to the theory's implications, there appears to be some relationship between location and identification for feature targets.

Looking at conjunction target results in the Distant column, we see that the results are, in one sense, in keeping with the theory's predictions. Identification of conjunctions with incorrect location responses at distant targets is, as predicted, at chance. However, we can also see that whereas the percentage is below chance at distant locations (.453), it is slightly above chance at adjacent locations (.582), and the latter is a statistically reliable difference. The theory does not predict differences between adjacent and distant mislocations for conjunction targets. One might argue that the differences are slight, and the major prediction of correct locations being well above chance, with incorrect locations being close to chance, is essentially correct. But the theory would not have predicted identification of integrated features that was even slightly above chance with incorrect location information.

What then can we conclude? Two things:

1. The feature data are consistent with the hypothesis that features are free-floating in the initial stage of processing in that they can be identified even without correct identification of location. However, there appears to be some relationship between location identification accuracy and feature identification, as indicated by the 20% drop in accuracy from correct to distant incorrect locations. If, as feature integration theory states, location information is obtained with focused attention, the small relationship between location identification accuracy and feature identification suggests that feature recording is not entirely attention free.

2. Detection of a conjunction of features does appear to occur jointly with the acquisition of location information. However, the results raise the possiblity that there may be a small amount of feature integration possible without location information.

The Role of Metaphor in Modifying a Theory. Treisman often described focal attention as a spotlight, and that is a metaphor used also by Posner and his colleagues (Posner, Snyder & Davidson, 1980). They would say that conjunctions are identified correctly in the correct location because the **spotlight** is focused on that location. The finding that conjunction targets are identified at above chance levels when location is displaced by one position could be viewed as reflecting the diameter of the beam. According to this view, focal attention is indeed required for correct identification, but the beam extends to adjacent locations.

A common role played by a metaphor that is advanced for an already existing theory is to suggest how the theory might be changed to accommodate unpredicted results. That is, a metaphor offers an analogous situation or process, in this example a search-light beam as an analogy of focused attention. The image offered by the metaphor can suggest new principles for the theory, in this instance being reminded of the existence of areas of reduced light at the edge of a beam. Thus a theorist/experimenter, thinking of the searchlight analogy, might consider adding principles of weak atten-tion at the edge of focused areas, to the theory. Additional research would be needed to support such an altered theory, beyond the results that indicated that the theory was, to some extent, at variance with the data. We now turn to further exploration of the theory, specifically in regard to the topic of attention.

Testing for Illusory Conjunctions: Experiments by Printzmetal, Presti, and Posner (1986)

According to feature integration theory, attention can be both present and absent in visual searches. The initial stage of processing is hypothesized to be preattentive, but focal attention is required for feature integration and object identification. In the studies discussed to this point, attention manipulations have not been employed, so there have not been any direct tests of whether attention plays the critical role asserted by the theory. The next two experiments by Printzmetal, Presti, and Posner (1986) do manipulate attention, but in the context of an interesting shift in the focus of the research.

Instead of looking at whether attention is required to successfully detect a briefly exposed conjunction of features, Printzmetal et al. looked at whether there are increases in the reporting of nonexisting conjunctions, when attention is distracted. That is, on the basis of feature integration theory, they postulated that the reporting of nonexisting conjunctions of features may be more readily enhanced by inattention than would the misperception of individual features.

For example, a subject might be asked to determine, in a brief visual exposure, whether a white X was in a stimulus array that contained four letters. Assume that the four letters consist of two white Os, one black O, and one black X (no white X present). If the subject reported seeing a white X, this could have occurred because the subject saw white, also saw an X, and mentally put the two together, erroneously forming a conjunction. The question being asked is whether that type of error experiences a greater increase with inattention than the misperception of individual letters, say misperceiving an *O* as an *X*. Of course, each type of error would have its own normal rate of occurrence. But would inattention have a greater effect on the incorrect reporting of conjunctions (when the subjects mistakenly combine individual features that are in the display) than on the mistaken reporting of individual features (when the subjects report individual features that are not present in the display)?

To answer this question, one could arrange for both focused and unfocused viewing of targets, and then compare how decreasing attention affected the error rates for two different types of errors: errors involving misperceptions of individual letters or colors (an *X* as an *O*, a pink letter as a blue letter), versus errors involving erroneous reporting of conjunctions (misperceiving individually present features as integrated features). Feature integration theory would predict that whatever the level of errors in the perception of individual features, it should remain the same regardless of whether the viewing was focused or unfocused (because the process is preattentive). By contrast, according to the theory, the process of integrating features requires focused attention, so erroneous integration of features should show a marked increase with misdirected or otherwise unfocused attention to the perceptual task.

This test was conducted by Printzmetal et al. (1986). Before discussing the details of two of their three experiments, we present some stimulus arrays that help to clarify the nature of the tasks that the subjects confronted in their experiments. These stimuli appear in Fig. 11.5.

The task in these experiments would be to state whether a conjunction target was present. We assume, for this example, that the conjunction target is a white *X*. In Fig. 11.5 the display on the far left, labeled "correct," is one that contains the target. The remaining three do not contain the target and so offer opportunities for errors involving the reporting of a nonexistent conjunction target. In the

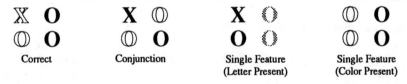

| Correct | Conjunction | Single Feature (Letter Present) | Single Feature (Color Present) |

FIG. 11.5. Four types of stimulus displays analogous to those used by Printzmetal et al. (1986). Subjects are instructed to say "yes" if a conjunction target is present (in this case, a white *X*), and "no" if it is not present in the display. The far-left display contains the target (white *X*), so a "yes" response would be correct. "Yes" responses to the other three displays would be incorrect, and offer three different types of error.

display labeled "conjunction," the individual features of the conjunction target are present, but the target itself is absent. That is, the display contains an X, and white letters. This type of error, a conjunction error, is called an **illusory conjunction**. This is the type of error that is expected to be increased by a lack of attention (misdirected focus). The third display from the left, labeled "Single Feature (Letter Present)," does not contain the color white (just black and grey letters). Thus, in order to come up with the percept of a white X during a brief visual exposure of the display, the subject would have to commit the error of incorrectly reporting the color white as present.

Because the letter feature of the target is in the display, this is called a letter-present single-feature display. This type of error is not expected to be affected by lack of attention, because the perception of individual features is presumed to be preattentive. The last stimulus display, labeled "Single Feature (Color Present)," indeed does contain the color white, but the letter X is absent, so again, in reporting a white X, the subject would have to commit an error of incorrectly perceiving something, in this case, an O as an X. Because this is just another example of a single-feature error, this too should not increase with lack of attention.

In the actual experiments by Printzmetal et al. (1986), colored letters were used in place of black, grey, and white. For example, one target stimulus was a pink X, with distractor items in pink as well as other colors. The stimuli were presented in the same type of stimulus arrays as seen in Fig. 11.5 (correct, conjunction, and single-feature arrays, the latter both in the letter-present and color-present form).

The task of the subjects was to say "yes" when they believed that the briefly exposed stimulus array contained the target, and "no" otherwise. The conditions of the experiment are summarized in Fig. 11.6, which shows a trial sequence for the first experiment of Printzmetal et al. (1986).

As can be seen in Fig. 11.6, subjects first received a target letter, X, for 1 sec. The X was presented in one of four colors, the presented color then becoming part of the conjunction target. The target was followed by a fixation point and a cue. The cue consisted of two arrows pointing to one of four locations in the display (top left or top right and bottom left or bottom right). The stimulus consisted of four letters, either an X and three Os, or four Os (as seen in black, white, and grey in Fig. 11.5). On all trials the subjects' task was to respond "yes" if they thought that the target, the X with the particular color, was one of the four letters in the display, and "no" if they did not observe the target among the four letters.

On some trials the subject's attention was misdirected away from the portion of the display where the stimulus was located (trials with

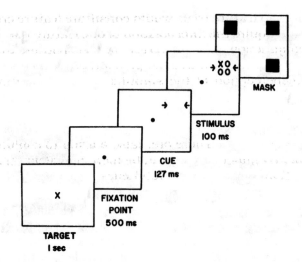

FIG. 11.6. Stimulus sequence for a valid trial in the Printzmetal et al. (1986) experiment. A target (X) is presented in one of four colors. The target is followed by a fixation point and then a cue. The cue consists of two arrows indicating a location in the display, in this case top right. The stimulus (four letters) follows the cue and it is either presented in the area designated by the arrows (valid cue), as it is in the example here, or in another area of the visual field (invalid cue). The subject's task is to indicate whether the target appeared in the stimulus display or not. From Printzmetal et al. (1986). Reprinted by permission.

invalid cues), and in others it was directed to the portion of the display where the stimulus was presented (trials with **valid cues**). Specifically, for two-thirds of the trials the cue was valid—that is, the area designated by the arrows was the area in which the stimulus was actually presented. For example, if the arrows pointed to the top right, that was where the four letters appeared. For the remaining one-third of the trials the stimulus was presented in one of the other three locations (invalid cue trials). Thus, there were two independent variables in this experiment: type of stimulus display (varied as in the displays previously seen in Fig. 11.5, except in color), and valid versus invalid cue trials.

Of major interest is whether there is an interaction between the two independent variables. The dependent variable selected was the proportion of false alarms. Remember from signal detection theory that a false alarm is an error in which a subject says that a signal was present but no signal was actually presented. In the present case a false alarm is when a subject says that the target (which combines two features, like a white X) was in the stimulus display when it was not ("yes" responses to conjunction and single feature displays in Fig. 11.5.).

False alarms to feature trials would constitute feature errors—that is, they would require the interpolation of one feature that was not in the target conjunction. A feature error would constitute the reported perception of a feature that was not present, and in that sense would involve a misperception of the stimulus. Because features are assumed to be detected preattentively, the proportion of false alarms to feature trials should not vary over cue-valid and cue-invalid trials.

Attention is required for determining whether features are correctly conjoined or not. Therefore, false alarms to conjunction displays (illusory conjunctions) should be more prevalent on trials with invalid cues than on trials with valid cues.

The results of the first experiment by Printzmetal et al. are graphically displayed in Fig. 11.7. The graph in Fig. 11.7 shows the proportions of false alarms as a function of the two levels of cue validity, seen on the X axis. Two separate lines are used, the upper line showing false alarm rates for conjunction targets, and the lower line showing false alarm rates for feature targets.

Data were analyzed by a two-factor repeated-measures analysis of variance. There was a main effect of type of display, with subjects making more errors to conjunction displays than feature displays. This is expressed in Fig. 11.7 by the entire conjunction target line being much higher than the feature target line. As we would have expected, there was also a main effect of cue validity, with subjects making more errors in cue-invalid than in cue-valid trials. This is expressed by the points above the cue-invalid position on the X axis being higher than those above the cue-valid position. There was also

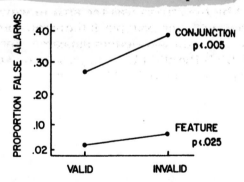

FIG. 11.7. Results of Printzmetal et al. (1986). Proportion of false alarms to conjunction and feature displays as a function of cue validity. False alarms to feature displays are feature errors that are thought to arise from misperceptions of the stimulus. False alarms to conjunction displays are illusory conjunctions that are thought to occur from recombining features in the stimulus. From Printzmetal et al. (1986). Copyright 1986 by the American Psychological Association. Reprinted by permission.

a cue validity by type of display interaction, with conjunction displays being more affected than the feature displays, by the change in the cue validity factor. This is seen in the steeper slope of the conjunction target line than the feature target line. A major prediction of feature integration theory, the cue validity by type of stimulus display interaction, is supported by the results of this experiment.

Although the overall interaction is significant, we need additional information about the interaction because feature integration theory makes specific predictions about the form that the interaction should take. The overall interaction tells us that the effects of cue validity differed over the two types of stimulus displays, feature and conjunction. However, feature integration theory holds that there should be a difference between cue-valid and -invalid trials for conjunction stimuli, but not for feature stimuli. In terms of the graph in Fig. 11.7, this means that we should have an upward-sloping line for the conjunction targets, but a horizontal line for the feature targets. We see a slight upward slant for the feature targets. Is this more than a chance variation from the horizontal? The significant interaction suggests that the slopes of the two lines are different, but only a simple effect test can give us information about a single line. The simple effect test would test the effect of cue validity for just one level of the other variable (in this case, for example, just for feature targets). A nonsignificant simple effect would imply that the line does not vary reliably from a straight horizontal line. The statistically significant interaction allows us to make simple effects tests (as discussed in chapter 6). The data of Printzmetal et al. are shown in a 2 × 2 table in Fig. 11.8, to provide a more helpful description of the two simple effects discussed here.

Simple effects tests supporting the theory would be an absence of a statistically significant difference between cue valid and invalid

	Type of Cue		
	Valid	Invalid	
Conjunction	.260	.380	$p < .005$
Feature	.036	.068	$p < .025$

Type of Stimulus

FIG. 11.8. Results of Printzmetal et al. shown in a 2 × 2 matrix. The data shown are the proportions of false alarms for feature and conjunction stimuli tested with valid and invalid cues. The analysis showed that there were significant differences between cue valid and invalid trials for both feature stimuli (bottom row) and conjunction stimuli (top row). The result of the simple effect test with feature stimuli ($p < .025$) is inconsistent with the prediction of feature integration theory.

trials for feature displays, and at the same time a statistically significant difference between cue valid and invalid trials for conjunction displays. However, as shown in Fig. 11.8, simple effects tests were significant for both conjunction and feature stimuli.

This is the same situation that we ran into in the second Treisman and Gelade experiment, where a main result supported the theory, but another result was inconsistent with the theory. Note that in both cases (Printzmetal et al., 1986; Treisman & Gelade, 1980) the inconsistencies have to do with the fact that the theory posits preattentive recording of features. If features were recorded preattentively, then we should not find an effect of cue validity (our way of manipulating attention) on feature false alarms. This result, along with that of the second Treisman and Gelade experiment, suggest that feature recording is not preattentive. That is the conclusion that Printzmetal et al. drew from their results. One might still argue from the results that less attention is needed for feature perception, but it does not appear to be attention free.

There is a question that can be asked about the internal validity of the Printzmetal et al. (1986) experiment. It is a question that was asked by the experimenters themselves, and led to their doing two more experiments. This concerns the definition of feature and illusory conjunction errors. Feature false alarms result when the subject says that a conjunction stimulus target was present in the display when only a single feature of the target (color or letter) was actually presented. For example, if a pink X were the target, a feature false alarm would occur if an X appeared in the display but the color pink was not present, and the subject reported that a pink X was presented. Feature false alarms are thought to result from misperceptions of the stimulus display. The display is only shown for 100 msec and it is followed by a masking stimulus, so it is not surprising that features are not always perceived correctly. However, the very finding of feature errors makes it difficult to interpret errors to conjunction stimuli. Feature integration theory's interest in false alarms concerns illusory conjunctions, that is, when errors to conjunction stimuli arise from combining two features incorrectly due to the lack of attention. But it is possible that, instead, some false alarms to a stimulus display that could allow for an illusory conjunction occur from the misperception of a stimulus feature. For example, look back at the conjunction display in Fig. 11.5. What if the subject saw the black X as a white X (when the white X was the target)? This would be a feature error, but it would appear to be a conjunction error because it occurred with the conjunction stimulus display. To the extent that some of the errors labeled as conjunction errors were feature errors, the test of the difference between feature error and conjunction error responses to cue manipulation would not reflect the actual difference between misperceiving a single feature, and mentally combining two features that were not conjoined in the display.

Printzmetal et al. recognized this possibility and conducted two additional experiments to remove errors to feature stimuli and make errors to conjunction stimuli more interpretable. The second of these two additional experiments accomplished that goal. This last experiment was very similar to the one just discussed, so we concentrate on differences.

In their final experiment, stimulus displays consisted of four letters, three Os and an F or an X. On each trial subjects were cued regarding location (80% valid, 20% invalid) and the cue was followed by a stimulus display and a mask. Subjects were asked to respond with the target identity, F or X, and target color. Conjunction errors were measured with the proportion of trials in which subjects responded with the correct letter but in a color of a nontarget letter. There were four types of feature errors that could occur: color (letter correct, color not present in the display); letter (letter incorrect, color correct); letter (letter incorrect, color in display); letter and color (letter incorrect, color not in display).

Adjustments in color and spacing between letters in the stimulus display were made to reduce feature errors. That is, brighter colors were used, and letters were placed further apart, and this resulted in a dramatic decrease in feature errors. Subjects identified the target incorrectly on less than 2% of the trials and reported a color that was not present in the display on less than 1% of the trials. Nevertheless, conjunction errors (false alarms, that is, saying the target is present, with color present in the display but not in combination with the target letter) occurred on 14.7% of the trials. Thus, a sizeable percentage of conjunction errors occurred under stimulus conditions in which there were almost no feature errors (no misidentifications of individual features).

As in the last experiment, conjunction errors varied with cue validity (11.9% on valid trials and 17.4% on invalid trials). This confirms the previous finding about sensitivity of conjunction errors to lack of attention, in an experimental context where it is clear that feature errors are not the cause of the false alarms. It offers a stronger case for the position that conjunction errors arise from incorrect combinations of features perceived correctly. Printzmetal et al. (1986) state: "An intuitive definition of conjunction errors involves situations where subjects clearly perceive the colors and letters in the display, but incorrectly combine this information. The present results, to us, satisfy this intuitive definition" (p. 366).

Where Are Illusory Conjunctions in the Real World?

The phenomenon of illusory conjunctions is certainly an interesting prediction from feature integration theory, and the empirical finding of illusory conjunctions is a source of support for the theory. Given the demonstration of illusory conjunctions in the laboratory, it is interesting to think of the notion of illusory conjunctions in our everyday life. Feature integration theory states that features are free-floating without focal attention. If attention is not directed to a specific location, then features can recombine and we see illusory conjunctions as described earlier. This suggests a chaotic picture of visual perception. We certainly do not direct focal attention to all locations within our visual field at all times. This suggests that we should experience illusory conjunctions on a regular basis. Why don't we experience illusory conjunctions under normal circumstances? Is it the case that we form illusory conjunctions but are unaware of them? Or are illusory conjunctions an interesting aspect of human information processing that appears only in carefully contrived laboratory experiments?

The model of visual information processing that we have been considering, feature integration theory, is primarily a bottom-up model. The term **bottom-up** refers to the fact that the model characterizes visual information processing in temporal stages starting with simple features and proceeding to more complex processing and finally to object identification. Meaning or object identification comes only after a lengthy sequence of analyses on the input. This approach to visual information processing is shared by many investigators. Bottom-up processing is contrasted with **top-down** processing, wherein meaning and object identity actually facilitate the identification of individual elements or features.

Numerous studies have indicated effects that suggest top-down processing. One reliable finding is the *word-superiority effect* (e.g., Reicher, 1969). In these studies subjects were asked to identify a letter. The letter was presented alone or was in a word. The word-superiority effect refers to the fact that subjects were able to identify the letter at shorter exposure durations more accurately when the letter was in a word than when it was alone. Somehow the word facilitates processing of the individual letter. (Controls for the possibility that the word simply makes it easier to guess the letter were included in these studies.)

Treisman (1986) used the concept of top-down processing to address the issue of illusory conjunctions with more meaningful, or life-related, stimuli. Treisman showed subjects three shapes flanked by a number on each side. The stimulus display was followed, 200 msec after it was removed, by a pointer and a random checkerboard masking stimulus. The pointer was oriented toward one of the three, now absent, shapes in the center of the display. Subjects were instructed to first report the two digits (on the left and right edge of the stimulus array) and then supply some object name for the shape that had been in the space designated by the pointer, and also report what its color had been. The function of the digits was to divert attention from the objects in the display.

Treisman and Schmidt (1982) had previously used a variant of this task with colored letters and found substantial illusory conjunctions (subjects, in their reports, combining the color of one object with the shape of another). The interesting aspect of the later experiment by Treisman (1986), described in the preceding paragraph, was in the different types of instructions given to subjects. One group was told that the three shapes in the middle of the stimulus display would consist of an orange triangle, a blue ellipse, and a black ring. This group is comparable to those tested previously with colored letters, in that shapes (geometrical in this case) are arbitrarily combined with colors. A second group was told that the display would consist of an orange carrot, a blue lake, and a black tire. The object-color pairings for this group are consistent with the prior knowledge and expectations of the subjects (and everyone else). One out of every four shapes was presented in the wrong color (from the point of view of ordinary expectations).

Feature errors were those in which shapes were reported in colors not in the display, whereas conjunction errors were those in which shapes were reported in colors present in the display but not in combination with the shape tested. There was a dramatic difference between the two groups in conjunction errors.

The group receiving arbitrary pairings of shapes and colors (e.g., blue ellipse) made many more conjunction errors (27%) than feature errors (13%). However, the number of conjunction errors made by the group receiving natural pairings of shapes and colors (e.g., blue lake) was not significantly greater than the number of feature errors. For the latter group, then, it is reasonable to posit that conjunction errors arose from misperceptions and not from incorrect recombinations of features present in the display. The most simple interpretation of these results is that prior knowledge and expectations constrain the way in which we combine features. Given arbitrary pairings, features are in some sense free-floating and can recombine readily with any other features. However, given common or familiar pairings, features are not free to recombine randomly. It is possible that illusory conjunctions can and do occur outside the laboratory, but not with features that are part of our organized information system— and most of the perceptual world of adults is organized.

CHAPTER SUMMARY

Feature integration theory is a theory of visual information processing developed by Treisman and her colleagues. The basic elements of the theory are as follows:

1. The first stage of visual information processing is feature recording. During this stage of analysis, features are recorded in parallel and this recording does not require attention. The output of this processing stage is the detection of isolated features that were present in a display, but does not include the locations of the features.

2. Features detected during the first stage are combined to form multifeatured objects in the second stage of processing. The process of feature integration or combination requires attention. Focal attention is directed to a location in the visual field and the features which are present in that location are glued together. Attention is a serial process.

We examined several predictions from feature integration theory. First, we looked at reaction times for subjects searching visual displays for features or conjunctions of features. Search times for features were invariant over different display sizes, but search times for conjunctions increased as a function of display size. These results are consistent with the theory suggesting that feature recording occurs in parallel and that feature integration is a serial process. Remember from chapter 10 that it is difficult to infer search types with complete confidence through analyses of reaction time data, as other types of search models make similar predictions. Second, we looked at the dependence of feature identity and conjunction identity on location. As predicted by the theory, conjunction identity was more dependent on location than was feature identity. However, feature identity was not independent of location. This result suggested that, contrary to feature integration theory, processing of features requires attention. Third, Printzmetal et al. (1986) postulated, on the basis of feature integration theory, that conjunction errors would be increased by misdirection of attention, although this would not be true for feature errors (using cue-valid and cue-invalid trials to manipulate attention). They found that conjunction errors were more strongly affected by misdirection of attention, but that there was some (smaller) effect on feature errors. As before, this result is inconsistent with feature integration theory, and indicates that feature analysis does require attention, or at least deteriorates in the absence of attention.

The errors of special interest to Printzmetal et al. were the errors of illusory conjunctions. The role of attention in correct combining of features for integrated percepts was the primary focus of most of this research. The finding that such errors can be readily demonstrated in the laboratory setting, and that such errors are increased by inattention, raised the question of why such errors are not more commonly experienced in natural settings. It was found that prior knowledge and expectations constrain or limit the ways in which features are likely to be combined. This may be what is responsible for the rarity of illusory combinations in natural settings.

Feature integration theory is a complex theory of visual information processing. Several predictions of the theory have been confirmed. The major weak point of the theory at this time is the tenet that feature recording (or detection) is preattentive. This aspect of the theory would appear to have been disconfirmed.

NEW WORDS AND PHRASES USED IN CHAPTER 11

attention
bottom-up processing
conjunctive
disjunctive
feature recording
feature integration
feature integration theory
focal attention
illusory conjunction
invalid cues
preattentive
spotlight
top-down processing
valid cues

CHAPTER 12

Applied Experimental Psychology: Examples of the Kinds of Questions Asked, and Experiments Done, When the Focus Changes from Theory to Application

The research covered in the preceding chapters of experimental content was theory driven. It offered an opportunity to examine the logic of drawing conclusions about the validity of theoretical ideas, and to become acquainted with the use of surrogate variables. In the present chapter we change the focus from theory-driven research to applied research. As a concrete example, we look at research designed to ease the task of a computer user searching through **computer menus**.

Searching through computer menus to find a needed command can be an onerous task, so software manufacturers have tried to simplify the process, with different manufacturers offering different menu arrangements. Rather than relying on people's assumptions as to which arrangements are best, it is reasonable to do research to find out which ones induce the fewest errors, or permit the quickest arrival at needed computer commands. An experimental psychologist can use such straightforward criteria to answer the question of which is the best menu arrangment for a given set of circumstances.

The function of a computer menu is the same as that of a restaurant menu—to provide us with a list of the available options. The restaurant menu facilitates the interaction between the chef and the customer. The customer gives a command to the chef, finding the command in the menu, and using the waiter in a loose analogy to a voice-controlled device. If a keyboard were placed on each table, the waiter's order-taking function could be eliminated.

Just as you cannot order what is not on the menu, you cannot give the computer a command that is not in its lexicon. The computer generally has a huge number of commands available, so it is reasonable to organize and list the commands in terms of function and contexts. On a restaurant menu the dishes are organized, or grouped, according to part of the meal (appetizer, soup, salad, entree, dessert), and type of food (meat, fish, pasta, etc.). One could conceive of a restaurant computer menu, with a main (initial) menu offering choices looking like Fig. 12.1.

Pressing a numbered key would offer a deeper (second level) menu, which would indicate, for example, just what salads are available, each type of salad numbered so it could be efficiently requested. The main menu would then reappear, so that the customer could then request a different class of items (the customer might only want to order salad and soup, or perhaps salad and entree, etc.).

When selection on a main menu leads to the appearance of an additional screen from which an additional selection is made, it is described as a **top-level menu**. It enables a user to become gradually more specific through the use of two or more successive choices on different menus. The two most common menu-driven computer applications are for **software-command** systems and **information-retrieval** systems. A computer program that is used to obtain information (e.g., "What is the population of Afghanistan?"), might list topics on one menu, geography being one of the choices; hemispheres or continents on a second, deeper menu; and countries on a third, still deeper menu. When the choice has been made of a

```
Press a numbered key to

see the individual items.


1     Appetizer

2     Soup

3     Salad

4     Entree

5     Dessert
```

FIG. 12.1. Main menu (initially viewed menu) for a computer menu in a restaurant.

particular country, a fourth menu might appear offering classes of information about countries, one choice being demographics, which would lead to a fifth menu offering the opportunity to ask questions about population sizes.

In using the computer to obtain a command in a software program (e.g., to do a particular statistical test with some data), the main (initial) menu might offer options including such things as organizing the data in various ways, or graphing possibilities, along with statistical analyses. Having chosen statistical analyses, a further (deeper) menu screen would offer choices among specific statistical analyses.

In summary, a computer menu allows users to search through a large set of options and retrieve a desired item. The item can be a point of information from a **database**, or a command from a large lexicon, which is needed to operate the computer. Thus the use of menus permits the operation of a computer by people with minimal prior preparation. Instead of learning commands before operating a computer, the menu screens offer the commands as needed. The earlier menus, with choices among relatively general terms, act as guides to the more specific information found at the end of the ever more restricted menu pathway. For example, an initial screen in a word processing package might have choices like EDITING, FILE HANDLING, GRAPHING, etc. Selecting EDITING might lead to CHANGING TEXT, FINDING TEXT, ALIGNING TEXT, etc. If CHANGING TEXT is chosen, the next screen might offer INSERT, DELETE, MOVE, etc.

The research presented in this chapter is in some ways similar to the instrument panel experiment discussed in chapter 7. It asks for the best way to accomplish a task, quickly, and with minimal errors. It illustrates how research is used to determine the features of menus that maximize performance. We are not as interested in specifying the internal psychological processes through which we achieve performance efficiency; therefore, most of the work in this chapter uses direct rather than surrogate variables.

It is important to point out that this research is not antitheoretical. Rather, psychological theory is not advanced enough to offer much guidance in designing good menu systems. If theories of perception, visual scanning, memory, and decision making were more powerful, we would start with these theories and use them to direct our approach. However, that is not the case, so we begin by testing whatever menu arrangements are currently used. In addition, we sometimes vary and exaggerate the differences to determine what dimensions are relevant. If we are able to think of new ways to construct menus, these too are tried and tested.

BREADTH AND DEPTH OF COMPUTER MENUS

One of the factors that varies in computer design is the breadth and depth of the menus. **Breadth** refers to the number of items on an individual menu frame (a screen), and **depth** refers to the number of successive frames (screens) that must be examined to find the desired item. With many menu-driven implementations the number of items in the database or the number of commands that might be executed are far in excess of what could be shown on a computer screen at one time. Therefore it is common for a user to go through a series of menus to find the desired selection. Often this takes the form of a main menu with a set of very general options. Each option refers to the contents contained on a deeper level submenu (perhaps like the example offered in Fig. 12.1). By selecting one submenu the user bypasses the items on other submenus. Thus, in Fig. 12.1, while choosing a soup, the user does not have to confront everything else that the kitchen produces. Later, when needing to know what entrees are available, the user selects a different submenu. If a person only wishes to have salad and soup, she is spared the trouble of having to look through the entrees, desserts, etc. Of course, the restaurant analogy is an artificial one. Restaurant menus are of relatively limited size. But given the potential number of computer commands, or amounts of information in some large databases, it becomes important to be able to limit the number of things that the user would have to sort through. This is accomplished by permitting the user to restrict viewing to some selected screens, by-passing most of what is contained in the database.

With a large number of items to be examined it would, at least intuitively, appear to be reasonable to begin to organize the responses into subsets, and possibly to place different subsets of the items on different frames. But what is a large number? What is too large a number for people to efficiently peruse on one screen? This is an empirical question that could only be answered through data collection.

We speak of menu systems with large numbers of items on each individual menu as **broad menus**, and menu systems that contain many levels (submenus that each have submenus that themselves have submenus) as **deep menus**. The use of menus can be seen as a search task. In chapter 11 we examined visual search for features and conjunctions of features. Treisman's findings were consistent with parallel search for features and serial self-terminating search for conjunctions of features. Words, commands and concepts are intrinsically complex, and likely to function as conjunctions of features.

Most models tie search for meaning (semantic search) to a serial search process. To the extent that models of visual search can be generalized to a computer menu task, we would expect some type of serial search in computer menu perusal.

Miller's Experiment on Menu Depth and Breadth

Miller (1981) conducted the first empirical investigation of menu breadth and depth. He was working with a menu situation more like that of an information retrieval situation than a search for computer commands. The **hierarchy** of words developed by Miller for his breadth-depth study is shown in Fig. 12.2. Note that there are six levels in this hierarchy, with two general categories (science and culture) in the first or top level and 64 specific instances of the categories in the sixth or lowest level. If a subject were to begin at Level I, he would be faced with just two choices at each level, with the path through the menu choices leading to a final pair of choices at Level VI.

A subject could also be started, say, at Level II, with four choices. Any choice made could lead to four more choices at Level IV (skipping Level III). A choice at Level IV would lead to a final four choices at Level VI (skipping Level V). In this, and similar ways, a subject could be given a set of six menus with 2 choices on each, three menus with 4 choices on each, two menus with 8 choices on each (using only Levels III and VI), or a single menu with 64 choices (all at Level VI).

In Miller's task, subjects were exposed to one of the four different menu systems just described. The task confronting each subject on each trial was to locate an initially presented target word at the end of the pathway of choices. This required choosing the right word on the earlier menus in order to end up confronting the desired target word. The question asked by Miller was, what is the optimum arrangement of menu breadth and depth for target detection? To address this question, Miller constructed the four different menu configurations described in the preceding paragraph, using the specific words in the semantic hierarchy shown in Fig. 12.2.

The four menu systems covaried in breadth and depth according to:

$$n = b^d, \tag{12.1}$$

where n is the total number of items in the domain (64 in this example), b is the breadth (the number of items displayed on a single menu), and d is the depth (the number of levels of menus that a user

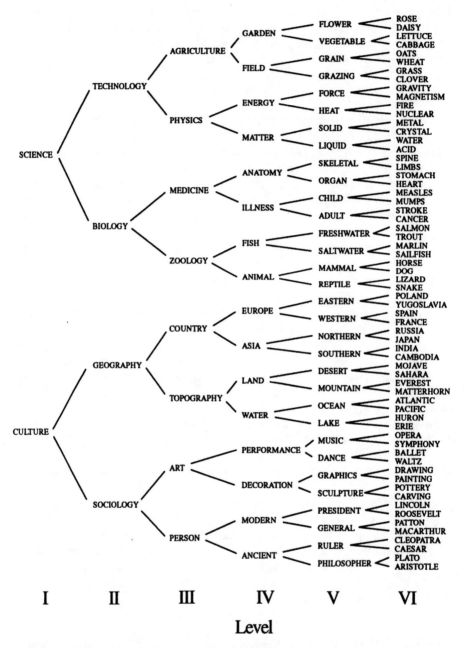

I   II   III   IV   V   VI

Level

FIG. 12.2. Word hierarchy developed for menu search by Miller (1980) and used in several studies reported in this chapter. From Miller (1980). Reprinted by permission.

of the menu system would have to access to reach the target item). Thus, given all the items on one menu, we have:

$64 = 64^1$

Given 8 items on each menu, we have:

$64 = 8^2$

Given 4 items on each menu, we have:

$64 = 4^3;$

Given just 2 items per menu, we have:

$64 = 2^6$

Table 12.1 summarizes the breadth and depth information for this example.

Equation 12.1 is sometimes restated as:

$$\ln n = d(\ln b) \qquad (12.2)$$

which is easily restated as

$$d = \frac{\ln n}{\ln b} \qquad (12.3)$$

These equations are used to compute either d from n and b, or b from n and d. Equations 12.1–12.3 are only useful with equal numbers of items on each frame (a constant value of b), which is not often the case in computer command menus. The main purpose of these equations is to offer some sense of the magnitude of the tradeoffs on breadth and depth (b and d), for any value of n.

Construction of Menus in the Miller Study. As suggested in Table 12.1, in the Miller study all 64 words in Level VI of Fig. 12.2 were presented at the same time, for the 64^1 menu. The 64 words

TABLE 12.1. Number of Options per Menu Frame (Breadth) and Number of Menu Frames (Depth) for the Four Menu Configurations used in the Miller (1981) Study

Menu	Options per Frame	Number of Frames
64^1	64	1
8^2	8	2
4^3	4	3
2^6	2	6

were presented in 8 columns of 8 words each. The 8 columns were arranged in two groups of 4 columns, one group above the other, with a space between the upper and lower groups of columns. The menu frames leading to the target word "heart" for the other menu configurations, 8^2, 4^3, and 2^6, are shown in Fig. 12.3a, b, and c, respectively.

In terms of experimental design we have a single factor, menu configuration, with four levels. Miller's experiment was a between-subjects design, so subjects were randomly assigned to one of the four menu arrangements for participation. Two dependent variables were measured, response accuracy (whether the target word was correctly located or not by the subject) and search time. Each subject received 256 target presentations. If a subject erred on a trial, that trial was repeated once at the end of the session.

What did Miller find? Note that we have not generated any predictions for the results of this experiment as we have for those covered in the last three chapters. This is because the Miller experiment was exploratory and was not testing a theory. Miller found significant differences between menu configurations for both response accuracy and response time (results of the experiment are shown in Fig. 12.4). The menu with 8 choices at two levels produced the most accurate performance (open bars in Fig. 12.4), followed in order by menus 64^1, 4^3, and 2^6. Error rates were very low in all menu configurations, but it should be remembered that subjects were given a second chance on each trial in which they made an error. That is, if a subject erred on the first trial with a target word but was correct on the second try, the error was thrown out and the trial was scored as correct. The second (correct) trial supplied the reaction time used for search times. Search times (striped bars in Fig. 12.4), were shorter in the two menus with intermediate levels of breadth and depth (8^2 and 4^3) than in the menus with extreme breadth (64^1) and depth (2^6). On the basis of the combined results for accuracy and time, Miller concluded that menus of intermediate breadth and depth (8^2 and 4^3) were optimal for menu design of the type studied in his experiment.

Confounding Factors in the Miller Study. Parkinson and his colleagues (Snowberry, Parkinson, & Sisson, 1983) noticed two problems with Miller's design. Both of these problems involve violations of Rule 2 for research presented in chapter 3. Remember that Rule 2 states that "there must be only one difference distinguishing different conditions of the experiment, that difference being variations of the factor." Variations in the number of words per frame and

MENUS 8^2

FRAME 1	*	• Agriculture • Physics • Medicine • Zoology	Country Topography Art Person	• • • •

- -

FRAME 2 (*Assuming the subject chose Medicine in Frame 1)	• Spine • Limbs • Stomach • Heart	Measles Mumps Stroke Cancer	• • • •

(b)

MENUS 4^3

FRAME 1	*	• Technology • Biology	Geography Sociology	• •

- -

FRAME 2 (*Assuming Biology in previous frame)	*	• Anatomy • Illness	Fish Animal	• •

- -

FRAME 3 (*Assuming Anatomy in previous frame)	• Spine • Limbs	Stomach Heart	• •

(c)

MENUS 2^6

FRAME 1	*	• Science	Culture •	
FRAME 2		• Technology	Biology •	*
FRAME 3	*	• Medicine	Zoology •	
FRAME 4	*	• Anatomy	Illness •	
FRAME 5		• Skeletal	Organ •	*
FRAME 6		• Stomach	Heart •	

FIG. 12.3. Menu frames for correct selections leading to the target word "heart" in menus 8^2 (a), 4^3 (b) and 2^6 (c). On each trial subjects are shown a target word (in this case "heart") and are asked to find the target word by searching through the options presented in the menu. Each menu frame shown is presented as it would appear to the subject (except for the asterisks and related comments). In sequential menus with more than one frame, only one frame is presented at a time and subjects are required to select an option that will lead them to the next frame. The sequences shown assume correct selections, as indicated by the asterisks. The dots next to the words represent response buttons, which the subjects push to indicate their selections. Fig. 12.2 illustrates how these sequences are generated from the hierarchy.

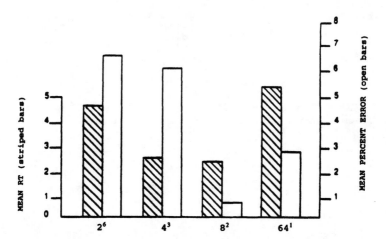

FIG. 12.4. Striped bars show response times in seconds, and open bars show mean percent error. From Miller (1981). From *Proceedings of the Human Factors Society 25th annual Meeting*, 1981. Copyright 1981 by the Human Factors and Ergonomics Society, Inc. All rights reserved. Reprinted by permission.

the number of frames should have been the only difference between conditions in the experiment. One clear additional difference between menu 64^1 and other menu configurations existed in the location of response buttons and in the specificity of the response. As shown in Fig. 12.3, the response buttons for menus 8^2, 4^3, and 2^6 were located to the sides of the words in the menu. This was not possible in the broadest menu, as the 64 words were arranged in two rows of four columns (see Fig. 12.5). As Fig. 12.5 shows, response buttons in the 64^1 menu condition were located at the top and bottom of columns of the display. Subjects were required to respond by pushing the button of the column in which the target word resided, rather than with a response directly to the target word.

A second difference concerns the method used for determining the location of items on a screen. In menus 8^2, 4^3, and 2^6 the placement of items on a screen was based on category membership. Items from the same category were grouped together, and within a category, items that were most similar to one another were located adjacent to one another in the display. Category grouping was not used to determine item location in menu 64^1; item placement was random in that condition. This then offers a second undesired difference between menu conditions.

These differences—categorical grouping, location of response buttons, and type of response (to the column rather than to the actual target)—are confounding variables; that is, they constitute differ-

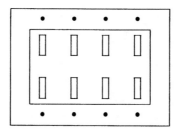

FIG. 12.5. Response button locations for menu 64[1] in the Miller (1981) study. Subjects were instructed to press the button above or below the column in which the target word appeared. From *Proceedings of the Human Factors Society 25th annual Meeting*, 1981. Copyright 1981 by the Human Factors and Ergonomics Society, Inc. All rights reserved. Reprinted by permission.

ences between different conditions in the experiment in addition to the manipulated factor.

Snowberry et al. (1983) investigated the importance of these confounding factors in another menu search study. Controlling the variable of category grouping differences, Snowberry et al. developed two menus in which all 64 words were presented simultaneously. In both menus, words were presented in four columns of 16 words. In one menu, 64 RAN, assignment of the 64 words in Level VI of Fig. 12.2 to columns was random. In the second menu, 64 CAT, the assignment of words to columns reflected the category grouping in the hierarchy. These two menus are shown in Fig. 12.6, with 64 CAT in the lower half of the figure. Looking back at Fig. 12.2, it can be seen that the 64 words in Level VI consist of eight instances of each of the eight categories presented in Level III (Agriculture, Physics, Medicine, Zoology, Country, Topography, Art, and Person). In Menu 64 CAT (Fig. 12.6), the assignment of words to columns was determined by the Level III category. Note the first column in Menu 64 CAT shown in the lower half of Fig. 12.6. The first eight words in the first column are from one category, Medicine, and the second set of eight words in that column are from another category, Zoology. Each column in Menu 64 CAT contains words from two categories, and all eight words within a category are in the same half of the column, top or bottom. Presenting these two different arrangements to subjects permitted a comparison of homogeneously grouped items in a menu, with items that were randomly grouped.

Snowberry et al. dealt with the problem of different response button arrangements by assigning a two-digit number to each word in Level VI (see Fig. 12.6), and subjects were instructed to type in the two-digit number of the target word when they located the target in

(11) ARISTOTLE	(31) WHEAT	(51) LETTUCE	(71) WALTZ
(12) POLAND	(32) ACID	(52) ATLANTIC	(72) CAESAR
(13) PATTON	(33) SAHARA	(53) PLATO	(73) MEASLES
(14) TROUT	(34) ROOSEVELT	(54) BALLET	(74) LIZARD
(15) WATER	(35) HURON	(55) MUMPS	(75) CAMBODIA
(16) NUCLEAR	(36) MARLIN	(56) SAILFISH	(76) SYMPHONY
(17) PACIFIC	(37) STOMACH	(57) METAL	(77) CARVING
(18) CANCER	(38) GRAVITY	(58) LIMBS	(78) CABBAGE
(21) DAISY	(41) ROSE	(61) RUSSIA	(81) YUGOSLAVIA
(22) INDIA	(42) EVEREST	(62) POTTERY	(82) SALMON
(23) PAINTING	(43) OPERA	(63) MACARTHUR	(83) CRYSTAL
(24) MATTERHORN	(44) SPAIN	(64) FRANCE	(84) MOJAVE
(25) STROKE	(45) ERIE	(65) FRANCE	(85) MAGNETISM
(26) HORSE	(46) SNAKE	(66) DOG	(86) GRASS
(27) FIRE	(47) SPINE	(67) HEART	(87) DRAWING
(28) JAPAN	(48) CLOVER	(68) LINCOLN	(88) OATS

(11) CANCER	(31) ACID	(51) CAMBODIA	(71) BALLET
(12) HEART	(32) CRYSTAL	(52) FRANCE	(72) CARVING
(13) LIMBS	(33) FIRE	(53) INDIA	(73) DRAWING
(14) MEASLES	(34) GRAVITY	(54) JAPAN	(74) OPERA
(15) MUMPS	(35) MAGNETISM	(55) POLAND	(75) PAINTING
(16) SPINE	(36) METAL	(56) RUSSIA	(76) POTTERY
(17) STOMACH	(37) NUCLEAR	(57) SPAIN	(77) SYMPHONY
(18) STROKE	(38) WATER	(58) YUGOSLAVIA	(78) WALTZ
(21) DOG	(41) CABBAGE	(61) ATLANTIC	(81) ARISTOTLE
(22) HORSE	(42) CLOVER	(62) ERIE	(82) CAESAR
(23) LIZARD	(43) DAISY	(63) EVEREST	(83) CLEOPATRA
(24) MARLIN	(44) GRASS	(64) HURON	(84) LINCOLN
(25) SAILFISH	(45) LETTUCE	(65) MATTERHORN	(85) MACARTHUR
(26) SALMON	(46) OATS	(66) MOJAVE	(86) PATTON
(27) SNAKE	(47) ROSE	(67) PACIFIC	(87) PLATO
(28) TROUT	(48) WHEAT	(68) SAHARA	(88) ROOSEVELT

Fig. 12.6. Menus 64 RAN (top) and 64 CAT (bottom) in Snowberry et al. (1983). Placement of words in columns in 64 RAN was random. In 64 CAT each column contained words from two categories. The two categories in each column were defined by the category names in Level III. A two-digit number was presented to the left of each word in the display. Subjects were instructed to type in the two-digit number when they located the target word.

the display. The two-digit number was located to the left of Level VI words in all menu configurations; thus, the type of response to the target word was held constant in this experiment.

The Snowberry et al. experiment was a mixed design with five levels of the menu variable manipulated between subjects (64^1 CAT, 64^1 RAN, 8^2, 4^3, and 2^6). Each subject in the Snowberry et al. experiment participated in two blocks of 64 trials, so trial block was a within-groups manipulation. Subjects were not allowed to repeat error trials in the Snowberry et al. experiment.

The results of the Snowberry et al. experiment, shown in Fig. 12.7 (Search Time) and Fig. 12.8 (Response Accuracy), indicate both a strong replication of Miller's findings and a dramatic difference. First, consider the replicated conditions, that is, Menus 64^1 RAN, 8^2, 4^3, and 2^6. Search times for these four conditions mirrored those found by Miller with shorter times for the two menus of intermediate

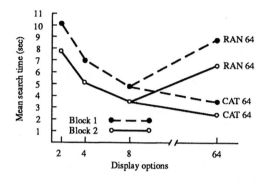

FIG. 12.7. Search time in the Snowberry et al. (1983) experiment. Block 1 was the first 64 trials and Block 2 the second set of 64 trials. From Snowberry et al. (1983). Copyright Taylor and Francis, Ltd., 1983. Reprinted by permission.

breadth and depth (8^2 and 4^3) and substantially longer times for the conditions with extreme breadth (64^1 RAN) and depth (2^6). The pattern of search accuracy across these four conditions was also very similar to that found by Miller. It should be noted that the error rate in the Snowberry et al. experiment was much higher than in the previous experiment. This is due to the fact that subjects were not allowed to repeat error trials in this experiment.

Whereas performances in replicated conditions produced results very similar to those found by Miller, the results with the new condition, 64^1 CAT, suggest a different interpretation of the pattern of findings. Subjects in the 64^1 CAT group showed the fastest search times in the experiment. It is often the case in speeded tasks that subjects trade accuracy for speed. That is, they respond very quickly, but at the expense of making a large number of errors. This tendency is called a **speed–accuracy tradeoff**. The rapid search of subjects in 64^1 CAT was not due to a speed–accuracy tradeoff, as search in that condition was also performed with very high accuracy.

Miller's results suggest that menus of intermediate breadth–depth configuration are optimal in terms of search speed and accuracy. The results of the present study suggest that the relatively poor performance found in the 64^1 menu was not due to breadth or the number of words on the screen, but rather to the organization of the words in the broadest configuration. Random organization results in slow search, and categorized organization results in very fast search. This is confirmation of what we would expect. What was not

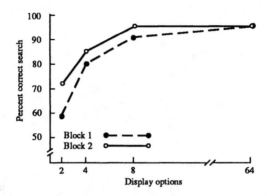

FIG. 12.8. Response accuracy in the Snowberry, et al. (1983) experiment. From Snowberry et al. (1983). Copyright Taylor and Francis, Ltd., 1983. Reprinted by permission.

predictable was that, when organized, 64 items on one screen would be processed more quickly than a two-level presentation, like the 8^2 menu condition, where a subject only had to scan through 16 items (8 on each of two screens).

In summary, confounding variables were detected in the Miller experiment. Snowberry et al. (1983) designed an experiment to remove or measure the effects of these confounding variables. Differences in response requirements between Menu 64^1 and other menus in the Miller study turned out not to be important, as the same pattern of results was found for those conditions by Snowberry et al. when type of response was held constant between all conditions. Organization of the 64^1 menu, however, proved to be an important determinant of performance. The results of Snowberry et al. suggest that menu search performance improves as a function of menu breadth if the items are presented in an organized fashion, when there are 64 items classified into eight categories. Separating the categories into different frames (decreasing breadth and increasing depth) slowed the performance.

This example incidentally illustrates the point that when confounding factors are recognized, they do not necessarily turn out to be important. This was the case with the varying button placements in the different conditions of the original Miller (1981) experiment. When a completed experiment is later recognized as having contained confounding variables, it is true that we can no longer be convinced of the relationships previously accepted, but it does not mean that we know the relationships to be false. Upon further study, the confounding variables could be found to have been innocent of influence, thus reinstating the original conclusions. In this example there were two confounding factors, but only one was found to have affected the outcomes.

An Advantage of Depth

What does adding depth to a menu accomplish? It decreases the total number of options to be viewed as it "**funnels**" (Paap & Roske-Hostrand, 1986) the user to a restricted domain at the lowest menu level. Imagine searching for a word in menu 64^1. Let us first assume an exhaustive search. You would search through all 64 words prior to making a response. Now consider the total number of words that you would need to search in an exhaustive serial search of menus 8^2, 4^3, and 2^6: 16, 12, and 12, respectively. A similar picture of progressively less words to be confronted, as depth increases, is found with the assumption of a self-terminating search. With the 64^1 menu, there would be $(b+1)/2$ words searched, on average, where b, the number of words per menu, is 64, yielding $65/2 = 32.5$ words per search. For menus 8^2, 4^3, and 2^6, respectively, the average numbers of words searched would be 9, 7.5, and 9. The decrease in the number of words to be searched as numbers of menus (depth) increase is only found with three or more items per menu.

In summary, assuming some constant total number of words or choices in the database, the deeper the menu, the fewer the total number of options (words, or choices) to be searched (as long as there are more than two words in any menu). Considering only the total number of words to be searched, depth usually offers an advantage. As we saw in Fig. 12.8 from the Snowberry et al. (1983) experiment, however, accuracy suffered with depth.

Now consider searches through the two different broad menus, 64^1 CAT and RAN. The words in these menus were presented in the same position on each trial, and subjects searched through the menu 64 times in each of two sessions. Initially, subjects had no knowledge about target locations. Through repeated searches for different target words, however, subjects in 64^1 CAT would find that words sharing many semantic features were located adjacent to one another in the display. Having engaged in a successful search for "heart" on trial n, the subject could then return to that general location on the screen on trial $n + 1$ when the target word was "spine." Organizing the words in a broad menu by category thus performs the same function as the funneling process with menu depth: It guides the subject to a restricted number of menu alternatives. No such knowledge is gained in a search through menu 64^1 RAN. Having just searched successfully for "heart", no restriction of alternatives is provided on trial $n + 1$. The only way that a subject searching a random menu can restrict alternatives is to learn the location of each individual target word.

If this view of the function of organization of a broad menu is correct, then other methods of organizing the words in a broad menu should also result in search benefits. But we would want to see empirical support for the advantage of any particular additional ways of organizing or grouping items. This is one of the topics of the next section.

ADDITIONAL FACTORS INFLUENCING MENU-AIDED PERFORMANCE

The results of Snowberry et al. (1983) indicate an advantage for broad menus in terms of both speed and accuracy when the menu is well organized. An immediate question that arises is, what exactly does *well organized* mean? In the previous study, well organized meant that words belonging to the same general category were presented adjacent to one another in the display. Poorly organized meant that knowledge about where a particular word was located in the display did not provide any information as to the likelihood of the location of another word. Organizing by category is one form of organizing a list of words. Organizing alphabetically is yet another way. Would an alphabetical listing of options prove to be an effective method of organizing information in a computer menu?

Additional issues with broad menus can be raised with regard to display format. For example, in the Snowberry et al. (1983) study, categories were arranged by column and there was no separation between the two categories presented in a single column. Would performance be improved if there were a separation between the two categories in a column? Categories could also be arranged by row rather than by column. Would a row arrangement prove more or less effective than organization by column? The effects of row and column arrangement and the effect of spacings or lack of spacings between categories was investigated in another study by Parkinson, Sisson, and Snowberry (1985). Type of organization, categorical or alphabetical, was also investigated in that study.

Ten different versions of the 64^1 menu were tested by Parkinson et al. In eight menus, words belonging to the same category (defined by menu Level III in Fig. 12.2) were presented together in the display (eight categories, eight words to a category). The order of words within categories in these eight menus was either alphabetized, or adjacent placement of words was based on semantic similarity. For example, in the TOPOGRAPHY category (a label taken from Level III in Fig. 12.2), the word order for the alphabetized versions was Atlantic, Erie, Everest, Huron, Matterhorn, Mojave, Pacific, and Sahara. In the versions in which order was based on semantic similarity for the same category, the order was Mojave, Sahara, Everest, Matterhorn, Atlantic, Pacific, Huron, and Erie. Note that in the order based on semantic similarity the first four words are land areas, with two deserts and two mountains, whereas the last four are bodies of water, with two oceans and two lakes.

The next basis for distinguishing categorized menus was the use of additional vertical spacing between categories, or an absence of additional spaces. In menus without spacings between category groups, words within and between categories were on adjacent lines. In menus with spacings, a blank line separated categories vertically. This permitted the two menus previously described (arranged alphabetically or according to semantic similarity) to be reconstituted two ways, half with and half without vertical spacing between categories, yielding four menus. Finally, these could be doubled to make eight menus, by juxtaposing the items in categories vertically (by column) or horizontally (by row).

Note that, in the alphabetized arrangements, it was groups of 8 words that were *semantically* similar that were alphabetized. To test exclusively alphabetized arrangements, in the 9th and 10th menus the entire 64-word array was arranged in alphabetical order (in one case the array was alphabetized by column and in the other by row).

Three analyses of variance were conducted on the menu data. Accuracy was over 97% for all menus tested, so analyses were only conducted on search time. The first analysis was conducted only on the eight categorized menus. This was a $2 \times 2 \times 2$ analysis where the three factors (each with two levels) were organization by row or column, spacing or no spacing between category groups, and arrangement of words within categories (alphabetical or semantic similarity). This analysis indicated significant main effects of type of organization (row or column) and spacing, but no effect of arrangement of words within categories. (That is, within sets of eight words that shared a general category, arrangments by alphabetization or semantic similarity were equally effective). Figure 12.9 omits the alphabetical/semantic similarity comparison, and summarizes only the statistically significant differences. Menus in which categories were organized by column were searched 1 sec faster than menus in which categories were organized by row (4.1 sec for row and 3.1 sec for column). Menus with spacings between category groups were searched 1 sec faster than menus without spacings (3.1 sec for spacing and 4.2 sec without spacing). None of the interactions between the factors were significant.

As there was no main effect for arrangement of words within categories (alphabetical versus semantic similarity) the data are collapsed over this factor in Fig. 12.10, which offers a little more detailed summary of the findings. *Collapsing* means that we treat the data as if the factor had not been manipulated in the study. This can be done when the main effect of the factor is not significant and when the factor does not interact with any other factor. Collapsing allows us to simplify our presentation of the data. Fig. 12.10 shows the differences between spacing and no spacing separately for menus organized by column and those organized by row.

Remember that there were 10 menus in the experiment, 8 categorized and 2 in which order was alphabetized across all 64 words. In the next two analyses, performances on the 2 menus in which the entire array was alphabetized, one by column and one by row, were compared to performances on the categorized menus. The menu in which the entire array was alphabetized by column was compared to the 4 categorized menus organized by column, and the menu in which the entire array was alphabetized by row was compared to the 4 categorized menus organized by row. The average search time for the menu alphabetized by column was 2.54 sec (see the placement of the asterisk in Fig. 12.10). Analyses indicated that this search time was significantly faster than for the categorized menus without spacings and was not significantly different from the categorized menus with spacings. The average search time for the menu alphabetized by row was 3.67 sec (see the placement of the plus sign in

ROW	VERSUS	COLUMN
4.1		3.1
SPACING	VERSUS	NO SPACING
3.1		4.2

FIG. 12.9. Mean search times among categorized menus, when comparing row versus column organization, and when spacing was present or absent between categories (both comparisons statistically significant).

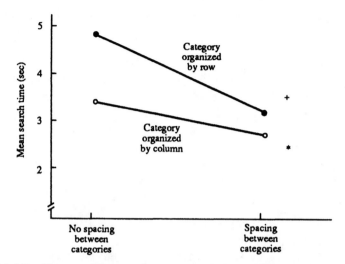

FIG. 12.10. Mean search times for categorized menus in which categories are arranged by column or row and where there is spatial separation or no spatial separation between categories. The two additional data points are for menus in which the entire array was alphabetized (* by column and + by row).

Fig. 12.10). Analyses indicated that this search time was significantly faster than for categorized menus without spacings and was not significantly different from categorized menus with spacings. In both cases involving comparisons between alphabetized and categorized menus, the alphabetized menu was searched at a rate not significantly different from the comparable menu with spacing between categories, and significantly faster than the menu without spacing.

In summary, the results of this experiment indicate that categorical organization by column is superior to categorical organization by row, and search is faster in both cases when spacing is provided between categories. Menus in which the entire array was alphabetized were searched at the same rate as categorized menus with spacing between categories and significantly faster than categorized menus without spacing.

In the previous study, Snowberry et al. (1983) found that organizing a broad menu by category resulted in accurate and rapid search. Organizing by category requires that groups of items (menu options) be similar in meaning or function. There could be cases where a menu is desirable but available options cannot be broken down conveniently into groups, the members of which are similar in meaning or function. The present results suggest that a simple alphabetical ordering of options can be effective in those cases.

IMPROVING PERFORMANCE IN DEEP-MENU SYSTEMS

We have previously seen that, given 64 items in a database, breadth should be maximized. That is, all items, if properly organized, can be handled with maximum efficiency on a single screen. However, there will often be databases that cannot fit on one screen. A reasonable question, then, is how can performance be improved when deeper menus have to be used? We examine that issue in this section.

Snowberry et al. (1983) found that performance on the deepest menu, 2^6, was both slow and inaccurate. In fact, in the first trial block, subjects only located the target word correctly on approximately 60% of the trials. A similar trend showing an increase in error rate with menu depth has been reported by Kiger (1984).

Why is search performance in deep menus so inaccurate? Consider how depth is provided in a menu. The items in the database (actual commands or sets of information) are subdivided according to semantic or functional similarity. A category descriptor term that corresponds to the shared meaning or function is selected, and subjects are given a list of these more general category descriptor terms at an upper level of the menu. Problems can arise in terms of how well the members of a group are described by the category descriptor term. For example, suppose that you are editing text and decide to underline a word. What is the appropriate command? If you are obtaining this information via a menu system, you would need to access the menu screen that contains the needed command as an option (say the command U for underline). The menu system probably has a main menu with terms like EDITING, FORMATTING, PRINTING, etc., from which you must select. You would have to choose, from among such terms, the one term that would lead to a second menu that contains the option to underline.

Difficulties arising from category descriptor terms at initial menu levels that are not clearly related to database terms become even more pronounced in deeper menus. Also, there are simply more opportunities to stray off the correct path. It is very easy to imagine subjects getting lost in deep menus, and that is exactly what does sometimes happen (Robertson, McCracken, & Newell, 1981).

What might be done to help subjects search through deep menus? The variability in directness of relationships between category descriptor terms and target words suggests two types of additional menu information that might be useful. When subjects get lost in menu systems, that means that they do not know what alternatives will direct them toward their targets deeper into the menus. They may not recall what selections they have previously made and therefore cannot retrace their paths and try again. We could minimize navigational problems of these kinds by providing the subjects with a map. The map could take the form of a record of the previous selections made on a trial, so that when confronted with a pair of options the subject would always know what previous selections got them to that particular point. Another type of map could inform the subject of the consequences of selecting an option. That is, given a set of options at menu level n, information could be provided that showed the options at menu level $n + 1$ for the various alternatives that might be selected at menu level n.

These two types of information could provide valuable aids to subjects as they attempt to select alternatives at various levels of the menu. The use of these two types of information assumes that the reason for inaccurate search in deep menus stems from weak associations between category descriptor terms and targets. There is another possible reason for the inaccurate search, and that is interference with short-term memory. There is a large body of literature that indicates that retention of an item over short periods of time is affected by subsequent information and processing. In one experimental paradigm, subjects receive a short list of to-be-remembered letters or words. Following presentation of the items to be remembered, subjects are asked to perform another task, such as counting backward by threes starting with a specific number. After a few seconds of counting backward the subject is asked to recall the item or items in the to-be-remembered set. Results indicate that recall accuracy drops off precipitously after only a few seconds of interpolated activity (counting backward). Now consider memory for the target word in the menu task. The subject sees the target word, and then the target word is turned off and menu frames are presented. In menu 2^6 the subject must search through five menu levels before he arrives at the frame with the target word in menu Level VI. It is possible that processing options through levels of the menu interferes with memory for the target word. Forgetting the target word might contribute to the inaccurate search typically found in deep menus.

The Effects of Help Fields

Snowberry, Parkinson, and Sisson (1985) conducted another study with the deepest menu, 2^6, to see if additional menu information would result in improved performance. Three types of help information were added to menu 2^6, with the original menu constituting the control condition. In the target condition, the target remained visible throughout the entire search from menu Levels I through VI. In the control condition for this experiment, and in the original experiment, the target was initially turned on, and then turned off prior to presentation of the first menu. In the previous selections condition, the previous selections made at each level of the menu within a trial were shown on the screen in addition to current options. In the upcoming selections condition, subjects were shown options one level deeper than the current menu frame in addition to the current options. Examples of each of the three experimental conditions are shown in Fig. 12.11.

Type of **help field** (control, target, previous selections, and upcoming selections) was a between-subjects manipulation, and trial block, 1 and 2, was a within-subjects factor. Separate analyses of variance were conducted on the two dependent measures, accuracy and search time. The results are displayed in Fig. 12.12. Overall results of the analysis of variance on accuracy indicated main effects of help field and trial block, and a help field by trial block interaction.

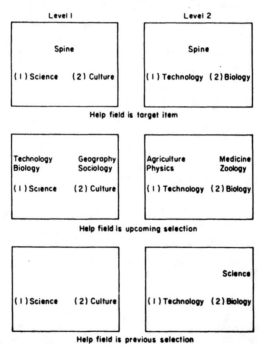

FIG. 12.11. Display formats for the first two menu levels of the three groups receiving help information. The target word is "Spine," and the correct choices are "Science" on Level I and "Biology" on Level II. From Snowberry, Parkinson, and Sisson (1985). Copyright 1985 by Academic Press, Ltd. Reprinted by permission.

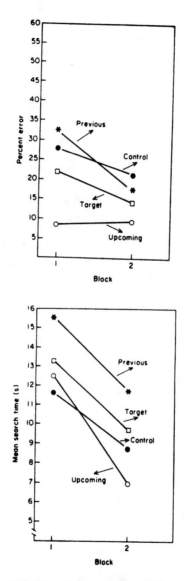

FIG. 12.12. Percent error (top panel) and search time (bottom panel) for three groups receiving help information and for control subjects searching through Menu 2^6 without any additional information. From Snowberry, Parkinson, and Sisson (1985). Copyright 1985 by Academic Press, Ltd. Reprinted by permission.

The main purpose of the experiment was to determine what type of additional information, if any, would improve performance relative to the standard deep menu, 2^6. Therefore, subsequent tests were conducted between the control and help field conditions on Trial Blocks 1 and 2. These analyses revealed that only the upcoming selections group searched with greater accuracy than the control group, and they did so in both trial blocks. Similar analyses were conducted on the search time data. Tests between the control group and help field groups showed different effects in Trial Blocks 1 and 2. In Trial Block 1 the group receiving help fields consisting of a record of previous selections actually searched more slowly than subjects in the control condition; no other groups were significantly different from control in the first trial block. In the second trial block the previous selections group was again significantly slower than control. Also in Trial Block 2 the upcoming selections group searched more rapidly than subjects in the control group.

In summary, performances of subjects on the standard deep menu, 2^6, were compared to those of subjects receiving three types of additional information in help fields: target, previous selections, and upcoming selections. Accuracy and latency data revealed that only upcoming selections benefited performance over that found with the standard menu.

The results of this study suggest that when menu depth is necessary, the adverse effects of depth can be reduced with information regarding consequences of each choice—that is, providing a look at the next level of the menu system.

APPLYING EXPERIMENTAL RESULTS TO MENU DESIGN

In this chapter the concern has been with solving some practical problems. It makes sense, therefore, to now ask how we would proceed in the future, given the research findings.

A basic tenet for computer menu design in the late 1970s and early 1980s was to present menu frames with no more than four or five options per frame (e.g., Schneiderman, 1980). The decision to restrict the number of options was based on the intuitions of programmers and design specialists, rather than on any empirical findings. Presumably, having more than four or five options on a frame was seen as being too confusing to the user. We can see from Equation 12.1, however, that for a large database of options, such decision making could lead to menu systems with extreme depth. The empirical findings in the present chapter lead to exactly the opposite conclusion, that is, menus should be constructed with the greatest possible breadth. Furthermore, within menus, items should be organized, if not categorically, then alphabetically. The categories should be separated by spaces, and the grouping should be arranged vertically (in columns).

On the basis of research, such as that presented in this chapter, and on observations of user performance with different types of commercial menus, researchers and designers have begun to emphasize the advantages of broad menus, and this trend is evident in current menu-driven systems.

DETERMINATION OF VISUAL SEARCH STRATEGIES IN COMPUTER MENU SELECTION

In previous sections of this chapter we have examined research directed at learning the advantages of particular menu configurations. We have not presented experimental manipulations that were conducted to analyze search processes. In this final section of the chapter we are going to change our orientation from an applied to a basic research focus and discuss research on search strategies in computer menu selection. Any light that can be shed will not have immediate application to the development of more efficient menu systems. But we can contrast what we learn in this situation with what we learned in the preceding chapters about the search process. We can also further contrast the kinds of questions being asked in basic research, where we raise questions about basic psychological processes, with applied research, where we just want to know how to get a particular task done most efficiently.

There are some recent studies (MacGregor, Lee, & Lam, 1986; Pierce, Parkinson, & Sisson, 1992) that have attempted to measure search strategies in computer menu selection, and we will cover methods and results from the MacGregor et al. study in this section. Both of these studies used a more direct measure of visual search than the indirect methods described in the last two chapters. In chapters 10 and 11 we presented attempts to describe and model memory search and visual search processes. Sternberg's (1966, 1969, 1970) memory search model was tested exclusively through analyses of functions relating number of alternatives in the memory set to reaction time. Relationships between number of items and reaction time were also used by Treisman in her studies of visual search and attention. Our conclusion after discussing these studies was that there was only limited evidence available to support hypotheses of specific types of search processes.

The study of computer menu selection to be presented here provides a more direct measure of search strategies by using sequential presentation of the items on an individual menu. That is, options on a single menu are presented sequentially, one at a time, and are under subject control. The options selected by a subject are recorded on each trial, allowing a direct determination of the type of search. Parallel search of alternatives is not possible with sequential presentation, because only one alternative is visible at a time. Three types of serial search are defined: exhaustive, self-terminating and **redundant**. If a subject views all options once prior to making a selection, the search is defined as *exhaustive*. If a subject makes a selection prior to viewing all options, the search is defined as *self-terminating*. If all options are examined, and some are reexamined prior to making a selection, the search is defined as *redundant*. These distinctions are possible because the subject only sees the items available on a menu screen by requesting them, one at a time.

MacGregor et al. (1986) used a mixed design with one between-groups and one within-groups factor to examine menu search performance. The between-groups factor was method of menu presentation and it had two levels, simultaneous and sequential. Twelve subjects were randomly assigned to each presentation condition. The within-groups factor was the number of alternatives per menu with four levels of the factor: 2, 4, 8, or 16 alternatives on each menu screen.

Subjects searched only one menu frame per trial, and had to make a selection on that menu. They were free to look at the choices on that menu frame, but in the sequential condition could only do that one item at a time. That is, the options on the frame were not visible, only numbers representing choices. If a subject moved the cursor to a particular number, the associated option became visible. In this way, subjects could go through all the options on that menu frame (that single screen), or could look at just a few, stopping when they thought they had the response they wanted; or they could reexamine any of the options. They eventually signaled a response (a final selection), leaving a record of what they needed to examine in order to make their final selection.

Final selection of an alternative on a trial resulted in either an indication of a correct response and termination of the trial, or an indication that the response was incorrect and that the subject should try again. All trials therefore ended in a correct response.

The menu alternatives presented and the questions asked were typical of an actual videotex information retrieval system. Videotex is an interactive information retrieval system designed to present textual and graphic information. The database used by MacGregor et al. (1986) consisted of general information on business, news, government, home, and community. Each trial started with a question asking the subject to select an information category that would lead to the specific information requested in the question. For example, subjects might be asked to "Find out what you can use instead of ground beef for a vegetarian hamburger." The question would be followed by a menu such as is contained in Fig. 12.13. Note that the question asks for specific information, whereas general information categories are presented as alternatives on the initial menu. The subjects were instructed to choose the alternative that would most likely lead them to the specific information desired (meat substitutes in this example). Each of the subjects searched through 40 different menu frames: 10 trials each with 2, 4, 8, and 16 alternatives per frame.

There are two important differences between the methods used in this experiment and those discussed previously in this chapter. First, in the previous studies subjects were given a target word and were instructed to search for that target word in a menu. The target word appeared at the lowest level of the menu searched. In the MacGregor et al. (1986) experiment there was no target word. Rather, subjects were given a question and they were asked to select one of a set of general alternatives that would most likely lead them to the answer to the question. Second, in the previous studies, subjects had many trials searching through the same menu for

```
FOOD PLANNING

    1.   Menu planning

    2.   Nutrition

    3.   Grocery list

    4.   Metric measures

    5.   Food dollar

    6.   Food dollar for specific foods

    7.   Meat substitutes

    8.   Delicatessens
```

FIG. 12.13.   An initial menu from the MacGreggor et al. (1986) experiment. From *Human Factors*, Vol. 28, No. 4, 1986. Copyright 1986 by the Human Factors and Ergonomics Society, Inc. All rights reserved. Reprinted by permission.

different targets. Subjects in the MacGregor et al. study had 40 different questions and 40 different menu frames.

We present the results from this study in two sections. Direct determination of search strategy is possible only with sequential presentation of menu alternatives, and we present the procedure and results of that condition in the next subsection. An indirect method to infer search strategies in the simultaneous condition will be discussed in the second subsection.

Direct Determination of Search Strategies with Sequential Presentation

All of the studies on menu search reviewed in this chapter have used simultaneous presentation of menu alternatives—that is, if there were two alternatives, they both appeared on the screen at the same time. The simultaneous presentation condition in the MacGregor et al. experiment was of the same type. In the sequential condition, however, subjects were given a question and were then shown an initial screen, which, as previously indicated, consisted of only the set of numbers corresponding to menu alternatives. The initial screen for the sequential presentation of the menu shown in Fig. 12.13 would contain only the numbers 1 through 8, which would tell the subject that there were eight alternatives in the menu. The alternatives themselves would not be present. Subjects were told that they were to request alternatives on the menu by moving the "up" and "down" special function keys. They could obtain an alternative by moving the cursor to one of the alternative positions and then hitting the space bar. That would result in the display of the alternative at that position. Moving the cursor to another position and hitting the space bar would erase the previous selection and present the alternative at the new position. Subjects were free to examine the alternatives in any order and as many times as they wanted prior to making a selection (done by pressing the "A" key followed by the number of the alternative selected).

The purpose of the sequential condition was to provide the experimenter with a complete record of the alternatives examined on each trial. The record of the alternatives selected was then used to infer the type of visual search strategy employed.

Remember that parallel search is not possible with sequential presentation as only one option is visible at a time. As stated earlier, three types of serial search were defined: exhaustive, self-terminating, and redundant.

The search strategy data from the sequential condition are shown in Fig. 12.14. There are several aspects of interest in this data. All 12 subjects in the sequential condition used more than one search strategy, and 8 of the 12 subjects used all three strategies. As shown in Fig. 12.14, search strategy varied with the number of menu alternatives. Separate repeated-measures analyses of variance were conducted on the three search types as a function of the number of menu alternatives. Self-terminating and redundant searches showed significant positive trends with the number of alternatives, whereas exhaustive searches revealed a negative trend. That is, as numbers of alternatives increased, subjects increased redundant searching, and tended, more so than with less alternatives, to terminate their searches before seeing all the alternatives. With only 2 alternatives, subjects searched exhaustively on approximately 90% of the trials. The exhaustive searches decreased to around 40% with 8 and 16 alternatives. Overall, 59% of the searches were exhaustive, 34% were redundant, and 7% were self-terminating.

Remember that the sequential mode of presentation provided a complete record of the alternatives searched on each trial, so the inference of search strategy is much more direct than through analyses of reaction time data. That all subjects used more than one search strategy and that search strategy varied with the number of alternatives suggests serious problems for interpreting reaction-time data when such direct measures of search strategy are not available.

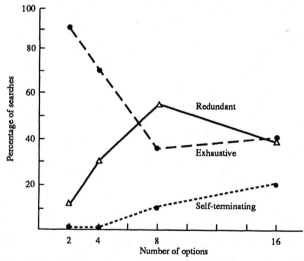

FIG. 12.14. Search strategy data showing percentage of different types of search as a function of the number of options (items) on menu pages. From *Human Factors*, Vol. 28, No. 4, 1986. Copyright 1986 by the Human Factors and Ergonomics Society, Inc. All rights reserved. Reprinted by permission.

In the studies of memory search and visual search mentioned previously, the functions relating reaction time and number of alternatives were averaged over many trials per subject and over several subjects. Did subjects in those experiments use more than one strategy? Unfortunately, we cannot determine whether multiple strategies were used in those studies. The fact that the MacGregor et al. (1986) study shows multiple strategies within the same task suggests the need for caution in intrepreting search data averaged over trials and subjects. The finding of multiple search strategies with sequential presentation has been replicated and extended by Pierce et al. (1992).

Indirect Assessment of Search Strategies with Simultaneous Presentation

MacGregor et al. tested two types of menu presentation, sequential and simultaneous. Direct measures of search type were possible only in the sequential condition. What was the purpose of the simultaneous method of presentation? All commercially available menu systems use simultaneous presentation of menu alternatives, and it is difficult to think of a situation in which we might want to present menu alternatives sequentially. The sole purpose of the sequential presentation condition in this experiment was to provide a more direct assessment of the types of search strategies involved in computer menu search. The reason for including the simultaneous condition was to determine if search processes measured directly in the sequential condition could be generalized to the simultaneous condition. The question being asked is whether the search processes found with sequential presentation are forced by that method of presentation or whether the same search processes are used in both presentation methods. How can such an assessment be made? Remember that search processes were measured only in the sequential condition so no direct comparison of search strategies across the two presentation conditions is possible. An indirect assessment is possible through correlational analysis. Subjects in each presentation condition searched through 40 menus, 10 each with 2, 4, 8, and 16 alternatives. The correct alternative in these menus was equally distributed over serial positions. If subjects in both presentation conditions engaged in similar search processes there should be a large correlation for search times between the two conditions across the 40 menus. If subjects in the two presentation conditions executed different types of searches (for example, exhaustive search with sequential presentation and a particular number of alternatives, and self-terminating search with simultaneous presentation and the same number of alternatives) there should be, at most, a modest correlation between search times. MacGregor et al. (1986) computed two correlations between simultaneous and sequential presentations. One used the search times to the time of the first option selected (regardless of whether it was correct or not), and the other used the search times required for the correct option to be selected. These two correlations between search times were .95 and .85, respectively. These are unusually high correlations, generally found only in repeated performances of the same task. We thus have support for the conclusion that the subjects used similar strategies in both cases. This type of indirect evidence is not sufficient to permit the unqualified conclusion that the same strategies were used in both tasks, but it can be considered as support for such a conclusion, and certainly is consistent with it.

CHAPTER SUMMARY

The computer menu is a popular interface for human-computer interaction. Computer menus are especially beneficial for novices and infrequent computer users, because the options available can be determined and accessed with minimal prior study of the software. The two most common menu-driven applications are software command systems and information retrieval systems.

Computer menus are typically arranged hierarchically, with general information categories at the top level of the menu and specific commands or sets of information at the lowest level. Given a database of fixed size and an equal number of options per menu frame, there is an inverse relationship between the number of options per frame and the number of levels in the menu hierarchy. The number of options per menu frame is referred to as menu breadth, and the number of menu frames needing to be accessed is called menu depth. There are apparent advantages to both breadth and depth. Broad menus require that fewer displays be presented, so subjects need to make fewer requests (for additional menus). Deep menus require fewer total items to be visually examined, because many of the items in the database are on menus that are bypassed through the submenu choice procedure.

The results of several experiments were examined that attempted to determine the depth and breadth of computer menus that optimize menu selection. It was concluded that menu search performance improves as a function of menu breadth, as long as the items are presented on the screen in an organized fashion. The studies used a maximum of 64 items grouped in sets of 8, so the conclusions would be limited to that number of items.

It was also found that organization of the items on the menu screens was critical. Additional research revealed that the organization could be based either on semantic similarity (items with similar meanings juxtaposed) or alphabetical listing. Further, it was found that homogeneous sets of items should be separated from other sets by additional spacing. The items should be arranged vertically (in columns) rather than horizontally.

Databases can be quite large, too large for all of the items to fit on a single screen. Thus, it is necessary to have deep menus for some databases. Because deep menus can create problems, a reasonable question is, how can performance be improved when deeper menus have to be used? A prior question is, what creates the difficulties with deeper menus? The problem appears to lie in the difficulty that users have in connecting the very general terms found in the choices on initial menus, or even second level menus, with the very specific items or commands being sought on the final menu. Thus subjects either take additional time while they try to make the necessary connections, or they sometimes make incorrect choices and get lost in the menu pathway.

Research was done to determine what sort of help fields (information on the menus) might be provided to reduce the problems with deep menus. It was found that the kind of information that was maximally helpful was information on what choices would be found at the next menu level. That is, when depth is necessary, search accuracy can be improved if subjects are shown options at level $n + 1$ of the menu system while they are considering options at level n.

As a contrast to the applied research in most of the chapter, basic research on the search process, in the context of computer menu searches, was discussed. It was found, somewhat surprisingly, that subjects appeared to be inconsistent in their choices of searching strategy. This was clear in the case of sequential choices, but sequential choices are atypical of what is found in real life circumstances, where choices are made while several options are simultaneously present. High correlations across sequential and simultaneous presentations of options lends support to the idea of inconsistency in search startegies, even in real life situations (where simultaneous choices would be found). This has implications for how data are collected and organized in studies of search processes. However, the evidence for the real life situations was indirect, so is suggestive rather than conclusive.

NEW WORDS AND PHRASES IN CHAPTER 12

breadth (number of options per menu frame)
broad menus
computer menu
database
deep menus
depth (number of menu frames)
funneling
help fields
hierarchy
information-retrieval menu
redundant search
software command menu
speed accuracy tradeoff
top-level menu

CHAPTER 13

Social Psychology I: Testing
Theories When Internal Events
Can Be Monitored or Manipulated

Social psychologists study the effects of one individual on another individual, and the relationships between individuals and groups. For example, social psychologists study altruistic behavior, which is an interaction between an individual and at least one other individual. They also study how one person can affect another person's attitudes, or what kind of general messages are more effective than others in changing people's attitudes. When looking at the influence of messages we might appear to be focusing on single individuals, but the influence of other individuals is implicit in the message. Social psychologists also study cognitive processes that are concerned with other individuals. For example, how are impressions formed of other people?

In addition, social psychologists examine cognitive processes that are less obviously socially interactive. For example, they study the factors that contribute to a person's perceptions of himself or herself, and how a person's self-perceptions affect his or her behavior. Factors affecting self-perceptions often include other people's responses, or even assumptions about other people's opinions. Thus it can be useful to view self-perceptions as products of social interactions, as well as offering predictions of future interpersonal responding.

DIRECT MEASUREMENT OF INTERNAL VARIABLES

Social psychological questions often focus on people's attitudes, preferences, beliefs, and self-perceptions (measured before and after experimental manipulations or before and after naturally occurring social change). These are internal variables that can often be examined directly through questionnaires or adjective checklists. They can also sometimes be measured behaviorally, for example, by recording people's choices (which offer a good indication of preferences). The particular methods of measurement of these internal variables can be questioned in any individual case. This issue is discussed in later sections. Here the important point is that it is sometimes possible to use direct observation of these internal events (attitudes, self-perceptions, etc.), rather than having to use inference.

When Theoretical and Experimental Variables Are Identical

The logical error of affirming the consequent was described in chapter 7. In each example, the problem encountered was that although the theoretical question concerned one or more internal variables, the experiment dealt exclusively with overt, directly observable variables (surrogate variables). The internal events were generally a critical part of some mechanism, which was hypothesized in an attempt to account for prior experimental results, or to aid in predicting new results. A frequently discussed example in that chapter concerned a pair of differently oriented stimuli, being compared (from memory) to determine if they were identical. Mental rotation of one member of the pair was hypothesized, to account for slowed reaction times. In all such cases where all that is manipulated and seen by the experimenter is a relationship between surrogate variables (like orientation differences between stimuli, and reaction times), it is always possible that a theoretical mechanism different from the one postulated could be the basis of the observed relationship. This is the heart of the problem in the logical error of affirming the consequent.

When the variables in the theoretical mechanism can be directly observed, confirmation of the events as theorized can be direct, and it is less reasonable to suggest that some other mechanism may be responsible for the observed relationship. For example, if some attitudes are directly manipulable and some decisions are directly observable, then it might be possible to have an unambiguous test of the relationship between the manipulation of the attitude and changes in decisions. Although the variables would constitute internal events, direct manipulation and measurement could permit less speculative reasoning about how the internal variables of attitudes and decisions relate to each other. The detailed logic of these direct tests is discussed in footnote 4 of chapter 7.

Although direct measurement of internal variables avoids the interpretive problems associated with the logical error of affirming the consequent, it too is beset with uncertainty of interpretation that stems from a different source. With direct measurement of internal variables, which is often possible in social psychology, the major source of uncertainty is the wide range of alternative definitions that usually exist for the variables. Advantages of direct measurement of variables and interpretive problems arising from alternative definitions of variables are illustrated in the following experiments by McArthur and Post.

The McArthur and Post Experiments

The example is taken from the literature on the *fundamental attribution error*. The fundamental attribution error is the error of exaggerating the role of other people's personal (dispositional) qualities when explaining other people's behavior, playing down the role of external (situational) factors, with the reverse bias when explaining one's own behavior. For example, I might explain your not studying as being lazy, but my not studying as due to a particularly good show on TV. If called upon to explain your loud voice, I might suggest that you are a gross and uncultured person; if called upon to explain my own loud voice, I might call attention to the surrounding noise, and state that it is necessary for me to shout in order to be heard.

The research example examined in this section consists of several related experiments by McArthur and Post (1977). The McArthur and Post experiments were an attempt to support the explanation of the fundamental attribution error that was first suggested by Jones and Nisbett (1972). This explanation suggests that the attribution error results from people being influenced to explain things in terms of what is most salient (focal or figural) for them. That is, they suggested that the factors that are most salient, most directly in view, play the major role in explanations. When an individual looks at a situation in which he or she is engaged, the person does not see him- or herself, but rather looks out at the environment. Thus, for the individual explaining his or her own actions, the environment should predominate in the explanation (if the salience explanation is correct). The pressures or temptations of life, the forces loose in the world, will predominate in explanations of an individual's own behavior (a situational explanation). But if an observer is looking at some other individual, that other individual's personal characteristics are likely to be more salient than the environment (we are by definition attending more to a person on whom we are focused than on the environment), and so personal dispositional factors would be offered as causative factors in explaining another's behavior. The person's ambition, honesty, dishonesty, or intelligence might be called on as an explanation.

There is a way to test the salience explanation of differential attribution that generalizes beyond the special case of self versus other. Assume a situation in which each subject observes two people. If the salience explanation is correct, then if anything causes one observed person to be more salient than another in the situation, there should be more dispositional attributions for that salient person. But for the individual who is somehow a background element in the situation, the situational factors should have a greater opportunity to predominate in an explanation. What McArthur and Post (1977) did, was have observers (the subjects) watch two people in a get-acquainted conversation. The observers had to judge how friendly and talkative the conversationalists were, and then indicate, for each conversationalist, to what extent the observed behavior was a function of dispositional factors ("personality, traits, character, personal style, attitudes, and mood") versus situational factors (being in an experiment, the getting-acquainted situation, the topic of conversation, etc.). A 9-point scale was used, with exclusively dispositional attributions as one end and exclusively situational attributions as the other. Thus, the experimental situation was simply the judging of the behavior of each of a pair of conversationalists, indicating the degree to which each person's behavior was influenced by dispositional versus situational factors.

The independent variable that was manipulated by McArthur and Post (1977) was the extent to which one or the other of the two conversing people was made salient by being more noticeable. In one of the manipulations one subject was placed in a brighter light than the other. In another manipulation one of the subjects sat in a rocking chair, rocking while the conversation took place, and the other person simply sat still in a regular chair. (Activity of this sort is sometimes used by actors who wish to upstage other actors, causing the audience to focus on the physically active actor, rather than on some other physically less active actor on the stage at the same time.) The two manipulations constituted two different but closely related experiments. It was really the same experiment done twice, each time using a different operational definition for a person's being salient. The dependent variable was the relative extent of dispositional versus situational attributions for each conversationalist. That is, in each experiment, each subject made two judgments on the 9-point scale, one judgment for the salient and one for the non-salient conversationalist. These two judgments were compared later in the data analyses.

As predicted, with both manipulations, the behavior of the figural individual was seen as primarily stemming from dispositional factors, whereas the behavior of the less salient conversationalist was seen as stemming more from situational factors.

Let us look at the experimental and theoretical variables here to see if they are the same. In the experiment, the independent variable is salience (using a brighter light, or having the person more active). The dependent variable is relative attribution of dispositional versus situational factors. The theory says that the salient individual should receive more dispositional than situational attributions. We see then that the variables in the theory are precisely the experimental variables of salience and attribution (of situational or dispositional factors); that is, the experimental and theoretical variables are identical. When McArthur and Post (1977) tested the relationship between variables in these experiments (the relationship between salience of the individual and the attributions made), they also were testing the theory. This was possible because the experimenters were able to manipulate an internal variable (what someone chooses to focus on, that is, they controlled what was salient) and to measure an internal variable (the attributions someone makes). If the focusing of the subjects was influenced as intended, and if we can trust the 9-point scale of attribution that was used, the relationship between two internal variables was directly tested.

Definitions for Social Psychological Variables. For social psychology the major source of uncertainty is the wide range of alternative definitions that usually exist for each of the variables. For example, in the first two experiments of McArthur and Post (1977), salience was defined in two different ways: a greater amount of light on one person than another, and greater physical activity (specifically, rocking in a rocking chair versus no rocking while sitting in a regular chair). The two definitions of salience in the McArthur and Post study are operational definitions in that they specify the operations that establish the presence of the variable (greater physical activity, or brighter light).

It is common practice in social psychology to repeat an experiment, each time using a different operational definition for one of the variables. This is desirable because an experimental outcome can sometimes be a result of some specific quality of a definition that is not relevant to what the experimenter is trying to test. Let us return to the McArthur and Post example of an operational definition of a manipulated variable. A rocking person might appear nervous, which might give rise to some special dispositional attributions having nothing to do with whether he or she was made the center of attention by the rocking, although this is not likely to be true of someone made salient through brighter lighting. This could result in observations of different relationships between salience and the tendency to make dispositional attributions, depending on the operational definition of salience.

Each definition of a variable has specific features that are not important for the generalization, as in the case of rocking to achieve salience. As another example, suppose an experimenter wanted to operationally define sense of humor in a study of the relationship between sense of humor and intelligence. Perhaps the ability to explain what is funny about jokes would be used as the criterion of a sense of humor. However, ability to verbalize would be a factor that would be included in this definition simply because of the way in which sense of humor is defined, and it might be this ability that is related to intelligence. If humor is not related to intelligence, such an operational definition would lead to the wrong conclusion. What if, instead, how long a person laughed at some jokes, or how loudly the person laughed, was used as the criterion? Long or loud laughing might be related to nervousness, as well as sense of humor. Thus, each operational definition can introduce new variables.

Almost any single operational definition will have some intrinsic aspects that tap some other quality in addition to what is intended. If only one definition is used, it is hard to know if an observed relationship between two variables is a relationship with the intended operationally defined variable, or with some other aspect of the particular definition. The best protection against this problem is to use more than one operational definition of a variable. That is, repeat the experiment, each time using a different operational definition of the variable. Only if the same relationship is found to exist with all or most of the definitions could some confidence be placed in an observed relationship. If most definitions yield evidence of the same relationship but there are one or two exceptions, this can serve to delineate the limits of the relationship or to better understand the nature of one of the variables (by recognizing when only some of the conceptualized operational definitions offer good representations of the variable).

McArthur and Post (1977) used more than the two definitions of salience previously mentioned (rocking and a brighter light). In a third experiment, salience was defined in terms of pattern complexity. The salient person wore a shirt patterned with a bold black and white horizontal stripe and the nonsalient person wore a solid grey shirt. In the final two experiments, salience was defined in terms of contextual novelty. Instead of two people being seen by observers, there were four people being observed. Only two of the four were engaged in the getting-acquainted conversation. The other two simply sat and listened, though they were also being observed as part of the same scene. The experimenter attempted to make just one of the two conversationalists nonsalient. This was arranged by having the nonsalient member of the conversing pair similar to the two people who only sat and listened. The salient person was (hopefully) made focal by being different from the other three people. Specifically, in the fourth experiment three of the people in the group wore shirts of the same color while the salient person had a different colored shirt. In the final (fifth) experiment three members of the group were of the same sex and the salient person was of the opposite sex. The results of Experiments 3, 4, and 5 were inconsistent with those of Experiments 1 and 2. Only Experiments 1 and 2 showed relatively greater dispositional attributions for behavior of the salient person. The results of the pattern complexity manipulation (Experiment 3) revealed no differences between the types of attributions for the behavior of salient and nonsalient persons. The final two experiments (4 and 5) yielded significant effects of salience, but in the opposite direction to those found in the first two experiments. That is, the person with a different colored shirt received relatively more situational and less dispositional attributions than the person with the same colored shirt as other members of the group. Likewise, the person of the opposite sex received more situational and less dispositional judgments than the person who was the same sex as other members of the group.

The results of the first two experiments by McArthur and Post (1977) were consistent with the theory that salience is the internal variable underlying attribution. However, the results of the final three experiments did not support the theory. According to the theory, *any* manipulation that induces salience should yield relatively more dispositional than situational attributions. According to the results, some manipulations that induce salience produce relatively more dispositional than situational attributions, some have the reverse effect, and at least one has no effect. Where does this leave us? There are several possibilities. First, it is possible that the theory is incorrect. That is, it is not salience, per se, that is the critical internal variable underlying differential attribution. The manipulations of salience may have been coincident with other inadvertent changes, one or more confounding factors being responsible for the observed effects. Or it is possible that the theory is correct but that the assumptions about how to produce salience were incorrect. For example, when observing two individuals talking, perhaps the individual who is similar to other people in the background becomes more focal, and the person who is different recedes into the background. An analogous situation where this is the case is when a person has, say, blue eyes, and wearing a blue shirt causes greater notice of the eyes. Having more than one person in the background wearing a particular color might draw attention to that color when worn by just one of the people in the foreground (brought to the foreground by their being engaged in conversation). How do we decide which of these two explanations of the experimental results is correct? There are undoubtedly many other possible explanations for these effects. When attempting to explain unexpected effects, we are sometimes aided in deciding which explanations are most reasonable by the use of manipulation checks, which are discussed in the next section.

Whatever the merits of the theory supported by two of the five experiments done by McArthur and Post (1977), it is a useful example for us.[7] It points up the place wherein uncertainty remains, even after a successful experiment that supports an explanation and avoids the error of affirming the consequent. Not only are there varied operations possible for making people salient, but there are many different ways of measuring attributions. As seen in this example, the relationship that appeared to exist (Experiments 1 and 2) may no longer be there with a different definition of one of the variables (Experiment 3), or the relationships might change, even reverse, with still other definitions (Experiments 4 and 5). Usually there are many different definitions possible for social psychological variables, such as attitudes, beliefs, preferences, and attributions.

---

[7]The fundamental attribution error, and related questions, were widely researched in the 1970s and 1980s. It appears to be broadly present in Western cultures, but less so in non-Western cultures (Fletcher & Ward, 1988). Further, even within Western cultures, there is wide individual variability (Block & Funder, 1986).

The conviction that a relationship between particular variables exists should wait until the relationship has been tested with a variety of definitions of the variables.

MANIPULATION CHECKS

Any independent means of assessing whether the planned manipulation functioned as expected is called a **manipulation check**. It is important to realize that a manipulation check must be independent of whether the theory expressing relationships between variables is correct or not.

In social psychological research the function of a manipulation is often to induce a particular internal state in the subjects participating in the experiment. The choice of the particular internal state follows from a theory that specifies certain consequences when the state is present. A manipulation check assesses the effectiveness of the manipulation in inducing the desired internal state. The manipulation check is not a test of the theory. Rather, the manipulation check informs the investigator whether the manipulation was or was not successful in producing the internal state. Successful induction of the internal state by the manipulation is a necessary prerequisite for testing the theory.

In the McArthur and Post (1977) study the theory was that the internal variable of salience was responsible for changes in the internal variable of attribution. This was tested through experiments with varied operational definitions of the variables. The question addressed with a manipulation check is whether the operational definitions of salience actually created salience. More specifically, was the person in a brighter light actually more salient or focal than the person in a dim light? Likewise, was the person of opposite sex actually more salient or focal than the person who was of the same sex as the other members of the group? If the manipulations were successful in influencing salience, then the investigators were actually testing the theory. Conversely, if the manipulations failed to influence salience, the investigators were not testing the theory. The experiments would not have had two groups differentiated on the planned independent variable. The experiments would have been a useless exercise. Because attentional focus is an internal variable, it would not have been obvious if the manipulations had been unsuccessful.

The use of a manipulation check is particularly important when the pattern of results is not as predicted, as in the case of the series of experiments by McArthur and Post (1977). Unfortunately, McArthur and Post did not include a manipulation check in their experiments, so it is not possible to tell whether any or all of the manipulations were successful in producing salience. The absence of the predicted outcome in Experiments 3, 4, and 5 in that series might be explained by the lack of success of the manipulation as well as by the poor predictive power of the theory. When drawing the conclusion that a theory has poor predictive power, it is particularly important to show that the theory has had a real chance to be tested, and so it would be ueful to have included a manipulation check in the McArthur and Post experiments. If, on the other hand, the results of an experiment are as predicted, the successful prediction itself offers some support for the contention that the manipulation functioned as planned (because, hopefully, the different groups are otherwise identical).

It would have been difficult to arrange for a manipulation check in the McArthur and Post study, which would have required confirming that the subject's attention was focused on the person chosen to be salient. Under some circumstances it is possible to secretly photograph eye movements. However, this is difficult to engineer in most circumstances. Furthermore, it is not clear that salience means only that an object will be stared at more than others. Salience implies an increased level of attention in a broader sense of attention, as when you look at someone's face but you are attending only to skin texture, or when you stare at someone but you are actually thinking about someone else. Attention in this sense is hard to measure.

Sometimes manipulation checks can be very direct. For example, often when moods are manipulated the subjects are asked to fill out brief questionnaires about their moods immediately after the experiment. They might be asked to respond to a scale such as, "On a 31-point scale, ranging from calm to tense, with 1 as calm and 31 as tense, how do you feel right now?" Other feelings and moods can be substituted, and differently numbered scales can be used. The procedures and forms for such scales are discussed in chapter 14.

It is often necessary to ask questions in disguised form for manipulation checks. For example, assume that the subjects had to deliver shocks to a second person who was actually an actor, but the actor was pretending to be a voluntary participant receiving shock. You would not ask the subject if he or she thought the person had actually received the shock, since that would call the deception into question. A proper question to put to the subject after the experiment would be, "Do you think that he (she) could have stood stronger shocks?" If the subject was not convinced, the subject would let you know this in response to such a question. At the conclusion of the Higgins and Marlatt (1975) experiment on alcoholism discussed in chapter 3, subjects were asked the following question: "Sometimes subjects feel that they are being deceived by experimenters and this affects their performance during the experiment. Did you feel that you were being deceived?" Higgins and Marlatt asked their subjects to rate the extent of their doubt. The data of those subjects with a confidence greater than 50% that they had been deceived were eliminated from the study.

In general, when a subject is found to have doubted the situation, that subject's data are omitted from the statistical analysis. The loss of 1 or 2 subjects in this way, out of 40 or 50, is not unexpected in an experiment involving deception. If, however, the loss surpasses 10%, the experimenter should consider redesigning the deception. If too many subjects are eliminated, those left can be seen as representing a special subpopulation, rather than as a representative sample of people from the sampled population. In such a case the data should not be used and the experimental manipulation should be redesigned.

A fairly common question, which can sometimes function as an indirect manipulation check, is a check of the subjects' impressions of the purpose of the experiment. Usually subjects are kept in the dark about detailed aspects of the experiment until they complete the experiment, and are then debriefed. The subjects are often asked, just prior to debriefing, what they believe was the true purpose of the experiment. This can lead to all sorts of speculative statements on the part of subjects. The usefulness of these statements is that they can indicate whether or not the subjects believed the rationale for the experiment given to the subjects when they volunteered. Also, their statements can reveal whether or not the manipulation was successful. Finally, subjects are usually quick to point out what they think were failed attempts to deceive them. This simple question can often indicate when an experiment has not succeeded in its attempted manipulations and/or has given indications to the subjects as to what responses were desired. Examples of manipulations and manipulation checks are presented in the context of the discussion of experiments on cognitive dissonance in this chapter.

SUBJECT BIAS

Checks on what the subjects believe to be the purpose of the experiment can be helpful in recognizing when subject bias has had some influence on the experimental outcome. **Subject bias** refers to the subjects' assumptions about what is expected or desired of them. For example, assume an experiment in which noise was used as a distracter, and at the same time other conditions, varied for different groups of subjects, were being assessed for their ability to protect against distraction. If a particular subject thought that the purpose of the experiment was to see if the subjects could identify the noise, and that this is what he or she will later be asked about, that subject's performance would be seriously affected by overattention to the noise. If many subjects had the same impression, the experiment could be sabotaged by subjects' assumptions.

Sometimes a subject's assumptions could actually aid in giving the experimenter the outcome that the experimenter desires. For example, the response being measured could be reaction time to a discrimination task. If the experimenter expects or hopes that one group will be faster than a second group and the subjects in the second group somehow assume that it is more important to be correct than fast, the experimenter could get the hoped-for results but for the wrong reasons. In fact, the experimenter might communicate his or her desires in some subtle fashion and encourage one group to be faster than the other. Thus, the experimenter's subtle communication of the desired results could lead to subject bias, which in turn could result in a misleading outcome.

Rosenthal (1966) brought together a good deal of evidence indicating that subjects can be biased by experimenters who are not aware of their own subtle influence. Most experimenters in their enthusiasm and hopes for their research can give inadvertent cues to the subjects as to what they (the experimenters) want. Subjects are often eager to please and without realizing it try to give the desired results.

Double-Blind Procedures

The usual way of avoiding the problem of experimenters communicating experimental purposes or desired outcomes is the use of **double-blind procedures**. Double-blind procedures are in effect when neither the subjects nor the experimenters in contact with the subjects are aware of the details of the experiment, the hypotheses, or which subjects are in which groups. Double-blind procedures are possible when the experimenter employs experimental assistants to give instructions to the subjects. The experimenter who designs the research does not have contact with the subjects and is careful to keep the experimental assistants uninformed about which groups receive which treatments, or what is the nature of the independent variable. For example, drugs and placebos would come in numbered bottles, not labeled as to their true contents. If assumptions of subjects were being manipulated through varied instructions the different instructions might be included in a packet of written materials passed to the subjects in sealed envelopes, with the experimental assistants unaware of the contents. This would at least leave the experimental assistants uninformed as to which conditions individual subjects were in. It would be still better if they did not even know what kind of assumptions were being manipulated.

After the experiment, questionnaires can be administered to the experimental assistants, as well as to the subjects. Specifically, the experimental assistants can be asked what they thought the experiment was testing, and they can also be asked to identify which subjects were in the experimental and control groups. This would be a check on the effectiveness of the double-blind procedures. Hopefully, it would indicate that the experimental assistants did not have any biasing information to communicate, or at least that they did not possess different assumptions about the different groups (that could have then been inadvertently communicated to the subjects in the different groups, constituting a differential influence, and therefore a potential confounding factor). Similarly, post-experimental questionnaires administered to the subjects could assess whether they harbored any assumptions or suspicions that might invalidate their data.

RESEARCH ON COGNITIVE DISSONANCE

One of the more fully developed social psychological theories is the theory of **cognitive dissonance**, initially developed by Leon Festinger (1957). Research on that theory offers some excellent examples of the use of moderator variables, where successfully predicted interactions are used as support for the theory. (Recall that the term *moderator variable* refers to a second independent variable involved in an interaction with another independent variable, which we will call the first independent variable. When the relationship between the first independent variable and the dependent variable is the focus of the study, and the nature of the relationship changes as a function of the level of the second independent variable, the second independent variable is called a moderator variable.) Research on the theory of cognitive dissonance also offers a case history of the evolution of an initial theoretical formulation that was nurtured and developed by the accumulating empirical findings. In this section some portions of that literature are examined.

Cognitive dissonance is the uncomfortable drive state (tension) believed to exist when an individual finds him- or herself apparently holding two psychologically inconsistent cognitions (ideas, beliefs, opinions, attitudes; Aronson, 1968). Festinger (1957) theorized that the practical impact, or effect, of this postulated uncomfortable state of tension is to cause the person to change one of the cognitions so as to reduce the inconsistency, and thereby reduce the personal discomfort.

Most often the inconsistency is found in an attitude or belief that is implied by some overt behavior that itself contradicts some verbalized or otherwise assumed attitude or belief. An example that Festinger offered is the following: Assume that a group of people are cigarette smokers. Assume further that they have heard that cigarette smoking causes cancer. We can also assume, for most people, that they would agree that the following statement is one that they can truthfully make: "I do not want to die of cancer." But this statement is psychologically inconsistent with the cognition that they smoke and cigarette smoking causes cancer. The smoker's behavior expresses an attitude of unconcern, which is inconsistent with the person's readily admitted desire not to die of cancer. If it were easy to stop smoking, it could be expected that the person would relieve the dissonance following from the inconsistency, by no longer smoking. However, this avenue is a difficult one for most smokers. It would seem reasonable that a person who cannot stop smoking will just accept the inconsistency. But the theory says that the inconsistency will cause discomfort and force some change in behavior or attitude. For example, the person might choose to doubt the information on the noxious effects of smoking, believing that filters will remove enough of the noxious elements to reduce the risk to a trivial level. Thus, one of the person's prior cognitions could be changed by the tensions of cognitive dissonance, resulting in rejection of the belief that cigarette smoking (at least with filters) is harmful. Denying that cigarette smoking is harmful has become harder to do in recent years, so it is more likely that it is the other cognition that will be changed for most contemporary smokers. For example, the smoker might say something like, "Everybody has to die sometime. Why not enjoy myself while I'm here?" Such a statement is an expressed change in the attitude of categorically not wanting to die of cancer.

Festinger (1957) recognized that if this mechanism worked as he postulated, it could be used to change people's attitudes. What this would require is some means of getting people to do or say things at variance with their attitudes. To remove the inconsistency a person might change his or her attitude in the direction of the induced inconsistent behavior, just as people appear to change their attitudes about health and longevity so that their health attitudes are consistent with their smoking behavior. A typical dissonance experiment that resulted from this thinking is one in which a subject is induced to write a **counterattitudinal essay**. A counterattitudinal essay is a written statement defending or rationalizing a position to which the writer is opposed, or supporting a person with whom the writer disagrees.

In the **counterattitudinal essay paradigm**, subjects are sought who have a clear stand on some issue (for example, they do not like a particular politician, or they are against an increase in school tuition). They are then asked to write an essay that is opposed to their own position. They might be asked to write an essay endorsing the politician they do not like, or to write in favor of an increase in school tuition. The request is always carefully rationalized so that it makes some sense to the subject. For example, Steele and Liu (1983), described this aspect of their experiment in the following way:

> The experimenter explained that this task would involve participation in a real survey being conducted by the Council for Student-Faculty Affairs in preparation for an upcoming orientation program for first-year students, during which the issue of a large tuition increase at the University of Washington would be discussed. In the interest of fully understanding the relevant arguments on both sides of the issue, the Council wanted students to list arguments favoring only one side. Ostensibly because the Council had already received so many arguments opposing an increase, it was now seeking arguments favoring the increase. Subjects were then told to take the next 10 minutes to list the strongest, most forceful arguments supporting a substantial increase in tuition at the University of Washington. (p.8)

The early research primarily established the kinds of situations that created dissonance. For example, Brehm (1956) showed that after making a difficult choice, people experienced dissonance. That is, a difficult choice implies that there are both advantages and disadvantages for each choice. A person confronting these facts would have to live with the doubts stemming from the negative facts about the choice they finally made. "I chose X, but there are some bad things about X. I did not choose Y, but there are some good things about Y." What Brehm found was that after making a decision, people emphasize the positive aspects of their choice and deemphasize the negative aspects of the chosen object, reducing the possibilities for dissonance. Aronson and Mills (1959) showed that if people go to a great deal of trouble to gain admission to a group that turns out to be dull and uninteresting, they will experience dissonance. To reduce dissonance they will distort their perceptions of the group, and will describe the group experience in more positive terms than it deserves.

A very large number of experiments were done, many of them yielding evidence consistent with the theory of cognitive dissonance. Confirming evidence of attitude change was found when people made difficult decisions; the subjects convinced themselves as much as possible of the desirability of their decisions. It was also found that when they worked hard or suffered for outcomes that were not worthwhile, the subjects convinced themselves that the outcomes were in fact in some ways worthwhile. Confirming evidence was also found when subjects made public statements that were at variance with their true feelings; the subjects changed their attitudes in the direction of their public statements. Many variations of each of these types of situations yielded support for the theory.

There were conditions under which support for cognitive dissonance was not found. But as with any theory, an important aspect of the research is identifying the limiting conditions for the effects. (When the bulk of the research supports the theory, it is reasonable to check to see if at least some of the negative findings might be defining limiting conditions.) A critical factor that was identified as a limiting condition for attitude change to take place with cognitive dissonance is the necessity of the counterattitudinal statement or behavior being voluntary (Linder, Cooper, & Jones, 1967). If the subjects are simply told to write a counterattitudinal essay there will not be any special change in their own attitudes. They have to be convinced that what they are doing is purely voluntary. To this end, each such study now includes statements assuring the subjects that what they are doing is voluntary. For example, if they are doing the experiment for course credit they are assured that if they do not complete this part of the experiment they will still receive their credit. Various verbalizations have developed over time that successfully apply subtle pressure to cooperate but still leave subjects convinced that they are not being pressured. It is now standard to also include a clearly nonvoluntary group in studies involving counterattitudinal statements, which then constitutes a control group in which no change in attitude is expected. This offers a comparison for the voluntary group in which the attitude change is predicted.

A further qualifier for the occurrence of cognitive dissonance is the requirement that the attitudes involve matters of personal import, some strongly held beliefs. Another is that, in the case of behaviors that are counterattitudinal because they lead to consequences that are personally unacceptable to the subjects, the unacceptable consequences of the acts must be recognized by the subjects before they act, in order for the attitude change to occur. For example, assume that S is a characteristically irresponsible person, who typically breaks rules at school, and seldom studies. Suppose that S, for some reason, reports T for those very same behaviors, and T is thrown out of school. The theory suggests that S will now become less tolerant of irresponsible behavior; but only if S knew before reporting the behavior of T that reporting the behavior could eventuate in T being thrown out of school.

Thus, moderator variables have been examined, and some of them (voluntarism, strength of personal belief, advance knowledge of personally unacceptable consequences) were found relevant to the presence or absence of attitude change under conditions of postulated cognitive dissonance. These moderator variables suggest limiting conditions for the theory of cognitive dissonance, and explain some of the theory's predictive failures. Further, these limiting conditions constitute additional assumptions that are added to the theory, and have, over time, suggested a fundamental change in the theory.

The important change that has been suggested in Festinger's original theory concerns the assumption that gave the theory its name. Festinger believed that the tension created in cases of cognitive dissonance is cognitively based. He postulated that people respond with tension to the awareness of a contradiction in their expressed attitudes (attitudes expressed verbally or implied behaviorally). Doubt about the cognitive basis for this relatively successful theory has been increasing.

The alternative rationale suggested in the later literature is that the inconsistency creating the inner tension of dissonance is ego based; that is, it involves a person's sense of personal worth rather than just an awareness of holding two conflicting ideas (Greenwald & Ronis, 1978; Steele & Liu, 1983). Let us look at an example. According to the original formulation of cognitive dissonance, a professor who found himself shouting at a student but who believed that professors should never shout at students would experience cognitive dissonance for the following reason: There is a logical contradiction between the idea of the self as not verbally abusing students, and the image of oneself actually doing it. The opposite of the professor's abusive behavior is what would follow logically from the professor's self-concept as someone who deals respectfully and kindly with students. This cognitive paradox is what is presumed to cause the uncomfortable inner tension, according to the original formulation. In contrast to the cognitively based interpretation, there is the ego-based interpretation. In this example the ego-based interpretation is that there is a self-perception of oneself as being worthy because of the self-concept of someone who deals respectfully and kindly with students. Seeing himself abuse a student, the professor would feel less worthy, and this would cause the inner tension.

Both interpretations would lead to similar attitude changes that would reduce the discrepancy in self-concept. For example, the professor might decide that he was not really shouting at the student but was sharing his enthusiasm, or trying to communicate his enthusiasm, or his devotion to the topic. The cognitive interpretation would see the self-image and the behavior as now less inconsistent. The ego interpretation would have the professor seeing his behavior more in line with what he values or admires.

In general, as one looks at the classic examples of cognitive dissonance, it is possible to see how the ego interpretation would fit as well as the cognitive interpretation. The ego interpretation is that when a person writes a positive essay about a disliked politician, the writer feels untrue to him- or herself in a moral sense. When a person works hard to get into an unworthy group, the person feels foolish. In these senses the tensions of dissonance are those of not wanting to feel immoral or stupid. The changes in attitude or beliefs are geared to permit the person to feel better about him- or herself. This potential interpretation of the research on cognitive dissonance was expressed by Greenwald and Ronis (1978) and was further articulated by Steele and Liu (1983), the latter offering strong empirical support for this newer interpretation.

Greenwald and Ronis (1978) further suggested that it might be improper to change a theory in response to empirical findings. Rather, they suggested, the theory should be tested in its original form, being rejected as a whole if it is not supported. By changing the theory to conform to the research findings, a new theory might emerge that is confirmed, but the old theory might not have been properly tested, perhaps prematurely abandoned.

The approach to theory testing tentatively suggested by Greenwald and Ronis might possibly protect some one or two worthy theories from premature rejection. But most testable psychological theories are initially very simple, involving few assumptions. There is little in the way of entrenched theory that would greatly upset the field if rejected. The relationships between variables uncovered during the testing of the theories usually outlasts the theories. The validated relationships then offer a firmer basis for later theorizing.

The gradually developed theory of cognitive dissonance, with its empirically developed moderator variables (voluntarism, strength of personal belief, etc.) and its changed basis for inner tension (from cognitive to ego-based dissonance), offers a much more powerful and useful theory than Festinger initially proposed. His initial theory was an inspired insight. His recognition of its potential use to deliberately change an attitude was probably of even greater importance. This concept of placing people in the position of having engaged in self-contradictory behavior, in order to examine the effect of the behavior on attitude, gave the field a new set of research designs. He and his students developed this experimental paradigm,[8] enlarged it, contributed clever operational definitions, and gave psychology a new way of studying attitude change.

Variations on the cognitive dissonance paradigm, repeatedly explored over 25 years, have produced a great deal of information about attitude change in the face of conflicting attitudes. The current formulation of cognitive dissonance has the benefit of this additional information. The conservative point made by Greenwald and Ronis (1978), that the theory should not have been changed in response to empirical findings but considered as either rejected or supported, would be more appropriate for a more mature science where a theory might start from better established assumptions. At the point in time when Festinger first presented his theory of cognitive dissonance, there was no history of a literature that had to be reconciled with the theory. There was little reason to expect that the initial version would stand unchanged after empirical exploration. Most of psychology's new theories are probably best treated as first passes at an

---

[8]An experimental paradigm is a model of research that is copied by many researchers who all tend to use the same variables, start from the same assumptions, and use similar special procedures. Those using the same paradigm tend to frame their questions similarly. Examples of experimental paradigms in psychology are rats (or pigeons) in a Skinner box pressing a lever (or pecking a key) for food or water that is usually contingent on some aspect of the response, human subjects learning paired associate nonsense syllables (or word pairs or picture-word pairs, etc.), rats being run through mazes, and ablation techniques to localize brain functions.

idea, immediately open to modification in response to research findings.

Whatever the eventual fate and status of the original theory of cognitive dissonance, the emerging theory follows from hundreds of experiments in many laboratories and offers a theory that has been modified by ingenious testing of alternative assumptions. As an example of this testing procedure, we examine a couple of experiments testing the assumption that cognitive dissonance is a phenomenon involving inner tension—that is, that the theory, in postulating a motivating discomfort, can be seen as implying that dissonance involves an actual physical discomfort, some physical tension that the subject attempts to lessen by the observed attitude change. Though there is some question as to whether this was intended in Festinger's original formulation, most researchers have accepted this as an implied assumption of the theory. This again presents us with an inner event as part of the explanation that a theory provides. Here again we see the attempt to directly assess whether in fact this postulated internal event does occur. Fortunately, the assumption of an internal physical event (of uncomfortable tension) is easier to test than the conceptual process initially emphasized by Festinger.

Evidence of Dissonance-Based Arousal

We have stated that the theory of cognitive dissonance assumes that the attitude changes of subjects, when motivated by cognitive dissonance, are attempts to get rid of the uncomfortable feelings of arousal (tension) created by the dissonance. This should reasonably follow only if the subjects are, at some level, aware of the dissonance as the source of the arousal. Zanna and Cooper (1974) decided to use the fact that subjects can be influenced to misattribute sources of arousal, to test this theoretical reasoning.

Zanna and Cooper gave three groups of subjects a placebo. One group was given the impression that the pill has side effects creating tension. A second was given the impression that it has side effects creating relaxation. A third was given the pill with the statement that there are no side effects (so the issue of tension or relaxation was not in any way broached). All groups were then placed into the classic counterattitudinal essay-writing situation. They were presented with the request to write an essay in favor of banning inflammatory speakers from campus. A separate sample of subjects on the same campus was asked their opinion on this issue, and it was clear that the students in general were opposed to such a ban. On a scale of 1 to 31, with 1 opposed and 31 strongly in favor, the sample gave an average response of 2.30. The subjects used in the experiment were not asked their opinion on the issue until after writing the counterattitudinal essay, but were assumed to be initially no different than the general campus population. Their scores on this same 31-point scale were the dependent variable, expected to increase with attitude change under the influence of cognitive dissonance. The mean scores of the various experimental groups could all be compared with each other, and also compared with the campus sample mean of 2.30, to identify those groups that did not have attitude shifts and those that did.

As has become the custom in cognitive dissonance research each group was divided in half, with half given the counterattitudinal task under clearly voluntary conditions, and the other half given the task and asked to do it with the assumption of compliance. In the voluntary condition subjects were repeatedly asked if they wished to participate and given formal opportunities to state their assent (which they all did). In the nonvoluntary group condition subjects were told, "I am going to ask you to do a small task" (p. 705), but it was then simply assumed that they would cooperate, with no formal opportunity to refuse (all did cooperate). The nonvoluntary group is included in the design as a baseline control condition with no attitude change expected. In the Zanna and Cooper experiment this created six groups, as seen in Table 13.1, which summarizes the results of this two-factor completely randomized design.

The one column in Table 13.1 that offers the usual test of cognitive dissonance is the middle column (headed "None"). Those subjects in the upper cell in that column, with high decision freedom (voluntary participation in writing a counterattitudinal statement), should evi-

TABLE 13.1. Means, for Each Group, of Subjects' Opinions Toward Banning Speakers on Campus

	Potential Side Effects of the Drug as Told to Subjects		
Decision freedom	*Arousal*	*None*	*Relaxation*
High	3.40$_a$	9.10$_b$	13.40$_c$
Low	3.50$_a$	4.50$_a$	4.70$_a$

Note. The subscript letters a–c are used to distinguish statistically different cells. Cells with different letters are statistically different from each other. Mean values in cells with the subscript letter *a* are not statistically different from the mean of 2.30 found in a campus survey. From Zanna and Cooper (1974). Copyright 1974 by the American Psychological Association. Adapted by permission.

dence the usual attitudinal shift expected under cognitive dissonance. Those with low decision freedom in that column (lower cell) were not expected to shift their attitude. The respective means of 9.10 and 4.50, statistically different from each other, support those expectations (the mean of 4.50 was not statistically different from the campus mean of 2.30). In contrast, it was expected that the group that was given the impression that any tension experienced was due to the pill (in the Arousal column of Table 13.1) would not have the attitude shift, regardless of whether the essay writing was voluntary or not. The reason is that any tension created by cognitive dissonance would be attributed to the pill, so they would have no motivation for shifting their attitude. On the other hand, the voluntary group given the expectation of feeling relaxed (in the Relaxation column) should find the tension created by cognitive dissonance all the stronger by contrast with their expectation of feeling relaxed. Thus, the voluntary group with the relaxation expectation should evidence an even greater attitude shift. The empirical means followed the predicted pattern of presence and absence of statistical significance.

Summarizing the expected and observed pattern of results, there should be a clear attitude shift in the High-None cell, and an even stronger one in the High-Relaxation cell (the two cells being significantly different from each other, as well as being significantly different from the sampled population mean of 2.30). All of the other cells should be similar to each other, that is, not different by statistical test and also not significantly different from the sampled population mean of 2.30, because none should evidence an attitude shift.

The data in the table are perfectly in accord with the prediction. A convenient way to summarize the statistical tests has been developed, and Table 13.1 offers an example of this form of communication. Subscript letters are placed in each cell. Cells with the same letters are not statistically different from each other, whereas those cells not sharing the same letters are different at a statistically significant level.

In this study Zanna and Cooper (1974) showed that manipulating misattribution of the arousal source, so that the arousal is not attributed to a dissonant attitude, behavior, or cognition (but rather to a pill that supposedly causes tension), can preclude dissonance caused attitude change. They have also shown that creating an expectation of relaxation in conjunction with dissonance can result in an unusually strong attitude change, ostensibly because the arousal is experienced as relatively large by the subject. The experimental evidence, summarized in Table 13.1, indicates that the theory successfully predicted the pattern of differences and lack of differences between the groups. By creating misattribution of feelings of tension (in the arousal group), the usual effects of cognitive dissonance were avoided. By increasing the relative strength of the tension (compared to expectations), the effects of cognitive dissonance were increased (in the relaxation group). The study thus offered support for the tension-based interpretation of cognitive dissonance effects. Although the outcome was as predicted, it is a case of affirming the consequent in that it was not a direct test of the occurrence of the inner event of tension after counterattitudinal statements. The theory predicted a pattern of outcomes, and that was what was observed. The intuitively stronger support here stems from the successful prediction of a pattern of findings, rather than just a single difference. But logically, all one can say is that the results were consistent with the theory.

There was, however, an opportunity to obtain somewhat more direct evidence of tension associated with cognitive dissonance as an incidental part of the manipulation checks in this study. For the manipulation checks, the subjects each had to fill out a 31-point scale labeled calm (1) at one end, and tense (31) at the other end, indicating how they felt "right now" (immediately after having written the counterattitudinal essay, and presumably before they had a chance to shift their attitudes to relieve any dissonance-based tension). We can look at the tension level self-ratings of those subjects who had not been given any information about side effects of tension and relaxation, that is, those who were in the usual cognitive dissonance conditions (high and low decision freedom in the None column of Table 13.1). Comparing these two groups on this 31-point scale of felt tension, there was a statistically significant difference in the expected direction; that is, the voluntary (high decision freedom) group experienced more tension. This is the group predicted to experience more tension (because they could feel responsible for their counterattitudinal statement), and thus should evidence attitude change (in an attempt to reduce the tension brought about by cognitive dissonance).

Recall that dissonance is posited to produce tension, which in turn is predicted to produce attitude change:

dissonance → tension → attitude change

The major analysis in the experiment, in terms of what was directly manipulated and measured, showed a relationship between the first part of that chain (dissonance) and the third part (attitude change).

The secondary analysis offered a direct measurement of, and confirmation of, the greater tension differences that were expected from the manipulation. Thus, strong support is offered here for the part of the theory that says that dissonance leads to inner tension.

Support for the second part of the theoretical chain, a relationship between tension and attitude shift, was found in the high decision group with no information about side effects, the subjects in the upper cell in the None column in Table 13.1. Within this group, which evidenced attitude change, presumably motivated by cognitive dissonance, a statistical correlation was computed between level of stated tension as seen in the tension manipulation check, and the expressed attitude. The correlation between attitude and degree of felt tension was high (.69) and statistically significant. This is support for a relationship between tension and attitude change, when the tension is caused by cognitive dissonance. However, tension was again a measured variable here (having the status of a subject variable), rather than a directly controlled (manipulated) variable. Although attitude change was manipulated in the study, between groups, the degree of attitude change in individual subjects within a condition was not manipulated, but measured, and so the measurement of attitude change was also a subject variable. The two subject variables do not offer conclusive evidence of a cause-and-effect relationship.

The two authors, joined by a third experimenter, undertook a still more direct attempt to prove the same point, using drugs to directly control tension, permitting cause-and-effect conclusions. Cooper, Zanna, and Taves (1978) used drugs in this second study, but convinced all of the subjects that they were each in the control group, each receiving only a placebo. In fact, one-third received amphetamine for arousal, one-third received a tranquilizer to induce relaxation, and one-third did receive just a placebo.

Subjects were told that the study was an investigation of the effects of drugs on memory; they agreed to take the drugs, and were given a simple memory task. After they had volunteered, all subjects were given the impression that they happened to be in the control condition, receiving a placebo rather than a real drug. They were told that the drugs would take time to work, so there would be a waiting period for the drugs to take effect. They were also told that in order to keep the different conditions of the experiment constant, all subjects in all groups would have the same waiting period.

Using the waiting period as an excuse (that there was some time available), subjects were asked to participate in "another experiment." In making this request, subjects were divided into voluntary and nonvoluntary conditions so that the nonvoluntary condition could offer a baseline control group with no attitude change. Those in the voluntary condition were given the option not to participate in the other experiment, with the voluntary nature stressed. Those in the nonvoluntary condition were simply given the task during the waiting period. This second task was the writing of a counterattitudinal essay (in this case, a statement in favor of the pardoning of Richard Nixon). As usual, the writing of this essay with which all of the students disagreed was well rationalized. Subjects participating in the experiment were then asked their attitudes subsequent to having written the essay, using a 31-point scale, with the higher numbers representing greater agreement. As in the Zanna and Cooper (1974) study, a campus survey was used to establish a baseline for the general campus attitude, so that shifts in attitude could be recognized as values above the campus average. Table 13.2 summarizes the design, and gives the mean attitude scores for the six groups in the study.

The results are in accord with the experimenters' predictions. The placebo group showed the usual cognitive dissonance, with the attitude shift in favor of the pardon only in the high-choice group, as expected. The group that was tranquilized (though they did not know that they had received a drug) did not evidence cognitive dissonance; that is, both choice levels had similar attitudes toward the pardon, and both were similar to the average response of 7.9 obtained from a random campus survey. (By similar we mean there was no statistically significant difference in a statistical test.) It appears that by chemically lowering arousal level, the usual attitude change did not occur, suggesting that physical arousal is necessary for the attitude change to take place. The only problematic results

TABLE 13.2.   Mean Scores of Attitudes Toward the Pardoning of Richard Nixon

	Drug condition		
Decision Freedom	*Tranquilizer*	*Placebo*	*Amphetamine*
High choice	8.6_a	14.7_b	20.2_c
Low choice	8.0_a	8.3_a	13.9_b

Note. Higher means on the 31-point scale indicate greater agreement with the attitude discrepant essay. Cell means with different subscripted letters are different from each other at the .05 level by the Newman-Keuls statistical procedure. The mean in a survey control group on the same campus was 7.9. All values in the table followed by a subscripted a are not significantly different from the campus mean of 7.9. From Cooper, Zanna, and Taves (1978). Copyright 1978 by the American Psychological Association. Reprinted by permission.

are in the amphetamine group. Here, not only did the expected very high shift in attitude occur for the high-choice group with amphetamine-enhanced arousal (significantly higher than all others), but even the low-choice group with amphetamine-enhanced arousal showed an attitude shift. The experimenters interpreted this as the low-choice amphetamine group having had nothing to attribute their arousal to but their writing of the counterattitudinal essay, so they manifested an attitude shift not unlike that of a group without drugs in a high-choice condition.

An alternative interpretation of this last finding is, however, possible. A manipulation check was given to all subjects in the study to see if only the voluntary groups subjectively experienced freedom of choice (as a test of the voluntarism manipulation). The subjects were asked to rate the extent to which they felt that they had freely decided to write the essay, on a 7-point scale. Three groups (the high-choice groups) had been told that they were free to participate or not, and all three indicated, on the 7-point scale manipulation check, that they had free choice. Three other groups (the low-choice groups) had merely been given a piece of paper on which to write the essay, with no discussion of freedom of choice. Two of these three groups rated their freedom of choice lower than the three groups that had free choice, in conformity with the intended experimental conditions. But the low-choice amphetamine group rated themselves as having had free choice. We therefore do not know whether the manipulation of lack of choice failed for that group, or if, feeling tension from the amphetamine, they simply reinterpreted their world as one where they must have done something to make themselves feel uncomfortable. Thus, in that cell of the design, we may have particularly strong evidence of the effect of experienced tension (induced here by amphetamine) in a cognitive dissonance paradigm, or may have a case of the low-choice manipulation failing for one group.

In Table 13.2, as in Table 13.1, the cells with different letters are different by statistical test, and those with the same letters are not significantly different from each other. The conclusion is that arousal is a critical factor in attitude change after the writing of counterattitudinal statements (the evidence being a lack of attitude change in the high-choice tranquilized cell), and that amount of arousal is related to amount of attitude change (increased attitude change in the high-choice amphetamine cell).

The theory of cognitive dissonance says that tension is an internal causal link in creating attitude change in cognitively dissonant situations (people changing their attitudes to reduce tension). The

Cooper et al. (1978) experiment directly manipulated tension with drugs, using drugs as a moderator variable. The theory says that in an experiment in which subjects are convinced to write counterattitudinal statements, the counterattitudinal statements create tension, which in turn fosters the attitude change (to reduce the tension). They used drugs to reduce tension in people writing such statements, and successfully prevented attitude change; they increased tension with drugs and got increased attitude change. Thus, they succeeded in directly testing the theory's predictive power by using drugs to directly manipulate an internal causal variable, tension. In this way, tension was present as an experimental variable (albeit through drug manipulation), rather than being only a theoretically operating internal variable. No surrogate variables were used. The variables in the experiment were the same as the variables in the theory (counterattitudinal statements, tension, and attitude change). The one remaining experimental variable, the moderator variable of voluntarism, is also a part of the current theory of cognitive dissonance.

The Zanna and Cooper (1974) study gave general support for the tension-based interpretation of cognitive dissonance. The secondary statistical analysis with the tension manipulation check gave good support for the theoretical linkage between cognitive dissonance and tension. The Cooper et al. (1978) experiment, with its direct manipulation of tension, gave strong support to the theoretical linkage between tension and attitude change. These experiments, plus the long history of other successful experiments, offer strong evidence in support of the theory. On the other hand, not all laboratories have had equivalent success in using cognitive dissonance predictively. Also, there are other theories that have been successful at times in explaining events that appear explainable as instances of cognitive dissonance. Only one alternative theory, however, has had a track record of many successes: Bem's self-perception theory (Bem, 1965, 1967, 1972). At this point, a reasonable view, articulated well by Fazio, Zanna, and Cooper (1977), is that each theory has a particular context (limiting conditions) in which its principles apply.

Special Design Features for Counterattitudinal Behavior

Cognitive dissonance research with counterattitudinal behavior has adopted a somewhat unorthodox but valid design that may also be useful in other situations. In ordinary research there is an independent variable defined by a manipulation that is present and absent in different groups, or else is present in different amounts in different groups, usually with one group in which it is completely absent so as to afford a clear control group. In dissonance research with counterattitudinal behavior, the manipulation being tested is the writing of a counterattitudinal essay. Yet it is common to have all groups exposed to the same dissonance situation. That is, there is no control group in the usual sense of an absence of the experimental treatment (here it would be a group that does not have to write a counterattitudinal essay). This absence of the usual type of control group is desirable only because the manipulation is such a strong one that it would be difficult to have a group not writing a counterattitudinal essay that is similar in all other respects to one that is convinced to write such an essay. The essay-writing groups, in the course of writing the essay, must not only think about the topic on which their attitudes will later be tested for change, but they must also come up with arguments opposite to their own current beliefs. Thus, there would be many other explanations available for their changing their attitudes, other than having made a counterattitudinal statement that led to inner tension. It is for this reason that simply having a group that did not write a counterattitudinal essay would not be useful as a control group.

The problem is solved by using the moderator variable of voluntarism to create a control condition, which is identical in the requirements of counterattitudinal behavior but removes the cognitive dissonance (discomfort from a counterattitudinal statement) by removing the voluntary component. This general design offers an interesting general solution to situations where the manipulation is a very strong one, or otherwise introduces potential confounding factors. Find a moderator variable that negates the effect, and then use it to form control groups with all subjects receiving the same manipulation, that is, the same level of the independent variable, but some groups differing on the moderator variable.

The use of the voluntarism manipulation does introduce another potential confounding factor in the investigation of counterattitudinal behavior. It is the possibility of poorer cooperation among those subjects not given freedom of choice in their participation. That is, the subjects have to write an essay with which they personally disagree. If the nonvoluntary subjects do not feel as cooperative as others, they might write less enthusiastic essays and think about the topic less. Because the subjects are later asked to indicate their opinions or attitudes on the topic on which they have written, those writing a more careful and serious essay favoring a point of view different from their own would be more likely to have simply thought of new arguments that would convince them to change their original point of view. To check on this possibility, it is common in such research to have people who are blind to the conditions of the subjects read the essays and rate them on convincingness, and at times also rate them on the level of writing, or on the measured length of the essays. Such checks were employed in both the Zanna and Cooper (1974) and Cooper et al. (1978) studies discussed earlier. No differences in essay quality were found, so degree of effort and involvement are not likely to have been responsible for the effects.

These checks on potential confounds are instructive for the example they offer of careful scrutiny of experimental conditions after the introduction of any new variable (such as the voluntarism manipulation). It is always possible that, in introducing one manipulation, additional variables could be inadvertently introduced, which also have an effect on the dependent variable, preventing clear interpretation of the experimental results. When we suspect that this is possible but cannot be sure we have prevented it, we can at least check on these potential effects, as was done in the case of seeing if the essays indicated differences in effort.

CHAPTER SUMMARY

The internal variables used in social psychological research often can be directly manipulated or measured. This in turn permits direct tests of relationships between internal variables. Under these circumstances theories that postulate internal events can be directly tested without having to commit the logical error of affirming the consequent. The McArthur and Post (1977) experiments offered an example of this type of experimentation.

Although social psychological research can sometimes avoid the logical error of affirming the consequent, another problem arises to replace the logical one. When measuring internal variables with questionnaires or behavioral indices, it is usually possible to define the internal variables through a number of different procedures. For example, one could ask people what they prefer, or else the experimenter can actually observe their choices. If a questionnaire is used, it can be constructed in more than one way. The problem that then arises is which operational definition to use to define an internal variable. The problem is further complicated by the occasional finding of different results when using different operational definitions. Because what is desired is general knowledge about the relationships between variables, different results with different operational definitions can play havoc with conclusions about relationships between variables.

The solution is to use several operational definitions, only drawing general conclusions when the results are not dependent on the way in which the variables are defined. In addition, when there has been consistency in the findings with most of the different definitions, one or two anomalous findings can serve to delineate the limits of the relationship, or to better understand the nature of one of the variables (by recognizing when only some of the conceptualized operational definitions offer good representations of the variable).

In social psychological research it is often important to have some independent means of assessing whether or not planned manipulations function as expected. The reason is that it is not often obvious whether the manipulation of an internal variable, such as an attitude, or mood, or expectation, has been successful. If the experimental results are as expected, there is some support for the assumption that the manipulation has been successful. When the experimental predictions are not borne out, this can be blamed on a failure of the manipulation, as well as on a failure of the theory. If the manipulation did not work, the theory would not have had a real test. The theory's rejection would then not be justified. It is therefore even more important to have manipulation checks when a theory fails. However, whenever internal variables are manipulated, it is desirable to include manipulation checks.

The specific manipulation checks used differ with the type of manipulation used in the experiment. A fairly common general check that can sometimes throw light on the success or failure of a manipulation is to ask subjects their impressions of the purpose of the experiment (just after the experiment). Their discussion can often make clear the extent to which they were or were not affected in the desired manner. In addition, subjects who are asked for their impressions or ideas about the experiment frequently inform the experimenter when they think that there has been an attempt to fool them.

The data of subjects who have not interpreted the experimental situation as intended, or have not been properly affected by an intended manipulation, are dropped from the analysis. The loss of a small number of subjects in this way is not considered to invalidate the findings. However, if too many subjects are lost in this way, then the subjects can no longer be considered to be a generally representative sample, limiting the generality of the findings. In such cases the study should be redesigned.

A topic that is in some ways related to the success or failure of manipulations is the issue of possible subject bias. Subject bias refers to the subjects' assumptions about what is expected or desired of them. Subject bias can influence the outcome in ways that could make it difficult to trust the experimental conclusions. Keeping the subjects in the dark as to the detailed purposes of the experiment, and which group they are in, is important in avoidance of subject bias. The subject is entitled to know the general purposes of the research before participating, but the detailed analysis of the variables under scrutiny can wait till after the subject's participation. Checking on the subjects' assumptions about the purposes of the experiment, in addition to shedding light on the success of manipulations, also is often a useful way of detecting the presence of subject bias. Detailed questions about what the subject thought various aspects of the experimental situation were for, prior to debriefing the subject, can also be useful. The data of subjects with bias can be removed, but it is important that this not be restricted to subjects with bias in only one direction, and also that the person removing subjects not be aware of their actual experimental performance when making the removal decision.

An important means of reducing the likelihood of subject bias is to use double-blind procedures. Double-blind procedures are in effect when neither the subjects nor the experimenters in contact with the subjects are aware of the details of the experiment, the hypotheses, or which subjects are in which groups. This generally requires the use of experimental assistants. Postexperimental questionnaires can be administered to the experimental assistants as well as the subjects, to see whether biasing information or cues were available to the subjects, along with the usual questionnaires to see what the subjects' beliefs were, about what was going on during the experiment.

Theory and research on cognitive dissonance were discussed in detail as an example of social psychological research, and used in a discussion of issues in theory development in psychology. The counterattitudinal essay paradigm was used as an example for a discussion of manipulations, manipulation checks, and design considerations.

Finally, the use of voluntarism as a moderator variable that removed an effect, to create a control group, was described. It was suggested that there may be other situations involving strong manipulations, where omitting a manipulation in order to form a control condition would offer too many differences between the control and experimental groups. In such cases, the use of a moderator variable that can remove an effect might offer a better control condition.

NEW WORDS AND PHRASES IN CHAPTER 13

cognitive dissonance
counterattitudinal essay
counterattitudinal essay paradigm
double-blind procedures
manipulation check
subject bias

CHAPTER 14

Social Psychology II:
The Measurement of Attitudes
and Construction of Tests for
Research

As seen in chapter 13, the principal question in the cognitive dissonance literature concerns the conditions that promote attitude change. Therefore, the dependent variable is almost always some attitude measurement. The measurement of attitudes is a frequent dependent variable in many areas of social psychology. Special tests are constructed on these occasions. Learning how to construct tests, of whatever sort, is useful information. In this chapter the most frequently used measurement techniques are described, along with detailed instructions on their use. The focus here is on assessing attitudes, but the same methods and concerns are appropriate for the construction of most psychological tests.

There are two very different ways in which attitudes are measured: questionnaires and behavioral indices. The questionnaire approach is examined first, in a discussion of the two most frequently used types of questionnaires, Likert scales and the semantic differential. These questionnaires yield an index of the extent to which subjects approve of, agree with, or believe some statement, or feel a mood or emotion that the statement describes, or approve of a person or a plan. Likert scales give the subject an opportunity for very direct expression of attitudes, whereas the semantic differential measures endorsement of attitudes in a more subtle way.

Both of these rating scales can be contrasted with another type of questionnaire that is much more indirect. This third approach focuses first on developing an ordered arrangement of some large set of statements or other stimuli, and with the aid of mathematical manipulation yields some indication of the distance between the ordered stimuli. In other words, attitude statements, or social events that can be evaluated, are placed on a scale where distance between items is indicated. Subjects are then themselves placed on a continuum by dint of the position of statements with which they agree. One common method asks subjects to compare all possible pairs among a set of stimuli, and then mathematical techniques are used to convert the large number of pairwise comparisons into a scaled continuum. The questions to the subjects can take the following form: "If you had to choose between candidates A and B, which would you choose? Between candidates B and C?," and so on. Other times the comparisons are more complex—for example, "Which of these many professions is twice as prestigeful as accountancy?" or "Which profession is midway in prestige between nutritionist and playwright?" Sometimes distance between stimuli is determined by the relative frequency of confusion of one with another; for example, in ordering confusability of voiced expressions of emotion, we could test the frequency with which people confuse the voice of someone surprised with the voice of someone happy. The less often two voiced expressions are confused, the further apart they are assumed to be. Each of these methods is accompanied by some mathematical assumptions and techniques that offer the logic and mechanisms to permit inferences about relative distance between the ordered stimuli. Using these methods, one can, for example, order severity of crimes; order politicians for electability, charm, or on a liberal/conservative continuum; or order professions for prestige.

These mathematical approaches are all useful for seeing how the relative positions of stimuli change. (For example, has the relative status of different professions changed over the years; or the opinions about the relative severity of different crimes, such as mugging as it has become more frequent in big cities?) These techniques are all ingenious and interesting, but require some mathematical sophistication, and extended discussion, for an adequate presentation. We therefore forego a detailed presentation of these methods, concentrating instead on simpler techniques. The interested reader with a need to scale attitudes should look at the introductory discussion by Dawes (1972, pp. 4–90).

After the discussion of Likert scales and the semantic differential, there is a discussion of the less structured but unendingly creative behavioral measurement of attitudes. The best of these examples of behavioral measurement of attitudes consist of observing behaviors that can serve as operational definitions of the attitudes of interest, often because they are examples of the attitude. A simple instance is the use of choice to define preference, because making a choice is an example of expressing an attitude (a behavioral statement of preferring X to Y). Defining an attitude through a specific behavior provides an unambiguous way of identifying the existence of the attitude. However, in most instances, a good deal of ingenuity is required to arrive at a clearly defined, representative, and easily observable behavior that can serve as an operational definition of the expression of an attitude. When such behavioral definitions are not available, behaviors or physical manifestations are used that may be correlated with an attitude in which there is interest. As some examples, experimenters have used dilation of pupils as an indication of interest; physical movement, such as leg jiggling, as evidence of anxiety; or, outside the laboratory, blushing has been taken as implying embarrassment.

The following sections offer detailed examination of the various approaches merely alluded to in the preceding discussion.

LIKERT AND OTHER DIRECT RATING SCALES

Likert scales ask subjects to indicate the strength or intensity of their attitudes directly, by having the subjects check a point on a scale, or having them choose the closest description of their feelings from among the choices given (Likert, 1932). The prototypical Likert scale is one in which people are asked to rate each of several statements on a 5-point scale, indicating the extent to which they agree with the statement, or some person or plan identified in the statement. For example, "On a scale of one to five, with one representing strong disapproval, and five representing strong approval, how would you rate the current American President?"

strongly disapprove (1)	disapprove (2)	undecided (3)	approve (4)	strongly approve (5)

Similarly, "On a scale of one to five, with one representing strong disagreement, and five representing strong agreement, how would you rate the President's position on tax reform?"

strongly disagree (1)	disagree (2)	undecided (3)	agree (4)	strongly agree (5)

The actual number of points on each scale item varies in use from one study to another, with researchers still referring to them as Likert scales, though sometimes using the term *Likert type scale*.

An example of a scale item that would not be called a Likert scale item is one where the basic statement is not a simple declaration with which the subjects can agree or disagree, and neither end point expresses approval or agreement. For example, the statement for the scale item can be presented as a question: "How free did you feel to refuse to participate in the experiment?" The end points of the scale for the subjects' responses could be "completely free to refuse to participate," and "no opportunity to refuse to participate." This scale item could be made more typical of a Likert scale item by rephrasing the question as a declarative statement, for example, "You were completely free to refuse to participate in the experiment," accompanied by scale items having end points of "completely agree" and "completely disagree."

Another example of a scale item that would not be a Likert scale item is the following:

very unhappy (1)	unhappy (2)	neutral (3)	happy (4)	very happy (5)

This could be converted to a Likert scale item by giving it the following form:

Concerning your feelings at this moment, check the number which indicates the degree of your agreement with the following statement:

"I am happy."

completely disagree (1)	(2)	(3)	(4)	completely agree (5)

The major feature that distinguishes a Likert scale item from items in other types of scales is the request to give a numerical rating overtly indicating the degree of agreement with, or approval of, a statement, or indicating accord with a person, a plan, or sentiment referred to in the statement.

Scales that ask for a numerical indication of degree of endorsement of some person, plan, idea, feeling, or attitude can take many forms. As seen in the preceding examples, they do not have to follow the form of the Likert scale, though that is one of the more common forms. In this text, all scales that offer unambiguous indications of attitudes and feelings, including Likert scales, are called **direct rating scales**. The label direct rating scale serves to differentiate clear and unambiguous statements of attitudes from a popularly used scale, discussed in a later section, that entails a less direct expression of attitudes.

A direct rating scale was used in the Zanna and Cooper (1974) study, in the form of a 31-point scale measuring subjects' agreement with the banning of inflammatory speakers on campus. Only the end points of the scale were verbally identified, with 1 opposed and 31 strongly in favor of the ban. In the closely related Cooper et al. (1978) study, a 31-point scale was again used, this time to indicate the extent to which subjects agreed with the pardoning of Richard Nixon (higher numbers meaning greater agreement). As a manipulation check for the voluntarism (free choice) variable, Cooper et al. asked subjects to indicate to what extent they believed they had freely decided to write the essay, using a 7-point scale. In all of these uses of scales only the end points were labeled. With a 5-point scale it is not difficult to label each numerical value, usually modifying verbs with adverbs (agree strongly, agree moderately, agree slightly, undecided, disagree slightly, etc.). With larger numbers of points in an item, it is difficult to construct verbalizations for all the different points.

The Number of Points in an Individual Scale Item

A 2-point item is seen in the alternative choices of yes or no, agree or disagree, approve or disapprove. Such dichotomous choices do not involve any numbers on the questionnaires given to the subjects; the subjects merely circle or check their verbal choice for each question. A third point can be introduced into a scale with an "undecided" category. A problem with having an undecided point in the middle of a scale item is that it offers a subject a chance to not answer some questions. When there is no such opportunity, the subject is forced to ferret out some slight preference and express it. In most situations people have some preferences, even if they are slight and based on very little information. For this reason many experimenters construct scale items with an even number of points, with no neutral or undecided center point. The desirability of the inclusion of such a center point has to be decided in the context of the question and the experiment. For example, a neutral point may be meaningful when we wish to see if a person retreats from a previous strongly held opinion. Also, being undecided may be realistic in the face of clearly contradictory information, or the absence of information.

Scale Reliability. **Reliability** is consistency in measurement. The **reliability of individual scale items** increases with the number of points in the item. The **reliability of the complete scale** increases with the number of items.

The smaller the number of scale items used to measure a single attitude, the larger the number of points per item that should be used. Conversely, the smaller the number of points per scale item, the larger the number of scale items that should be used. Thus, if dichotomous items are desirable because of the nature of the issue, then it is particularly important to have many items in the scale (in order to have a reliable scale).

Nunnally (1967, p. 523) recommended at least 10 points when using a single-item scale. (Recall that Zanna & Cooper, 1974, used a 31-point single-item scale, as did Cooper et al., 1978, for measuring agreement with an attitude. The latter group, however, used just a 7-point single-item scale in the manipulation check of freedom of choice.) Although large numbers of points are desirable for single item scales, Nunnally (1967, p. 521) said that when several items are used in the scale to assess a single attitude, there is little to be gained by having more than 11 points per item. In the case of an attitude scale with several items all testing the same attitude, he suggested that the real gains in reliability from more points per scale item are in the increases from two through seven points. In summary, if there are very few items in a test, the individual items should each have a large number of points, in order to maximize the reliability of the test. If there are only 2, or 3, or even 5 points per item, it is particularly important to have many items.

Scale Validity. **Validity** is correctness, or truthfulness, in measurement. A valid scale, or a valid test, is one that measures what it claims to measure; that is, if it is labeled as measuring something, say, anxiety, then it is valid if it measures anxiety. Perfect validity, which is measurement of precisely what is intended, is not expected in psychological tests. A test with strong validity (a more realistic expectation) primarily measures what is intended, although other (unidentified) factors are also influencing the scores. The extent to which other factors influence the scores is the extent to which validity is compromised. Validity, like reliability, is a question of degree.

The Influence of Reliability on Validity. In order for a test to have some degree of validity, it must have some degree of reliability. That is, reliability is necessary for validity. A test must measure something with consistency, in order to be measuring something validly. If you heard, or read, that a test had no reliability, you would know that it is also not a valid test.

Although reliability is necessary for validity, it does not guarantee validity. That is, a test can be very reliable, in the sense of being very consistent, always giving the same scores to the same people, but yet be measuring (with this great consistency) something other than the test is claimed to measure. For example, a test could be used to measure grade-school children for intelligence, utilizing group administration. Such a test would require adequate reading skills (so the children could follow the instructions, and understand the individual items on the test). The high-scoring children might turn out to be those with good reading skills, those with lesser reading skills scoring lower. The test would then be a test that measures reading skills. It is possible that it would in fact be a better test of reading skills than of intelligence. If it measured the children consistently, it would be a reliable test, but possibly with low validity as a measure of intelligence. Thus, validity is determined by the extent to which the test or scale measures what it is claimed to measure. Reliability is determined from the consistency of the measurements, being necessary for validity, but not sufficient to guarantee it.

Summative Scales

The best way to maximize reliability is to have several items asking the same question, each in a slightly different way. In a Likert scale the simplest way to do this is to use the same basic statement for approval/disapproval, but vary the evaluative terms. For example, one item could ask for degree of approval/disapproval, another for degree of support/opposition, and a third for extent of agreement/ disagreement. When the same question is repeated, the scale values that have been checked are summed. Thus, if using a three-item questionnaire, with 11 points in each item, the maximum obtainable score is 33. When the points checked on each item are added together in this way the scale is called a **summative scale**. This is the proper technical name for what we have been informally calling a scale (as differentiated from a scale item or a single-item scale). Any measuring device assigning a score on a range of potential numerical values is a scale. It could consist of a single quantitative item. Where there are several items a procedure is needed for deriving a single score. When the points obtained from individual items are added it is called a summative scale.

Most of the scales discussed to this point used verbs concerning accord and its opposite (with polar terms such as agree/disagree, approve/disapprove, support/oppose). But adjectives suggesting moods (happy, depressed, angry, etc.), can also be used, as in the earlier example that had end points of very unhappy and very happy. Zanna and Cooper (1974) asked subjects to indicate how they felt, "right now," on a 31-point scale ranging from calm to tense. More often than not, adjectives are employed in a more subtle measurement of attitudes, called the semantic differential (Osgood, Suci, & Tannenbaum, 1957). This approach is an indirect one, as is apparent from the form of the questions. The semantic differential is particularly useful in providing a variety of scale items testing the same attitude.

OSGOOD'S SEMANTIC DIFFERENTIAL

The full appreciation of the range of scale labels that could be used to express an attitude stems from the introduction of Osgood's **semantic differential** (Osgood et al., 1957). Charles Osgood and his associates developed this measurement technique while working on a theory of meaning. Their scale consists of the presentation of some concept, say labor unions, or politicians, or the United Nations, followed by a series of scale items, perhaps a half dozen or as many as 20, each bound by bipolar adjectives, and each used to evaluate the same concept. It might look like the scale presented in Fig. 14.1 (although perhaps with more items).

In the example in Fig. 14.1 all of the adjectives used to define the poles of the scale items have an underlying dimension in common: an implication of ranging from bad to good. Osgood spoke of adjec-

```
                              LABOR UNIONS

bad        -----|-----|-----|-----|-----|-----|-----  good
                1     2     3     4     5     6     7

useless    -----|-----|-----|-----|-----|-----|-----  useful
                1     2     3     4     5     6     7

dishonest  -----|-----|-----|-----|-----|-----|-----  honest
                1     2     3     4     5     6     7

foolish    -----|-----|-----|-----|-----|-----|-----  wise
                1     2     3     4     5     6     7

unfair     -----|-----|-----|-----|-----|-----|-----  fair
                1     2     3     4     5     6     7
```

FIG. 14.1. Example of a 5-item semantic differential scale on attitude (positive or negative) on labor unions.

tives sharing the bad to good implication as representing the evaluative dimension. Each pair of adjectives has other implications besides the bad-good dimension, so the evaluation component is not as clear as in direct rating scales. However, because all of the items share the evaluative dimension, collectively they can offer an attitudinal bottom line. The numbers representing the subjects' choices on the different scale items are simply added to produce a summed value (a summative scale) representing the subject's evaluation of that institution, or concept, on the dimension of bad to good.

Osgood did not restrict his adjectives to those suggesting an evaluative dimension. He had subjects respond to statements by choosing points between many pairs of adjectives, and used statistical techniques (primarily factor analysis) to see which pairs of adjectives formed groups that seemed to be measuring something in common. From this grouping of pairs of adjectives he identified three dimensions that emerged most frequently. These were the evaluative dimension, a potency dimension, and an activity dimension.

Examples of adjectives sharing the potency dimension are strong/weak, thick/thin, large/small, rugged/delicate. Examples of the activity dimension are active/passive, quick/slow, excitable/calm, tense/relaxed. Although other dimensions sometimes emerged with variations in the stimuli being evaluated, the evaluative, potency, and activity dimensions were the ones they found most frequently, even when they varied the language and the culture in which they administered such scales. The potency and activity dimensions are not discussed further here, because it is the evaluative dimension that is most frequently used in psychology.

The semantic differential has found widespread use even in areas outside of social psychology, particularly political science. Within social psychology, findings derived from the use of the scales have had an influence on a number of theoretical issues. However, its broadest influence has been a modest but highly useful one: expanding the pool of labels for scales using the evaluative dimension from the more restricted set seen in direct rating scales, to a much larger set. As Nunnally (1967, p. 537) recognized, "The evaluative factor [in the semantic differential] almost serves as a definition for the term attitude, and consequently scales on the evaluative factor should serve well as measures of verbalized attitudes."

As one example of the use of a semantic differential scale, McFarland, Ross, and Conway (1984) did a study investigating some of the factors that could have an effect on enduring attitudes, such as attitudes about brushing one's teeth after every meal, and attitudes toward vigorous exercise. (They introduced some interesting manipulations that they hypothesized would have an effect on those particular attitudes.) To measure the attitudes of the subjects toward tooth brushing and vigorous exercise they used 9-point scales, with the end points being important/unimportant, healthy/unhealthy, beneficial/harmful. Petty and Cacioppo (1984) offered another example of the use of a semantic differential scale. Testing the effects of numbers of arguments (the independent variable) on attitude change (the dependent variable), they measured attitudes toward instituting comprehensive exams for seniors in their major subject as a requirement for graduation. They also used 9-point scales, but with the end points of good/bad, beneficial/harmful, foolish/wise, and unfavorable/favorable.

THE PHYSICAL FORM OF SCALES

A scale generally begins with instructions indicating how to fill out the form, for example, telling subjects to circle the numbers, or to place check marks in one of the provided spaces, and making it clear that they can, or cannot, check points between the numbers. Most frequently the scales are presented horizontally, with discrete steps, along with instructions to specifically select one of the numbers on the scale. One form of presentation is the following:

```
Completely                                        Completely
approve ---------:---------:---------:---------:---------:--------- disapprove
              1      2      3      4      5      6
```

In this example only the end points are labeled. Under these conditions the numerical values are often identified with verbalizations elsewhere, perhaps placed with the instructions for completing the scale. For example, in the instructions for the questionnaire, the following equivalence can be indicated:

1. Completely approve
2. Mostly approve
3. Slight approval
4. Slight disapproval
5. Mostly disapprove
6. Completely disapprove

If there is just one item being administered, or each item verbalizes agreement differently, the label generally appears directly above the numbers, as in the following example:

strongly support 1	moderately support 2	slightly support 3	slightly oppose 4	moderately oppose 5	strongly oppose 6

The statement to be evaluated could appear at the top of a page, and the individual scale items to be checked by the subjects could appear below the statement on the same page, each item using different verbal end points. If the end points are so similar that the question appears redundant, slightly altered verbalizations of the same question can be interspersed throughout the questionnaire, separated by other questions.

Sometimes the points on the scale are represented on a drawing of a thermometer, or are given individual boxes to be checked. There is no clear evidence that one or another visual presentation is preferable. It is merely important that the instructions be unambiguous, requiring little effort for complete understanding, and that the positive and negative poles be clearly indicated, so that subjects do not get the two ends confused and forget which number means strong support. If smaller numbers on a scale item imply agreement with the statement on that scale item, this should not be changed from statement to statement, or subjects will sometimes check agreement when they mean disagreement and vice versa. If agreement is on the left for one item, it should be on the left for all items.

The Nature of the Items

In attitude measurement within the context of experiments, the subjects are generally asked to express their attitude toward some single issue. Most experimenters using a direct rating scale in experiments have used just a single item, as in the case of the question of how people felt about President Ford's pardon of former President Nixon. In most experiments the issue being examined is not of any importance to the experimenters. They are not really doing a general survey to find out what people think. They take some arbitrary issue about which people have identifiable attitudes, and investigate different methods for changing attitudes.

In cognitive dissonance research they have used single readily verbalized issues, such as the subjects' attitudes toward a group they had to go through some trouble to join; attitudes toward a college tuition increase; attitudes toward some political issue, and so on. The questions can therefore be quite straightforward—for example, "To what extent do you agree or disagree with the pardoning of

Richard Nixon?" or "How interesting or dull did you find the group discussion?" The scale can then include the verbs or adjectives that are used in the question (agree/disagree, interesting/dull), merely adding modifiers (strongly, moderately, slightly), to create different levels, or to identify extreme poles. Often the question is presented as a statement, with the extent of the subject's agreement with the statement indicated by the position on the scale that is checked, for example: "Please indicate the degree to which you are or are not in accord with the following statement: 'The President of Iraq cannot be trusted to maintain an agreement.' " The scale choices then range from strongly agree to strongly disagree.

There are three issues of concern in constructing items. The first, and most obvious, is that the question or statement must be clear. Suppose the preceding example of a statement were shortened to the following: "The President of Iraq cannot be trusted." One subject might interpret this to mean that he will treat many of his own citizens badly (oppressing them, or torturing them). Another subject might interpret it to mean that Iraq will mount a sneak attack against Kuwait. A third might think it refers to not maintaining signed treaties and other agreements. A fourth subject might wonder what it refers to, and therefore have trouble answering. The question must be unambiguously and simply stated; otherwise different subjects will, through personal interpretation, be answering different questions, or subjects might become irritated at not being able to answer the question.

The second issue is closely related to the first. This second issue is the inadvertent asking of two questions at once. For example, suppose attitudes toward the president of the country were being solicited with a scale, and the instructions read: "Indicate the extent of your agreement or disagreement with the following statement: The President is doing a poor job and he should not run again." If the subject were a very conservative person, and the president was only moderately conservative, the subject might be inclined to evaluate the president's performance as poor, therefore wanting to agree with the first part of the question ("The President is doing a poor job . . . "), yet wish that the President would run again, because the other potential candidates are all more liberal. The result would be a desire to disagree with the second part of the question, but agree with the first part. The double nature of this question is fairly clear. Let us look at one that is a little more subtle. "Indicate the extent of your agreement with the following statement: Most people do not realize the extent to which their success or failure is completely out of their own control." A person might believe that people are at the mercy of forces outside themselves, but may believe that in fact most people know this. If someone held those two views, that person would be in agreement with the second part about lack of control, and in disagreement with the first part that says "Most people do not realize . . . . " Such double-barreled statements should be avoided wherever possible.

Yet there are situations where a second clause is necessary in order to make a question more specific. Examples are found in complex political issues, such as disarmament, where the nature of the proposal must be specified. (Is the proposal one of bilateral or unilateral disarmament? Is it gradual? etc.) If the experimenter is in a position to select the issue, he or she should select an issue that can be stated unambiguously in a single sentence without a second clause.

The third issue is one of possible **response bias**. Assume for the moment a scale consisting of several questions measuring agreement on some issue, each item requesting a response on a scale with the end points of agree and disagree, support and oppose, approve and disapprove, and so forth, with, say, 7 points on each item. Response bias is a tendency to respond in one direction with some neglect of the statement being rated. The research evidence suggests that on tests and questionnaires response bias most often occurs as a tendency to agree with the statement when the subject is unsure of his or her own position on the issue. Thus, something besides the person's belief, attitude, or opinion can occasionally influence and bias an answer. One way to prevent this from having an effect on the results is to make sure that the statement being agreed with, or disagreed with, is stated as its own converse half the time. As an example, let us look at two items in a questionnaire that would be intended for use in a study using people's attitudes toward smoking on airlines as the dependent variable. We assume that there are some subjects who are not certain of how they feel about the issue, so some of them might be prone to simply be more agreeable than not (yielding examples of response bias). The example is illustrated in Fig. 14.2.

Note that in Fig. 14.2 agreement (support) is on the right for both items. It is the verbalization of the statement that is reversed for the second item on smoking. By reversing verbalizations in this way, a person with a tendency to agree (and give a response closer to 5 on both questions due to this tendency) would numerically inflate his or her response to both sides of the issue. On item 1 there would be increased agreement with permitting smoking, and on item 5 there would be increased agreement with prohibiting smoking. The av-

PERSONAL OPINION SURVEY

Please indicate the degree to which you are or are not in accord with each of the following statements by placing a check mark above the number that most closely represents your opinion.

1. Smoking should be permitted on airlines.

Strongly
Disagree   -----|-----|-----|-----|-----   Strongly
           1   2   3   4   5   Agree

2. (This, and a few other items, would ask for opinions on other issues.)
.
.
.

7. The airlines should prohibit smoking on all flights.

Strongly
Oppose   -----|-----|-----|-----|-----   Strongly
           1   2   3   4   5   Support

FIG. 14.2. Example of two items, with reversed verbalizations, in a questionnaire of attitudes towards smoking in airplanes.

erage response would therefore not be biased, and could reflect the person's attitude about smoking on airplanes (including being uncertain).

In the questionnaire in Fig. 14.2, for a person to be consistent on the smoking items, the same subject that selects a 5 for Item 1 would be expected to select a 1 for Item 7. That subject, with the strongest possible responses in support of smoking, would have a total score of 6 on the two items. If another subject selected number 1 for Item 1, and number 5 for Item 7, that subject, with the strongest possible responses for prohibiting smoking, would also obtain a score of 6 for the two items. Thus, when reversing verbalizations to avoid response bias, the numerical index produced by the questionnaire is useless, unless **transformed scores** are used for the reversed items. A transformed score, in this context, is a score whose value is changed so that it affects the summed total in the opposite direction. A transformed score of 5 on a scale from 1 to 5 becomes a 1, and vice versa. By transforming the scores of the appropriate items, a response offering maximum agreement with permitting smoking contributes the same amount to the total as a response offering maximum disagreement with prohibiting smoking. In this way all responses in favor of one side of the issue take the total in one direction (maximizing the total), and all responses favoring the other side of the issue take the total in the other direction (minimizing the total).

Transforming Scores. The explanation of how scores are transformed is clearer if it is assumed that the implications of all answers will consistently conform with the phrasing and numbering of the first item. Specifically, in the first item in the Personal Opinion Survey on smoking in Fig. 14.2, the higher numbers suggest a preference for smoking being permitted. Thus, in all items, the final result should be that higher numbers mean a preference for permitting smoking.

The transformation is simple. First, a 1 is added to the number of points in the item; call this new number "plus 1." Then the numerical response given by a subject to each item that is to be transformed is subtracted from plus 1. In the example in Fig. 14.2, there are 5 scale points on each item, so the responses to the reversed (transformed) items are each subtracted from 6. The remainder after subtracting the person's response from 6 is the transformed numerical score for that scale item. If a person strongly supported prohibiting smoking, and so checked number 5 on Item 7, the 5 would be transformed to a 1 by subtracting it from 6. If that person responded consistently, that same person who responded with a 5 to Item 7, transformed to a 1, would be expected to respond with 1 on Item 1, which would not be transformed. This would yield a summed score for the two items of 2, the smallest possible sum for the two items (representing the strongest possible stand against permitting smoking.) On the other hand, if he or she consistently strongly supported permitting smoking, that subject would respond with a 5 to Question 1, and a 1 to Question 7, the latter transformed via 6–1 to 5. This would yield a summed total of 10 for the two items, the maximum possible total for the two items, representing the strongest possible stand in favor of permitting smoking.

Measuring Interitem Reliability

In the construction of tests, an important question is whether or not all of the items intended to measure the same dimension actually do so. When they all measure the same thing, this is called **interitem agreement**. There are a number of statistical tests to measure the degree of interitem agreement. In the days before the ready availability of computers and statistical software, the **split-half reliability coefficient** was probably the best known of these, because of its ease of computation. The split-half reliability coefficient is simply the correlation between two arbitrary halves of the same test (with a correction for the loss in reliability that occurs when using fewer items, as is the case when only half of the test is treated as the test itself).

The best of the reliability tests is **coefficient alpha**. Coefficient alpha reflects the average correlation among all the individual items—that is, the average value if the correlation of each item with every other item is computed, averaged, and then corrected for the number of items in the test (the more items, the higher the reliability, assuming everything else is equal). With most psychological tests in which each item, though measuring the same thing, probably has a very different form, or taps the dimension of interest by asking a different kind of question than some other item, we expect only modest correlations between individual test items.

For Likert-type scale items all testing the same attitude, it is likely that the items, all cloned from the same basic statement, are all very similar to each other. The variations in Likert scale items are afforded by slight variations of the labels and reversal of implication for half of the statements. In such a case, high interitem correlations are expected. But the interitem correlations should still be checked. As with any test for which the scores will be summed, it is important to know that the numerical values being summed do in fact reflect the same attitude. Only if agreement with one version of a statement coincides with agreement with another version of the same statement does it makes sense to combine, and specifically to add, the scores.

A second reason for checking the interitem reliability is to identify any items that may have been inadvertently changed in implication from the change in scale labels, or from having inverted the statement. This suggests that what is desired is not just an overall statement of reliability such as is obtained from coefficient alpha or the split-half reliability, but also a specific check of each item for its agreement with the remaining items. This is accomplished by computing individual correlations between the scores on individual test items and the sum of all other items. This would offer **individual item reliabilities**. To obtain individual item reliabilities, for each subject the score of the item being tested is subtracted from the subject's total score (obtained from summing all items). This yields the sum of all other items. A Pearson product moment correlation is then computed between this sum of all other items and the sub-tracted items's score, using this set of paired scores over all subjects.

This procedure is repeated for each item, yielding the values for the correlations between each of the individual items and the rest of the questions. Often this is not as difficult as it seems, because frequently there are only a few items used in questionnaires examining attitudes for experiments. This is a repetitive task, so computers can do all of the correlations efficiently when there is a large number of items. If the items for the questionnaire have not been used before, this procedure is highly desirable. It is generally conducted before the experiment, with a different group of subjects, so as to have a maximally useful questionnaire for the experiment. It is not unusual to find one or two items that may be far lower in correlation than the rest and need to be reworded or discarded.

BEHAVIORAL MEASUREMENT

Instead of developing a questionnaire-based test of an attitude, it is sometimes possible to observe a person's behavior and infer an attitude from the nature of the behavior. We call this **behavioral measurement of attitudes**. Earlier, the statement was made that the choice of one thing rather than another can be a direct expression of an attitude. If the person chooses A over B, the person prefers A over B. Although there are conceivable conditions under which this would not be true, such exceptions are sufficiently infrequent that choice can often be used as a good operational definition of preference. A **good behavior-based operational definition of an attitude** does two things: (a) It specifies the conditions indicating when the attitude is present, and (b) it functions as an example of the attitude. In addition, it should be based on a general definition of what is meant by the attitude in the real world.

These qualities can be recognized in our example of choice as an operational definition for preference. If asked for examples of instances in which, say, John preferred beer to wine, we would answer by enumerating instances in which he chose the one over the other. Such instances would specify when that preference was present, constitute examples of what is meant by preference for beer, and fit people's definition of preference.

It has previously been stressed that an operational definition must be highly specific so that others can know precisely how the manipulation was carried out, or precisely what measurement procedures and criteria were used. This would enable interested scientists to accurately reproduce the study, or knowledgeably critique it. In addition, having the operational definition define an attitude as usually defined in the real world, and/or being an example of the attitude, helps to ensure that it is a relevant definition, not just a clear or reproducible one.

Behavioral Measures as Operational Definitions

This section begins with examples from the altruism literature. The major independent variables in experiments on altruism are most often personal qualities that are being tested to see if they are, at least in part, responsible for altruism; examples of such independent variables are empathy and mood. Usually these qualities are induced within the subjects (manipulated, rather than subject variables). To induce empathy, some experimenters vary the apparent similarity between the subject and some other person in the situation. To vary mood, subjects are sometimes asked to think of very sad, or very happy events. At other times they are unexpectedly rewarded to improve their mood.

The operational definitions of the dependent variables in the altruism literature offer interesting examples of behavioral measures. Altruism, as defined by most people in most circumstances, involves being helpful to someone else, at personal cost (of time, trouble, discomfort, or valuables). However, a part of the definition that is in dispute is whether we should also expect there to be an absence of personal gain in order for us to call an example of helpfulness, altruism. In fact, this is one of the issues that motivates much of the research. Can we identify situations in which people are helpful without even covert types of gain? If covert gain is present, what is its nature?

The operational definitions of altruism used in research tend to confine themselves to helpfulness to others at some personal cost, with no overt payment or gain. The experiments then try to shed light on the conditions of such helpfulness, including the issue of whether some covert personal gain is necessary, or what else motivates or promotes such behavior.

A tough part of arranging for the potential occurrence of altruism in research is the necessity of having some situation develop, during the experimental session, that convinces the subjects that some individual really needs help (and that this is not part of the experiment). To this end, it is generally necessary to describe the experiment, to the subject, as having some other purpose, perhaps pretending that it is a learning experiment. Then, during what appears to be a learning task, an experimental assistant, or a friend of the experimental assistant, expresses some dire need, for example, having to complete some other experiment or project by some deadline. Cialdini, Darby, and Vincent (1973) had a "student" (actually an experimental assistant) express a need for subjects to agree to do some phone interviews, in order for a class project to be completed on time. The experimenters then were able to monitor two closely related dependent variables: whether or not subjects agreed to do at least one phone interview, and also a quantitative measure of number of phone interviews for which subjects volunteered, as a function of different conditions of the experiment (which were being tested to see if they promoted altruism). A variation on requests for help is to ask people to come back for a second session of the experiment, at a very inconvenient time (middle of the night, early morning hours, Saturday night, etc.). This type of request can be rationalized in a variety of ways, for example, "because I have to complete my research project by the end of this week so that I can complete my degree by the end of this semester, in order to take a great job that will not wait for me." If people will not normally be willing to do such things, but experimental circumstances can be manipulated to increase the occurrence of such behavior, then variables have been identified that are relevant to the occurrence of that behavior.

The Cialdini et al. (1973) study that used willingness to volunteer to give phone interviews as evidence of altruism found evidence that altruism can apparently function to make the altruistic person feel better. One often sees what appears to be altruism in people witnessing someone being harmed, or someone experiencing some sudden loss. Cialdini et al. concluded that witnessing such pain creates a negative feeling in observers, which people can sometimes get rid of by doing something nice for somebody else. Cialdini and Kenrick (1976) thought that if subjects were directly made to feel bad, not by seeing someone in discomfort, but merely by having their mood influenced, this might produce altruism. That is, perhaps people who simply feel sad will be more altruistic, if altruistic (helpful) behavior is a way of making oneself feel better. Cialdini and Kenrick's rationale for this use of altruism is that the use of altruism by individuals to make themselves feel better is the result of people having been reinforced, while growing up, for behaving nicely to others; eventually this reinforcement is internalized—that is, altruistic behavior is simply associated with feeling good (because of its earlier association with praise). However, if this is true, they reasoned that such learning takes time, so this phenomenon should not be seen in young children in the first three grades in elementary school; it might be seen to some small degree in preadolescents; but it will be seen full-blown in adolescents. Thus they used three different age groups for their subjects.

What Cialdini and Kenrick (1976) did was manipulate mood for the subjects, by having them think of sad or neutral events. In the same situation the subjects were given coupons that could be redeemed for prizes after their participation, and were told that "The more coupons you have, the better the prize you can get with them" (Cialdini & Kenrick, 1976, p. 909). To provide the opportunity for the potential altruistic act (the dependent variable), a box that was labeled "coupons for the other students" was placed in the room. The participating subjects were told that because there were other students at the school who would not have the opportunity to participate in this study and so could not obtain the prizes, participating students could share their coupons with those other students by dropping some of their coupons in the box. (The experimenter was not in the room at the time when there was an opportunity for the subjects to drop coupons in the box, so that this was maintained as a private altruistic act, rather than as a response to social pressures.) The purpose of this design was to show that altruism would increase even without witnessing or causing harm (the conditions under which it had been traditionally observed in other experiments). All that would be required is a sad mood in the subjects. Subjects would then perform altruistic acts, it was hypothesized, to make themselves feel better. The results of the study supported the hypothesis. That is, sad mood resulted in greater giving (altruism) than a neutral mood for the adolescents. As they had predicted, it did not have this effect among very young children, but had a small effect among preadolescents, among whom it could be assumed that only limited social learning had occurred.

Note that one example of altruism mentioned previously, volunteering to do phone interviews, involves sacrificing time and trouble. The coupon example involves the voluntary loss of valuables. Both of these examples involved personal sacrifice of some sort, in the service of someone who had no overt way of offering something in return, and so are behaviors that correspond to a verbal definition of altruism that most people would accept.

Batson, Duncan, Ackerman, Buckley, and Birch (1981) provided another definition of altruism, in an experiment on the role of empathy in altruism. They gave subjects an opportunity to volunteer to take some of the electric shocks in place of another person who appeared to be particularly vulnerable to harm from the shocks.

This is an example of a relatively strong self-sacrificing act for a stranger. As still another example, willingness to help injured people has been used in a number of studies as a behavioral index of altruism. The occurrence of each of these behaviors offers good evidence of what most people would call an altruistic act.

There is another area in social psychology, the area of persuasion (which often overlaps with the cognitive dissonance literature), which offers an interesting example of behavioral measurement. In the persuasion literature the receptivity of listeners to various messages is one of the questions examined (for example, for differences in receptivity when the subjects do or do not agree with the message). Variables that may affect people's willingness to hear a message are tested. Brock and Balloun (1967) developed an ingenious behavioral measure of a subject's desire to hear a message. They had subjects listen to tape-recorded talks that were partially masked with static. The subjects were led to believe that they could remove some of the electrical interference by pressing a button, with more presses removing more static. (The static was explained by saying that the talks were recorded on a small tape recorder.) Subjects were told that the purpose of the experiment was to have the talks rated by the subjects. Thus, ratings were used, but they were not the real dependent variable. Instead, the number of presses to remove static from a particular talk, indicating desire to hear the talk, was the dependent variable. Note that expending effort to hear the talk more clearly constitutes a reasonable definition of desire to hear the talk, so that more button pressing can be used as an operational definition of this desire.

The independent variable in the Brock and Balloun (1967) study was agreement versus disagreement with the message. Specifically, subjects who did or did not smoke and subjects who were or were not religious (using frequency of both prayer and church attendance to define religiousness) listened to a talk that disputed the smoking-cancer link, and another talk that affirmed that link, and also listened to a message attacking Christianity (each subject hearing several talks). Subjects were informed of the point of view of each talk before hearing it. It was found that "smokers pressed more than nonsmokers to remove static from a message disputing the link between smoking and lung cancer; smokers made fewer attempts than nonsmokers to clarify a message affirming a smoking-cancer link; persons having considerable recourse to prayer and church attendance pressed less to clarify a message attacking Christianity than persons weakly committed to religion" (p. 413). The study did show that people work more to hear a message when the message is consistent with their behavior and implicit beliefs. For our purposes the major point of interest is the clever operational definition that the experimenters created.

It has been stated previously that when a behavioral measure is an operational definition of an attitude, and the behavioral measure defines that attitude in the context of the experimental situation, it is usually also an example of the attitude. This can be recognized in the many examples of helpful behavior as an operational definition of the presence of an altruistic attitude. This is the case also in the Brock and Balloun study, where taking action to better hear something (pressing the button to clear away the static) is both an example of wanting to hear something, and an operational definition of that desire. Yet each specific behavioral definition of an internal state can reflect other things as well. Refusing to help someone who is a student needing to complete a project, and refusing to help a drunk who has hit his head on the sidewalk, can reflect other attitudes besides a rejection of altruistic impulses. A person might be offended by drunkenness, or afraid of derelicts, or believe students should make it on their own. Each example of an operational definition of an attitude is capable of reflecting some other considerations and other attitudes. Although a good operational definition will usually reflect what it is expected to reflect, it will not do this perfectly, and will also have additional implications. The operational definitions presented here are high correlates of their respective attitudes, but they are not perfectly correlated with their attitudes.

In this section the discussion has dealt with operational definitions of dependent variables. In the discussion in chapter 13 of the McArthur and Post (1977) study, examples were given of operational definitions of an independent variable (salience defined via added light, or movement on stage, or being dressed differently). The point was made in that earlier discussion that when testing relationships between variables, the use of multiple operational definitions is always desirable in order to be certain that the observed relationships are not just relationships with unique properties of a particular operational definition. This is also true when dealing with operational definitions of dependent variables. When each of several operational definitions of the same attitude can be used as a dependent variable, it is important to determine if the same results are obtained with the varying operational definitions. Thus, with dependent variables as with independent variables, it is important to use multiple operational definitions. There are good examples of the use of varied operational definitions for dependent variables in the altruism literature, with its use of taking another's electric shocks, giving away valuables, and giving time and labor to others, all as measures of altruism.

Nonreactive (Unobtrusive) Measurement

In the Brock and Balloun (1967) study a strong attempt was made to deflect the subjects from any awareness that frequency of button pressing was the important behavior being monitored. Another behavior (rating the talks) was presented as the purpose of the study. This study offers a clear example of a type of behavioral measure that was initially called **unobtrusive measurement**, and is now usually called **nonreactive measurement** (Webb, Campbell, Schwartz, Sechrest, & Grove, 1981; many examples of studies using nonreactive measures are found in the Webb et al. reference, which also offers a broad discussion of the topic of nonreactive measurement.) The terms unobtrusive and nonreactive measurement signify that the subjects do not know that they are being observed for the targeted behavior, and therefore are less likely to be reacting to being observed. The response then is more likely to be a truer reflection of each subject's normal response to that class of situations, rather than being a special response created for the experimental situation (thus offering greater external validity, that is, greater generalizability of the experimental results to other situations).

The experimenters in social psychological research often attempt to make the actual experiment appear to be a part of a spontaneous interaction among people. As seen in the altruism experiments, this is done by having the subject initially recruited for an experiment that is different than the true experiment. The true experiment is disguised as a spontaneous event that just happens to take place in the course of the subject coming to participate in the experiment. Perhaps another subject (who is actually an experimental confederate) makes some personal request of the subject. In these cases the apparent experiment is therefore just a screen for the events the experimenter wishes to record. Care was taken in the Cialdini et al. (1973) study to keep the request for doing phone interviews separate from the experiment (by having someone who appeared to be unconnected with the experiment ask for help). In the Cialdini and Kenrick (1976) study the use of a box labeled "coupons for the other students" worked as a nonreactive measure for children, but it would probably have raised suspicions for adults. Manipulation checks or postexperimental interviews are desirable in such situations to determine whether or not the subterfuge was successful.

There are many examples in the social psychological literature of nonreactive measurement. These are by their nature always behavioral measures rather than paper and pencil tests. A good deal of ingenuity is required to construct such measures. Most of these measures have been used in nonmanipulative studies, or surveys, or when examining the relationship between variables in natural situations. For example, Latané and Darley (1970) discretely recorded the percentages of people in public places who would offer assistance. The independent variables that they manipulated were number of people present, the type of assistance requested, or the place. Piliavin, Rodin, and Piliavin (1969) measured the percentage of people in a public place who would help a person if he appeared injured or drunk. These nonreactive measures are all operational definitions of behavior that are highly correlated with altruistic attitudes. They are also measures that are easily obtained. A more difficult measurement situation is described in an interesting example by Webb et al. (1981): "Gump (1962) reports that Chinese jade dealers . . . determined a potential buyer's interest in various stones by observing the dilation of his pupils as pieces were shown . . . . " A number of studies have been done using pupil dilation as an indication of interest, although "Recent studies have cast some doubt on the exact meaning of the measure" (Webb et al. 1981, p. 260).

To the extent that pupil dilation could be a reflection of interest, it would be an example of a behavioral event that is associated with interest, rather than in itself defining interest. It would not be the kind of behavior people would normally use as an example of interest. Behaviors that are not good examples of the attitude, and that do not fit some general definition of the attitude, usually have low correlations with the attitude. However, this is not necessarily the case. If pupil dilation had a high correlation with interest it could be used just as any good operational definition of an attitude. But when the operational definition does not fit a general definition of the attitude, and is not a good example of what is meant by the attitude, it is important to have some data on just how well the behavior correlates with the attitude. Without such data we would not know whether we are measuring what we think we are measuring.

Associated Behaviors

When a behavior does not define an attitude, but is associated with that attitude, we will identify such behavior as **associated behavior**, as differentiated from a behavioral operational definition of an attitude. Associated behaviors, though most often only weakly associated with particular attitudes, have the advantage of frequently being nonreactive.

Some examples of associated behaviors are people's selection of seats in a group, or how close they stand to each other, which are sometimes taken as signifying how they feel about each other. Fidgeting is sometimes interpreted as reflecting anxiety, and at other times as impatience. The use of behaviors that are associated with attitudes or other internal states, as evidence of the presence of these internal states, requires careful testing of the assumed associations.

An interesting example of a test of whether a relationship exists between an overt measurable behavior and attitudes is seen in a pair of studies by Cialdini and Baumann (1981). In a study examining people's littering with fliers (handbills), Cialdini had noticed that subjects threw the fliers away out of view of the person who had handed them the fliers, but not necessarily out of view of other people. When questioned about this, the subjects indicated that they did not wish to discard the handbill in front of someone committed to the handbill's message. Cialdini recognized that people saw their own littering behavior as a potential message, communicating an attitude of disrespect for the person or the message. He wondered whether people would only express this disrespect (tossing the flier on the ground) when they disagreed with the message. Cialdini and Baumann decided to test whether littering a flier was correlated with feelings about the message on the flier, recognizing that if it was, it would offer a potential nonreactive measure of attitude toward an issue.

One special value of a nonreactive measure is the absence of social pressure to give what the subject interprets as the response that the experimenter desires. To see if their nonreactive measure did circumvent social pressure, Cialdini and Baumann (1981) did an experiment in which they compared responses overtly obtained under social pressure for a particular response, with responses indirectly obtained by interpreting attitudes through handbill disposal. The social pressure was created by having an interviewer who had a clear stake in the subjects' responses. The situation is described as follows.

Cialdini and Baumann placed four different kinds of fliers on cars in a parking lot, one on each car. Two of the fliers concerned the equal rights amendment ("Support the Equal Rights Amendment" or "Oppose the Equal Rights Amendment"); the other two concerned a controversial local football coach's reinstatement ("Support the Reinstatement of Frank Kush" or "Oppose the Reinstatement of Frank Kush"). The coach issue was a control condition, which was not expected to yield the difference between the interview and nonreactive measures (for reasons discussed later). The fliers were color coded so that a remote observer could identify each of the four types. The observers recorded whether or not each student returning to a car in the parking lot littered or carried the flier away (there were no trash baskets available), and also the type of flier that had been on their car.

According to the hypothesis, those receiving fliers containing a message in keeping with their attitudes should be less likely to litter than those receiving fliers opposed to their attitudes. To obtain the interview data, the subjects were interviewed as they approached the parking lot by a woman dressed in a manner that would be congenial with being pro equal rights amendment (pro-ERA). The interviewers, female students, "were instructed to dress as a feminist might" (Cialdini & Baumann, 1981, p. 256). It was assumed that this would create social pressure for a pro-ERA response. The subjects, all males, were told that the interviewer was conducting a survey and, for one half of the subjects, asked whether they supported or opposed the ERA, and, for the other half, asked whether they supported or opposed the reinstatement of Frank Kush. Although it was assumed that there was some implicit social pressure for the subject to respond in a pro-ERA manner, there was no pressure to respond in any particular way for those who were asked about the coach.

Thus, social pressure was assumed to be operating for one half of the interviewees, and not operating for the other half (who were asked about a different issue). Those asked about the coach issue were a control group in which it was expected that their interview data would offer the same responses as that implied by their littering behavior. Someone not in favor of reinstating the coach should indicate this when speaking to the interviewer, as well as indirectly by throwing away a handbill in favor of reinstatement, or by keeping a handbill against reinstating the coach. For the ERA issue, there should be a discrepancy between the two means of obtaining opinions.

The data were organized by first defining a favorable response. A favorable response refers to being favorable toward the issue (being either pro-ERA or supporting the reinstatement of the coach). A favorable response was therefore recorded when a subject retained a flier supporting the issue, or littered a flier opposing the issue. The interview responses were also scored as favorable toward ERA or not, and favorable toward the coach's reinstatement or not.

Collating the flier response data and the interview data, it was found that within the sample of subjects asked about the coach issue who had received a flier on that issue, 58% were reported as favorable by the interview method, and 56% were reported as favorable by the littering method. Here it was expected that the size of the favorable responses should be similar from both methods, and it was. By contrast, within the sample of subjects asked about the ERA issue who had received a flier on that issue, 75% were reported as favorable by the interview method, and 46% were reported as favorable by the nonreactive littering method. A statistical test of the results showed this to be a nonrandom difference—that is, the results achieved statistical significance.

The nonreactive measure, littering behavior, does not fit a general definition of a favorable (or unfavorable) attitude, and would not normally be used as an example of a favorable or unfavorable attitude. Thus, it does not fit our prior definition of an operational definition of an attitude, but it has been shown in this experiment to be correlated with favorable/unfavorable attitudes. It therefore fits the definition of an associated behavior. Having established the association, the next question is just how high the correlation is between the associated behavior and the attitude.

Cialdini and Baumann (1981) did provide the material for computing a statistical test of the degree of association between littering behavior and attitudes toward presidential candidates, in an initial study that they reported within the same journal article. In this other study they placed fliers on cars that were in a parking lot at a polling station during the presidential contest between Carter and Ford. The fliers advocated voting for either Carter or Ford. Again observers noted which flier each subject received when he or she went to his or her car, and noted whether or not the subject littered (the fliers were color coded). Cars were required to stop at a stop sign when leaving the parking lot. At that point they were approached by an interviewer who claimed to be conducting a poll as part of a university survey, and asked for whom the subject had voted in the election. It was found that there was a relationship between the person for whom subjects said they voted, and whether or not they kept the flier. These data are summarized in Fig. 14.3.

The conclusion was that subjects were more likely to refrain from littering with a flier supporting a candidate for whom they had voted and more likely to litter with a flier supporting a candidate they had voted against. The results were statistically significant at better than the .001 level. This offers support for the validity of littering as a nonreactive measure of voting behavior and as an index of preference.

What the Flier Represented

	The candidate the subject voted against	The candidate the subject voted for
Littered	63%	37%
Did not litter	33%	67%

Total N = 227

FIG. 14.3. Results from Cialdini and Baumann (1981), initial experiment.

As can be seen in Fig. 14.3, there was not perfect correspondence between whether or not the flier favored the person's voting choice (preference) and whether or not the person littered. Although the article only reported the significance level, it was possible to use the data in the article to roughly estimate the size of the correlation between reported voting behavior and flier behavior. The computed correlation (phi coefficient) was estimated as .30, suggesting that the proportion of variance in littering behavior associated with candidate preference is on the order of 10%. Although the finding of statistical significance forces the conclusion that there is an association between the associated behavior (littering) and the attitude (candidate preference), the low correlation implies that it is a weak relationship.

The problem with this low correlation is that it refers to the relationship between an underlying attitude (preferring a candidate) and a manifestation of it (littering behavior). This is the correlation of a variable with one of its measures. If it is a weak correlation, we only have weak information.

For example, assume that we were interested in knowing whether there is a relationship between income (obtained from income tax records) and presidential preference. If we had strong information on people's voting, we could easily establish the truth or falsity of the relationship. But if we only had people's littering behavior with fliers of presidential candidates, we would lose much of our information about voting behavior in the low relationship between the littering behavior and the presidential voting. Some of the people voting one way would have disposed of their fliers as though they had voted another way. The problem is, instead of actually knowing how a person voted, we would be observing something that is only loosely related to voting behavior. The statistical strength of the relationship between littering behavior with presidential fliers and income would be less than that which exists between actual voting and income. The weaker relationship might be too weak to obtain statistical significance, even though the underlying events were related. In summary, only very strong relationships between variables could be detected with measures that are themselves only lightly related to the underlying constructs being examined.

Low correlations between an attitude and a measure of it are likely to be what we will find for most behavioral measures that are merely associated with an attitude. In each instance an empirical test is needed for an estimate of the correlation. Low correlations do not mean that such behavioral indices should not be used. Rather, low correlations mean that associated behaviors should be used like the items of a test, which individually have low correlations with any other criterion, but when used together can offer reliable measures. Thus, whenever possible, low or moderately correlated associated behaviors should be used with other indices, being in some way combined as though a test were being constructed. When a few such behaviors can be observed, each by its presence or absence indicating the presence or absence of the same attitude, they can simply be summed, with a 1 indicating presence and a 0 indicating absence, as is often done with the yes/no response items in a test or questionnaire.

In general, the development of behavioral measures has been one of the more interesting and impressive aspects of psychological research. The kinds of events in which psychologists are interested, inner events such as attitudes and opinions and cognitive processes, are clearly difficult things to measure. Yet they must be measured to find out to what other variables they are related.

Most frequently, tests are used to measure inner events. But their purposes are often transparent, and so can be influenced by social desirability. Further, subjects are often unaware of, or confused about, their internal states. Thus behavioral measures that can reflect attitudes, particularly nonreactive measures of attitudes, are usually worth the considerable creative effort that is frequently required for their development.

CHAPTER SUMMARY

Likert scales were described. A Likert scale is one in which people are asked to rate each of several statements on a 5-point scale, indicating the extent to which they agree with the statement. The same label is also often applied when more or less than 5 points are used. A Likert scale item is always a request to give a numerical rating overtly indicating the degree of agreement with, or approval of, a statement, or person, or plan, or concordance with a feeling. There are other kinds of scales that also request numerical ratings but are not phrased in terms of approval/disapproval or agreement/ disagreement. In this text, any scale that offers an unambiguous indication of an attitude, belief, feeling, or mood, including a Likert scale, is called a direct rating scale. Direct rating scales are distinguished here from the semantic differential, which offers a less direct way of measuring attitudes.

The concepts of reliability and validity were introduced. Reliability is consistency in measurement, and validity is correctness, or truthfulness, in measurement. Reliability is necessary for validity, but does not by itself guarantee validity.

The reliability of individual scale items increases with the number of points in the item. The reliability of the complete scale increases with the number of items. When there are more items in the scale it is possible for the individual items to have less points, but with very few items each item should have many points. For a single-item scale the item should have at least 10 points. Examples were given in which 31 points were used for each item. When the scale has several items, little is gained by having more than 11 points per item, with the major gain in reliability coming in the increase from 2 to 7 points. With a 5-point scale item it is easy to label each point on the scale, but for larger scale items just the end points are labeled.

Because it is desirable to have many items testing the same thing (to maximize reliability), it is important to have many ways to ask the same question. One way to do this is to have the same basic statement, and vary the nature of the evaluative statements that are presented with it. For example, subjects can be asked to respond to a statement expressing an attitude, checking a point on an approval/ disapproval scale, then on an agreement/disagreement scale, and then on a support/opposition scale. The numerical values of the responses are then summed, offering a summative scale indicating each subject's level of accord with the attitude expressed in the statement.

Response bias is a tendency to respond in one direction with little regard for the item itself, which tends to occur when subjects are unsure of their own position on the issue. To minimize response bias, half of the items are reversed in implication, so that some statements favor a particular stance, or point of view, whereas others are opposed to that position. The reversal must be restricted to the verbalization of the item (that is, whether it speaks for or against some action). The left and right sides of the items must remain constant in regard to numbers and favorability. Thus, if on the first item the left side has a number 1, the right side has a number 5, and higher numbers mean more favorable, that must be the same throughout the scale. The verbally reversed responses have to be mathematically transformed in order to properly sum the scale with its reversed verbalizations but constant numbers. The method of transformation was detailed.

Response bias is one of three issues to be concerned about in constructing items. The other two issues discussed were clarity (lack of ambiguity) in the question, and avoidance of asking two questions at once.

Osgood's semantic differential was discussed as another way of constructing test items for measuring attitudes. The semantic differential consists of the presentation of some concept, institution, or person (abortions, labor unions, or a particular politician), followed by a series of scale items, each bound by polar adjectives. Each pair of adjectives is used to evaluate the same concept. The adjectives, when used to tap the approval/disapproval dimension, could be things like bad/good, useless/useful, or dishonest/honest. Because the adjectives have other implications besides approval/disapproval, the measurement of approval/disapproval is less direct than in the case of the Likert scales, or other direct rating scales. In the use of the semantic differential, because of the fact that each item only partly measures the intended dimension, more items are needed than when working with a direct scale.

Interitem agreement is the extent to which all of the items measure the same dimension. This is the central concept in the idea of reliability. There are many measures of reliability of a test. The split-half reliability was mentioned, because it used to be popular and is still mentioned in the older literature. Its principle advantage was its simplicity in calculation, which is less critical in the computer era. Coefficient alpha is the best of the reliability tests. It measures the average correlation of each item with every other item in the test, and, using this as a base, corrects for the number of items in the test (the more items, all else being equal, the higher the reliability). For the brief tests used in experiments to measure attitudes and attitude change, it is useful to obtain the correlation of each item in the test with the sum of all of the other items (using the Pearson product moment correlation in the manner described in the text). In this way any items that are not measuring the same thing as the remaining items can be identified and rewritten or deleted.

When possible, it is desirable to use behavioral measurement of attitudes, rather than tests. A good operational definition of a behavioral measure of an attitude specifies when the attitude is present, and is also an example of this attitude. In addition, it expresses what is meant by that attitude in the real world. When practical, various operational definitions of the same attitude should be used in repeated tests of the same experimental question.

It is desirable to use nonreactive (i.e., unobtrusive) measurement so that the responses are less likely to be a response to being observed. In keeping with the importance of this issue, social psychologists usually try to make the critical part of the experiment look like it is not part of the experiment. Both the invention of nonreactive measures and the creation of situations that look like they are not part of the experiment require a great deal of ingenuity.

Sometimes behaviors are used as reflections of attitudes, although the behaviors are not typical examples of what is meant by the behavior, and do not offer definitions of the behavior. These are cases where some behaviors are simply associated with the attitude in which there is some interest. These associated behaviors tend to have smaller correlations with the attitudes than the more direct behavioral measures. They can, however, be useful. Because of their small individual correlations, several should be used in the same study, where possible, to maximize reliability.

NEW WORDS AND PHRASES IN CHAPTER 14

associated behaviors
behavioral measurement of attitudes
coefficient alpha
direct rating scales
good behavior-based operational definition of an attitude
individual item reliabilities
interitem agreement
Likert scales
nonreactive measurement
reliability
reliability of individual scale items
reliability of the complete scale
response bias
semantic differential
split-half reliability coefficient
summative scale
transformed scores
unobtrusive measurement
validity

CHAPTER 15

Clinical Psychology: The
Research Problems Encountered,
and Procedures Used, in
Treatment Outcome Research

Clinical psychology is the subspecialty that offers assistance to people with psychological problems. It is clearly an applied discipline. But it has had the unhappy task of being called to fulfill its mission before an adequate set of therapeutic methods has been fully developed. It had its start as a recognized subdiscipline during World War II (circa 1940). Psychologists were used by the military for the purpose of testing people, as well as for counseling. Initially there was little in the way of theory or technique that these early clinical psychologists could call upon, other than the various psychoanalytic approaches. They were in a position similar to that of physicians in the early years of medicine: It was possible that they were in danger of hurting their patients as well as helping them, because they had no independent assessments of the efficacy of the techniques they used.

Their task was made harder by the somewhat vague nature of the problems that were recognized as needing treatment (e.g., various forms of neurosis). In recent years the situation has improved through the development of therapeutic techniques that target more specific problems, with measurable symptoms, such as phobias, debilitating test anxiety, or lack of assertiveness. We can, for example, measure how close a person will come to a phobic object, before and after therapy, or check whether he or she is willing to touch the object. Debilitating test anxiety can be measured both physiologically and through test performance. The targeting of specific measurable symptoms has made success or failure of the therapies easier to identify. This greater specificity of therapeutic goals has been accompanied by the gradual development of research paradigms for testing and comparing therapeutic techniques. The findings from this very large body of research suggest that there are at least some problems for which psychosocial treatments appear useful. Examples of successfully treated problems are the aforementioned phobias, lack of assertiveness, many forms of anxiety (e.g., speech anxiety, test anxiety), and some forms of depression.

The perplexing part of the research findings is that the different methods that have been tried all seem equally effective (e.g., see Sloane, Staples, Cristol, Yorkston, & Whipple, 1975; Strupp & Hadley, 1979). Although some studies find differences, for instance, one finding that cognitive restructuring is better than desensitization, another could be located that finds the reverse. Kazdin and Bass (1989) suggested that the problem may be that the differences in effectiveness may be real, but small. In that case they would not be detectable unless large samples were used to maximize the power of the statistical tests. It is possible that they are correct. However, the general conclusion from massive reviews has usually been that there is no consistent evidence of superiority of one technique over another (Luborsky, Singer, & Luborsky, 1975; Smith, Glass, & Miller, 1980, chapter 5). The differences that appear to exist in some summarizing analyses of the research data (called meta-analyses) are not found in other analyses (e.g., see Shapiro & Shapiro, 1982; Berman, Miller, & Massman, 1985). Berman et al. (1985) provided data suggesting that where differences are found they may be a function of the preferences or expectations of the experimenters, who are often the therapists.

The lack of differential effectiveness is puzzling in that many of the treatments are very different from one another; for example, some stress reexamination of maladaptive beliefs, whereas others attempt to identify consistent relationships between precipitating environmental events and a patient's unwanted behaviors. Those reexamining maladaptive beliefs focus on cognitive changes to achieve desirable changes in behavior. Those searching for precipitating environmental events rely more on direct changes of behavior (e.g., learning new responses to old situations, and/or changing some situations). Within just these two broad classes of therapy there are a number of widely divergent variations. Then there are the even wider differences between either of these classes of psychotherapy and the many different psychodynamic-interpretive therapies. If what is effective is common to all these different forms of therapy, should therapists take seriously any of the details of their own therapeutic training?

There is also the problem that success with any one form of therapy is only a sometime thing, and there is as yet little knowledge of with whom and under what conditions a therapeutic intervention will or will not be successful, with contradictory answers coming from different studies. Contradictory findings suggest that we still have not identified the major factors that are relevant to effectiveness. Further, psychological problems framed in the more traditional way, involving problems in personality, personal growth, or the meaning of life and general feelings of self-dissatisfaction, offer greater problems in measurement, and so it is harder to know if any forms of therapy are generally effective for these less specific discomforts or maladies.

The result is that contemporary clinical psychologists have some validated techniques available that are useful for some classes of problems, but they are not sure what it is that they do that is effective, nor do they know the conditions under which these treatments are most likely to be effective. On the other hand, the slowly increasing number of validated methods, the increasing tendency to test each treatment in specific contexts, and the continuing attempt to understand, through research, just what aspects of what therapists do that are effective, suggest that the distant future is bright. However, this also means that contemporary clinical psychologists need to attend closely to the research literature. It is in the empirical literature that clinicians will learn what new methods have been validated for specified contexts. The researchers also might eventually be successful in providing valid explanations of why things work, which can be critical information for therapists shaping, and sometimes improvising, treatment for individual patients.

In psychological journals volunteers conduct the review process for submitted articles. The only external reward is professional recognition. Many reviewers are very busy people, not always having all the time they would like to have for reviewing a manuscript. Although this tends to be an effective procedure, it is possible, within this system, for flawed experiments, or improper conclusions from experiments, to find their way into the literature. For this reason, clinicians need to be critical readers, and this means having a thorough understanding of research methods.

As evidenced in the earlier chapters on experimental and social psychological research, the different subareas can require sophistication that is unique to an area. This is also true for clinical research. For example, there is no question about the desirability of placebo control groups in psychological research where drugs are used, but the question of whether or not placebo control groups are desirable in clinical research on psycho-social treatment is often raised (Parloff, 1986; Parloff, London, & Wolfe, 1986; Wilkins, 1986; the placebo issue is discussed later in this chapter). There are other special considerations in clinical research that require some unique approaches. This chapter discusses some of the research techniques that are relevant to the design and evaluation of research in the area of treatment efficacy, generally referred to as outcome studies. Psychotherapy outcome studies raise some questions that have not been encountered in our previous discussions of research in experimental and social psychology.

There are many other areas of research in clinical psychology besides outcome studies, such as the causes of various forms of psychological disturbance, community mental health, behavioral medicine, and personality (which is an area of equal interest to social psychologists). Each area has a few of its own special research problems and methods, though there is also a great deal of overlap.

APPLYING THE RULES OF RESEARCH TO OUTCOME STUDIES

If we think of wanting to test the efficacy of a particular form of treatment, we would probably think in terms of the first three rules of research: (a) multiple conditions, say at least a treatment and a control condition; (b) avoidance of confounding factors, that is, having only one difference between the treatment and control condition; and (c) random assignment of subjects to the different conditions, that is, assign subjects randomly to the treatment and control conditions and run the conditions randomly. Different subjects would be assigned to different groups in a treatment outcome study, so we would use a completely randomized design.

$$R \mid T \quad O$$
$$R \mid \quad\;\; O$$

The R implies random assignment, the T is the treatment, and the O represents measurement. An alternative is the pretest-posttest completely randomized design with a control condition, as when symptoms are measured both before and after the treatment, or some

other measure of mental health or mental illness is obtained both
before and after treatment.

$$R \mid O_1 \quad T \quad O_2$$

$$R \mid O_1 \qquad O_2$$

We immediately run into problems with either of these two
designs. There are ethical issues that have to be confronted in
suggesting a control condition in which people do not receive a
treatment, when the subjects are people who need treatment. Thus,
we are often not in a position to assign people randomly to a
treatment or no-treatment condition. Instead, the people on the
waiting lists in the clinics are used as the control group subjects.
This is called, as one might expect, the use of **waiting list controls**.
The problem with waiting list controls is that often people are put on
a waiting list because they do not need help as badly as those who
are seen more quickly. This could create a second difference between
groups, a potential confounding factor.

But let us assume for the moment that we are working with a clinic
in which there has been no selective placement into the waiting list
or treatment groups. The treatment group subjects expect to be
better at the time that the first posttherapy measurements take
place, whereas the no-treatment controls do not. This expectation
difference is another potential confounding factor. To create a control condition with equivalent expectations, it is common to include
a placebo control group, which is usually formed with people who
think they are receiving treatment, but in fact are in a control
condition. The problems in making such placebo control conditions
convincing are discussed in the following section.

THE TRADITIONAL USE OF PLACEBO CONTROL
GROUPS IN PSYCHOLOGY

In accordance with research Rules 1 and 2, experiments on treatment
effectiveness normally include a control group that contains just one
difference from the experimental group. When this is not possible, it
is usually because the application of the treatment inadvertently
introduces other differences between the groups (such as the expectation of being helped). When this cannot be avoided, that is, when
we cannot remove these additional incidental differences from the
treatment condition, we then add them to the control condition. As
indicated in chapter 3, this is what differentiates the placebo control

condition from an ordinary control condition such as a waiting list control. A placebo control group attempts to include those influences that are incidental, unintended influences in the experimental (treatment) group, factors that are not central to the experimental question, but that cannot be avoided when the treatment is applied.

The most familiar use of placebo controls is in the studies of the effectiveness of drugs, where one group of patients (subjects) receives a placebo (a sugar pill that looks like the drug). The expectation of getting better is added to the control condition to make it more exactly like the experimental condition. However, when we use analogous procedures to eliminate differences in expectation between groups in psychotherapy outcome studies, we run into a problem. How do we provide a convincing pseudo-psychotherapy that would be analogous to a sugar pill in a drug study? If we offer people a useless treatment, they are likely to be aware of it. For example, relaxation training is a standard part of some phobia treatment. It was incorporated by Ashby and Wilson (1977) as part of their weight reduction program. However, their patients described that part of the treatment as useless. This suggests that patients can make such distinctions.

Not only do the subjects have to be convinced that some useless activity is a genuine therapy, but the "therapist" in the placebo control condition has to somehow avoid giving the game away. We have previously discussed the problem of an informed experimenter's influence, when that experimenter interacts with the subjects and knows who is in the experimental group, and who is in the control group. This is normally avoided by the use of double blind procedures. However, double blind procedures are not possible in the usual forms of therapy which require that trained therapists conduct the therapy. The therapists would know which treatments are useless, and could convey their lesser expectations to the subjects. In addition, as the previously cited Ashby and Wilson (1977) study shows, useless tasks can sometimes be recognized as useless even when presented as part of a therapeutic program. All of this suggests that it is often not possible to construct realistic and convincing placebo groups that are truly identical in all ways other than the application of a treatment.

On the other hand, creative experimenters occasionally have come up with apparently convincing placebo conditions. When a placebo control condition is used, it is important that some checks also be used, to see if the placebo condition was in fact seen as a convincing form of therapy (or at least as convincing as the actual therapy conditions). This was done by Holroyd (1976), in a well-designed doctoral dissertation examining two forms of therapy for test anxiety. There were five groups in the study: one form of therapy (systematic desensitization), another form of therapy (rational emotive therapy), the two therapies combined (each slightly condensed to keep the treatment times equal for the three groups), a placebo control group using a form of meditation as a pseudotherapy, and a waiting list control.

Systematic desensitization pairs deep muscle relaxation with instructed imagination of the anxiety-inducing event, beginning with scenes that produce minimal anxiety, and gradually working up to imagining scenes that are capable of producing maximum anxiety. The theory assumes that the deep muscle relaxation will prevent the occurrence of the anxiety, providing that the hierarchy of frightening scenes is ascended sufficiently slowly. In this way the subject gradually confronts the formerly anxiety-provoking situation without anxiety, extinguishing the anxiety response (in the Holroyd example, to a test situation).

The other form of therapy focuses on modifying cognitive and attentional components of the test situation, based on the theory that worry is what debilitates test performance because it is attentionally demanding and distracts the student's attention during the test. This cognitive therapy therefore trained subjects to become aware of their distracting thoughts and then taught them to emit self-statements (admonitions and other comments to themselves) that would help them to keep a productive focus. It also used other related cognitive procedures based on rational-emotive therapy. The combined therapy condition involved exposure to slightly shortened versions of both techniques.

The placebo group was told that meditation exercises would allow group members to achieve a mental state that could not be disturbed by test anxiety.

> The exercises required clients to (a) concentrate on various sensations of the hands, arms, and body to "increase body awareness"; (b) imagine commonplace situations such as "sewing a button on a pair of pants" to develop "mental control"; and (c) engage in simultaneous mental control and body awareness exercises for "meditation proper." (Holroyd, 1976, p. 994).

The waiting list control group was simply told that the response to the call for subjects was so large that there would be some delay before they would receive the therapy, and that the selection of the people who had to wait was random.

Before beginning any treatment, all of the subjects were put in an analogue test situation, under pressure (told that the task was a measure of intelligence and academic ability), as a behavioral test of their actual performance. That is, they were given a decoding task that is known to be disturbed by anxiety. This was repeated after the treatment phase of the study, and again at the 1-month follow-up. As an unobtrusive behavioral measure, the pre- and posttreatment school grades of the subjects were obtained, without their knowledge. Thus there were two behavioral measures of whether or not the test anxiety had been reduced (school grades, and performance in an analogue test situation).

Immediately following the analogue test (test performance under anxiety provoking conditions), a self-report measure of anxiety was administered, and was clearly labeled as such. Note that performance on the analogue test is a measure of the experience of anxiety, whereas the self-report test is a measure of personal expectations of being anxious, along with the actual experience of anxiety. Thus, differences in anxiety on the analogue test before and after treatment would indicate a difference in the influences of anxiety on performance, whereas differences in the self-report test would reflect differences both in treatment effects and in expectation of improvement.

Holroyd included a second measure of expectation of improvement, developed by McReynolds and Tori (1972). As an excuse for this measure, the subjects were first given a test that merely involved crossing out 2s and 6s from closely spaced numbers on a page. The subjects were told that this causes frustration, and falsely told that their frustration tolerance could be affected by the anxiety treatment. They were then given, right after the task, what they were told was a frustration thermometer, a self-rating scale that is in fact not reflective of anxiety. If, however, subjects believed that the frustration thermometer did reflect anxiety, frustration thermometer ratings should reflect less frustration after the treatment, in line with the subjects' expectations. This latter test then offered a measure of expectation that was not confounded with actual treatment effects.

In summary, the analogue testing situation and the self-administered anxiety test offered two measures both of which were responsive to anxiety, the latter being expectation sensitive. The "frustration" task (crossing out numbers) and its accompanying self-administered test (the frustration thermometer) offered two indices that were not responsive to anxiety, though the frustration thermometer was responsive to expectations. In this way, Holroyd could monitor actual test anxiety changes (in the analogue test situation and unobtrusively in his measurement of grades before and after the treatment), and expectation effects in two situations, one where expectation and treatment effects should influence the scores (on the self-report anxiety test), and one where only the expectation should influence the scores (on the frustration thermometer). Furthermore, only in the analogue testing situation and the pre- and posttreatment grades should the actual treatments be superior to the placebo effects, while in the behavioral frustration (letter crossing task) there should be no differences between any groups. In the two self-administered tests (of anxiety and frustration), if expectation shows its usual powerful effects where self-reports are used, the placebo groups should show the same effects as the therapy groups, and they should all be different from the waiting list controls. In summary, the therapies should appear more effective than the placebo condition on measures of therapeutic impact, and the placebo should appear equal to the therapies in self-report measures. The results were precisely in line with these predictions. (In this study the rational-emotive therapy was superior to the desensitization therapy, which in turn was superior to the placebo condition. For unknown reasons, the combined therapy using both approaches turned out to not be effective in this study.)

Holroyd used an additional measure, one that can easily be used in many outcome studies, to ascertain whether the subjects believed that the placebo condition offered a legitimate therapy. At the end of the study he merely asked the subjects whether or not they would recommend the treatment that they had received to a test-anxious friend. The placebo group subjects answered "yes" as frequently as the subjects in the three treatment groups. Thus, no difference was found in belief in therapeutic efficacy. This is an interesting check on the ability of the placebo pseudotherapy to pass as a real therapy for the subjects. Unfortunately, a single-item test usually has weak reliability. Weak reliability implies a weak statistical test. Thus, differences could be present, but the test could be too weak to reveal them (a Type II error). Stated another way, using a single-item test, or any other form of test that might have weak reliability, is not a good idea when you hope to show an absence of statistical significance. When what is being demonstrated is a lack of differences between groups, it is important to minimize the probability of a Type II error. In this example the particular single-item test was clever, and may have been a reliable test. But, in general, attempts should be made to find additional measures, which should then be combined into a single test, for which reliability could then be statistically assessed. If the results show a statistically significant difference between groups, the issue of a weak test is not relevant (because a Type II error would not be possible). But when what is being demonstrated is a lack of a statistically significant difference, potential weakness in the measurement device is an important issue.

Regardless of what conclusions we can take away about the substantive issues examined by Holroyd, it is his methods that are instructive for our purposes. All of his many extra measures show how creative use can be made of both behavioral and self-report tests to tease apart expectation and treatment effects.

Alternatives to Traditional Placebo Groups

The definition of placebo control groups that is offered in this text is somewhat broader than any of the traditional definitions. There are roughly three common definitions of placebo controls. The first one, stemming from its original use in medicine, is that of an inert substance, which has now been generalized to any procedure that is assumed to be ineffective. A second definition is that of any procedure lacking a specific identifiable treatment component (sometimes called a *nonspecific* treatment). A third definition is that of a procedure which contains only those therapeutic components that are common to all forms of therapy. This third definition has received a great deal of attention (see Critelli & Neumann, 1984; Frank, 1973; Kazdin, 1979; and Shapiro, 1971, for discussions of the placebo concept in psychotherapy, and discussions of various definitions of placebo control conditions).

The common therapeutic components that are found in almost all forms of psychotherapy are called **common factors**. Two examples of common factors are the patients' knowledge that they are receiving treatment, and attention from the therapist. Critelli and Nemann (1984) offered telling criticisms of the use of most of the traditional definitions in the application of the placebo concept to psychotherapy research, drawing the conclusion that the only useful definition for psychology was the common factors definition. However, Horvath (1988) presented an equally strong argument against the usefulness of the common factors definition, demonstrating that many examples of placebo control conditions in the literature do not conform to the common factors definition.

Recall the definition advanced here: A placebo control condition is a condition not receiving any known effective treatment, but to which are added the inadvertent by-products of introducing the experimental manipulation (without the manipulation itself). That is, whatever is incidentally added as a function of applying the treatment is also added to a control group to transform it into a placebo control group. This definition fits all uses found in the literature, and offers greater flexibility in defining placebo controls. The most common confounding factor in treatment research is the knowledge of being treated, leading to optimism about recovery. Instead of placing control subjects into a sham therapy condition, a group of patients could be given an optimistic prognosis as a placebo condition. They could be told, perhaps after a series of "tests," that their condition is clearly improving and can be expected to last no longer than t, where t is the time required for the therapy that is being given to the experimental group.

By focusing on the ways in which the experimental treatment provides the inadvertent confounding factors, the experimenter is encouraged not only to try adding these components to a placebo control condition, but, alternatively, to invent creative methods for removing these components from the experimental condition, while leaving the manipulation otherwise intact. This broader definition of placebo controls has been implicitly used in some instances in the literature, along with novel attempts to extract the confounding factors from treatment conditions. Examples of such attempts are now discussed, to illustrate the advantages of this view of placebo controls.

One procedure that is sometimes used is called **counterthera-peutic instructions** (Diament & Wilson, 1975), or *subtractive expectancy placebo* (Suedfeld, 1984). In this approach, rather than bolstering the control condition so that it contains an optimistic ingredient, the therapeutic condition is made to appear as something other than therapy, or as preparation for therapy, or as part of an initial measuring process.

Diament and Wilson (1975) used countertherapeutic instructions. They wanted to do a very careful test of whether covert sensitization is effective in weight control. In covert sensitization, vivid imagery of unpleasant scenes, involving a target food (aversive conditioning), is used to develop a negative response to the food. They had some doubts about the treatment's effectiveness (apart from expectancy). To test their doubts they used countertherapeutic instructions for their subjects in a treatment group undergoing the aversive conditioning, and in a placebo group undergoing similar imagery training but without the aversive components. Their purpose was to see if the aversive conditioning therapy was no better than the placebo group, when countertherapeutic instructions were used to remove the expectation difference from the two groups.

Diament and Wilson introduced countertherapeutic instructions by telling the subjects in both their therapy and placebo groups that the procedures they were using for weight control and taste aversion would have no effect until after all of the procedures were completed (a 3-week period). At the same time, subjects were weighed and food aversion measured, both before and after this period, with the explanation that the experimenters wanted to establish consistent baseline measures. There was also a waiting list control, and, for all subjects, an unobtrusive measure of amount of the target food eaten.

With countertherapeutic instruction as used by Diament and Wilson (1975), a pseudotreatment is still used for the placebo group, but with an attempt to remove expectation of improvement from both the placebo and experimental groups. This is intended to keep both the treatment and placebo control groups, in regard to expectations, the same as the no-treatment (waiting list) control. Thus, if the expectation removal is successful, there should be no expectation differences between any of the groups.

Suedfeld (1984), in a variation on this approach, suggested that the experimental group with the expectation removed be used instead of a placebo group (though he still called it a placebo group). That is, rather than a pseudotreatment for the placebo group, he suggested that the placebo group be identical to the treatment group, but with the expectation removed. (Whereas traditionally a placebo group means a nontreatment group with expectation of improvement, in Suedfeld's recommended use, placebo would mean a treatment group without expectation of improvement.) He also recommended an actual treatment group, with expectation, along with a no-treatment control.

With the arrangement suggested by Suedfeld, the placebo group without expectation can be used for a comparison with a waiting list control, which also lacks expectation of improvement. This offers a comparison of pure treatment effect (application of treatment with no expectation of improvement) against a no-treatment condition also lacking expectation, yielding an estimate of the effect that is specific to the form of the treatment, and independent of expectation.

A measurement of the expectation effect can be obtained by subtracting the postexperimental placebo group scores (treatment but no expectation) from the postexperimental treatment group scores (which include expectation). The full clinical impact of expectation plus treatment-specific effect can be obtained by comparing the waiting list control with the treatment group, as you would in any traditional design.

Suedfeld (1984) offered an example of how countertherapeutic instructions (which he called a subtractive expectancy procedure) can be implemented. Assume that the problem is a phobia and the therapy being used is systematic desensitization, which we have previously described as involving both muscle relaxation and the gradual introduction of anxiety-provoking scenes of the phobic object. The muscle relaxation component of the therapy could be rationalized as being used to reduce anxiety before treatment begins. Similarly, the gradual introduction of anxiety provoking scenes could be represented as accustoming the client to confronting the issues and situations that will be discussed when therapy begins. Thus the therapy could proceed with the patient under the impression that therapy had not yet started. Of course, a postexperimental check on the actual expectations of the subjects would be important, to make sure that the lack of expectation of improvement during therapy was successfully engineered.

A limitation on countertherapeutic instruction is that it is only likely to appear credible with very brief forms of therapy, because subjects would not normally continue to believe that a preexperimental measurement process, or preparation for therapy, was being conducted over an extended period of time. However, a way that this might be arranged for longer periods of therapy is that people could be told that they are on a waiting list, but that to remain on the waiting list they must be willing to submit to weekly or semiweekly interviews for the purpose of some research. If the therapeutic process could be cloaked as information gathering for the research, it might be possible to keep the subjects convinced that therapy had not yet started. A waiting list control might then be sufficient for comparing groups to see whether there are any treatment-specific effects independent of any expectation. A therapy group with the expectation could also be used, because it is possible that there is some positive interaction between the therapy-specific effects and positive expectations. If it was feared that there might be some other unknown effects besides expectation that are operating for the groups receiving interviews, a control condition with some neutral interview sessions could be used, along with the waiting list control.

Emmelkamp and Walta (1978) used the pretense of research in a different way, but for a similar purpose. By making some subjects think that they were in a research situation where physiological responses were being measured, the concept of therapy was completely bypassed for some subjects, removing the expectation of getting well. Unfortunately, Emmelkamp and Walta omitted a no-treatment control group. They just had two treatment groups (exposed to two different forms of aversion therapy), both of which had the expectation of being helped, which were compared to two identically treated groups without the expectation of being helped (who thought they were in a physiological psychology experiment). Their question was whether expectation of being helped was important to these forms of therapy.

It was possible with this design to learn if expectation added something to therapeutic effectiveness. But what if therapy itself did nothing, and only expectation was effective? In their design there was no way to tell whether there was anything operating other than expectation; that is, we could not know whether factors specific to the particular form of treatment were effective. We call effects that are obtained through procedures that differentiate one therapy from another **treatment-specific effects**. What Emmelkamp and Walta needed in their design was a no-treatment control condition. We could then compare the nonexpectation/treatment group with the no-treatment control, to see if without expectation the treatment still had some effect, some treatment-specific effect. Without a difference between a no-treatment control and the nonexpectation/treatment group, there is no evidence that the treatment has any effect other than an expectation effect. If there were differences found between all three groups, with the expectation/treatment group doing best and the no-treatment control group worst, then in addition to the evidence of an expectation effect from the expectation/treatment group's superiority over the nonexpectation/treatment group, we would also know that there is a treatment-specific effect operating. If a difference was found between expectation/treatment and non-expectation/treatment groups, but the nonexpectation/treatment group was not superior to the no-treatment control, it would mean that the only effect found was an expectation effect. If no difference was found between the two treatment groups, but both were superior to the no-treatment control, this would imply that there are some treatment-specific effects, but that expectation was not necessary in that it did not add anything.

It should be clear from all of the preceding examples that setting up placebo groups, or making other arrangements to isolate expectancy from treatment-specific effects in a therapy outcome study, is a difficult task. There is not only expectation of improvement as a possibly therapeutic component of all therapies, but the attention and concern of the therapist. There are now many researchers who believe that it is not necessary to demonstrate nonspecific effects as distinct from treatment-specific effects in tests of the effectiveness of different forms of treatment (Parloff, 1986). Kirsch (1985) made a particularly strong case for the role of expectation of absence of fear, as a factor in successful therapy for anxiety-related conditions. Because this expectation of reduced anxiety can also be a factor in many placebo conditions, the clear distinction between placebo conditions and therapy conditions can be lost. For some researchers this means careful scrutiny of the role of expectations in all conditions of the experiment. For others, the arguments of people like Parloff (1986) and Kirsch (1985) suggest that it is often desirable to omit placebo control groups. We now examine the rationale and logic for treatment outcome research that omits placebo control groups.

Comparative Studies Without Placebo Groups

The varied forms of available treatment are often very different from each other, yet research suggests that all of them are equally effective. How much can the unique components of individual therapies contribute to their effectiveness when there is no consistent evidence of differential effectiveness? Combining the doubts raised by this question with the frequent lack of differences between placebo and treatment groups has led some psychologists (e.g., Frank, 1973; Kirsch, 1985) to a controversial conclusion. The conclusion is that the main therapeutic components of psychotherapy are the common factors, those components of the interaction that are found both in all therapies and in convincing placebo conditions (such as the patient's expectation of improvement, or someone showing great interest in the patient's problems).

If all therapies are at least to some degree effective, an obvious question is which ones are more or less effective. In line with this thinking, many therapy outcome studies omit any placebo group, and simply compare several therapies against each other. Another reason that outcome studies sometimes take this form is that there is an ethical problem in denying treatment to placebo control group patients who would otherwise be placed in treatment groups.

The ethical issue has been the major reason for the use of a similar approach in medicine; that is, when a particular treatment has been found even modestly effective, it replaces the placebo groups in future studies. In this way the researchers avoid the ethical issue of not treating some patients. The assumption that every psychotherapy treatment can be relied on to at least have some positive impact suggests that any treatment can take the place of a placebo group. A new treatment is then tested to see if it at least measures up to the old treatment. It may be no better, but it might be faster, or require less training for the therapist. Or, it may be better, and in fact have some unique treatment effects beyond the influence of the common factors. If the assumptions about the old therapy being at least minimally effective are correct, then this does represent a logical position.

The problem with this approach is that although it may be true that in general most psychotherapies are at least minimally effective, that is, better than no treatment, this may not be true in every experiment. For example, a particular therapist could lack competence with a particular treatment and change its effects, eliminating the usual common factors, either not causing any improvement or possibly making people worse. This could only be recognized through comparison with a no-treatment control. Without such information, differences observed between treatments could be misinterpreted. For example, with two treatments looking different, the difference could be a function of one having made people worse, and the other not having had any effect, rather than both having been effective, but one more than the other. The need for a no-treatment control is therefore especially critical with a new and unusual form of therapy, where negative effects or possible absence of common factors are more of a risk. When the circumstances permit it then, comparative treatment studies that lack placebo groups should include a waiting list or other no-treatment control.

In addition to simply comparing several treatments, there are two more strategies for using treatment methods in place of placebo conditions. One is an approach called the **construction strategy**, and the other is called the **dismantling strategy**.

Construction Strategy. Sometimes the effectiveness of a single treatment component is established (e.g., self-monitoring of caloric intake for weight watchers). It is then possible to use this single component as a baseline measure, a control group against which to test more elaborate programs that include this useful procedure. For example, we could compare self-monitoring of caloric intake, with self-monitoring of caloric intake plus a social support group of other people monitoring calories, with self-monitoring plus social support plus exercise, and so forth. When several groups using overlapping techniques are compared but they differ in the number or combinations of techniques for each group, it is called a construction strategy. Although the single component can be used as a good control condition, a no-treatment control should also be present, if possible. The reasoning here is similar to that offered in the preceding section. The construction strategy is used less often than a closely related approach, called the dismantling strategy.

Dismantling Strategy. Most psychotherapies are born as packages of therapeutic intervention, consisting of a variety of therapist responses and initiatives (several therapeutic procedures). Therefore, when deciding to test a particular therapeutic approach, it is common to start by testing the complete package. Once it has been established that a therapeutic package is useful, it is then desirable to investigate its components, to see which of the component parts are necessary. This is called the dismantling strategy. The dismantling strategy can have three advantages: It can indicate what is critical to the therapy and so lead to improvements in the therapy by eliminating some unnecessary components; this in turn can be useful in the training of new therapists; and, finally, it can help to support or disconfirm the theories that often accompany the various therapeutic approaches.

For example, in systematic desensitization for the treatment of phobias, which, as previously indicated, involves imagining gradually more fearful images of the phobic object while being completely relaxed, the relaxation was assumed to be necessary because it was believed that complete relaxation precludes an anxiety response, resulting in extinction of the fear response. The finding that the process could also work without the relaxation called into question the theoretical basis for the therapy. Understanding the theoretical basis of a therapy is important because we always want to improve the therapy, for example making it effective with more people, or effective more quickly. If we have an accurate understanding of why something works sometimes, it is a lot easier to improve it so that it works more often.

Like construction, dismantling involves the comparison of different groups that each have different though overlapping components. In the case of dismantling we know what the complete package is like, and so can simply compare its efficacy to that of different subpackages. By dropping out one or another single component, the complete package is being compared with a package with one component missing; both of these are being compared with a third group that has a different single component missing; and similar comparisons are possible with a fourth group that has a different combination of just some of the components, and so on. In this way it is possible to identify any useless components, and any particularly effective combinations.

If there are only two components, there would only be three groups (the combined pair of techniques, and each technique alone). For example, Lichtenstein, Harris, Birchler, Wahl, and Schmahl (1973) dismantled the sometimes successful technique for smoking cessation, rapid smoking with warm smoky air. To their surprise they found that either component alone (extended exposure to warm smoky air, or rapid smoking) was as effective as the combination.

In summary, both the dismantling and the construction approaches provide sets of comparable methods that could all afford a similar level of expectation from subjects. Moreover, if there is successful differentiation of effective from noneffective components, it not only improves the therapy, but probably offers some further understanding about the nature of the therapeutic process associated with that therapy.

DESCRIBING FORMS OF TREATMENT

An issue that is frequently a problem for psychotherapy research is a clear description of the form of the treatment. There is great variability in the way in which treatment programs with the same label are carried out by different therapists. When one of the therapies being compared is a general form of therapy, such as rational-emotive therapy, or, more vaguely, individual insight-oriented therapy, then the form that the therapy took during the treatment is essentially unknown to anyone trying to learn from the research, unless special efforts are made both to describe the procedures, and also to check on whether the procedures were carried out as intended. "There has been little reason to believe that the variability among therapists within a school of therapy is less than the variability among therapists across different schools" (Parloff et al., 1986).

To convert situation-specific knowledge that one treatment was more successful than another into generally useful information, we have to be able to reproduce the more successful treatment. Unfortunately, there are some forms of therapy that are so much a function of apprentice training that we cannot readily communicate what the form of treatment is, if in fact there is some single identifiable form of treatment, as opposed to general guidelines that can be interpreted differently by different therapists. But for many of the behavioral programs that we see in specific goal oriented therapies, it is possible to be specific about the treatment programs. It is easiest to do this when there is a **treatment manual** describing the treatment procedures. Occasionally manuals are provided by researchers, who use the manuals to train their therapists for the research, and make the manuals available for other researchers. Treatment manuals are also available in the literature describing particular forms of treatment, such as Beck, Rush, Shaw, & Emery (1979), offering a description of a cognitively oriented form of treatment for depression, and Klerman, Weissman, Rounsaville, & Chevron (1984), offering a description of a psychodynamically oriented form of treatment for depression.

It is useful, in research contexts, to be able to check and see if the therapists actually carried out the varied forms of therapy as intended in the experimental design. Having blind raters evaluate random sections of recorded sessions and classify the form of treatment, seeing if each treatment is recognizable to blind raters, would offer one way to do this. Unfortunately, implementing this procedure is difficult and time-consuming.

THE UNIQUE CONCERNS OF TREATMENT RESEARCH

Although the form of the therapy can be, at times, only vaguely described, in contemporary psychotherapy it is often quite easy to specify the goals of the therapy, which occasionally involves the client and therapist in a contract as to what is to be accomplished. The agreement about goals is particularly easy to reach when a client is concerned about appetitive problems, such as obesity, alcoholism, or smoking, and wants help in controlling the behavior. This specificity makes research on therapies for controlling appetitive behaviors easier, in some respects. However, there are some special difficulties encountered in treatments for this class of problems: The patients often have to implement aspects of the therapeutic procedures outside of therapy. For people doing research on the effects of such therapies, this creates a problem of treatment manipulations that have to be self-administered. Also, because so much of what is occurring takes place outside of a laboratory, the measurements of client progress often require self-monitoring. The problems of self-monitoring, and self-administration of aspects of the manipulations, are unique to research in the treatment area. To acquaint the reader with how these problems are handled, we devote most of the remainder of this chapter to the discussion of some of the issues in outcome studies for smoking cessation and weight reduction.

Smoking Cessation

We first need to identify people who have been smoking habitually for some time and who wish to stop. More often than not this is achieved through advertisements in newspapers, or at times on school bulletin boards. Sometimes people responding to such adds are invited to a general session on smoking cessation, at which time they are told something about the treatment methods being re-searched, or about smoking cessation in general. They might be given forms on which to record their smoking frequency during a preexperimental period in which they are told to smoke as usual. They then bring this material to a second session at a later date. This helps to filter out people who only have a momentary desire to stop and showed up the first time on impulse. Sometimes a **returnable fee** is charged, usually in the form of a postdated check, brought by the subjects to the second session and returned to the subjects at the end of the study, preferably after the last follow-up interview, although sometimes at the end of therapy. The subjects are told that the check will be returned if they stay with the therapy and comply with the therapeutic and recording procedures. It is not uncommon to find, among volunteer smoking subjects, people who have tried to stop smoking in the past. They will likely have succeeded for some short period, often just a matter of weeks, rarely for as much as a few months. (Of course, there are many people who successfully quit smoking on their own, without joining therapy groups. The rate of quitting among self-quitters is not particularly impressive, and is consistent with the overall reduction in smoking seen over the past few years, 3–4% per year Cohen et al., 1989.)

The preexperimental level of smoking is called the baseline, and the records of smoking prior to beginning treatment are the **base-line data**. This is likely to be a reduced level of smoking, because merely monitoring smoking for people anxious to quit could result in some reduction in smoking. A measurement that affects what is being measured is called a **reactive measurement** (the opposite of a nonreactive measurement, defined in the preceding chapter). Because monitoring one's own cigarette smoking can be reactive, it is necessary to tell people to smoke at their normal level during the baseline recording period. However, if they do reduce their smoking somewhat, this merely makes it harder to prove the effectiveness of the treatment, and such conservative bias is acceptable.

Measurement Issues.   How do we measure the amount of smok-ing? It is best to have the data in the form of individually recorded cigarettes. Thus, you would want to give the subjects some easily maintained record system permitting the notation of each cigarette smoked. Marston and McFall (1971) used small pads, the size of cigarette packs, that could be slipped into the cellophane wrapping of a cigarette pack. The slips on the pad had room for name and date, and 24 blocks representing hours of the day. Each cigarette smoked was to be recorded in the appropriate block. Marston and McFall, like many other researchers, had the subjects obtain all their cigarettes from the experimenters during the course of the experiment (though they were charged for these cigarettes). The subjects were informed that this would get them out of the habit of buying cigarettes. Although breaking up habits associated with smoking is often part of the treatment, having the subjects purchase their cigarettes from the experimenters also offered a partial check on the number of cigarettes reported smoked by the subjects.

It is difficult to know if the subjects' own recordings of their smoking frequencies are accurate. In fact, such information is often not accurate, though this is not a severe problem if the inaccuracy is fairly constant across groups in the experiment. It is easiest to check on accuracy when subjects achieve, or claim to achieve, complete abstinence. Schmahl, Lichtenstein, and Harris (1972) took a random sample of their subjects, and had these (nine) subjects "provide the name of an informant (not a relative) who was familiar with their smoking habits." The experimenters then contacted these informants and had them verify the smoking reports. Friends in frequent contact can verify whether or not a person has stopped smoking. Biochemical means can also be used to detect whether or not a person is smoking. There is a carbon monoxide assessment and a saliva nicotine procedure (Cohen et al., 1989). If we wished to verify specific levels of smoking, this would be more difficult, not only because of the inaccuracies in self-reports, but because the practical biochemical measures do not offer that kind of quantitative information. The self-report accuracy can be improved by giving the subjects the impression that the biochemical tests are a check on their accuracy.

Follow-Up. Almost all smoking treatments lead to some immediate reduction in smoking, most of which is lost over a period of a few months. Thus, to merely show that some new therapy reduced smoking is to offer very little useful information. A follow-up is usually employed, which is remeasurement of the subjects, after some time has passed following the posttreatment measurement. If the therapy succeeded in obtaining a high percentage of total abstainers, and this was maintained over a 6-month follow-up, or longer, this would be impressive. Even drastic reductions (cutting nicotine intake in half), if sustained for a long time, would be of some interest. Abstinence rates, given entrance into a treatment program, tend to cluster around 20% at 6- and 12-month follow-ups, only occasionally yielding 30% quit rates (Cohen et al., 1989). Meaningful confirmation of any type of success requires that there be at least a 6-month follow-up, with a 1-year follow-up desirable.

Cohen and Lichtenstein (1990) used an interesting procedure for maximizing subjects' participation in all of the follow-up sessions. They paid subjects a nominal fee for each session. But, in addition, subjects who participated in all six evaluation sessions were eligible to win a video recorder in a drawing.

It is important that the follow-ups have the data collected in the same way as the earlier data. Thus, if the earlier data were obtained by having the subjects record each time they smoked over a period of a few days, the follow-up data should be obtained in the same form. It would not do to merely call up people 6 months later and ask them for an estimate of smoking rate. Rather, they would have to be sent the same forms that they had used previously, and asked to fill them out. When subjects are initially recruited, it is a good idea to obtain the name and phone number of someone who would know where they would be in case they moved. In this way, at the end of the follow-up period you would have a way of tracing subjects who had moved.

Drop-Outs.   There is always the question of how to treat **drop-outs**. Drop-outs are people who have stopped coming, have stopped supplying data, have otherwise stopped cooperating during the study, or with whom contact has been lost. One might only wish to know how effective a treatment is, given that people have completed the treatment. In that case, there would be some reason to exclude drop-outs from the analysis. However, when there is a large number of drop-outs, it raises the question of whether those remaining are a special class of person. If the treatment was effective, this special class of person (who remained in treatment) would have to be defined in order to know for whom the treatment would be useful. Further, excluding the drop-outs from the data analysis results in much more impressive rates of success (McFall & Hammen, 1971).

It is usually appropriate to record drop-outs as treatment failures. This is particularly true when treatment is aversive, which is often the case in smoking cessation treatment. A sometimes successful method is the rapid smoking technique put forward by Lichtenstein and his colleagues (Lichtenstein et al., 1973; Schmahl et al., 1972), which is quite aversive. It entails inhaling every 6 sec, continuously, until the subject cannot stand it. Then there is a brief rest, until the subject can tolerate another cigarette, and the procedure is repeated.

This continues until the subject feels physically ill, or dizzy, or feels that another cigarette would cause vomiting, etc. This is repeated on consecutive days, or done a few times a week, with no ordinary smoking during intervening periods. Because the aversive quality is an integral part of the treatment, having people drop out is an integral part of a weakness in the treatment. It is therefore appropriate to simply count drop-outs as people who are still smoking.

Control Conditions.   Control conditions can be varied treatments, including cold turkey quitting, in which subjects are merely told about the necessity of using will power (which is generally considered to be useless advice). There are also various pills and sprays that can make smoking unpleasant. Those that are considered to be ineffective are sometimes used as placebo control conditions. It is of course desirable that the conditions in the control group be as similar as possible to the treatment conditions with the exception of the treatment components that you are testing. For example, if a form of psychotherapy only incidently includes the opportunity to discuss the problems that people are having with quitting smoking, you would want the control conditions to also have such opportunities for group discussion (unless the group discussion of difficulties with stopping was the experimental treatment being tested).

Finally, there is the occasional use of waiting list controls. There is a problem with that type of control condition for appetitive therapy research that is not generally acknowledged. The reason for a control condition is to see what would happen if therapy was absent, but everything else was the same. If a group of people all apply for treatment, they are all probably motivated. However, those who are put on a waiting list are in essence informed that their problem will be dealt with, but later. This could tempt people who are worried about the problem (and therefore volunteer for treatment) to forget about the problem for a time. Thus their motivation for change would be put in abeyance. Compare this with a hypothetical third group, one that volunteered for treatment, and was turned down (rather than told that they will be treated at a later date). The rejected volunteers would probably still want help, and their motivation might be sufficiently high for some of them to help themselves (if they did not find alternative professional help). They would be more similar to those who are currently going into therapy and are being told in therapy that they will have to be active participants in their own cure, than would a waiting list control group. That is, there might be a higher rate of spontaneous self-help in groups denied therapy, and groups in therapy, than in a waiting list group told that their treatment is to be delayed. Thus, a waiting list group might show a lower than average spontaneous remission or self-cured rate, making an ineffective treatment condition look effective, in a comparison of the number of cures in the two groups. For this reason, waiting list controls, though often the most readily available of control conditions, are probably the least desirable in smoking cessation or other types of appetitive therapies.

Weight Reduction

As in smoking research, the subjects are often recruited from advertisements. Care is taken to be sure that the subjects do not have a physical illness that would preclude their participation in a weight reduction study. In addition, some criteria are used to accept people as subjects, which differ from study to study. As an example, it could be required that subjects be at least 10% overweight (using the Metropolitan Insurance Company Standards), not taking diet pills, and not now participating in any other weight reduction program.

A baseline level of weight is established, usually through a period of repeated weight measurement, prior to beginning any weight reduction program. The evidence indicates that weighing oneself is not a reactive measurement (Romancyzk, 1974), though it is often not accurate (Brownell, 1982). When weight is measured, it should be measured by the research staff. Subjects are often placed into a few blocks, according to percentage overweight. They are then randomly assigned to treatment groups in equal numbers from the various blocks, to keep the various treatment groups reasonably similar in regard to percentage overweight. The reason for this is that the greater the percentage overweight, the greater the probable weight loss in absolute pounds. When there is such a known influence on the dependent variable, it is important to keep it relatively constant across treatment groups, rather than permitting it to vary randomly.

The issue of measurement can be somewhat complex in weight reduction research. Weight can vary from day to day on the basis of such things as fluid intake and fluid retention; however, it is an easily obtained measurement. Many researchers avoid using just the amount of weight lost in the statistical analysis. Instead, they use the amount lost relative to how much overweight a person is, also taking into account the absolute weight of the person. An index that does this is the weight reduction index (Feinstein, 1959; Wilson, 1978):

$$\text{Weight reduction index} = \frac{\text{Pounds lost}}{\text{Pounds overweight}} \times \frac{\text{Initial weight}}{\text{Ideal weight}} \times 100$$

The ideal weight in the weight reduction index is taken from the Metropolitan Life Insurance Standards. Despite some theoretical arguments for using the weight reduction index rather than simply pounds lost, in many studies they give about the same results (Wilson, 1978, p. 689). Percentage overweight is also used, primarily because it is the most easily understood.

Skin fold measures of excess fat are also used in some studies, although such measurement requires special training, and possession of appropriate calipers. The advantages of skin fold measures are that they are independent of amount of fluid temporarily retained, and also they differentiate fat from muscle weight. That is, if a person both diets and exercises to lose weight, some of the fat can be converted to muscle tissue, which weighs more than fat tissue, so the fat loss might not be recorded as weight loss. If the treatment program includes exercise that can develop muscle tissue, skin fold changes probably should be used, rather than weight, as the criterion of effectiveness.

One common finding is great variability among subjects in weight loss, even among subjects in the same treatment condition. Group means are therefore not as informative as in the case of other dependent variables. This makes the use of analysis of variance less appropriate. An intuitively satisfying statistic that has become common is the percent of people losing different amounts of weight, for example, 0–10 lbs, 11–20 lbs, 21–30 lbs, and so on, in each group.

The final issue on measurement is the question of follow-up. As with smoking, it is common to find some initial improvement, that is, initial weight loss, at the end of almost any treatment program. The problem is that it does not last. Not only do we find a quick end to continued weight loss, but much of the weight lost is soon regained. Thus, to know if a program is really effective, there must be a prolonged follow-up period.

As with smoking research, a fee is sometimes charged that is returned if the subject cooperates throughout the program. It is best to postpone return of the fee until after the completion of the follow-up. This helps to maximize both the appearance of subjects at the therapy sessions and their cooperation in giving follow-up data. As with smoking, subjects lost during the program should be treated as failures. For example, in computing the percentage of people in a particular treatment group who lost various amounts of weight at the end of treatment, the people in that group who dropped out would be counted as those in the lowest interval (which would include zero), for example, 0–10 lb. If some people who had stayed with the treatment just until the end of treatment, and successfully lost, say, 25 lb, dropped out during follow-up (not returning for follow-up weight checks), they would be counted at the end of the treatment period as having lost 21–30 lb, but counted as 0–10 in the follow-up data. (If there was a failure or no weight-loss-category, they would be placed in that category at follow-up.) The data could be treated in a chi-square analysis. Each subject would be in a particular cell of the matrix in Fig. 15.1. An identical matrix would be used at follow-up.

The use of a chi-square analysis with 15 cells (as in Fig. 15.1) would only be appropriate with enough subjects so that at least a few subjects are represented in each cell. With small numbers of subjects the classifications would be combined (for example, 0–10, 11–30, 31–50), to avoid having cells with less than approximately five subjects.

Self-Administered Treatment. In most weight reduction programs the major treatment is self-administered. For example, people might be told to eat very slowly, not to do anything else while eating (such as reading), to individualize each bite, perhaps putting down the fork between bites, and to always eat in the same room. Self-monitoring of caloric intake is also used to control weight. That is, whereas merely keeping track of weight does not appear to be reactive, checking calories does seem to have an effect. Furthermore, it has been concluded that recording caloric intake before eating food is more effective in reducing caloric intake than when it is recorded

POUNDS LOST AT END OF TREATMENT

		0–10	11–20	21–30	31–40	41–50
T R E A T M E N T	A					
	B					
	CONTROL					

FIG. 15.1. Chi-square matrix for analysis of weight control results, at end of treatment, when the subjects have been classified into groups according to weight loss. The pictured example assumes two therapy groups and a control group, and assumes no losses greater than 50 pounds.

after the food is eaten (Bellack, Rozensky, & Schwartz, 1974). But when the experimenters ask different subjects to behave in these different ways, how do they know that the groups are all complying equally? If you want to eat something, it is possible, for example, that it is easier to eat it and then record the information, than to first stop and do the recording. The problem of fidelity to instructions is a general one in weight reduction research, and so a number of methods are used to maximize conformity with instructions, or to obtain some evidence of conformity.

A common procedure is to give subjects pocket-sized pads with name, date, and so on, making recording of caloric intake easier. They are also given addressed and stamped envelopes, and told to mail each day's records every day. This can help to insure the daily recording that is part of the program. It is harder to insure compliance with requests for changes in eating habits. It might be possible, in the middle of the experimental period, to arrange for some controlled situations involving eating, so as to see how comfortable subjects are with the new procedures. Unfortunately, this would not guarantee similar behavior when the subjects are on their own.

A good practice is to ask subjects, at the end of the experiment, to rate themselves on the degree of compliance with the special instructions, say on a scale of 1 to 10, 10 meaning complete compliance. An advantage of using ratings, rather than asking whether or not they complied, is that ratings avoid the embarrassment of having to simply say that you did not comply. A rating scale permits some face saving by suggesting at least some degree of cooperation, and thus is more likely to contain some information about noncompliance.

A question that arises when using a rating scale of compliance is, what range of values would indicate that there should be some concern about compliance? A preliminary study, using family members as informants, might indicate which self-rating values of compliance are suggestive of insufficient cooperation. More important, perhaps, is the opportunity to learn if certain conditions of the experiment, certain types of treatment, tend to yield less compliance than others. Differences in effectiveness of some treatments might, at times, be explainable by differences in the degree of cooperation that the different treatments promote. In these circumstances compliance ratings could be helpful even when a criterion of what constitutes adequate compliance cannot be agreed upon.

It would be possible to eliminate subjects who are recognized as not having complied, if some prior self-rating value was identified as a basis for dropping subjects. However, if this were to cause more than two or three subjects to be eliminated, a situation analogous to having drop-outs would be created. Discounting them would mean that the subjects used represent a special population. For this reason, compliance self-ratings are more useful as indicators of possible differences between the practical advantages of different treatment conditions.

Maintaining Distinct Treatment Groups. A problem that can arise in weight control research is the need to keep the different treatment groups truly different from each other procedurally. For example, suppose that one group is to simply monitor their calories, while another is to meet as a group and talk about the problems that they are having in losing weight, and a third is to use social support within the group to increase motivation. What if some of the people in the group devoted to talking about the problems that they are having losing weight decide to discuss the possibility of counting calories? Does the therapist discourage this to keep the groups pure in their differences? Would this attempted inhibition of a natural group process change the character of the group so that it might then be unreal? What if people in that same group begin to offer each other social support and motivational aids? Is the therapist to discourage this? Such therapeutic interference can make the therapy unrealistic. In designing the study, and in selecting the kinds of treatments to be compared, the ability to realistically omit and sustain varied procedures has to be considered by an experienced therapist.

The Body's Resistance to Weight Loss. The biggest problem in creating long-term weight loss is the issue of the body's resistance to accepting new weight levels. The evidence is that when you begin to lose more than 5–10% of your weight, your metabolism slows down, and your body begins to conserve calories, so that far more severe dieting is necessary to lose the second 10 pounds than the first 10 (Keesey & Powley, 1986). It appears to get still worse as the body gets still further below its set point (your body's accustomed weight), which is different for different individuals. The evidence on whether this set point can be altered when individuals keep themselves at new weights for a prolonged time is equivocal. There are at least some individual cases where set points do appear to change. The only way to combat this slowed down metabolism is to exercise, which on its own increases metabolic rate. But the conservatism of the body, in regard to accepting new weight levels, is a formidable obstacle in achieving long-term weight loss.

Most activities in which great effort is required—for example, developing a new skill—offer increased rewards as greater success is achieved. By contrast, as a weight loss program succeeds for an individual, that person's body rebels and fights the continuation of the process. This is what makes it so critical to have long-term follow-ups in weight reduction programs, or to have some long-term intermittent treatment that also has to be evaluated for its success in maintaining the weight loss.

Personal Factors in Success or Failure. Weight reduction is similar in some respects to attempts at smoking cessation. We find that although most therapy programs are only marginally success-ful, there are individuals in these programs who do succeed. Simi-larly, there are people who stop smoking on their own, or who lose weight and maintain the weight loss on their own, despite the more common experience of failure after some brief initial success. At-tempts to see who will or will not maintain a weight loss have not uncovered any useful personality factors. The only dimension that possibly has some promise is the very general one of motivation. For example, it has been found that those who lose the most weight in the initial week of a treatment program are likely to lose the most at the end, and maintain the loss longest. However, this could just as well reflect some physiological difference in the quick weight loss individuals.

Mausner (1971), in discussing the motivating factors responsible for success in smoking cessation, suggested that what may be involved is "a feeling of humiliation at the stupidity of smoking" (p.168). Similarly, people who can successfully lose weight may have become ashamed of their bodies, or frightened for their health. We frequently see people who could never keep their weight down, suddenly find that after a heart attack they can successfully lose weight. On the other hand, there are people who experience great shame and painful interpersonal interactions over excess weight, and appear to be deeply motivated, but cannot maintain appreciable weight loss. The difference may be in the intensity of the physical resistance. For example, addiction to cigarettes causes the body to resist the attempt at change. But a person with a half pack a day habit is, by definition, less dependent on the cigarettes, less a slave to the habit, than a two pack a day smoker. The half pack a day smoker does usually find it easier to quit (Cohen et al., 1989). Similarly, a person who has been slim most of his life, and gains weight in middle age, may find it physically easier to lose weight than someone who has been heavy his entire life. Even more generally, women seem to naturally gain weight with age, more frequently than men. There may be some physiological factor that makes it more difficult for women to lose weight than men, even with equal motivation in both. To the extent that psychological factors could be discovered that would be helpful, they would probably have to be very powerful factors, to help those who most need the help. Motivation is undoubtedly relevant, but it can only be seen as one factor, and often a weak one relative to physical variables. Perhaps, in the future, our understanding and control of motivation will be increased, or new useful variables will be identified.

PROCESS RESEARCH

This chapter has concentrated on the problems encountered, and procedures used, for evaluating whether various therapeutic interventions work. The reader should be aware of another general approach to the evaluation of therapy, called **process research**. Psychotherapy process research examines the therapist/patient interactions that can be observed or measured in therapy sessions. For example, this type of research has looked for relationships between therapist behaviors such as interpretation, or reassurance, or reflection of feelings, and patient behaviors such as self-exploration, resolution of conflicts, and changes in attitudes or states of mind. Other interactions examined have included depth of interpretation and client resistance, or the effects of therapist orientation on patient behavior.

Some attempts have been made to relate the observed changes in behavior found in process research to overall effectiveness of the therapeutic interventions. But to date most process research has been primarily focused on identifying relationships between therapist interventions and short-term, or within-session, changes in the behavior of patients. (A special issue of the *Journal of Consulting and Clinical Psychology* [Beutler, 1990] contains a series of articles discussing psychotherapy process research. It includes an article by Garfield [1990] that discusses process research in regard to the outcome issue.)

CHAPTER SUMMARY

The usual assumption of random assignments to groups is not always possible in treatment outcome research. This can result in differences in condition severity in waiting list controls, a potential confounding factor. Even with random assignments, there is a problem of different expectations among subjects on a waiting list (as compared to subjects in treatment). Thus the use of waiting list controls is especially prone to confounding factors. The traditional solution to this problem is the use of placebo control groups. A placebo control group is a nontreated group to which have been added any inadvertent influences that are incidently added to the treatment group as a function of applying the treatment. This is usually a form of pseudo-treatment. Pseudo-treatments are not always convincing, so some checks should be included to determine whether the subjects in the placebo control condition believed that they were being treated. An alternative option is to remove these undesired components from the treatment condition during experimental tests of the treatment. For example, countertherapeutic instructions are used. In this approach, the therapeutic condition is made to appear as something other than therapy, or as a preparation for therapy, or as a preliminary measurement process.

There is a term in the psychotherapy literature that is frequently encountered in discussions over whether placebo groups are in fact different from therapy groups. The term is *common factors*. Common factors in therapy are those influential procedures and situational components that are common to all forms of therapy, and may be present in placebo conditions that produce better outcomes than waiting list controls. The questions about possible therapeutic qualities in placebo groups have been prompted by the frequent failure of studies to show treatments as superior to placebo controls, although the treatments generally are superior to waiting list controls. The view that it is the common factors that are critical for therapy has been bolstered by the frequent lack of consistent differences between therapies in effectiveness. A related term in these discussions is *treatment-specific effects*. Treatment-specific effects are those therapeutic effects that are obtained only from particular treatments.

One result of the belief in the efficacy of the common factors has been the assumption that almost any therapy should be effective (particularly if the patient believes that he or she is being treated). The next question is whether there are any treatment-specific effects to be identified for particular treatments. Therefore, most contemporary studies involve comparisons between two or more different forms of therapy. Given the ethical problems in using placebo control groups, many of these studies are done without placebo controls, simply comparing two or more different treatments for efficacy. When one or more of the treatments has previously been found effective, it further justifies its use as a standard against which to compare other therapies. However, a problem still exists in that a treatment's effectiveness in one setting with one therapist, or group of therapists, may not justify the assumption of its effectiveness in another setting. This is particularly important in case a particular treatment is potentially harmful. A no-treatment control might help to identify this unusual type of situation. Thus, there should always be some sort of no-treatment control used in a study comparing different therapies for effectiveness.

Rather than comparing different therapies, it is possible to compare components of therapies. Two similar ways of doing this were described, one called the construction strategy and the other called the dismantling strategy. The construction strategy involves a comparison of increasing numbers of overlapping therapy components, using one component as a baseline, and then adding additional components in other groups. The dismantling strategy begins with a form of therapy containing two or more components, comparing the intact therapy with subsets of its components, including single components. The two approaches are clearly similar, with the dismantling strategy being more common, because researchers are more likely to be comparing the separate components of an already developed systematic approach. A no-treatment control should be used with both of these strategies.

The importance of clarity as to the form of the treatment was discussed. Treatment manuals describing the treatments are particularly useful. Having raters blindly rate the sessions as to form of treatment was suggested as one way of determining whether the treatments are as specific in practice as in theory.

To provide concrete examples of outcome research, problems and procedures in testing treatments for smoking cessation were described. The use of returnable fees to discourage drop-outs and the importance of counting drop-outs as failures were mentioned. Obtaining a baseline measure of pretreatment smoking was discussed, along with the fact that self-monitoring of the amount of smoking is a reactive measure, so that participants should be encouraged to smoke at their normal level during the baseline period. Problems in measuring the amount of smoking were described, along with some solutions. Because the point at which failure most often becomes apparent is after the treatment program is over, the importance of follow-up measurements, where measurement procedures are not changed, was stressed.

Research on the efficacy of weight reduction programs was discussed. The special problems when treatment has to be self- administered (as when learning to eat only under certain conditions, or to put the fork down between bites, etc.) were discussed, as were means of making caloric counts easier, and the use of self-ratings on degree of compliance. The occasional difficulties in keeping the different groups distinct in this type of research were also mentioned. People meeting in groups, as is often the case in weight reduction programs, can lead to all sorts of group decisions or processes that were not planned by the research team. The importance of long-term follow-ups was stressed for weight reduction research, as it was for smoking cessation research. This point is relevant for all appetitive research.

The special problems of waiting list controls with therapies for appetitive problems were mentioned. This is the problem of the possibility of larger rates of spontaneous self-help among groups thinking that they are being treated, when compared to waiting list controls that are in a sense encouraged to put such efforts on hold. The use of waiting list controls for these types of therapy is therefore discouraged. On the other hand, if there are no control conditions available other than a waiting list control, such a control condition would be better than none.

Finally, brief mention was made of a very different approach to the examination of psychotherapy, called process research. Psychotherapy process research examines the therapist/patient interactions in ongoing therapy sessions, in hopes of learning how the former have impact on the latter.

NEW WORDS AND PHRASES IN CHAPTER 15

baseline data
common factors
construction strategy
countertherapeutic instructions
dismantling strategy
drop-outs
follow-up
process research
reactive measurement
returnable fee
treatment manual
treatment-specific effects
waiting list controls

APPENDIX A

The Proper Form When Submitting Experiments for Publication

A research report in psychological journals usually has six sections. The first five sections are the abstract, the introduction, the method, the results, and the discussion. The sixth section is a list of articles and books that were mentioned in the article, giving sufficient information so that they can be located in a library or obtained from a publisher. Because articles are frequently reviewed without the reviewer being informed of the identity of the author or authors, a separate title page is needed that includes the title, the author (or authors), and the author's (or authors') professional affiliation. For example:

Memory for Events Experienced Under Stress
John J. Jones
University of Southern Arizona

would appear on a separate page, centered within all four margins of the page, and treated as page 1 of the manuscript. The second page contains only the abstract, and the manuscript proper begins on the third page, preceded by the title, centered between the left and right margins, and followed by the rest of the article, as described in this appendix. The author's name does not appear anywhere in the manuscript other than the title page. The various sections are now described in some detail.

ABSTRACT

The abstract is a brief summary, generally a somewhat dense paragraph of 100–150 words, which offers a sentence or two about the nature of the problem that was researched, states the major hypotheses (if there were any), and gives a skeletal description of the design, the major results, and the central conclusions. As previously suggested, the abstract appears on a separate page. It has its own heading, Abstract, centered, with only the first letter upper case. The abstract, like the rest of the article, is typed with double spacing. The headings are separated from the body of the manuscript by a double space. (The only possible exceptions to double spacing in the manuscript are equations, which may sometimes be separated by more than a double space.)

INTRODUCTION

The first extended section of the report is the introduction. Here the author identifies the problem being explored, mentions and briefly describes any previous relevant research, and cites and summarizes the findings of those whose research results, or theoretical suggestions, inspired the hypotheses of the present experimenter. If other researchers introduced the techniques to be used in the current article, their original articles are referenced. In addition, the experimenter indicates her or his hypotheses (the preexperimental expectations). The general nature of the variables should be apparent from this discussion, although the precise definitions are not given. Thus, it might be clear that empathy and altruism are being examined, although how empathy is manipulated, and altruism measured, would not be discussed until the method section.

Sometimes statements are made in the introduction section concerning the importance of the problem being investigated. For example, the research might be an attempt to settle a long-standing controversy, or it might be an attempt to explain why one group of experimenters did not get the same results as another group of investigators. The introduction does not have its own heading; it simply follows the title of the article, on Page 3 of the manuscript (Page 1 being the title page and Page 2 containing the abstract).

METHOD SECTION

The next section is the method section. This section does have its own title, "Method," centered on the page. In the method section the details of the experimental procedures are offered in sufficient detail so that other experimenters can reproduce the same experiment. The operational definitions of the variables also appear here. After reading the method section a reader should know whether manipulated or subject variables were used to differentiate groups, should be able to differentiate independent and dependent variables, and should know precisely how each of the variables is defined and/or measured.

When some of the materials that were used are too long and detailed for inclusion in the article (for example, detailed instructions to judges), a footnote generally indicates where copies of these materials can be obtained (usually from the senior author). When the material is important but distracting to the main argument (e.g., a mathematical proof or a new questionnaire), the material is placed in an appendix.

The experimental design is detailed in the Method section, and includes such things as the number of subjects, how they were obtained, and some facts about them such as sex or age if that is relevant. The procedures are detailed and include the instructions to the subjects, the manipulations to which the subjects were exposed, the details of time of exposure to stimuli, light or sound levels when relevant, and so on. Sometimes the procedures are sufficiently complex and unique that they are given a separate subsection labeled procedure, under the method heading, along with other subheadings such as subjects, materials, and apparatus, when the details under these subheadings are sufficiently extensive to warrant a separate paragraph or two under each subheading. The subheadings appear flush with the left margin and are underlined, for example:

Subjects
or
Materials.

The descriptions of subjects or materials follow immediately under the subheading, separated from the subheading by just the usual double space.

RESULTS SECTION

The results section presents the findings without editorial comment, that is, without commenting on whether the experimenters' expectations were met, and without discussing implications. It simply presents the outcomes of all of the statistical tests, indicating which statistical tests were used, which were statistically significant, and at what probability levels. Frequently the means and standard deviations for the different groups are also given. Usually the data is summarized in tables, with the text redundantly verbalizing the important findings that are at the same time visible in the tables. Clear tables, with appropriate commentary about what they contain, are important to having a communicative results section. Graphs of the data, when useful, also appear here. Graphs have the function of giving readers a quick intuitive picture of the results. The heading for this section, Results, like headings for the other sections, is centered.

DISCUSSION SECTION

The next section is the discussion section, and it too receives a centered heading, "Discussion." Here the experimenter discusses the implications of the findings, commenting on what was only described, without interpretation, in the results section. The hypotheses are usually reiterated, indicating which ones were and were not supported. These results are related to the initial discussion of the problem in the introduction, and to the findings of other people in the literature. The author also discusses the theoretical implications of the research, and may engage in a limited amount of theoretical speculation. When some of the hypotheses are not supported, it is not uncommon for the experimenter to offer some ideas or rationalizations about why the results came out as they did. The experimenter might point out any limitations in the research that can now be recognized from hindsight, and might make recommendations for future research.

The discussion section includes the author's perspective on the research. In contrast, the method section and the results section offer the basic hard facts of the research. For this reason, the discussion section has to be read with a certain degree of skepticism. It is possible for readers to reach different conclusions than the author about some of the implications of the research, or to be less or more willing to dismiss unexplained or perplexing parts of the results. Often very interesting and thoughtful comments occur in the discussion section, so it is an important part of the report of the research. However, it is the point where rationalism and empiricism meet, so the reader should take pains to distinguish between the two.

LISTING OF REFERENCES

The list of references follows the discussion section and has the centered heading "References" (unless there is only one reference, in which case the heading is "Reference"). The references in psychological journals appear in alphabetical order. Most of the references are either journal or book references. Journal references list last names first, then initials (if more than one initial, they are separated by a period and a space), with a comma and a space between names, the last name followed by a double space and then the year of publication in parentheses, a period, and a double space; then the title of the article (only first letter of first word capitalized) followed by a period and a double space; then the journal name, underlined, the volume number, underlined, and finally the pages, ending in a period. For example:

Cooper, J., Zanna, M. P., & Taves, P. A. (1978). Arousal as a necessary condition for attitude change following induced compliance. Journal of Personality and Social Psychology, 36, 1101–1106.

Note that the first line is flush with the left-hand margin, but subsequent lines in the same reference are all indented three spaces.

Book references list the authors' names followed by the year of publication, just as for journals, followed by the book title, underlined, a period, a double space, then the home office of the publisher, then a colon and a double space, followed by the name of the publisher, ending in a period. For example:

Rosenthal, R. (1966). Experimenter effects in behavioral research. New York: Appleton-Century-Crofts.

Occasionally an article or a chapter that is cited is contained within a book, slightly complicating the reference. In the body of the referencing article it is treated as any other citation, that is, the last name of the author of the cited work, and year of publication of the book in which it appears, are given. The reference at the end of the article takes the following form: author's or authors' names, followed by the year of publication in parentheses as for any other article; then the title of the work being cited, ending in a period. After two spaces, this is followed by the word *In*, followed by the editors of the book containing the cited work, with their initials preceding their names. The names are followed by the parenthetical *(Ed.)* or *(Eds.)*, assuming an edited book, followed by a comma, followed by the title of the book containing the cited work, underlined, followed by the page numbers of the cited work, in parentheses, followed by a period. Finally, as for other books, we have the city of publication, a colon, a double space, and the publisher, followed by a period. An example follows:

> Likert R. (1967). The method of constructing an attitude scale. In M. Fishbein (Ed.), Readings in attitude theory and measurement. (pp. 90–95). New York: Wiley.

A source that is frequently cited is the *Annual Review of Psychology*, which appears in the form of an edited annual book. The articles in the volume each consist of a chapter, which might appear to require citation in the form of articles or chapters in edited books; however, the *Annual Review of Psychology* is treated as a journal, each issue having a volume number, so the articles are cited in journal article form.

Sometimes a monograph or book is a product of the joint effort of committees within an organization. In such instances there may not be any identifiable individual authors. In those cases the organization is listed as the author. For example, this appendix is based on the publication manual of the *American Psychological Association*. This manual contains additional detail on the correct form for submitting articles to journals published by the American Psychological Association. The reference to that monograph takes the following form:

> American Psychological Association. (1984). Publication manual of the American Psychological Association. Washington, DC: Author.

The word *Author* at the end of the reference, following the colon, is in lieu of the name of a publisher. That is, the organization is both author and publisher. Instead of repeating the name of the organization, the word *Author* is used.

Sometimes an author, or an identical group of authors, is cited more than once in an article, each time referring to different articles (or books). In these cases, the separate references are ordered by year of publication, the earlier references preceding the later ones. If two or more identically authored references were published in the same year, they are then ordered alphabetically, using the title of the article for this purpose. A letter is then appended to the year, to differentiate the two references for purposes of separate identification within the text (discussed further in the next section). For example, two references, the title of one beginning with the letter *C*, and the other with the letter *L*, might be listed in the following ways:

Greene, J. P. (1991a).   Changes in attitude . . .

Greene, J. P. (1991b).   Loss of control . . .

The appended letters are a, b, c, and so on, in keeping with the alphabetical order of the titles.

CITATIONS WITHIN THE BODY OF THE ARTICLE

Citations within the article take the form of the authors' last names, plus the year of publication, all in parentheses. An example for one author is (Tanner, 1950); for two authors (Black & Whyte, 1979); for more than two authors (Brown, Greene, & Gray, 1978). When there are several citations at the same point, they are separated within the parentheses by semicolons, for example, (Black & Whyte, 1979; Tanner, 1950). When authors are being mentioned at the point in the article at which their article is being cited, only the year is placed in parentheses, for example, "As shown by Jones and Smith (1981), ... "

When the same author is cited for more than one article in the same year, the citation within the text includes both the year and the added letter that was used to indicate the order in which the references appeared in the reference section, for example, "The previously discussed work on loss of control under pressure (Greene, 1991b) gave a more detailed . . . ," or, "Greene's (1991a) article on changes in attitude showed . . . . "

APPENDIX B

Statistical Tables

TABLE 1   Random Numbers

5461	0962	3535	5131	7035	6812	5219	8414
2518	8666	0431	1797	2212	7674	8028	0073
4833	1032	4776	4350	6980	4988	2169	7283
4849	6034	0180	4174	3285	2810	7225	5684
7446	7879	2469	4569	9343	2654	2184	1154
2734	9051	9377	1746	1754	0540	7283	6805
8909	0841	4600	7822	8096	5268	9866	7428
8058	8773	6996	1924	2457	8203	8675	2164
8565	4668	8722	8244	5492	0346	3864	1105
2696	1712	2526	7994	6460	1182	7236	5566
0931	8013	4187	1077	8730	4916	4221	3124
8567	7599	9012	8035	0834	4691	0541	5041
7474	6858	1708	9711	1172	8997	3742	4562
9251	4041	7843	1250	8794	1601	9056	4585
7777	8859	6048	5802	0727	6364	6841	5166
6353	2353	9883	6552	6050	6165	1419	3341
3226	3413	6334	8524	4012	7486	3310	7581
0387	8443	5240	3348	3734	1184	7836	6964
7871	3183	5364	9339	7554	7587	0874	0720
7327	0700	1609	4694	8373	4057	9139	4322

9122	7517	5568	1622	4368	9702	3057	7382
7236	3222	2494	2491	6466	6169	4443	4029
7700	0065	8608	5501	5538	5381	4226	5050
1996	8289	1937	2885	6152	4980	8608	0848
3084	6421	5988	7904	1122	4311	5212	3012
1309	0604	9421	0482	6323	4021	0306	9117
5508	8168	3522	0213	5690	4646	0670	7754
9372	2654	2698	1316	3969	9817	1378	2602
5756	0109	0022	2513	6095	1892	0746	6885
3931	5092	8432	9431	2383	5479	4966	1045
7755	4452	4551	3830	3240	0577	4859	7790
2561	3115	2321	6363	6569	2863	9759	4711
3616	1189	9097	2631	3061	6592	8875	6828
4191	6830	0313	7262	8586	1779	5939	3555
4038	1828	3668	8696	5940	6420	0609	1939
3029	0609	7572	6151	9513	0700	7959	9297
0589	9250	3466	8845	3753	1478	7943	9747
8794	6854	0633	9033	4422	1483	2248	0209
2400	9094	4158	7238	8292	7196	4405	4994
4325	3709	9425	2297	8728	2867	8968	0385
7741	2125	2198	1683	6103	9601	9354	7995
8463	2363	1192	5267	2835	4960	5073	0016
6733	5198	2311	5697	4836	5591	8256	8968
3011	3628	4634	9766	0161	3826	6087	3532
2447	5123	2867	2389	0333	3172	2780	4957
0404	3582	7038	7108	9059	8460	4875	9052
5350	0347	7614	0188	8193	0236	7719	4166
5449	3362	4816	7290	9768	7054	1929	2510
9601	2995	8408	5191	4265	5892	0759	4883
6824	3805	2001	6216	2350	5989	7983	5115
1737	1543	2038	4876	3485	1240	4066	9760
8893	1970	8808	6056	4461	2374	2485	1955
1015	3488	3268	4300	9666	5800	6439	0642
8811	5380	5474	7748	2957	3468	7377	5311
8240	1951	7464	2485	5825	1766	1275	2642
4845	3076	6308	9273	3322	5610	8294	6716
7752	8746	2558	3345	8410	1100	0259	3672
2790	0595	8605	9069	8581	9148	9517	7662
8606	0951	3693	2986	1354	6334	1814	9741
5267	6267	2211	2652	3515	2579	5383	7847

(continued on next page)

TABLE 1   *(Continued)*

7018	5568	9921	4864	0302	1667	6753	6184
2170	2222	7687	6478	8396	2258	1204	0548
2482	7416	0081	5464	4844	2609	8261	5338
9749	5789	5335	8258	4646	5516	1583	7286
9721	4197	7335	9121	1064	6603	3304	2260
8866	1725	0282	1395	7540	2396	6714	8676
3693	2221	6304	5359	7955	8179	4392	1067
7428	6086	1867	0336	2247	7878	2550	0977
2027	2867	3084	4877	4143	3137	3448	6875
9087	5460	1602	1938	1807	1312	6903	2524

TABLE 2   **Table of Probabilities Under the Normal Curve**

z	Area from Mean	Height of Curve at z (Ordinate)	z	Area from Mean	Height of Curve at z (Ordinate)
0.00	.0000	.3989	0.25	.0987	.3867
0.01	.0040	.3989	0.26	.1026	.3857
0.02	.0080	.3989	0.27	.1064	.3847
0.03	.0120	.3988	0.28	.1103	.3836
0.04	.0160	.3986	0.29	.1141	.3825
0.05	.0199	.3984	0.30	.1179	.3814
0.06	.0239	.3982	0.31	.1217	.3802
0.07	.0279	.3980	0.32	.1255	.3790
0.08	.0319	.3977	0.33	.1293	.3778
0.09	.0359	.3973	0.34	.1331	.3765
0.10	.0398	.3970	0.35	.1368	.3752
0.11	.0438	.3965	0.36	.1406	.3739
0.12	.0478	.3961	0.37	.1443	.3725
0.13	.0517	.3956	0.38	.1480	.3712
0.14	.0057	.3951	0.39	.1517	.3697
0.15	.0596	.3945	0.40	.1554	.3683
0.16	.0636	.3939	0.41	.1591	.3668
0.17	.0675	.3932	0.42	.1628	.3653
0.18	.0714	.3925	0.43	.1664	.3637
0.19	.0753	.3918	0.44	.1700	.3621
0.20	.0793	.3910	0.45	.1736	.3605
0.21	.0832	.3902	0.46	.1772	.3589
0.22	.0871	.3894	0.47	.1808	.3572
0.23	.0910	.3885	0.48	.1844	.3555
0.24	.0948	.3876	0.49	.1879	.3538

z	Area from Mean	Height of Curve at z (Ordinate)	z	Area from Mean	Height of Curve at z (Ordinate)
0.50	.1915	.3521	0.90	.3159	.2661
0.51	.1950	.3503	0.91	.3186	.2637
0.52	.1985	.3485	0.92	.3212	.2613
0.53	.2019	.3467	0.93	.3238	.2589
0.54	.2054	.3448	0.94	.3264	.2565
0.55	.2088	.3429	0.95	.3289	.2541
0.56	.2123	.3410	0.96	.3315	.2516
0.57	.2157	.3391	0.97	.3340	.2492
0.58	.2190	.3372	0.98	.3365	.2468
0.59	.2224	.3352	0.99	.3389	.2444
0.60	.2257	.3332	1.00	.3413	.2420
0.61	.2291	.3312	1.01	.3438	.2396
0.62	.2324	.3292	1.02	.3461	.2371
0.63	.2357	.3271	1.03	.3485	.2347
0.64	.2389	.3251	1.04	.3508	.2323
0.65	.2422	.3230	1.05	.3531	.2299
0.66	.2454	.3209	1.06	.3554	.2275
0.67	.2486	.3187	1.07	.3577	.2251
0.68	.2518	.3166	1.08	.3599	.2227
0.69	.2549	.3144	1.09	.3621	.2203
0.70	.2580	.3123	1.10	.3643	.2179
0.71	.2612	.3101	1.11	.3665	.2155
0.72	.2642	.3079	1.12	.3686	.2131
0.73	.2673	.3056	1.13	.3708	.2107
0.74	.2704	.3034	1.14	.3729	.2083
0.75	.2734	.3011	1.15	.3749	.2059
0.76	.2764	.2989	1.16	.3770	.2036
0.77	.2794	.2966	1.17	.3790	.2012
0.78	.2823	.2943	1.18	.3810	.1989
0.79	.2852	.2920	1.19	.3820	.1965
0.80	.2881	.2897	1.20	.3849	.1942
0.81	.2910	.2874	1.21	.3869	.1919
0.82	.2939	.2850	1.22	.3888	.1895
0.83	.2967	.2827	1.23	.3907	.1872
0.84	.2995	.2803	1.24	.3925	.1849
0.85	.3023	.2780	1.25	.3944	.1826
0.86	.3051	.2756	1.26	.3962	.1804
0.87	.3079	.2732	1.27	.3980	.1781
0.88	.3106	.2709	1.28	.3997	.1758
0.89	.3133	.2685	1.29	.4015	.1736

(continued on next page)

TABLE 2 *(Continued)*

z	Area from Mean	Height of Curve at z (Ordinate)	z	Area from Mean	Height of Curve at z (Ordinate)
1.30	.4032	.1714	1.70	.4554	.0940
1.31	.4049	.1691	1.71	.4564	.0925
1.32	.4066	.1669	1.72	.4573	.0909
1.33	.4082	.1647	1.73	.4582	.0893
1.34	.4099	.1626	1.74	.4591	.0878
1.35	.4115	.1604	1.75	.4599	.0863
1.36	.4131	.1582	1.76	.4608	.0848
1.37	.4147	.1561	1.77	.4616	.0833
1.38	.4162	.1539	1.78	.4625	.0818
1.39	.4177	.1518	1.79	.4633	.0804
1.40	.4192	.1497	1.80	.4641	.0790
1.41	.4207	.1476	1.81	.4649	.0775
1.42	.4222	.1456	1.82	.4656	.0761
1.43	.4236	.1435	1.83	.4664	.0748
1.44	.4251	.1415	1.84	.4671	.0734
1.45	.4265	.1394	1.85	.4678	.0721
1.46	.4279	.1374	1.86	.4686	.0707
1.47	.4292	.1354	1.87	.4693	.0694
1.48	.4306	.1334	1.88	.4699	.0681
1.49	.4319	.1315	1.89	.4706	.0669
1.50	.4332	.1295	1.90	.4713	.0656
1.51	.4345	.1276	1.91	.4719	.0644
1.52	.4357	.1257	1.92	.4726	.0632
1.53	.4370	.1238	1.93	.4732	.0620
1.54	.4382	.1219	1.94	.4738	.0608
1.55	.4394	.1200	1.95	.4744	.0596
1.56	.4406	.1182	1.96	.4750	.0584
1.57	.4418	.1163	1.97	.4756	.0573
1.58	.4429	.1145	1.98	.4761	.0562
1.59	.4441	.1127	1.99	.4767	.0551
1.60	.4452	.1109	2.00	.4772	.0540
1.61	.4463	.1092	2.01	.4778	.0529
1.62	.4474	.1074	2.02	.4783	.0519
1.63	.4484	.1057	2.03	.4788	.0508
1.64	.4495	.1040	2.04	.4793	.0498
1.65	.4505	.1023	2.05	.4798	.0488
1.66	.4515	.1006	2.06	.4803	.0478
1.67	.4525	.0989	2.07	.4808	.0468
1.68	.4535	.0973	2.08	.4812	.0459
1.69	.4545	.0957	2.09	.4817	.0449

z	Area from Mean	Height of Curve at z (Ordinate)	z	Area from Mean	Height of Curve at z (Ordinate)
2.10	.4821	.0440	2.50	.4938	.0175
2.11	.4826	.0431	2.51	.4940	.0171
2.12	.4830	.0422	2.52	.4941	.0167
2.13	.4834	.0413	2.53	.4943	.0163
2.14	.4838	.0404	2.54	.4945	.0158
2.15	.4842	.0396	2.55	.4946	.0154
2.16	.4846	.0387	2.56	.4948	.0151
2.17	.4850	.0379	2.57	.4949	.0147
2.18	.4854	.0371	2.58	.4951	.0143
2.19	.4857	.0363	2.59	.4952	.0139
2.20	.4861	.0355	2.60	.4953	.0136
2.21	.4864	.0347	2.61	.4955	.0132
2.22	.4868	.0339	2.62	.4956	.0129
2.23	.4871	.0332	2.63	.4957	.0126
2.24	.4875	.0325	2.64	.4959	.0122
2.25	.4878	.0317	2.65	.4960	.0119
2.26	.4881	.0310	2.66	.4961	.0116
2.27	.4884	.0303	2.67	.4962	.0113
2.28	.4887	.0297	2.68	.4963	.0110
2.29	.4890	.0290	2.69	.4964	.0107
2.30	.4893	.0283	2.70	.4965	.0104
2.31	.4896	.0277	2.71	.4966	.0101
2.32	.4898	.0270	2.72	.4967	.0099
2.33	.4901	.0264	2.73	.4968	.0096
2.34	.4904	.0258	2.74	.4969	.0093
2.35	.4906	.0252	2.75	.4970	.0091
2.36	.4909	.0246	2.76	.4971	.0088
2.37	.4911	.0241	2.77	.4972	.0086
2.38	.4913	.0235	2.78	.4973	.0084
2.39	.4916	.0229	2.79	.4974	.0081
2.40	.4918	.0224	2.80	.4974	.0079
2.41	.4920	.0219	2.81	.4975	.0077
2.42	.4922	.0213	2.82	.4976	.0075
2.43	.4924	.0208	2.83	.4977	.0073
2.44	.4927	.0203	2.84	.4977	.0071
2.45	.4929	.0198	2.85	.4978	.0069
2.46	.4930	.0194	2.86	.4979	.0067
2.47	.4932	.0189	2.87	.4979	.0065
2.48	.4934	.0184	2.88	.4980	.0063
2.49	.4936	.0180	2.89	.4981	.0061

(continued on next page)

TABLE 2　*(Continued)*

z	Area from Mean	Height of Curve at z (Ordinate)	z	Area from Mean	Height of Curve at z (Ordinate)
2.90	.4981	.0060	3.20	.4993	.0024
2.91	.4982	.0058	3.21	.4993	.0023
2.92	.4982	.0056	3.22	.4994	.0022
2.93	.4983	.0055	3.23	.4994	.0022
2.94	.4984	.0053	3.24	.4994	.0021
2.95	.4984	.0051	3.25	.4994	.0020
2.96	.4985	.0050	3.26	.4994	.0020
2.97	.4985	.0048	3.27	.4995	.0019
2.98	.4986	.0047	3.28	.4995	.0018
2.99	.4986	.0046	3.29	.4995	.0018
3.00	.4986	.0044	3.30	.4995	.0017
3.01	.4987	.0043	3.31	.4995	.0017
3.02	.4987	.0042	3.32	.4995	.0016
3.03	.4988	.0040	3.33	.4996	.0016
3.04	.4988	.0039	3.34	.4996	.0015
3.05	.4989	.0038	3.35	.4996	.0015
3.06	.4989	.0037	3.36	.4996	.0014
3.07	.4989	.0036	3.37	.4996	.0014
3.08	.4990	.0035	3.38	.4996	.0013
3.09	.4990	.0034	3.39	.4996	.0013
3.10	.4990	.0033	3.40	.4997	.0012
3.11	.4991	.0032	3.41	.4997	.0012
3.12	.4991	.0031	3.42	.4997	.0012
3.13	.4991	.0030	3.43	.4997	.0011
3.14	.4992	.0029	3.44	.4997	.0011
3.15	.4992	.0028	3.45	.4997	.0010
3.16	.4992	.0027	3.46	.4997	.0010
3.17	.4992	.0026	3.47	.4997	.0010
3.18	.4993	.0025	3.48	.4997	.0009
3.19	.4993	.0025	3.49	.4998	.0009

TABLE 3   Critical Values of *t*

Degrees of Freedom	One-Tailed			
	.05	.025	.01	.005
	Two-Tailed			
	.25	.10	.05	.02	.01
1	2.414	6.314	12.706	31.821	63.657
2	1.604	2.920	4.303	6.965	9.925
3	1.423	2.353	3.182	4.541	5.841
4	1.344	2.132	2.776	3.747	4.604
5	1.301	2.015	2.571	3.365	4.032
6	1.273	1.943	2.447	3.143	3.707
7	1.254	1.895	2.365	2.998	3.499
8	1.240	1.860	2.306	2.896	3.355
9	1.230	1.833	2.262	2.821	3.250
10	1.221	1.812	2.228	2.764	3.169
11	1.214	1.796	2.201	2.718	3.106
12	1.209	1.782	2.179	2.681	3.055
13	1.204	1.771	2.160	2.650	3.012
14	1.200	1.761	2.145	2.624	2.977
15	1.197	1.753	2.131	2.602	2.947
16	1.194	1.746	2.120	2.583	2.921
17	1.191	1.740	2.110	2.567	2.898
18	1.189	1.734	2.101	2.552	2.878
19	1.187	1.729	2.093	2.539	2.861
20	1.185	1.725	2.086	2.528	2.845
21	1.183	1.721	2.080	2.518	2.831
22	1.182	1.717	2.074	2.508	2.819
23	1.180	1.714	2.069	2.500	2.807
24	1.179	1.711	2.064	2.492	2.797
25	1.178	1.708	2.060	2.485	2.787
26	1.177	1.706	2.056	2.479	2.779
27	1.176	1.703	2.052	2.473	2.771
28	1.175	1.701	2.048	2.467	2.763
29	1.174	1.699	2.045	2.462	2.756
30	1.173	1.697	2.042	2.457	2.750
40	1.167	1.684	2.021	2.423	2.704
50	1.164	1.676	2.009	2.403	2.678
60	1.162	1.671	2.000	2.390	2.660
90	1.158	1.662	1.987	2.368	2.632
120	1.156	1.658	1.980	2.358	2.617
Infinity	1.150	1.645	1.960	2.326	2.576

TABLE 4 **Critical Values of Chi-Square**

Degrees of Freedom	Level of Significance			
	.10	.05	.01	.001
1	2.71	3.84	6.63	10.83
2	4.61	5.99	9.21	13.82
3	6.25	7.81	11.34	16.27
4	7.78	9.49	13.28	18.47
5	9.24	11.07	15.09	20.52
6	10.64	12.59	16.81	22.46
7	12.02	14.07	18.48	24.32
8	13.36	15.51	20.09	26.12
9	14.68	16.92	21.67	27.88
10	15.99	18.31	23.21	29.59
11	17.28	19.68	24.72	31.26
12	18.55	21.03	26.22	32.91
13	19.81	22.36	27.69	34.53
14	21.06	23.68	29.14	36.12
15	22.31	25.00	30.58	37.70
16	23.54	26.30	32.00	39.25
17	24.77	27.59	33.41	40.79
18	25.99	28.87	34.81	42.31
19	27.20	30.14	36.19	43.82
20	28.41	31.41	37.57	45.31
21	29.62	32.67	38.93	46.80
22	30.81	33.92	40.29	48.27
23	32.01	35.17	41.64	49.73
24	33.20	36.42	42.98	51.18
25	34.38	37.65	44.31	52.62
26	35.56	38.89	45.64	54.05
27	36.74	40.11	46.96	55.48
28	37.92	41.34	48.28	56.89
29	39.09	42.56	49.59	58.30
30	40.26	43.77	50.89	59.70

TABLE 5 Critical Values of F

Degrees of Freedom for Denominator	Degrees of Freedom for Numerator									
	1	2	3	4	5	6	7	8	9	10
					$\alpha = .05$					
1	161	200	216	225	230	234	237	239	241	242
2	18.51	19.00	19.16	19.25	19.30	19.33	19.35	19.37	19.38	19.40
3	10.13	9.55	9.28	9.12	9.01	8.94	8.89	8.85	8.81	8.79
4	7.71	6.94	6.59	6.39	6.26	6.16	6.09	6.04	6.00	5.96
5	6.61	5.79	5.41	5.19	5.05	4.95	4.88	4.82	4.77	4.74
6	5.99	5.14	4.76	4.53	4.39	4.28	4.21	4.15	4.10	4.06
7	5.59	4.74	4.35	4.12	3.97	3.87	3.79	3.73	3.68	3.64
8	5.32	4.46	4.07	3.84	3.69	3.58	3.50	3.44	3.39	3.35
9	5.12	4.26	3.86	3.63	3.48	3.37	3.29	3.23	3.18	3.14
10	4.96	4.10	3.71	3.48	3.33	3.22	3.14	3.07	3.02	2.98
11	4.84	3.98	3.59	3.36	3.20	3.09	3.01	2.95	2.90	2.85
12	4.75	3.89	3.49	3.26	3.11	3.00	2.91	2.85	2.80	2.75
13	4.67	3.81	3.41	3.18	3.03	2.92	2.83	2.77	2.71	2.67
14	4.60	3.74	3.34	3.11	2.96	2.85	2.76	2.70	2.65	2.60
15	4.54	3.68	3.29	3.06	2.90	2.79	2.71	2.64	2.59	2.54
16	4.49	3.63	3.24	3.01	2.85	2.74	2.66	2.59	2.54	2.49
17	4.45	3.59	3.20	2.96	2.81	2.70	2.61	2.55	2.49	2.45
18	4.41	3.55	3.16	2.93	2.77	2.66	2.58	2.51	2.46	2.41
19	4.38	3.52	3.13	2.90	2.74	2.63	2.54	2.48	2.42	2.38
20	4.35	3.49	3.10	2.87	2.71	2.60	2.51	2.45	2.39	2.35

(continued on next page)

TABLE 5   *(Continued)*

| | | | | Degrees of Freedom for Numerator | | | | | |
Degrees of Freedom for Denominator	1	2	3	4	5	6	7	8	9	10
					$\alpha = .05$					
21	4.32	3.47	3.07	2.84	2.68	2.57	2.49	2.42	2.37	2.32
22	4.30	3.44	3.05	2.82	2.66	2.55	2.46	2.40	2.34	2.30
23	4.28	3.42	3.03	2.80	2.64	2.53	2.44	2.37	2.32	2.27
24	4.26	3.40	3.01	2.78	2.62	2.51	2.42	2.36	2.30	2.25
25	4.24	3.39	2.99	2.76	2.60	2.49	2.40	2.34	2.28	2.24
26	4.23	3.37	2.98	2.74	2.59	2.47	2.39	2.32	2.27	2.22
27	4.21	3.35	2.96	2.73	2.57	2.46	2.37	2.31	2.25	2.20
28	4.20	3.34	2.95	2.71	2.56	2.45	2.36	2.29	2.24	2.19
29	4.18	3.33	2.93	2.70	2.54	2.43	2.35	2.28	2.22	2.18
30	4.17	3.32	2.92	2.69	2.53	2.42	2.33	2.27	2.21	2.16
32	4.15	3.29	2.90	2.67	2.51	2.40	2.32	2.25	2.19	2.14
34	4.13	3.28	2.88	2.65	2.49	2.38	2.29	2.23	2.17	2.12
36	4.11	3.26	2.87	2.63	2.48	2.36	2.28	2.21	2.15	2.11
38	4.10	3.24	2.85	2.62	2.46	2.35	2.26	2.19	2.14	2.09
40	4.08	3.23	2.84	2.61	2.45	2.34	2.25	2.18	2.12	2.08
42	4.07	3.22	2.83	2.59	2.44	2.32	2.24	2.17	2.11	2.06
44	4.06	3.21	2.82	2.58	2.43	2.31	2.23	2.16	2.10	2.05
46	4.05	3.20	2.81	2.57	2.42	2.30	2.22	2.15	2.09	2.04
48	4.04	3.19	2.80	2.57	2.41	2.29	2.21	2.14	2.08	2.03
50	4.03	3.18	2.79	2.56	2.40	2.29	2.20	2.13	2.07	2.03

55	4.02	3.16	2.77	2.54	2.38	2.27	2.18	2.11	2.06	2.01
60	4.00	3.15	2.76	2.53	2.37	2.25	2.17	2.10	2.04	1.99
65	3.99	3.14	2.75	2.51	2.36	2.24	2.15	2.08	2.03	1.98
70	3.98	3.13	2.74	2.50	2.35	2.23	2.14	2.07	2.02	1.97
75	3.97	3.12	2.73	2.49	2.34	2.22	2.13	2.06	2.01	1.96
80	3.96	3.11	2.72	2.49	2.33	2.21	2.13	2.06	2.00	1.95
90	3.95	3.10	2.71	2.47	2.32	2.20	2.11	2.04	1.99	1.94
100	3.94	3.09	2.70	2.46	2.31	2.19	2.10	2.03	1.97	1.93
125	3.92	3.07	2.68	2.44	2.29	2.17	2.08	2.01	1.96	1.91
150	3.90	3.06	2.67	2.43	2.27	2.16	2.07	2.00	1.94	1.89
200	3.89	3.04	2.65	2.42	2.26	2.14	2.06	1.98	1.93	1.88
300	3.87	3.03	2.63	2.40	2.24	2.13	2.04	1.97	1.91	1.86
400	3.86	3.02	2.63	2.39	2.24	2.12	2.03	1.96	1.90	1.85
1000	3.85	3.00	2.61	2.38	2.22	2.11	2.02	1.95	1.89	1.84
10000	3.84	3.00	2.61	2.37	2.21	2.10	2.01	1.94	1.88	1.83

TABLE 5 *(Continued)*

$\alpha = .01$

Degrees of Freedom for Denominator	Degrees of Freedom for Numerator									
	1	2	3	4	5	6	7	8	9	10
1	4052	4999	5403	5625	5764	5859	5928	5981	6022	6056
2	98.50	99.00	99.17	99.25	99.30	99.33	99.36	99.37	99.39	99.40
3	34.12	30.82	29.46	28.71	28.24	27.91	27.67	27.49	27.35	27.23
4	21.20	18.00	16.69	15.98	15.52	15.21	14.98	14.80	14.66	14.55
5	16.26	13.27	12.06	11.39	10.97	10.67	10.46	10.29	10.16	10.05
6	13.75	10.92	9.78	9.15	8.75	8.47	8.26	8.10	7.98	7.87
7	12.25	9.55	8.45	7.85	7.46	7.19	6.99	6.84	6.72	6.62
8	11.26	8.65	7.59	7.01	6.63	6.37	6.18	6.03	5.91	5.81
9	10.56	8.02	6.99	6.42	6.06	5.80	5.61	5.47	5.35	5.26
10	10.04	7.56	6.55	5.99	5.64	5.39	5.20	5.06	4.94	4.85
11	9.65	7.21	6.22	5.67	5.32	5.07	4.89	4.74	4.63	4.54
12	9.33	6.93	5.95	5.41	5.06	4.82	4.64	4.50	4.39	4.30
13	9.07	6.70	5.74	5.21	4.86	4.62	4.44	4.30	4.19	4.10
14	8.86	6.51	5.56	5.04	4.69	4.46	4.28	4.14	4.03	3.94
15	8.68	6.36	5.42	4.89	4.56	4.32	4.14	4.00	3.89	3.80
16	8.53	6.23	5.29	4.77	4.44	4.20	4.03	3.89	3.78	3.69
17	8.40	6.12	5.19	4.67	4.34	4.10	3.93	3.79	3.68	3.59
18	8.29	6.01	5.09	4.58	4.25	4.01	3.84	3.71	3.60	3.51
19	8.18	5.93	5.01	4.50	4.17	3.94	3.77	3.63	3.52	3.43
20	8.10	5.85	4.94	4.43	4.10	3.87	3.70	3.56	3.46	3.37

21	8.02	5.78	4.87	4.37	4.04	3.81	3.64	3.51	3.40	3.31
22	7.95	5.72	4.82	4.31	3.99	3.76	3.59	3.45	3.35	3.26
23	7.88	5.66	4.76	4.26	3.94	3.71	3.54	3.41	3.30	3.21
24	7.82	5.61	4.72	4.22	3.90	3.67	3.50	3.36	3.26	3.17
25	7.77	5.57	4.68	4.18	3.85	3.63	3.46	3.32	3.22	3.13
26	7.72	5.53	4.64	4.14	3.82	3.59	3.42	3.29	3.18	3.09
27	7.68	5.49	4.60	4.11	3.78	3.56	3.39	3.26	3.15	3.06
28	7.64	5.45	4.57	4.07	3.75	3.53	3.36	3.23	3.12	3.03
29	7.60	5.42	4.54	4.04	3.73	3.50	3.33	3.20	3.09	3.00
30	7.56	5.39	4.51	4.02	3.70	3.47	3.30	3.17	3.07	2.98
32	7.50	5.34	4.46	3.97	3.65	3.43	3.26	3.13	3.02	2.93
34	7.44	5.29	4.42	3.93	3.61	3.39	3.22	3.09	2.98	2.89
36	7.40	5.25	4.38	3.89	3.57	3.35	3.18	3.05	2.95	2.86
38	7.35	5.21	4.34	3.86	3.54	3.32	3.15	3.02	2.92	2.83
40	7.31	5.18	4.31	3.83	3.51	3.29	3.12	2.99	2.89	2.80
42	7.28	5.15	4.29	3.80	3.49	3.27	3.10	2.97	2.86	2.78
44	7.25	5.12	4.26	3.78	3.47	3.24	3.08	2.95	2.84	2.75
46	7.22	5.10	4.24	3.76	3.44	3.22	3.06	2.93	2.82	2.73
48	7.19	5.08	4.22	3.74	3.43	3.20	3.04	2.91	2.80	2.71
50	7.17	5.06	4.20	3.72	3.41	3.19	3.02	2.89	2.78	2.70

(continued on next page)

TABLE 5 *(Continued)*

$\alpha = .01$

Degrees of Freedom for Denominator	Degrees of Freedom for Numerator									
	1	2	3	4	5	6	7	8	9	10
55	7.12	5.01	4.16	3.68	3.37	3.15	2.98	2.85	2.75	2.66
60	7.08	4.98	4.13	3.65	3.34	3.12	2.95	2.82	2.72	2.63
65	7.04	4.95	4.10	3.62	3.31	3.09	2.93	2.80	2.69	2.61
70	7.01	4.92	4.07	3.60	3.29	3.07	2.91	2.78	2.67	2.59
75	6.99	4.90	4.05	3.58	3.27	3.05	2.89	2.76	2.65	2.57
80	6.96	4.88	4.04	3.56	3.26	3.04	2.87	2.74	2.64	2.55
90	6.93	4.85	4.01	3.53	3.23	3.01	2.84	2.72	2.61	2.52
100	6.90	4.82	3.98	3.51	3.21	2.99	2.82	2.69	2.59	2.50
125	6.84	4.78	3.94	3.47	3.17	2.95	2.79	2.66	2.55	2.47
150	6.81	4.75	3.91	3.45	3.14	2.92	2.76	2.63	2.53	2.44
200	6.76	4.71	3.88	3.41	3.11	3.89	2.73	2.60	2.50	2.41
300	6.72	4.68	3.85	3.38	3.08	2.86	2.70	2.57	2.47	2.38
400	6.70	4.66	3.83	3.37	3.06	2.85	2.68	2.56	2.45	2.37
1000	6.66	4.63	3.80	3.34	3.04	2.82	2.66	2.53	2.43	2.34
10000	6.64	4.61	3.78	3.32	3.02	2.80	2.64	2.51	2.41	2.32

References

Aronson, E. (1968). Dissonance theory: Progress and problems. In R. Abelson, E. Aronson, W. McGuire, T. Newcomb, M. Rosenberg, & P. Tannenbaum (Eds.), *Theories of cognitive consistency: A source book* (pp. 5–27). Chicago: Rand McNally.

Aronson, E., & Mills, J. (1959). The effect of severity of initiation on liking for a group. *Journal of Abnormal and Social Psychology, 59,* 177–181.

Ashby, W. A., & Wilson, G. T. (1977). Behavior therapy for obesity: Booster sessions and long term maintenance of weight loss. *Behavior Research and Therapy, 15,* 451–463.

Ashcraft, M. H. (1989). *Human memory and cognition.* Glenview, IL: Scott, Foresman & Co.

Averbach, E., & Coriell, A. S. (1961). Short-term memory in vision. *Bell System Technical Journal, 40,* 309–328.

Baddeley, A. (1990). *Human memory: Theory and practice.* Needham Heights, MA: Allyn & Bacon.

Baron, R. M., & Kenny, D. A. (1986). The moderator-mediator variable distinction in social psychological research: Conceptual, strategic, and statistical considerations. *Journal of Personality and Social Psychology, 51,* 1173–1182.

Barker, R. G., Dembo, T., & Lewin, K. (1941). Frustration and regression: A study of young children. *University of Iowa Studies in Child Welfare, 18,* 1–314.

Batson, C. D., Duncan, B. D., Ackerman, P, Buckley, T., & Birch, K. (1981). Is empathic emotion a source of altruistic motivation? *Journal of Personality and Social Psychology, 40,* 290–302.

Beck, A. T., Rush, A. J., Shaw, B. F., & Emery, G. (1979). *Cognitive therapy of depression.* New York: Guilford Press.

Bellack, A. S., Rozensky, R., & Schwartz, J. (1974). A comparison of two forms of self-monitoring in a behavioral weight reduction program. *Behavior Therapy, 5,* 523–530.

453

Bem, D. J. (1965). An experimental analysis of self-persuasion. *Journal of Experimental Social Psychology, 1,* 199–218.

Bem, D. J. (1967). Self-perception: An alternative interpretation of cognitive dissonance phenomena. *Psychological Review, 74,* 183–200.

Bem, D. J. (1972). Self-perception theory. In L. Berkowitz (Ed.), *Advances in experimental social psychology* (Vol. 6, pp.1–62). New York: Academic Press.

Berman, J. S., Miller, R. C., & Massman, P. J. (1985). Cognitive therapy versus systematic desensitzation: Is one treatment superior? *Psychological Bulletin, 97,* 451–461.

Berkowitz, L. (1989). Frustration-aggression hypothesis: Examination and reformulation. *Psychological Bulletin, 106,* 59–73.

Beutler, L. E. (Ed.). (1990). Special series: Advances in psychotherapy process research. *Journal of Consulting and Clinical Psychology, 58,* 263–303.

Block, J. & Funder, D. C. (1986). Social roles and social perception: Individual differences in attribution error. *Journal of Personality and Social Psychology, 51,* 1200–1207.

Brehm, J. W. (1956). Postdecision changes in the desirability of alternatives. *Journal of Abnormal and Social Psychology, 52,* 384–389.

Brock, T. C., & Balloun, J. L. (1967). Behavioral receptivity to dissonant information. *Journal of Personality and Social Psychology, 4,* 413–428.

Brown, J. L. (1965). Afterimages. In C. H. Graham (Ed.), *Vision and visual perception.* New York: Wiley.

Brownell, K. D. (1982). Obesity: Understanding and treating a serious, prevalent, and refractory disorder. *Journal of Consulting and Clinical Psychology, 50,* 820–840.

Campbell, D. T., & Stanley, J. C. (1963). *Experimental and quasi-experimental designs for research.* American Educational Research Association. Chicago: Rand McNally.

Chow, S. L. (1985). Iconic store and partial report. *Memory and Cognition, 13,* 256–264.

Cialdini, R. B., & Baumann, D. J. (1981). Littering: A new unobtrusive measure of attitude. *Social Psychology Quarterly, 44,* 254–259.

Cialdini, R. B., Darby, B. L., & Vincent, J. E. (1973). Transgression and altruism: A case for hedonism. *Journal of Experimental Social Psychology, 9,* 502–516.

Cialdini, R. B., & Kenrick, D. T. (1976). Altruism as Hedonism: A social development perspective on the relationship of negative mood state and helping. *Journal of Personality and Social Psychology, 34,* 907–914.

Cohen, J. (1962). The statistical power of abnormal-social psychological research: A review. *Journal of Abnormal and Social Psychology, 65,* 145–153.

Cohen, J. (1988). *Statistical power analysis for the behavioral sciences.* (2nd ed.). Hillsdale, NJ: Lawrence Erlbaum Associates.

Cohen, S., Gary W. E., Krantz, D. S., & Stokols, D. (1980). Physiological, motivational, and cognitive effects of aircraft noise on children. Moving from the laboratory to the field. *American Psychologist, 35,* 231–243.

Cohen, S. & Lichtenstein, E. (1990). Partner behaviors that support quitting smoking. *Journal of Consulting and Clinical Psychology, 58,* 304–309.

Cohen, S., Lichtenstein, E., Prochaska, J., Rossi, J., Gritz, E., Carr, C., Orleans, T., Schenback, V., Biener, L., Abrams, D., DiClemente, C., Curry, S. J., Marlatt, G. A., Cummings, K. M., Emont, S., Giovino, G., & Ossip-Klein, D. (1989). Debunking myths about self-quitting: Evidence from ten prospective studies of persons quitting smoking by themselves. *American Psychologist, 44,* 1355–1365.

Coltheart, M. (1980). Iconic memory and visible persistence. *Perception and Psychophysics, 27,* 183–228.

Coltheart, M., Lea, C. D., & Thompson, K. (1974). In defence of iconic memory. *Quarterly Journal of Experimental Psychology, 26,* 633–641.

Cook, T. D., & Campbell, D. T. (1979). *Quasi-experimentation. Design and analysis issues for field settings.* Chicago: Rand McNally.

Cooper, J., Zanna, M. P., & Taves, P. A. (1978). Arousal as a necessary condition for attitude change following induced compliance. *Journal of Personality and Social Psychology, 36,* 1101–1106.

Critelli, J. W., & Neumann, K. F. (1984). Conceptual analysis of a construct in transition. *American Psychologist, 39,* 32–39.

Crowder, R. G. (1976). *Principles of learning and memory.* Hillsdale, NJ: Lawrence Erlbaum Associates.

Dawes, R. M. (1972). *Fundamentals of attitude measurement.* New York: Wiley.

DiLollo, V. (1980). Temporal integration in visual memory. *Journal of Experimental Psychology: General, 109,* 75–97.

DiLollo, V. & Dixon, P. (1988). Two forms of persistence in visual information processing. *Journal of Experimental Psychology: Human Perception and Performance, 14,* 671–681.

Diament, C., & Wilson, G. T. (1975). An experimental investigation of the effects of covert sensitization in an analogue eating situation. *Behavior therapy, 6,* 499–509.

Dollard, J., Doob, L., Miller, N., Mowrer, O., & Sears, R. (1939). *Frustration and aggression.* New Haven, CT: Yale University Press.

Efron, R. (1970). The relationship between the duration of a stimulus and the duration of a perception. *Perception and Psychophysics, 8,* 231–234.

Emmelkamp, P. M. G., & Walta, C. (1978). Effects of therapy set on electrical aversion therapy and covert sensitization. *Behavior Therapy, 9,* 185–188.

Engel, G. R. (1970). An investigation of visual responses to brief stereoscopic stimuli. *Quarterly Journal of Experimental Psychology, 22,* 148–160.

Eriksen, C. W., & Collins, J. F. (1967). Some temporal characteristics of visual pattern perception. *Journal of Experimental Psychology, 74,* 476–484.

Estes, W. K. (1980). Is human memory obsolete? *American Scientist, 68,* 62–69.

Fazio, R. H., Zanna, M. P., & Cooper, J. (1977). Dissonance and self-perception: An integrative view of each theory's proper domain of application. *Journal of Experimental Social Psychology, 13,* 464–479.

Feinstein, A. R. (1959). The measurement of success in weight reduction: An analysis of methods and a new index. *Journal of Chronic Diseases, 10,* 439–456.

Festinger, L. (1957). *A theory of cognitive dissonance.* Stanford, CA: Stanford University Press.

Fletcher, G. J. O., & Ward, C. (1988). Attribution theory and processes: A cross-cultural perspective. In M. H. Bond (Ed.), *The cross cultural challenge to social psychology,* (pp. 230- 244). Newbury Park, CA: Sage.

Frank, J.D. (1973). *Persuasion and healing* (rev. ed.). Baltimore, MD: Johns Hopkins University Press.

Garbarino, J., & Asp, C. E. (1981). *Successful schools and competent students.* Lexington, Ma: Lexington Books.

Garfield, S. L. (1990). Issues and methods in psychotherapy process research. *American Psychologist, 58,* 273–280

Green, D. M., & Swets, J. A. (1974). *Signal detection theory and psychophysics.* Huntington, NY: Kreiger.

Greenwald, A. G., & Ronis, D. L. (1978). Twenty years of cognitive dissonance: Case study of the evolution of a theory. *Psychological Review, 85,* 53–57.

Greenwald, A. G., Pratkanis, A. R., Leippe, M. R., & Baumgardner, M. H. (1986). Under what conditions does theory obstruct research progress? *Psychological Review, 93,* 216–229.

Grossberg, J.M., & Grant, B. F. (1978). Clinical psychophysics: Applications of ratio scaling and signal detection methods to research on pain, fear, drugs, and medical decision making. *Psychological Bulletin, 85,* 1154–1176.

Gump, R. (1962). *Jade: Stone of heaven.* New York: Doubleday.

Haber, R. N., & Standing, L. (1969). Direct measures of short-term visual storage. *Quarterly Journal of Experimental Psychology, 21,* 43–54.

Higgins, R. L., & Marlatt, G. A. (1973). Effects of anxiety arousal on the consumption of alcohol by alcoholics and social drinkers. *Journal of Consulting and Clinical Psychology, 41,* 426–433.

Higgins, R. L., & Marlatt, G. A. (1975). Fear of interpersonal evaluation as a determinant of alcohol consumption in male social drinkers. *Journal of Abnormal Psychology, 84,* 644–651.

Holding, D. H. (1970). Guessing behavior and the Sperling store. *Quarterly Journal of Experimental Psychology, 22,* 248- 256.

Holding, D. H. (1975). Sensory storage reconsidered. *Memory and Cognition, 3,* 31–41.

Holroyd, K. A. (1976). Cognition and desensitization in the group treatment of test anxiety. *Journal of Consulting and Clinical Psychology, 44,* 991–1001.

Horvath, P. (1988). Placebos and common factors in two decades of psychotherapy research. *Psychological Bulletin, 104,* 214-225.

Hsu, M. L. (1989). Random sampling, randomization, and equivalence of contrasted groups in psychotherapy outcome research. *Journal of Consulting and Clinical Psychology, 57,* 131–137.

Hull, C. L. (1943). *Principles of behavior.* New York: Appleton-Century-Crofts, Inc.

Irwin, R. J. (1992). More than Psychophysics. A review of N. A. MacMillan and C. D. Creelman (1991). *Detection Theory: A User's guide. New Zealand Journal of Psychology, 21,* 80–81.

Irwin, R. J. & Whitehead, P.R. (1991). Towards an objective psychophysics of pain. *Psychological Science, 2,* 230–235.

Jones, E. E., & Nisbett, R. E. (1972). The actor and the observer: Divergent perceptions of the causes of behavior. In E. E. Jones, D. E. Kanouse, H. H. Kelley, R. E. Nisbett, S. Valins, & B. Weiner (Eds.), *Attribution: Perceiving the causes of behavior* (pp. 79–94). Morristown, NJ: General Learning Press.

Julesz, B. (1971). *Foundations of cyclopean perception.* Chicago: University of Chicago Press.

Kazdin, A. E. (1979). Nonspecific treatment factors in psychotherapy outcome research. *Journal of Consulting and Clinical Psychology, 47,* 846–851.

Kazdin, A. E., & Bass, D. (1989). Power to detect differences between alternative treatments in comparative psychotherapy outcome research. *Journal of Consulting and Clinical Psychology, 57,* 138–147.

Keesey, R. E., & Powley, T. L. (1986). The regulation of body weight. *Annual Review of Psychology, 37,* 109–133.

Kiger, J. I. (1984). The depth/breadth trade-off in the design of menu-driven user interfaces. *International Journal of Man-Machine Studies, 20,* 201–213.

Kintsch, W. (1967). Memory and decision aspects of recognition learning. *Psychological Review, 74,* 496–504.

Kirsch, I. (1985). Response expectancy as a determinant of experience and behavior. *American Psychologist, 40,* 1189-1202.

Klerman, G. L., Weissman, M. M., Rounsaville, B. J., & Chevron, E. S. (1984). *Interpersonal psychotherapy of depression.* New York: Basic Books.

Kling, J. W., & Riggs, L. A. (1971). *Woodworth & Schlosberg's experimental psychology*, (3rd ed.) New York: Holt, Rinehart and Winston.

Kroll, N. E. A., Parks, T., Parkinson, S. R., Bieber, S. L. & Johnson, A. L. (1970). Short-term memory while shadowing: Recall of visually and of aurally presented letters. *Journal of Experimental Psychology, 85*, 220–224.

Latané, B., & Darley, J.M. (1970). *The unresponsive bystander. Why doesn't he help?* New York: Appleton-Century- Crofts.

Levine, G. (1961). The effects of two verbal techniques on the expression of feelings. *Journal of Consulting Psychology, 25*, 270–271.

Lichtenstein, E., Harris, D. E., Birchler, G. R., Wahl, J. M., & Schmahl, D. P. (1973). Comparison of rapid smoking, warm, smoky air, and attention placebo in the modification of smoking behavior. *Journal of Consulting and Clinical Psychology, 40*, 92–98.

Likert, R. (1932). A technique for the measurement of attitudes. *Archives of Psychology*, Whole No. 140.

Linder, D. E., Cooper, J., & Jones, E. E. (1967). Decision freedom as a determinant of the role of incentive magnitude in attitude change. *Journal of Personality and Social Psychology, 6*, 245–254.

Loftus, G. R., & Hogden, J. (1988). Picture perception: Information extraction and phenomenological appearance. In G. H. Bower (Ed.), *The psychology of learning and motivation* (vol. 22, pp. 139–191). San Diego: Academic.

Loftus, G. R., & Hanna, A. M. (1989). The phenomenology of spatial integration: Data and models. *Cognitive Psychology, 21*, 363–397.

Long, G. M. (1980). Iconic memory: A review and critique of the study of short-term visual storage. *Psychological Bulletin, 88*, 785–820.

Luborsky, L., Singer, B., & Luborsky, L. (1975). Comparative studies of psychotherapies: Is it true that "everyone has won and all must have prizes?" *Archives of General Psychiatry, 32*, 995–1008.

Luce, R. D. (1986). *Response times: Their role in inferring elementary mental organization*. New York: Oxford University Press.

MacGregor, J., Lee, E., & Lam, N. (1986). Optimizing the structure of database menu indexes: A decision model of menu search. *Human Factors, 28*, 387–399.

MacMillan, N. A. & Creelman, C. D. (1990). Response bias: Characteristics of detection theory, threshold theory and "nonparametric" indexes. *Psychological Bulletin, 107*, 3, 401–413.

MacMillan, N. A. & Creelman, C. D. (1991). *Detection theory: A user's guide.* Cambridge (England): Cambridge University Press.

Madsen, K. B. (1984). The hypotheses quotient: A quantitative estimation of the testability of a theory. In J. R. Royce & L. P. Mos (Eds.), *Annals of theoretical psychology* (Vol. 2, pp. 185–202). New York: Plenum.

Marston, A. R., & McFall, R. M. (1971). Comparison of behavior modification approaches to smoking reduction. *Journal of Consulting and Clinical Psychology. 36*, 153–162.

Mausner, B. (1971). Some comments on the failure of behavior therapy as a technique for modifying cigarette smoking. *Journal of Consulting and Clinical Psychology, 36*, 167–170.

McArthur, L. Z., & Post, D. L. (1977). Figural emphasis and person perception. *Journal of Experimental Social Psychology, 13*, 520–535.

McFall, R. M., & Hammen, C. L. (1971). Motivation, structure, and self-monitoring: Role of nonspecific factors in smoking reduction. *Journal of Consulting and Clinical Psychology, 37*, 80–86.

McFarland, C., Ross, M., & Conway, M. (1984). Self-persuasion and self-presentation as mediators of anticipatory attitude change. *Journal of Personality and Social Psychology, 46,* 529–540.

McReynolds, W. T., & Tori, C. A. (1972). A further assessment of attention-placebo effects and demand characteristics in studies of systematic desensitization. *Journal of Consulting and Clinical Psychology, 38,* 261–264.

Merikle, P. M. (1980). Selection from visual persistence by perceptual groups and category membership. *Journal of Experimental Psychology: General, 109,* 279–295.

Metzler, J. (1973). *Cognitive analogues of the rotation of three-dimensional objects.* Unpublished doctoral dissertation, Stanford University.

Metzler, J., & Shepard, R. N. (1974). Transformational studies of the internal representations of three dimensional objects. In R. L. Solso (Ed.), *Theories of cognitive psychology: The Loyola Symposium.* Hillsdale, NJ: Lawrence Erlbaum Associates.

Miller, D. P. (1981). The depth/breadth tradeoff in hierarchical computer menus. *Proceedings of the 25th Annual Meeting of the Human Factors Society,* 296–300.

Miller, D. P. (1980). *Factors affecting item acquisition performance in hierarchical systems: Depth vs breadth.* Unpublished doctoral dissertation, Ohio State University, Columbus.

Miller, G. A. (1956). The magical number seven, plus or minus two: some limits on our capacity for processing information. *Psychological Review, 63,* 81–97.

Neisser, U. (1967). *Cognitive psychology.* New York: Appleton- Century-Crofts.

Nisbett, R. E., & Ross, L. (1980). *Human inference: Strategies and shortcomings of social judgment.* Englewood Cliffs, NJ: Prentice-Hall.

Nunnally, J. C. (1967). *Psychometric theory.* New York: McGraw Hill.

Osgood, C. E., Suci, G. J., & Tannenbaum, P. H. (1957). *The measurement of meaning.* Urbana: University of Illinois Press.

Paap, K. R., & Roske-Hofstrand, R. J. (1986). The optimal number of menu items per panel. *Human Factors, 28,* 377–385.

Parkinson, S. R., Sisson, N., & Snowberry, K. (1985). Organization of broad computer menu displays. *International Journal of Man-Machine Studies, 23,* 689–697.

Parkinson, S. R. (1972). Short-term memory while shadowing: Multiple-item recall of visually and of aurally presented letters. *Journal of Experimental Psychology, 92,* 256–265.

Parks, T. E. (1966). Signal-detectability theory of recognition-memory performance. *Psychological Review, 73,* 44–58.

Parks, T. E., Kroll, N. E. A., Salzberg, P. M., & Parkinson, S. R. (1972). Persistence of memory as indicated by decision time in a matching task. *Journal of Experimental Psychology, 92,* 437–438.

Parloff, M. B. (1986). Placebo controls in psychotherapy research: A sine qua non or a placebo for research problems? *Journal of Consulting and Clinical Psychology, 54,* 79–87.

Parloff, M. B., London, P., & Wolfe, B. (1986). Individual psychotherapy and behavior change. *Annual Review of Psychology, 37,* 321–349.

Petty, R. E., & Cacioppo, J. T. (1984). The effects of involvement on responses to argument quantity and quality: Central and peripheral routes to persuasion. *Journal of Personality and Social Psychology, 46,* 69–81.

Pierce, B. J., Parkinson, S. R., & Sisson, N. (1992). Effects of semantic similarity, omission probability, and number of alternatives in computer menu search. *International Journal of Man-Machine Studies, 37,* 653–677.

Piliavin, I. M., Rodin, J., & Piliavin, J. A. (1969). Good samaritanism: An underground phenomenon? *Journal of Personality and Social Psychology, 13,* 289–299.

Pollard, P., & Richardson, J. T. E. (1987). On the probability of making Type I errors. *Psychological Bulletin, 102,* 159–163.

Posner, M. I., Boies, S. J., Eichelman, W. H., & Taylor, R. L. (1969). Retention of visual and name codes of single letters. *Journal of Experimental Psychology Monograph, 79* (1,Pt. 2), 1–16.

Posner, M. I., Snyder, C. R., & Davidson, B. J. (1980). Attention and the detection of signals. *Journal of Experimental Psychology: General, 109,* 160–174.

Printzmetal, W., Presti, D. E., & Posner, M. I. (1986). Does attention affect visual feature integration? *Journal of Experimental Psychology: Human Perception and Performance, 12,* 361–369.

Reicher, G. M. (1969). Perceptual recognition as a function of meaningfulness of stimulus material. *Journal of Experimental Psychology, 81,* 275–280.

Robertson, G., McCracken, D., & Newell, A. (1981). The ZOG approach to man-machine communication. *International Journal of Man-Machine Studies, 14,* 461–488.

Rogers, C. R. (1942). *Counseling and psychotherapy.* Boston: Houghton Mifflin.

Romanczyk, R. G. (1974). Self-monitoring in the treatment of obesity: parameters of reactivity. *Behavior Therapy, 5,* 531-540.

Rosenthal, R. (1966). *Experimenter effects in behavioral research.* New York: Appleton-Century-Crofts.

Rutkowski, G., Gruder, C., & Romer, D. (1983). Group cohesiveness, social norms, and bystander intervention. *Journal of Personality and Social Psychology, 44,* 545–552.

Schmahl, D. P., Lichtenstein, E., & Harris, D. E. (1972). Successful treatment of habitual smokers with warm, smoky air and rapid smoking. *Journal of Consulting and Clinical Psychology, 38,* 105–111.

Schneiderman, B. (1980). *Software psychology: Human factors in computer and information systems.* Cambridge, MA: Winthrop.

Shapiro, A. K. (1971). Placebo effects in medicine, psychotherapy, and psychoanalysis. In A. E. Bergin & S. C. Garfield (Eds.), *Handbook of psychotherapy and behavior change: Empirical analysis* (pp. 439–473). New York: Wiley.

Shapiro, D. A., & Shapiro, D. (1982). Meta-analysis of comparative therapy outcome studies: A replication and refinement. *Psychological Bulletin, 92,* 581–604.

Shepard, R. N., & Cooper, L. A. (1982). *Mental images and their transformations.* Cambridge, MA: MIT Press.

Shepard, R. N., and Metzler, J. (1971). Mental rotation of three-dimensional objects. *Science, 171,* 701–703.

Smith, M. L., Glass, G. V., & Miller, T. I. (1980). *The benefits of psychotherapy.* Baltimore, MD: Johns Hopkins University Press.

Sloane, R. B., Staples, F. R., Cristol, A. H., Yorkston, N. J., & Whipple, K. (1975). *Psychotherapy versus behavior therapy.* Cambridge, MA: Harvard University Press.

Snowberry, K., Parkinson, S. R., & Sisson, N. (1983). Computer menu displays. *Ergonomics, 26,* 699–712.

Snowberry, K., Parkinson, S. R., & Sisson, N. (1985). Effects of help fields on navigating through hierarchical menu structures. *International Journal of Man-Machine Studies, 22,* 479–491.

Sperling, G. (1960). The information available in brief visual presentations. *Psychological Monographs, 74,* 11 (Whole No. 498).

Sperling, G. (1963). A model for visual memory tasks. *Human Factors, 5,* 19–31.

Steele, C. M., & Liu, T. J. (1983). Dissonance processes as self-affirmation. *Journal of Personality and Social Psychology, 45,* 5–19.

Sternberg, S. (1966). High speed scanning in human memory. *Science, 153*, 652–654.

Sternberg, S. (1969). The discovery of processing stages: extensions of Donders' method. In W. G. Koster (Ed.), *Attention and performance* II. *Acta Psychologica, 30*, 276–315.

Sternberg, S. (1970). Memory-scanning: mental processes revealed by reaction-time experiments. In J. Antrobus (Ed.), *Cognition and Affect* (pp. 13–58). Boston: Little, Brown & Co.

Sternberg, S. (1975). Memory scanning: New findings and current controversies. *Quarterly Journal of Experimental Psychology, 27*, 1–32.

Strupp, H. H., & Hadley, S. W. (1979). Specific vs. nonspecific factors in psychotherapy. *Archives of General Psychiatry, 36*, 1125–1136.

Suedfeld, P. (1984). The subtractive expectancy placebo procedure: A measure of non-specific factors in behavioral interventions. *Behavior Research and Therapy, 22*, 159–164.

Swets, J. A. (1973). The relative operating characteristic in psychology. *Science, 182*, 990–1000.

Swets, J. A. (1986). Indices of discrimination or diagnostic accuracy: Their ROCs and implied models. *Psychological Bulletin, 99*, 100–117.

Swets, J. A. (1988). Measuring the accuracy of diagnostic systems. *Science, 240*, 1285–1293.

Swets, J. A., Tanner, W. P., Jr., & Birdsall, T. G. (1961). Decision processes in perception. *Psychological Review, 68*, 301–340.

Taylor, J. A. (1953). A personality scale of manifest anxiety. *Journal of Abnormal and Social Psychology, 48*, 285–290.

Townsend, J. T. (1990). Serial vs. parallel processing: Sometimes they look like tweedeldum and tweedledee but they can (and should) be distinguished. *Psychological Science, 1*, 46–54.

Townsend, J. T., & Ashby, F. G. (1983). *Stochastic modeling of elementary psychological processes.* Cambridge: Cambridge University Press.

Townsend, V. M. (1973). Loss of spatial and identity information following a tachistoscopic exposure. *Journal of Experimental Psychology, 98*, 113–118.

Treisman, A. (1986). Features and objects in visual processing. *Scientific American, 255* (5), 106–115.

Treisman, A., & Gelade, G. (1980). A feature integration theory of attention. *Cognitive Psychology, 12*, 97–136.

Treisman, A., & Gormican, S. (1988). Feature analysis in early vision: Evidence from search asymmetries. *Psychological Review, 95*, 15–48.

Treisman, A., & Schmidt, H. (1982). Illusory conjunctions in the perception of objects. *Cognitive Psychology, 14*, 107–141.

Treisman, A., & Souther, J. (1985). Search asymmetry: A diagnostic for preattentive processing of separable features. *Journal of Experimental Psychology: General, 114*, 285–310.

Turvey, M. T. (1973). On peripheral and central processes in vision. *Psychological Review, 80*, 1–52.

Uttal, W. R. (1988). *On seeing forms.* Hillsdale, NJ: Lawrence Erlbaum Associates.

Webb, E. J., Campbell, D. T., Schwartz, R. D., Sechrest, L., & Grove, J. B. (1981). *Nonreactive measures in the social sciences* (2nd ed.). Boston: Houghton Mifflin.

Wilder, R. L. (1965). *Introduction to the foundations of mathematics* (2nd Ed.). New York: Wiley.

Wilkins, W. (1986). Invalid evidence for expectancies as causes: Comment on Kirsch. *American Psychologist, 91*, 1387-1389.

Wilson, G. T. (1978). Methodological considerations in treatment outcome research on obesity. *Journal of Consulting and Clinical Psychology, 46,* 687–702.

Woodworth, R. S. (1938). *Experimental psychology.* New York: Henry Holt & Co.

Zanna, M. P., & Cooper, J. (1974). Dissonance and the pill: An attribution approach to studying the arousal properties of dissonance. *Journal of Personality and Social Psychology, 29,* 703–709.

Author Index

Subject Index